Franz Xaver Weninger

A manual of the Catholic religion

For catechists, teachers and self-instruction

Franz Xaver Weninger

A manual of the Catholic religion
For catechists, teachers and self-instruction

ISBN/EAN: 9783742892522

Manufactured in Europe, USA, Canada, Australia, Japa

Cover: Foto ©Lupo / pixelio.de

Manufactured and distributed by brebook publishing software (www.brebook.com)

Franz Xaver Weninger

A manual of the Catholic religion

A

MANUAL

OF THE

CATHOLIC RELIGION,

FOR

CATECHISTS, TEACHERS

AND

SELF-INSTRUCTION.

BY THE

REV. FATHER F. X. WENINGER, D. D.,

MISSIONARY OF THE SOCIETY OF JESUS.

SIXTH EDITION

CINCINNATI.
JOHN P. WALSH,
PRINTER, PUBLISHER AND BOOKSELLER,
170 SYCAMORE STREET.
1867.

I have read and examined the "Manual of the Catholic Doctrine," by Rev. F. X. Wenninger, S, J., with a great deal of pleasure and delight. I know of no work more clear and explicit, or that better meets the exigencies of the times than this; hence, I would exceedingly like to see it translated into English, and freely circulated within the diocese.

† JOHN HENRY LUERS,
Bishop of Fort Wayne.

Entered according to Act of Congress, in the year 1861,
By D. & J. SADLIER & CO.,
In the Clerk's Office of the District Court of the United States, for the Southern District of New York.

THE AUTHOR'S PREFACE.

In the following work, I offer to the Catholic public a book which contains in brief a complete exposition of the whole of the Christian doctrine, so that, whoever has mastered its contents, may be called, and truly is, a perfectly instructed Christian. But why do I write a new book for this purpose? Have we not already a multitude of good Catechisms and very solid catechetical works? Doubtless we have. But doubtless, also, something remains to be done. I thought that a Manual as complete, brief, clear, and systematical as possible, adapted equally for teachers and for self-instruction, was a desideratum.

I felt, especially in all the catechetical books with which I am acquainted, the absence of a regular system, that is, a system in which the development follows throughout the nature of the subject, and connects the several parts into one complete whole. I hope it will be difficult to detect in the present work a defect in this regard. I have also remarked in this kind of books, that proofs drawn from tradition are almost totally neglected, or at least, much less attended to than proofs taken from scripture. I have endeavored in the present Manual to place them on an equal footing.

How far, in other respects, I have succeeded in giving to the book the perfection of completeness, united with brevity and clearness, others will judge.

For myself, it is encouraging to know that I place my

readers on a safe and well-tried road. For in preparing this Manual, I made use of a work entitled, "Summa Doctrinæ Christianæ," written by me about thirteen years ago. I had the consolation of receiving a letter for it from his Holiness Pope Gregory XVI., in which the Holy Father deigned to express himself thus: "Purissimis fidei catholicæ principiis juventutem erudire satagis." The Holy Father, therefore, is pleased to call the principles of religion set forth therein, the purest principles of Catholic faith, and I am confident, that in preparing this Manual, I have not deviated in the least from the principles of faith contained in the Latin edition.

Instruction in religious matter is the great want of our time, particularly among the otherwise better educated classes of the laity. The present work is intended to supply this want, to enable every one who is willing to study, and is fit for self-instruction, to render an account of his faith on all occasions, and, in fine, to make people understand what influence faith is to exert on their conduct.

As the book was printed in the absence of the author, some additions were overlooked, and consequently have been added at the end of the work.

Should the Manual obtain a favorable reception from the public, especially the reverend clergy, it will be followed, God willing, by other instructive books which I have written in German for popular instruction, and which are intimately connected with the present work.

May Mary, who is the seat of Divine wisdom, bestow her benign and maternal benediction upon this book and its readers!

CONTENTS.

Introduction .... Page 9

PART I.

ON THE WAY OF SALVATION.

CHAPTER I.

ON FAITH.
    Definition and Necessity of Faith........................ 14
    Sources of Faith.. 16
    Holy Scripture... 16
    Tradition.. 19
    The Apostles' Creed.................................... 24

FIRST ARTICLE OF FAITH.
    Of the Attributes of God............................... 25
    Of the Trinity of God.................................. 31
    Of the Creation.. 35
    Of the Angels.. 39
    Of Man in the State of Original Justice................ 42
    Of Man's Fall, and of Original Sin..................... 44
    Of the Exemption of Mary from Original Sin............. 45

SECOND ARTICLE OF FAITH.
    Jesus Christ the promised Redeemer as to His Mission... 50
    Jesus Christ the Son of God as to His Person........... 57

THIRD ARTICLE OF FAITH.
    Jesus Christ both God and Man as to His Nature......... 63

FOURTH ARTICLE OF FAITH.
    Jesus Christ the Redeemer of Man, by His Life, Passion and Death.. 68

FIFTH ARTICLE OF FAITH.
    Jesus Christ the Vanquisher of Hell, the Deliverer of the Just from Limbo, and the glorious Conqueror of Death.. 71

SIXTH ARTICLE OF FAITH.
    Jesus Christ the King of Glory ascending into Heaven... 75

SEVENTH ARTICLE OF FAITH.
    Jesus Christ the Judge of the Living and the Dead...... 77

EIGHTH ARTICLE OF FAITH.
    The Holy Ghost the Third Person of the Blessed Trinity.... 81

NINTH ARTICLE OF FAITH.
The Church of Christ.. 85

MARKS OF THE CHURCH.
The Catholic Church the only true Church................. 87
The Catholic Church the only Immutable and Infallible Church.. 101

GOVERNMENT OF THE CHURCH.
The Ecclesiastical Hierarchy................................ 102
The Roman Pontiff the Head of the Catholic Church....... 103
His Infallibility in Deciding on Matters of Faith............ 105
His Supreme Jurisdiction in Governing the Church......... 106
The Communion of the Members of the Church............ 109
Purgatory.. 110
The Veneration of Mary and of the Saints.................. 113
"   "   Holy Pictures and Relics............... 115
The Catholic Church the only Sanctifying Church......... 122

TENTH ARTICLE OF FAITH.
The Remission of Sin to the Supernatural and Spiritual Life of the Soul.. 126

ELEVENTH ARTICLE OF FAITH.
The Resurrection of the Body to the Supernatural, Incorruptible Life of the Body.............................. 128

TWELFTH ARTICLE OF FAITH.
Everlasting Life of the Blessed in Heaven as regards both soul and body...
The Eternal Pains of the Damned in Hell in regard to soul and body.. 131

CHAPTER II.

HOPE.
Definition and Necessity of Hope......................... 141
Prayer the most sublime Act of Hope..................... 142
The Lord's Prayer.. 146
Explanation of its Seven Petitions........................ 148
Invocation of Mary... 163
The Hail Mary.. 165
Explanation of the Solutions and Petitions contained therein. 166

CHAPTER III.

CHARITY.
Definition and Necessity of Charity....................... 171
The Two Principal Commandments of Charity............ 173
The Ten Commandments.................................... 175
The First Commandment................................ 177
" Second " 181
" Third   " 186
" Fourth " 188

	Page
The Fifth Commandment	199
" Sixth "	202
" Seventh "	204
" Eighth "	208
" Ninth "	208
" Tenth "	216
The Commandments of the Church	217
The First Commandment	218
" Second "	221
" Third "	224
" Fourth "	227
" Fifth "	230

PART II.

ON THE MEANS OF SALVATION.

CHAPTER I.

GRACE.

Of Grace in general	231
Of Actual Grace	233
Of Sanctifying Grace	236

CHAPTER II.

THE HOLY SACRAMENTS.

Of the Sacraments in general	243
" Sacrament of Baptism	246
" " Confirmation	255
" " the Altar or the Holy Eucharist	259
" Presence of Christ in the Blessed Sacrament	260
Of Transubstantion	261
Of the Offering it up in the Holy Sacrifice in the Mass	263
Of Communion	267
Of Adoration	275
Of the Sacrament of Penance in general	276
Of Contrition	278
Of Confession	282
Of Satisfaction	297
Of Indulgences	303
Of Extreme Unction	307
Of Holy Orders	310

CHAPTER III.

OF MATRIMONY.

Of the Sacrament of Matrimony	316
Of Celibacy	325

CHAPTER IV.

The Sacraments.
Of the Sacraments in general.................... 327
Of Benedictions................................. 327
Of Blessings.................................... 328
Of Ceremonies................................... 330
Of the Solemn Usages of the Church.............. 331

PART III.

ON THE CARE OF SALVATION.

CHAPTER I.

The Avoiding of Evil.
Of Sin in general............................... 343
Of the Seven Capital Sins....................... 350
" Sins of Participation........................ 365
" " against the Holy Ghost.................... 367
" " that cry to Heaven...8.................... 370
" Atonement for Sin............................ 372

CHAPTER II.

Good Works.
Of Good Works in general........................ 373
Of Virtue....................................... 376
Of the Divine Virtues........................... 376
" Moral Virtues................................ 377
" Four Cardinal Virtues........................ 377
" Seven Principal Virtues...................... 381
" Eight Beatitudes............................. 581

CHAPTER III.

The State of Christian Perfection.
Of the Seven Gifts of the Holy Ghost............ 389
" Twelve Fruits of the Holy Ghost.............. 392
" Three Evangelical Counsels................... 392
" Practice of exciting Fervor.................. 401

ADDITIONS.

The Jubilee..................................... 405
Of the Sacramentals............................. 405
The Ecclesiastical Year and its Festivals....... 406
Missions.. 409

MANUAL

OF

THE CATHOLIC RELIGION.

INTRODUCTION

Question. What is Christian doctrine?
Answer. Christian doctrine is a short, clear, and methodical summary of those truths of faith and morality which every Christian should know, in order to be able to live according to faith; and to answer the questions proposed to him concerning it.

Q. Who is called a Christian, and is so in the true sense of the word?
A. He who, after the reception of the sacrament of Baptism, believes in Jesus Christ and his doctrine, and professes the same in the true Church.

Q. Whence is it that we are called Christians?
A. From Christ, the founder of the faith, and the author of our salvation.

Q. To what does the name of *Christian* oblige us?
A. It obliges us to *render thanks* to God for the inestimable favor of being called to the true faith.

It obliges us to *know* all that the law of Christ commands us to believe and to do.

It obliges us, moreover, to *lead a life* corresponding to this name; for if any one should pride in the name of Christian, and, nevertheless, live the life of a heathen, such a one would only bear that name for his greater responsibility and condemnation.

And finally, it obliges us to *suffer* every thing, and to be ready to lay down even our lives for Christ, and for the truth of our holy faith, just as Christ suffered and laid down his life for us.

Q. By what sign, in particular, may we know a Christian?

A. By the sign of the holy cross, with which he is wont to sign himself, and the use of which dates by constant practice and tradition, from the time of the Apostles.

Q. How do you make the sign of the cross?

A. Whilst signing ourselves, with the right hand, with the sign of the cross, we say: In the name of the Father, and of the Son, and of the Holy Ghost. *Amen.* The signing with the sign of the cross is twofold; namely: If we sign ourselves with the greater sign of the cross, we place our left hand extended upon the breast, and touch, with the extremities of the fingers of our right, likewise extended, first our forehead, saying: *In the name of the Father;* then with the same hand the middle of the breast, saying: *and of the Son;* and finally, we pass the hand in a right line from our left shoulder to the right, saying: *and of the Holy Ghost;* and joining our hands, and inclining the head, we say: *Amen.* When we make the lesser sign of the cross, we also place the left hand upon the breast, as said above, but with the thumb of the right hand we make a small sign of the (✠) cross upon our forehead, saying: *In the name of the Father;* next, in the same manner, a (✠) cross upon our mouth, saying: *and of the Son;* and finally, a (✠) cross on the middle of our breast, saying: *and of the Holy Ghost;* and conclude by joining our hands and saying: *Amen.*

Q. Why is it that we thus make the sign of the cross?

A. Signing our forehead, we say: In the name of the

actions, and desires, for the honor and glory of the most Holy Trinity. But signing ourselves with the greater or so called "Latin" sign of the cross, we pronounce the words: *and of the Son, and of the Holy Ghost*, whilst signing ourselves over the breast; because the Son, coming down from heaven, became man in the womb of the ever blessed Virgin Mary, through the co-operation of the Holy Ghost. We pass the hand across the breast, from the left side to the right, because the left signifies the state of sin—the right, that of grace. But Christ brought us from the state of sin to that of grace by means of his redemption on the cross.

Q. Has the signing with the sign of the cross any other significations?

A. Yes; for we say, In the "*name*" and not "in the *names*," in order to express, by means of the singular number, the unity of God: and the expression "In the name" is significant of the divine power and majesty, which, in all the three divine persons, is one and the same. Whereas the words: *of the Father, and of the Son, and of the Holy Ghost*, mark the distinction of the three divine persons in the one and undivided Trinity.

Moreover, because the signing itself is made in the form of a cross, we are put in mind of the Passion, and, consequently, of the Incarnation of the Son of God. And the making of the sign of the cross, from the left to the right, reminds us, as already stated above, that by the Passion of our Lord, we were restored to life again, from the death of sin, and are now called upon to abandon perishable goods for the possession of goods eternal.

Q. Why do we sign ourselves with the sign of the cross?

A. In the first place, to make an open profession of our being Christians, and, indeed, soldiers of Christ, who is our chief and leader, and whose victorious banner is the sign of the cross.

2d. We sign ourselves with this sign, in order to call, by means of it, for divine assistance. For the signing with the holy sign of the cross is a short but at the same time, a powerful invocation of the most Holy Trinity, through the merits of the precious passion of Christ; on which account pious Christians are wont to arm themselves with this holy sign on all occasions, as in rising from bed, in leaving the house, in sitting down at table, and particularly in any affair of importance; and this is the very same practice, to which already in the earliest times of Christianity, St. Cyril (first catechist, afterwards archbishop of Jerusalem,) invited the faithful; for he says in his thirteenth catechesis: "Let no one be ashamed of professing Christ crucified, but let him, full of confidence, make with his fingers the sign of the cross upon his forehead, and let the sign of the cross be made before every thing we do, as: when food or drink is taken, going out or coming in, lying down and rising, taking a walk or sitting still;" *i. e.*, use the sign of the cross often, and with confidence to obtain God's blessing for all your actions.

Finally, make use of the sign of the cross as a weapon against all temptations of the evil spirit; since, through the cross, Christ has vanquished hell, and accomplished his victory. For, " when the evil spirits," says the same St. Cyril, in his fourth catechesis, "perceive this sign of the Supreme King, they are terrified, and take to flight." By this holy sign, therefore, man may be freed from many dangers of body and soul, if he use it with faith and confidence in the mercy of God manifested thereby, and in the merits of Christ who died upon it.

Practice—Rejoice, in thy vocation to the kingdom of God, and honor the holy sign of the cross, that triumphant banner of faith, hope, and holy love, which waves from Sion of the holy Church. Excite, too, in thy breast the greatest desire, not only to show thyself every where by the use of this sign, as a Christian, but also as one who is perfectly versed in the science of salvation, that, living a true follower of Jesus Christ crucified, thou mayest be saved through Him.

Q. Into how many principal parts may the Christian doctrine be divided?

A. Into three general parts. For in matters of religion a three-fold question is chiefly to be answered; and only the Christian doctrine answers it satisfactorily. The first question is: Which is the way that leads us to eternal life and happiness, our last end?

2d. Which are the necessary means, and

3d. In what manner, and with what perfection are we to proceed for reaching this end?

Hence the whole of the Christian doctrine divides itself naturally into three principal parts. The first part defines and expounds the way of salvation, and treats of Christian wisdom and justice in general, declaring what and how we are to believe, to hope, and to love, in order to work out our salvation. This part contains, therefore, three chapters, namely: that on Faith, on Hope, and on Christian Charity.

The second part treats of the means of salvation, by the right use of which, we truly walk in the path of faith, hope, and charity, and consequently work out our eternal salvation. This second part is also subdivided into three chapters; the first, treating of Grace; the second, of the divinely instituted means of Grace, or of the holy Sacraments; and the third, of the Sacramentals; *i. e.*, different practices instituted by the church for the sanctification of the faithful.

The third part treats of the care and solicitude we ought to have concerning our eternal salvation, proposing the manner in which we may be guided in the practice and acquisition of Christian wisdom and justice, and thus arrive at the height of Christian perfection. The third part is likewise subdivided into three chapters, the first of which lays before us the manner of avoiding evil, the second that of doing good, and the third the virtues of Christian perfection.

In conclusion, we are reminded of those things which should be especially considered, in order that we may carry on the work of salvation with vigilance, and under the guidance of Christian zeal and prudence.

These are the principal parts and divisions of the Christian doctrine which every well-instructed Christian ought to know, in order to show himself worthy of his name, and to be able to give an account of his faith and his practice.

We have chosen to take and to lay down this plan of the Christian doctrine, rather than any other, because it seemed to us to correspond best with man's destiny, and the relation regarding his end. For we are, as the Apostle so earnestly reminds us, and as the whole order of divine providence in the work of our salvation clearly evinces, we are, I say, essentially travellers and pilgrims on the road to our country, to our home, which is heaven. Now, since the order, by which salvation is obtained, points out the way of eternal happiness, and he who journeys in it can only be interested in the three questions mentioned above, to wit: Which is the true way to salvation? Which are the means necessary for obtaining it? and, With what care are they to be employed? it is plain that the whole Christian doctrine of salvation follows naturally and readily this division.

FIRST PART.

THE WAY OF SALVATION.

CHAPTER I.

ON FAITH.

Q. What is Christian faith?
A. Christian faith is a gift of God, and a supernatural light, by which man, enlightened, professes and firmly believes, all that God has revealed, be it written or not, because God teaches us so by his Church.

Faith does not rest on the experience of the senses, nor on human power and intelligence, but on the authority of God revealing himself; because the eternal truth, which is God, can neither deceive, nor be deceived. And hence it is the property of faith, to subject the understanding, in obedience to Christ, to the teaching of the Church, not admitting even a shadow of doubt.

Q. Is faith necessary for salvation?
A. Yes; for St. Paul says: "Without faith it is impossible to please God." *Heb.* xi. 6. The foundation of our salvation is faith, without which we can neither know, nor invoke and serve God as we ought. "If you will not believe, you shall not continue." *Isaiah* vii. 9.

"For he that cometh to God, must believe," says St. Paul, xi. 6. "He that believeth not, shall be condemned," and "is already judged." *Mark* xvi. 16; *John* iii. 18.

Q. But does man know nothing at all about God and the affair of his salvation, without faith?
A. He knows indeed something, but by no means all, and

that which, by the light of reason and the voice of conscience, he does know about God and his holy will, for doing good and avoiding evil, and which is called *natural* religion, even this he does not know sufficiently well, as to be by himself capable of doing always what is right, particularly in strong temptations. For by the mere light of reason he cannot discover the source, whence, the perversions of our inclinations and passions, the wickedness of the world, the corruption of human nature, derived their origin. Of himself, man is likewise unable to find means of reconciliation after falling into sin; and he knows nothing of his condition after death, in the world eternal. All these questions, our holy faith can alone answer with certainty. The best proof of this is the nations of the world, that lived before Christ, and walked in the night of heathenism during a period of four thousand years. Even the wisest of their philosophers could not resolve those vital questions, either for themselves, or for the people. Another proof we have even at the present day, in the nations that have not as yet opened their eyes to the light of the Gospel. The same darkness of heathenism is yet brooding over them, over the learned as well as the unlearned. They are abiding not only in ignorance, but in the mists of their own inventions—for, deciding on matters of religion without faith, will necessarily produce a mixture of the most absurd assertions and fables. Another proof of this is finally furnished by those learned men, who, despising the blessed inheritance of faith, reject the truths of revelation; and, as soon as they have done so, fall back into the night of ignorance, as regards those essential questions which relate to salvation.

Q. Is faith alone sufficient for salvation?

A. By no means; in order to enter eternal life, it is necessary, besides, that we keep the Commandments of God and those of the Church, or, in other words, we must also do good *works* and diligently practise all those virtues, which, by the duties of religion and those of our state of life, we are bound to fulfill. For it is this which faith teaches and obliges us to do.

"If thou wilt enter into life," says our Lord, "keep the Commandments." *Matt.* xix. 17. And again: "Not every one that saith to me, Lord, Lord, shall enter into the kingdom of heaven, but he that doeth the will of my Father who is in heaven, he shall enter into the kingdom of heaven." *Matt.* ii. 7–21. And, speaking of the last day, Jesus Christ says expressly: "Then will he render to every man according to his works." *Matt.* xvi. 27. St. James, in his epistle, lays down the same doctrine: "Even so," says he, "faith, if it have not works, is dead in itself; for, as the body without the spirit is dead, so also faith without good works." *James* ii. 17–26.

Q. What, then, must the qualities of faith be, in order that we may be saved by it?

A. It must be a *living* faith, namely, practical and productive of good works. It must be a full faith, or our faith must also be *entire*—that is to say, we must believe *all* that God proposes to us by the Church; for this the authority of God demands of us—that authority which, with regard to every article of faith revealed to us, is always the self-same supreme, divine authority.

Q. How many sources are there from which we derive our knowledge in matters of faith?

A. In general, there are two sources, namely: The Holy Scripture and Tradition.

Q. What do you understand by Holy Scripture?

A. By Holy Scripture, I understand all those books or sacred writings, the contents of which have been written under the inspiration of the Holy Ghost, from the beginning, through Moses and the Prophets, down to the times of the Apostles, and which have been acknowledged and accepted as such by the Church.

Q. How many books of this kind are there?
A. Seventy-three.

Q. How are they divided?
A. They are divided into the Old and New Testaments.

Q. Which books belong to the Old, and which to the New Testaments?

A. To the Old Testament belong those which were written by Moses, David, Solomon and the Prophets, and by other holy men, under divine inspiration, before the coming of Christ.

Q. How many of them are there, and how are they divided?

A. The Old Testament is made up of forty-six books, and they are divided into historical, prophetic, and moral or instructive books.

Q. Which are the historical books of the Old Testament?
A. The historical books are:
The Book of Genesis, or the Creation,
" " Exodus, or the departure from Egypt.
" " Leviticus,
" " Numbers,
" " Deuteronomy, or the Book of Laws.
" " Josue,
" " Judges,
" " Ruth,
The 1st book of Kings *alias* I. of Samuel.
" 2d " Kings.
" 3d " Kings.
" 4th " Kings.
" 1st " Paralipomenon, *alias* I. of Chronicles.
" 2d " Paralipomenon.
" 1st " Esdras.
" 2d " Esdras, *alias* Nehemias.
" book of Tobias.
" " Judith.
" " Esther.
" " Job.
" 1st " Machabees.
" 2d " Machabees.

Of these historical books, those from Genesis to the first book of Esdras, contains the history of the world, and that of the people of God, till the Babylonian captivity.

The books of Esdras, and those of the Machabees, contain the history of the people of God after the Babylonian captivity.

The books of JOB, RUTH, TOBIAS, JUDITH, and ESTHER, contain each the history of an individual, written by a special disposition of divine providence, under the inspiration of the Holy Ghost, because all the events relating to those persons are calculated to excite, to strengthen, and to animate our confidence in the providence of God; that confidence stood, especially in the Old Testament, in need of a particular support, because all hope of salvation rested on the Redeemer that was to come.

Q. Which are the prophetical books?
A. They are the following:
ISAIAS,

Jeremiah, together with The Lamentation, and the book of Baruch.
Ezechiel,
Daniel,

These four, because their prophecies are more extensive, are styled the four greater Prophets.

Next follow the books of the twelve minor or lesser Prophets, who are so called, because their prophecies are not so extensive as those of the first. They are Osee, Joel, Amos, Abdias, Jonas, Micheas, Nahum, Habacuc, Sophonias, Aggeus, Zacharias, and Malachias.

Q. Which are the books of moral instruction?
A. The books of moral instruction are these:

The book of the Psalms of David.
" " Proverbs of Solomon.
" " Ecclesiastes.
" " Canticle of Canticles.
" " Wisdom.
" " Ecclesiasticus.

Q. What books constitute the sacred writings of the New Testament, and how are they divided?
A. The New Testament is made up of twenty-seven books: their order is as follows:

1. The four Gospels, bearing respectively the names of St. Matthew, St. Mark, St. Luke, and St. John.

2. The Acts of the Apostles, written by St. Luke.

3. The Epistles of St. Paul, which are fourteen in number, namely:

The Epistle to the Romans.
" 1st " " Corinthians.
" 2d " " Corinthians.
" " " Galatians.
" " " Ephesians.
" " " Philippians.
" " " Colossians.
" 1st " " Thessalonians.
" 2d " " Thessalonians.
" 1st " " Timothy.
" 2d " " Timothy.
" " " Titus.
" " " Philemon.
" " " Hebrews.

4. The remaining canonical Epistles of the Apostles, namely:—

    The Epistle of St. James.
    " 1st " St. Peter.
    " 2d " St. Peter.
    " 1st " St. John.
    " 2d " St. John.
    " 3d " St. John.
    "   " the Apostle St. Jude.

5. The Apocalypse, or Revelations of St. John.

Q. Who has guaranteed all those books of the Old and New Testament as divinely inspired?

A. The Church, from the earliest times of Christianity, as the Holy Council of Trent has declared; which Council, in its Fourth Session, pronounces the sentence of excommunication on those who refuse to accept as divine and canonical those books, with all their parts, just as the Catholic Church receives them, and as they are contained in the Latin edition of the Vulgate.

Q. Where, then, do we find the Holy Scriptures?

A. In the Catholic Church, which, after receiving them directly from the Apostles, has, by the assistance of the Holy Ghost, preserved them inviolate. All the sects which sprung up afterwards took the Bible with them from the Catholic Church. Suppose the Church not to be true, whence would they know that they themselves had the true Bible?

Q. Are the Holy Scriptures the only source and rule of faith?

A. By no means; for first: they do not contain all that God has revealed, as they themselves bear witness, by referring to oral tradition.

In the Epistle to the Thessalonians, St. Paul writes thus: "Stand firm; and hold the traditions which you have learned, whether by word or by our Epistle." 1 *Thess.* ii. 14. And for this reason he praised the Corinthians in these words: "Now I praise you, brethren, that in all things you are mindful of me, and keep my ordinances as I delivered them to you." 1 *Cor.* xi. 2.

Moreover, he exhorts the Thessalonians "to withdraw themselves from every brother, walking disorderly, and not according to the tradition which they had received from the Apostles." 1 *Thess.* iii. 6.

In the same manner does St. John make mention of the tradition of the Apostles, and gives us to understand that more is contained in it than in the Holy Scriptures. For in one of his Epistles, he writes thus: " Having more things to write to you, I would not by paper and ink, for I hope that I shall be with you, and speak face to face." *2 John*, 12. In his third Epistle, he repeats the very same; *3 John*, 13. And he concludes his Gospel with these memorable words: " But there are also many other things which Jesus did ; which, if they were written every one, the world itself, I think, would not be able to contain the books that should be written." *St. John*, xxi. 25. From this it is plain that all that the Apostles delivered to the Church is not contained in the Holy Scriptures.

Christ, our Lord, himself wrote nothing at all. And many of the Apostles likewise did not write ; whereas, all of them preached to the nations, as St. Paul assures us: " Verily," says he, " their sound went over all the earth, and their words unto the ends of the whole world." *Rom.* x. 18. Their spoken word the Church received, and keeps with infinite respect, teaching her ministers, to whom she has intrusted the office of promulgating the divine word; and to teachers sent by the Church is applicable now, and to the end of time, the command of our Lord Jesus Christ: " He that heareth you, heareth me ; and he that despiseth you, despiseth me." *Luke* x. 16. " By this," writes St. John, " we know the Spirit of truth, and the spirit of error." 1 *John*, iv. 6. That is, by this submission to the lawful ministry of the Church, we may know the believer and the unbeliever, and discern between them.

Secondly. The Holy Scripture is not written sufficiently plain for all to understand it. Every one that reads the Scripture must be aware of this, and the Holy Scripture itself testifies it. When the Apostle Philip, approaching the chariot in which the courtier of the queen of Candace was sitting, in the act of reading the prophet Isaias asked whether he understood what he was reading, the courtier answered thus: "How can I, unless some one show me?" *Acts*, viii. 31. Now, if a man of such high standing as he, who lived eighteen centuries ago, and was, moreover, an inhabitant of the East, did not understand the Scriptures of the Old Testament, how is it possible that, at the present day, every man should be able to understand it? And the Apostle St. Peter, himself, says of the Epistles of St. Paul, that in them "there are some things hard to be understood, which the unlearned and unstable wrest, as also the other Scriptures, to their own perdition." 2 *Pet.* iii. 16. "Whence else spring all heresies, than because the Holy Scripture, in itself good, is badly understood." Thus St. Augustine.

Thirdly. The Holy Scripture is written in a language which is not now spoken, and he who does not know this language is not competent to judge whether a translation is correct.

Fourthly. In point of controversy, the Holy Scripture cannot interpret itself, since it is but a book, the meaning of which any one may wrest as he pleases. For, of what use would it be to place a book of laws in the judgment-hall, and say: Let every one who has a lawsuit, decide his case from the law-book. Certainly there would be no end to litigation, and every one might contend that the right was on his side. St. Jerome has already said: "There has never been a heretic who did not quilt a pillow for his errors from the text of Holy Scripture."

Fifthly. The Holy Scriptures were not known or circulated before the fourth century.

Sixthly. The Holy Scripture was an exceedingly rare book till the invention of printing in the fifteenth century, and cost such a price, that it was only the rich who were able to procure it. And yet the Gospel was, according to Christ, to be preached, in a special manner, to the poor.

Seventhly. The greater part of mankind were unable to read then, as they are even now. What benefit, therefore, could those people derive from the Bible alone?

Q. Is it right, then, that any one may choose for himself, from Scripture alone, whatsoever he wishes to believe, and interpret the same as he pleases?

A. No, every one is bound to submit to the interpretation of the Church, to whom God entrusted the Holy Scriptures—that Church which is "the pillar and the ground of truth." 1 *Tim.* iii. 15. "Our mother, the holy Catholic Church, preserves, and always will preserve, the truth in its purity; for she is governed and taught by God, and she is the only teacher of salvation." Thus St. Cyprian to the bishops assembled at Carthage.

Q. Is every one allowed to read the Scriptures at the pre-

A. The Church wishes that the Christian people should read the Holy Scripture, for their instruction and edification; but in order that they may understand what they read, she wills that the people should read the Scripture with explanations authorized by herself, in order that they may really read it with profit, and not run the risk of receiving harm from reading inconsiderately what they do not understand, and may misinterpret to their own destruction.

Q. How do we come to know that portion of God's revelation, which is not contained or found recorded in Holy Scripture?

A. By means of oral transmission or tradition.

Q. What is the opinion of the holy Fathers, concerning tradition?

A. Irenæus, one of the earliest Fathers of the Church, writes thus in his book against the Heretics: ".All those who wish to see the truth, see in every Church the Tradition of the Apostles which is spread throughout the whole world; for it has come down to us, through the uninterrupted succession of the bishops ordained by the Apostles." And again: "Those bishops and priests are the guardians of our faith, and the interpreters of the Sacred Writings to us, without any danger of error." It was through the succession of the bishops, to whom the Apostles gave in charge the Churches established in every place that the true and genuine interpretation of Holy Writ was propagated without addition or diminution, and so delivered to us. And thus the reading of the Scripture is now safe and secure, and its text free from distortion.

Tertullian writes in the same manner in his book, entitled, "De Præscriptione." He says: "Jesus Christ sent his Apostles to preach; no other preachers than those whom Christ invested and commissioned to preach, are to be received, for what he revealed is sufficient. But that which those preached, and which Christ revealed, needs, in my opinion, no other proof than that of the very Churches which the Apostles established, partly by the living word, partly by subsequent Epistles." And again: "We do believe what those apostolic Churches believe; for we are in communion with them, and this our doctrine is true."

Origen, in his first book, styled: "Periarchon," writes thus: " We must not believe heretics, because they quote the

Holy Scriptures; nor are we allowed to swerve from the ecclesiastical tradition, or to believe it otherwise than the Church of God delivered it to us through the succession."

St. Basil, in his book of the Holy Ghost, chap. ii. 27, writes: "We have some articles of faith from the Holy Scripture, others we received by the Tradition of the Apostles . . . which the Apostles preached, the Fathers believed and the martyrs confirmed with their blood."

In support of our article of faith, regarding the unwritten doctrine of the Catholic Church, St. John Chrysostom expresses himself briefly and forcibly thus: "It is the Tradition—do not ask, therefore, any further." *Hom.* iv. *on* 2 *Epist. to the Thess.*

Justly, then, did the first General Council of Nice already declare: "The ecclesiastical Traditions are to be kept unanimously and inviolably, whether they be written or not." And all the Councils and Fathers of our holy Church give the same unanimous decision in this regard; and this truth, as shown by the above cited definition of the Council of Trent, is an article of faith.

Q. Where are the Traditions of the Church to be found?

A. In the living ministry of the Church, in the writings of the holy Fathers and in the approved ecclesiastical writers of the first centuries of Christianity. The best known are the following: St. Hermas, St. Clement of Rome, St. Ignatius the Martyr, St. Polycarp, St. Justin the Martyr, Athenagoras, St. Irenæus, St. Cyprian, Tertullian, St. Athanasius, St. Hilary, St. Basil, St. Ephrem, St. Cyril of Jerusalem, St. Gregory Nazianzen, St. Ambrose, St. John Chrysostom, St. Jerome, St. Augustine and a host of others down to the time of St. Bernard, St. Thomas Aquinas and St. Bonaventure.

Of all these, St. Augustine, St. Ambrose, St. Jerome and St. Gregory the Great, are called, by way of distinction, the four Doctors of the Church.

Q. But might not the holy Fathers err?

A. Individually they might, but if all of them agree, they could not; for then they stand forth as witnesses of the universal doctrine of the holy Church, which is infallible, and hence it is that no man is allowed to interpret the Holy Scripture in opposition to the unanimous doctrine of the holy Fathers, as the Council of Trent, in the decree of the Fourth Session, expressly teaches and decrees.

Q. Is there a short summary of the chief things that we are bound to believe?

A. Certainly there is, viz.: the Apostles' Creed, of which the Church has made use ever since the time of the Apostles; because it contains, in brief, all the most necessary truths of the Christian doctrine.

Q. What is the Apostles' Creed?

A. 1. I believe in God, the Father Almighty, Creator of heaven and earth.

2. And in Jesus Christ, his only Son, our Lord;

3. Who was conceived by the Holy Ghost, born of the Virgin Mary;

4. Suffered under Pontius Pilate, was crucified, dead and buried;

5. He descended into hell; the third day He rose again from the dead;

6. He ascended into heaven; sitteth at the right hand of God the Father Almighty;

7. From thence He shall come to judge the living and the dead.

8. I believe in the Holy Ghost;

9. The Holy Catholic Church; the Communion of Saints;

10. The forgiveness of sins;

11. The Resurrection of the body;

12. And life everlasting. Amen.

Q. For what is the Apostles' Creed intended?

A. To place before our eyes a short summary of all those facts which give us a knowledge of God and His works, and which we must necessarily know, in order to lead a truly Christian life, and thereby work out our salvation. But to effect this, it is necessary to know the most Holy Trinity, and confess our belief in it; and the division of the Apostles' Creed into its three principal parts correspond wonderfully well with this knowledge of the most Holy, undivided Trinity: the first part acknowledging the Creation; the second, the Redemption; the third, the Sanctification of man through the operations of the Three Persons of the one and undivided Trinity. The whole is concluded by professing our belief in that life everlasting, which we shall commence to live, when we shall see the Triune God in His glory, face to face, as He is. 1 *John*, iii. 2.

Practice.—Thank our Lord, from the depths of your heart,

for the gift of faith, and endeavor to animate it within you, in order that you may live the life of faith. Think, thereby, of St. Peter, the martyr, who gave his life for the faith, and who, in the hour of combat, whilst reciting the Creed, fell bleeding to the ground, and wrote thereon at the moment of his death, with his own blood, the words: "I BELIEVE."

I.

THE FIRST ARTICLE OF FAITH.

Q. Why do we say in this article: "I believe?"

A. Because *to believe* is the first act of the Christian life, and the foundation of our salvation; hence when the courtier of the queen of Candace desired to be baptized, St. Philip answered him first of all: "If thou believest . . . thou mayest." And the eunuch said: "I believe," and he was immediately baptized by Philip. *Acts*, viii. 37–38.

Q. What is it to believe?

A. To believe is to assent firmly, with heart and mind, to all that God has revealed, as soon as the holy Catholic Church proposes it to us as an article of faith. The reason of this belief is: Because God, who is the truth, has given the Church to us as a mother and instructor.

Q. What is God?

A. God is the self-existing, eternal, infinitely perfect being, who gave existence to all other things. "Yet to us there is but one God, the Father, of whom are all things." *St. Paul*, 1 *Cor.* iii. 5–6.

Q. How do we obtain a clearer and more distinct knowledge of God?

A. By considering the infinite perfections or attributes of the divine nature in three persons.

Q. Which are the attributes of God?

A. They are the following:

God is eternal. That is to say: God had never any beginning, but always was, is, and ever shall be. In the divine nature there is no succession of time. GOD IS!! Admirably does St. Augustine express himself on this subject: "God is, as He was, and thus He shall be for ever; or rather, there is no past or future in Him, the undivided eternal being." "Before the mountains were made, or the earth and the world were formed; from eternity and to eternity thou art God." *Psalm*, lxxxix. 2.

God is immense and omnipresent. That is to say: Even as God has no limits as to time, and is infinite, neither is He confined within the bounds of space. God *is*, and is on that account, *everywhere* present with his essence and His power.

"Do not I fill heaven and earth, saith the Lord." *Jeremiah*, xxiii. 24. "Whither shall I go from Thy spirit? or whither shall I flee from Thy face? If I ascend into heaven, Thou art there: If I descend into hell, Thou art present." *Psalm*, cxxxviii. 7–8.

God is a pure spirit. That is to say: God is a being absolutely indivisible, having an infinitely perfect understanding and will, but no body and no parts. "God is a spirit," says Jesus Christ himself. *John*, iv. 24.

God is omniscient. That is to say: He knows all things, the past, the present, and the future. He knows the most secret things. He knows every thought and every desire of our heart. He knows even all things that are merely possible, and all the conditions under which they are, or are not possible. God knows every thing. "Neither is there any creature invisible in His sight; but all things are naked and and open to His eyes." Thus St. Paul, *Hebrews*, iv. 13. "The Lord searcheth all hearts, and understandeth all the thoughts of minds." 1 *Paralip.* xxviii. 9.

God is Almighty. That is to say: He can do all things, by the mere power of His will, without instruments, without labor, without loss of time; the very moment He wills anything, it is. "Whatsoever the Lord pleased He hath done, in heaven, in earth, in the sea, and in all the deeps." *Psalm*, cxxxiv. 6. "He spoke, and they were made; He commanded, and they were created." *Psalm*, cxlviii. 5. "I am the Almighty God." *Genesis*, xvii. 1.

God is all-wise. That is to say: He wills only what is best, and to that end, He always chooses the best means. "How great are Thy works, O Lord! Thou hast made all things in wisdom." *Psalm*, ciii. 24. "O the depth of the riches, of the wisdom, and of the knowledge of God." *Romans*, ii. 33.

God is infinitely holy. That is to say: God is himself the law of all good; so that, whatever accords with His will, is good and holy, and whatever does not accord is bad. He is the essential holiness; and for that reason, He abhors the least evil, and is pleased with the least good, in any of His creatures.

"I am the Lord your God: be holy, because I am holy." *Leviticus*, ii. 44. " Holy, holy, holy, Lord God of hosts; all the earth is full of his glory." *Isaias*, vi. 3.

God is infinitely good. That is to say: He is the essential as He is the infinite and the supreme good. He is not only infinitely perfect himself, but He wills also of himself nothing but what is good for His creatures. All good comes to them only from Him. "None is good but God alone." *St. Luke*, xviii. 19. "Great is the Lord, and greatly to be praised: and of His greatness there is no end." *Psalm*, cxliv. 3. "Every best gift, and every perfect gift, is from above, coming down from the Father of lights." *James*, i. 17.

God is infinitely true and faithful: God is truth itself; *i. e.*, in God there can be no falsehood; in him there can be no deceit or no delusion, but whatever He says is true, and whatever He promises he fulfils.

"God is not as a man that He should lie, nor as the son of man that He should be changed. Hath He said, then, and will He not do? Hath He spoken and will He not fulfil?"

God is infinitely merciful. That is to say: He pardons the sinner all the guilt contracted by sin, if he be willing, by the aid of divine grace, to quit his evil ways, to do penance, and atone for his sins.

" O the Lord, the Lord God, merciful and gracious, patient and of much compassion, and true." *Exod.* xxxiv. 6.

"And His mercy is from generation to generation, to them that fear Him." *Luke*, i. 50. "As I live, saith the Lord God, I desire not the death of the wicked, but that the wicked return from his way, and live. Turn ye, turn ye from your evil ways." *Ezech.* xxxiii. 11.

God is infinitely just. That is to say: He rewards and punishes every one according to his merits without regard to persons.

" Who, without respect of persons, judgeth according to every one's works." 1 *Peter*, i. 17. "His justice continueth for ever and ever." *Psalm*, cx. 3.

God is infinitely free. That is to say: All that God does, He does not by necessity or by chance, but according to the counsel of His most perfect will.

"Whatsoever the Lord pleaseth He hath done." *Psalm*, xxxiv. 6. "Who worketh all things according to the counsel of His will." *Ephes.* i. 11.

God is life and supreme happiness. That is to say: God possesses with the most perfect consciousness the essence of His infinite perfections; He is also the source of the life and the happiness of His creatures. "As the Father hath life in himself, so He hath given to the Son also to have life in himself." *John*, v. 26. Thus Christ himself, "Who giveth to all life, and breath, and all things." *Acts*, xvii. 25.

God is infinite Majesty. That is, by saying, God is infinite Majesty, we mean to express the most glorious state of His nature, emanating directly from the infinite perfections of the Deity. This majesty of God is called by the theologians the internal glory of God. But from this must be distinguished the external glory, by which we understand the majesty of God, as it shines forth in the creatures of the universe which are created by Him, and which He rules and preserves by His Fatherly care and providence; on account of this greatness God is to be acknowledged, adored, praised, and glorified by all rational creatures. Holy Scripture everywhere praises this majesty of God. Thus it was that Isaias saw, in a vision, the Lord in this His Majesty as seated on a throne of glory, and at the same time heard the canticle of praise of the heavenly Seraphim: "Holy, holy, holy, the Lord God of hosts; all the earth is full of His glory." *Isaias*, vi. 3. And the prophet Baruch says: "God will bring Israel with joy in the light of His Majesty . . . . that cometh from im." *Baruch*, v. 9. And St. Paul in his epistle to Timo\]y: "Which in his time he shall show, who is the Blessed .nd only Mighty, the King of kings, the Lord of lords." *Tim.* vi. 15. And again: "For of Him, and by Him, and in Him, are all things: to Him be glory for ever. Amen." *Rom.* xi. 36.

God is immutable. That is: He can never change, because as He is infinitely perfect, there can never be change or alteration in Him.

"With whom there is no change, nor shadow of vicissitude." *St. James*, i. 17.

Q. But does it not raise a difficulty, that we cannot conceive those attributes of the Divine nature, as clearly as the attributes of creatures?

A. By no means; for how could the infinite,—and God is infinite,—be perfectly conceived or comprehended by the finite, namely, by limited human intelligence? On the contrary, reason requires that the attributes of God should be above our comprehension, because they are infinite. The attributes of God are incomprehensible, and they must be so, because they are infinite; but to reason it is equally plain, that attempting to deny or to limit those attributes in God, involves such a contradiction that it would subvert the very notion or idea of God. For instance, that God is eternal, is inconceivable to reason, and it must be so; for the idea of eternity denotes the infinite. But asserting that God is not from eternity, but had a beginning, reason recognizes as thorough absurdity; for, who would have created God, or how could God, from nothing and through nothing, possibly pass into existence!! The same holds good with regard to all the other attributes of God: all of them are unfathomable to reason, and necessarily are so; but to doubt or to deny them, reason perceives to be a direct contradiction. Although, therefore, reason does not fully comprehend the Divine attributes in their nature, yet it perceives, with certain conviction, their reality and their unavoidable necessity; and hence, in silent adoration, subjecting the limited understanding of the creature, rejoices in acknowledging and praising a God whose greatness is beyond our comprehension. Moreover, you should not be surprised that here on earth, you do not clearly comprehend the nature of God, since you do not even understand yourself, in regard to your soul, not knowing, namely, how, in union with the body, it can exercise its powers; because, generally, the essence of things, and the manner of their actions, is to us a secret. Or, do you understand how the grass grows and creatures are formed, etc.?

All this we shall know hereafter, when we shall see God himself in that knowledge in which we ourselves are known to him. As for the rest, it should be the aim of our whole life, and of all our actions, as children of God, to imitate and show forth in our conduct the excellence of the Divine attributes, by the practice of virtue, according to what we read in the Book of Wisdom: "To know Thee, is perfect justice; and to know Thy justice and Thy power, is the root of immortality." *Wisd.* xv. 3. And to this we are also exhorted by the words of the Lord: "I am the Lord: be holy, because I am holy."

Lev. xi. 44. And again: "Be you, therefore, perfect, as also your heavenly Father is perfect." *St. Matt.* v. 48.

For this purpose, consider the following points and exhortations: God is eternal, He is of himself the most perfect of beings; you come from nothing, and you were from all eternity nothing; humble yourself accordingly. God is immense, He is everywhere; walk in His presence. God is a spirit, you are a spirit, His image, rejoice in this excellent likeness, which He stamped upon you, and endeavor to render yourself more and more like unto God, by a most faithful observance of His commandments, and a diligent practice of virtue. God is All-knowing; try, before all other things, to increase in the knowledge of Him; for only this knowledge can serve for salvation, and as a means of perfection. God is Almighty; trust in Him. He is infinitely wise;—throw yourself confidently into the arms of His divine providence. God is infinitely holy; strive always to attain to greater sanctity. God is good, He is the essential goodness: give, then, as much as you can to those who want, and be good and beneficent to all. God is infinitely true and faithful: be a lover of truth, and keep your word with God and man. God is infinitely merciful; be you merciful to others. God is infinitely just; think often of the judgment to come, and take care that you may be able to stand before His judgment-seat; especially try to have a holy and pure intention in all that you do. God is infinitely free; see that no inordinate passion or inclination keeps you captive. God is life and supreme felicity; seek your joy and happiness in communion with Him by prayer and an interior life. God is immutable; be unshaken and resolute, especially in temptations. God is the supreme majesty and the infinite glory: ALL FOR THE GREATER GLORY OF GOD, let this be the motto of your life.

Q. Can man attain to the knowledge of God by the light of reason alone, and without revelation?

A. Certainly he can, by the contemplation of the universe No rational being could imagine that this great world could have come from nothing, and by nothing, into existence, or have existed without a beginning from all eternity. From nothing, and by nothing, nothing can ever come. Further. where a number does exist, there can exist no infinity; where no infinity exists, there can be no eternity; and where no eternity is, there is a beginning. But in the world every thing exists in a certain number. Every new day increases the number of days, therefore, as true as time is time, so true is it that the world is not eternal, but had a beginning, and, consequently, a Creator. The harmony and order in the duration of the world proves the same thing. Hence it is with reason that the Psalmist says: "The fool hath said in his heart: There is no God." *Psalm*, xiii. 1. And St. Paul truly says of the pagans, that they have no excuse if they do not believe in God; "for the invisible things of Him, from the creation of the world, are clearly seen, being understood by the things that are made." *Rom.* i. 20. In a similar language does the Book of Wisdom speak, chap. vii., and the Acts of the Apostles, xiv. 16, where mention is made of the sermon of St. Paul at Lystra. But, besides all this, the voice of conscience clearly admonishes us of a most just Judge, who placed this voice within us, and who is—God!

But this knowledge of God is obscure and very imperfect, and is brought into full light only by the word of revelation, which assists us to penetrate deeper into the nature and character of God. A special proof of this is the mystery of the most Holy Trinity, which we can perceive only by the eyes of faith.

Q. Is there more than one God?

A. There is but one God in the divine nature. "Hear, O Israel, the Lord our God is one Lord." *Deut.* vi. 4. "Thou art great, and dost wonderful things: Thou art God alone." *Psalm*, lxxxv. 10. "This is life everlasting; that they may know Thee, the only true God." *St. John*, xvii. 3. "But God is one." *Gal.* iii. 20.

Q. Why do we say, God is one in His nature and essence?

A. Because we distinguish, in the one divine nature, three Divine persons.

Q. Which are the three Divine persons?

A. They are: the Father, the Son, and the Holy Ghost.

Q. Whence do we know that there are three persons in God?

A. From the revealed word of God, which teaches us that in one essence there subsist three, to whom the one divine nature undividedly belongs. They are called: the Father, the Son, and the Holy Ghost. For our Lord himself says: "Baptize them in the name of the Father, and of the Son, and of the Holy Ghost." *Matt.* xxviii. 19. And St. John writes: "There are three that give testimony in heaven; the Father, the Word, and the Holy Ghost: and these three are one." 1 *John*, v. 7.

We confess the most Holy Trinity generally in the Apostles' Creed, and particularly in the Athanasian Creed, thus: "The Catholic faith is this, that we worship one God in the Trinity, and the Trinity in the Unity."

Q. Since, then, there are three persons in the divinity, is each of them God?

A. Yes, each.

Q. Why, then, is it not allowed to say: There are three Gods?

A. Because all three of them have but one and the same undivided nature.

Q. Are the three Divine persons distinguished in regard to their perfection?

A. No, they are equal in perfection.

Q. Was any one of the Divine persons prior to the other?

A. No; but all three are, simultaneous, from eternity, as the nature of God. This mystery of the most Holy Trinity we have to acknowledge and to adore as such, in the fullness of faith, because God himself revealed it to us; but we should not seek, curiously, to fathom its nature, for such an attempt on the part of St. Augustine was rebuked by an angel himself, which happened in this way: When Augustine, as the legend goes, being one day on the sea-shore, was searching into the mystery of the most Holy Trinity, because he was then writing his books on the Trinity, he saw a beautiful little child pouring the water of the sea into a hole by means of a ladle. Augustine said, smiling: "My child, what is that you are doing? The sea is great, and your ladle and the hole into which you pour the water are very small!" "But," replied the child, "it is easier to do, than that which you have in your mind. For you study to compress into a little book an inexhaustible mystery; but before you have succeeded in that, I shall have put the water of the sea into this hole." Thus the child spake and disappeared. But Augustine praised God, and understood how truly the angel, under the form of a child, had spoken. *Cansip.* ii. *Book, Apum* c. 48.

In truth, God would not be infinite, if it were possible for us to comprehend him. Reason itself clearly understands that the nature of God must remain a veiled mystery to man, till we shall see Him as He is, surrounded by the light of His glory. "We see now through a glass in an obscure manner," says St. Paul, "but then face to face. Now I know in part; but then I shall know, even as I am known." 1 *Cor.* xiii. 12. If, however, we wish for some image or similitude of this most sublime mystery of God, we find one in our soul itself; which, being created according to the likeness of God, its Maker, possesses three principal powers: the will, the memory, and the understanding, which three constitute the one undivided soul. Other images of the Trinity may be found in innumerable objects of nature.

Q. How do you distinguish the three Divine persons, one from the other?

A. By the procession of the one from the other. Namely: The Son proceeds from the Father by generation, and is from eternity perfectly equal to him, but the Holy Ghost proceeds from the Father and the Son simultaneously, and is the reciprocal Divine Love essential to both.

Q. What do we mean by saying, the one Divine person proceeds from the other from all eternity?

A. We mean by it the everlasting subsistence of the one person through the other in the entity of God. This, instructed by the word of God, we believe, but dare not rashly scrutinize: and he who attempts it, exposes himself to the censure of folly, and deserves to be rebuked in the words of St. Gregory Nazianzen; in his third book on the Divinity, he says: "You who are not even able to understand your own generation, how could you possibly understand that of God?" St. Augustine, speaking of the Procession of the Holy Ghost, in his third book against Maximin, testifies the same thing. He writes: "Not every thing that proceeds is born, though all that is born proceeds. This I know; but how to discern between the generation of the Son, and the Procession of the Holy Ghost, I know not; I can not do it, for the plain reason that both are incomprehensible."

Q. What do we ascribe to each of the three Divine persons?

A. 1. The Divine Nature,
    2. The Divine Attributes,
    3. The Name of God,
    4. The Divine Operations.

Q. Which are the outward operations of God, and to which persons are they specially ascribed?

A. The outward works of God are: the Creation, the Preservation, and the Government of the world. As these works have reference to the operations of the Divine nature, which belongs undividedly to each person, we necessarily ascribe them equally to all the three persons in common. If, therefore, the works of Might are referred to the Father, those of Wisdom to the Son, and those of Love to the Holy Ghost, it is done only nominally; namely, in as far as that has reference to the relation of the Divine persons. But, since the Incarnation, immediately regards the person, namely, the the Second Person of the Trinity, it is, therefore, in this view, ascribed to the Son of God. Neither the Father, nor the Holy Ghost, but the Son of God, assumed our human nature in Christ in an inseparable union. But, on that account, the second Divine Person did not receive an increase of glory, in preference to the other persons; for not the Divine, but the *human*, nature was elevated by this union; the eternal nature of God remained and remains immutable, as well in as after the Incarnation.

Q. What rules are to be observed, in order to avoid any offence against the definitions of faith regarding the mystery of the Most Holy Trinity?

A. First: In speaking of this most sublime mystery of faith, always employ the expressions of the Church.

Second: Do not use the titles of God in the plural; for instance, do not say: Three Creators, &c.

Third: Verbs may be used either in the singular or plural number. For instance, we say correctly: The Father, the Son, and the Holy Ghost *governs* or *govern* the world.

Fourthly. Neither is it allowed to say: God is *threefold*, but *triune*.

Fifthly. In general we must avoid any expression which would destroy the distinction of persons or the equality of their nature.

Q. How are the Three Divine Persons called, when taken together?

A. They are called "the most Holy Trinity."

Q. Does human reason, naturally, know nothing about this mystery?

A. Human reason, enlightened by faith, finds arguments

for professing the mystery of the Trinity, but without revelation it could never have attained to a sure and distinct knowledge of this mystery. Reason infers from the idea of an eternal and infinite act of understanding and will, a triune principle in the nature of God. It finds also that singleness does not include in itself the idea of the most perfect happiness, as the Trinity does in the unity of God, by a full, reciprocal communication of Divine perfection, knowledge and love. Reason, moreover, finds in the very powers and actions of the soul, the image of God, an indication of this relation of the divine essence. For the understanding, the will and the memory, have, as it were, a threefold and distinct subsistence in the soul, and they are but one soul. In like manner, the inquiring mind of man finds in light, in sound and in innumerable other objects of the outward world, images of that *Trinity;* but, without revelation, man would never have arrived at the certain knowledge of the existence of the most Holy Trinity. This our reason understands clearly, that in what faith teaches us of this mystery, there is not, or never can be, contradiction; because nothing is thereby asserted contrary to one and the same subject in the same relation.

Q. Why do we add to the first article of the Apostles' Creed the word "Father?"

A. Because the Father, as already mentioned, is the First Person of the Deity, and is really the Father of his only-begotten divine Son—of whom we have to speak in the Second Article at greater length. Further, because He is the Father of all the good by adoption; and finally, because He is, by creation, the author of all things, which He preserves and rules with the highest wisdom, bounty and goodness.

Q. Why is *Almighty* added?

A. God has as many divine names as He has attributes; to wit: Eternal, Immense, Omniscient, &c. . . . nevertheless, God is here called *Almighty,* because we are disposed by this acknowledgment, to receive, without hesitation, all that is proposed to us in the First Article of faith, respecting creation.

Q. What do we mean to profess by the term "Creator?"

A. That God has called into existence all things out of nothing, by His word only: "He spoke, and they were made; He commanded, and they were created." *Psalm,* xxxii. 9. God also made all things that are ; and they depend, incomparably, more on Him than on the light of the sun ; for, if God should withdraw, but for a moment, His power, by which the world is preserved, it would fall that instant into nothing. Angels may make something and destroy it again; the evil spirits even can do so ; but none of them are capable of producing any thing, without using pre-existing matter. They may use it, to form something else of it; but to annihilate that matter is not in their power. Thus an architect may build a house of stone, of wood or of any other material ; but he cannot call anything into existence from nothing, by his will only, without instruments, and in an instant; nor can he entirely destroy the matter of which he built the house; all he can do is, to reduce it again to its component parts. It is, therefore, God alone who can be called the Creator, because He alone is capable of producing things by his mere will, and of destroying and annihilating them again if He pleases.

Q. What do we understand by the expression, " heaven and earth ?"

A. We understand by it all the works of God, which He called into existence by His mere will, out of nothing, without help, without labor, without tools, without any waste of time.

But we say : " of heaven and earth," because heaven and earth are the two principal parts of the universe, in regard to rational beings. The angels and the blessed inhabit heaven. The earth is inhabited by men; it is a place of probation for them during the time of this transitory life. All other beings whatsoever have been created only in reference to this twofold species of rational creatures—namely, the angels and men.

Q. When and in what order did God create the world ?

A. God, who stands in need of nothing, because He is, of His own nature, infinitely happy, by a most free act of His will, created the world in the beginning of time—about six thousand years ago, in the order recorded in the Book of Creation, (Genesis).

Namely : " In the beginning God created heaven and earth, and God said : ' Be light made,' and light was made. *Gen.* i. 1–3. Then, within six days, God created all the other things according to their kind and species—namely, the firmament, the earth, the sea, the rivers, the trees, and all beings in the animal kingdom. Finally, on the sixth day, God created Adam, the first man, whose body he framed of the slime of the earth, breathing into it the breath of life—a spirit created of nothing, according to His own image and likeness. Then God sent a deep sleep over Adam, took a rib from his side, and made of it the body of Eve, endowing it with a rational soul. Thus he made man a living, rational being, the most noble of all that live upon earth. "And God created man to His own image; to the image of God He created him, male and female He created them." *Gen.* i. 27.

Q. Did God create anything else besides this visible world?

A. Besides this visible world, God also created the spiritual and invisible world, to wit: the heavenly spirits, or angels, anterior to the visible creation. For we read in Job thus: "All the sons of God," *i. e.*, the heavenly spirits, "made a joyful melody" (*Job*, xxxviii. 7) when they saw the wonders of God's omnipotence so gloriously manifesting itself at the creation of the visible world. "And on the seventh day God ended His work which He had made; and He blessed the seventh day." "These are the generations of the heaven and the earth, when they were created in the day that the Lord God made the heaven and the earth." *Gen.* ii. 2, 3, 4.

Q. Why did God create the world?

A. For the sake of manifesting His internal glory, and in order to bestow happiness on all those of His rational creatures, who do faithfully keep His commandments.

Q. Who governs and preserves the world—that is, all creation?

A. God, by His Almighty power and wisdom: "Thy providence, O Father, governs it." *Wisd.* viii. 1. "He hath equally care of all." *Wisd.* vi. 8. "Cast all your solicitude upon Him; for He hath care of you." 1 *Pet.* v. 7. Christ himself assures us that, though "five sparrows are sold for two farthings," yet "not one of them is forgotten before God." That "the very hairs of our head are numbered," and that none of them falls to the ground without His knowledge. That it is He who makes the lilies grow and clothes the grass, and who, therefore, knows and governs all things." *St. Luke*, xii.

Q. What do we call this tender care of God for the propagation and preservation of his creatures?

A. The Divine Providence.

Q. In what appears, in a special manner, the providence of God for man?

A. In the work of Redemption. In the Old Testament by those noble works done on behalf of his chosen people for the welfare of the whole human race, and in the New Testament by the protection of His holy Church.

Q. Why does the providence of God permit so much evil in the world?

A. In order that the sinner may know the justice of God and be converted; and the virtuous may have opportunity of practising the most sublime and meritorious virtues, especially by an entire abandonment of themselves to the will of God, who ordains and permits such trials. "Gold and silver are tried in the fire, but acceptable men in the furnace of tribulation." *Eccles.* ii. 5. "My brethren, count it all joy, when you shall fall into divers temptations, knowing that the trying of faith worketh patience: And patience hath a perfect work." *James,* i. 2–4.

Q. Why is it that the providence of God often suffers the wicked to live in abundance and wealth?

A. 1. God rewards the natural virtue which they exercise whilst living in sin, by means of temporal goods; in eternity they have to expect nothing, save the consequences of sin and their eternal punishment.

"The Lord patiently expecteth, that when the time of judgment shall come, He may punish them in the fulness of their sins." 2 *Mach.* vi. 14.

2. But God also desires by His exceeding mildness to bring them to repentance, and make them return to Him. "Knowest thou not that the benignity of God leadeth thee to penance?" *Rom.* ii. 4.

Q. Why does the providence of God sometimes permit that the good also enjoy riches and temporal prosperity?

A. St. Augustine answers; "In order to remind us that He is the Lord who guides every one on His way through life, and who as the Lord and Ruler of the world, distributes His gifts as He pleases. But also, in order that they may succor the poor by means of their wealth, and perform other good works for His honor and glory."

Q. How is God's providence manifested to each individual?

A. By the experience of each one's life. He who does not acknowledge this, has never examined his life; and he who does not thank the Lord for this watchful care, has no gratitude in his heart.

Practice.—Praise the astonishing works of God in the creation, and use all creatures to the honor and service of God, after the example of the saints. All creatures proclaim His power, wisdom and goodness. Love particularly to look often up to the spangled heavens, and think what a kingdom of glory God has prepared for you beyond that starry ocean. You serve the Almighty who calls them all by name; consider, therefore, how all nature strictly fulfilling His word, faithfully operates according to its innate powers, agreeably to the will of God. Endeavor to do the same of your own free will. Yes, thank God often in union with all creatures, for the decree of His eternal love and mercy, according to which, He created you to His own image and likeness, and the whole world for you as a means to aid you in serving Him, in order that you might be happy with Him for ever in heaven.

Return thanks to God, moreover for all that His divine providence ever did, since the days of creation, for the preservation and welfare of all creatures, but especially for His paternal solicitude for mankind and for yourself in particular. Never complain of His divine dispensations; never be troubled or fearful. God knows what is best for us; His ever benign providence directs all to the greater good for those who are of good will and walk before Him in humility and trust.

Q. Which are the most excellent beings that God created?
A. The Angels and men.
Q. What are the Angels?
A. The Angels are pure spirits, that is to say, they are beings created after the image and likeness of God, endowed with understanding and free will, but having no body. They are, therefore, by their nature, more elevated than man: "Who makest Thy Angels spirits," says the Psalmist. *Psalm*, ciii. 4. St. Paul writes in similar terms: *Heb.* i. 7. The same Apostle mentions also their superiority over man, according to the Psalmist: "Thou hast made him (man) a little lower than the angels." *Heb.* ii. 7. And St. Peter writes: "Though they," the angels, "are greater than man, in strength and power." 2 *Peter*, ii. 11. "The nature of the angels," writes St. Augustine, "is superior in dignity to all that God created besides." *Book* II., *on The City of God*.

Q. How many angels are there, and how are they distinguished among themselves ?

A. There is an innumerable multitude of angels. "Thousands of thousands ministered before Him : and ten thousand times a hundred thousand stood before Him." *Daniel*, vii. 10 ; *Apoc.* v. 11. There are distinctions amongst them, however, because some of them have been adorned with greater gifts and graces in their creation than the others. The holy Fathers following the Holy Scripture, distinguish nine degrees of dignity among the angels, and hence as many choirs of angels, constituting together three great divisions, each of which comprises three choirs. Beginning with the highest division, we have :

In the first order : The Seraphim, the Cherubim, and the Thrones.

In the second order : The Dominations, the heavenly Powers, and Dominions.

In the third order : The Principalities, the Archangels, and the Angels.

Q. What is the condition and the destiny of the Angels ?

A. The Angels are destined to know and to love God, and to enjoy eternal happiness in His sight. Besides, God makes use of them in the guidance of the visible world, and many of them are the guardian angels of men upon earth, to assist and protect them in dangers of soul and body. "He hath given his Angels charge over thee; to keep thee in all thy ways," says the Psalmist. *Psalms*, xc. 11. And St. Paul writes : "Are they not all ministering spirits, sent to minister for those who shall receive the inheritance of salvation ?" *Hebrews*, i. 14. And Christ himself says : "For I say to you, that their Angels in heaven always see the face of my Father who is in heaven." *Matthew*, xviii. 10.

"It is, in truth, a great honor for the souls of men," says St. Jerome, " that for each of them, from the very instant of creation, there is appointed a protecting Angel." In Com. *Matthew*, xviii. 10. And Origen : "At the side of every one of us, even of him that is the least in the Church of God, stands a good Angel, an Angel of the Lord, who directs, admonishes, and guides him, and who sees daily the face of the Father who is in heaven, for the direction of his acts, and the attainment of special favors in his regard." Homil. xx. in *Matthew*, iii. B.

Q. Is the lot of all the Angels a happy one?

A. All of them were created by God in a state of sanctity and justice, that is in the state of sanctifying grace; but all of them did not remain faithful to God; many of them suffered themselves to be puffed up with pride, and sinned, following the seductive example of Lucifer, the prince of the angels. On account of which they were, on the instant, hurled down from heaven by the good angels, with the Archangel St. Michael at their head, into the woful abyss of hell, where they are now suffering the well-merited punishment of their rebellion against God.

"I saw," says Jesus Christ, "Satan as lightning falling from heaven." *St. Luke*, x. 18. And St. John writes in the Apocalypse: "Michael and his angels fought with the dragon; and the dragon fought, and his angels; and they prevailed not; neither was their place found any more in heaven." *Apoc.* xii. 7–8. And St. Peter in his Second Epistle says: "God spared not the angels that sinned, but, having cast them down into the place of torments, delivered them into the chains of hell to be tormented." 2 *Peter*, ii. 4.

Now the devil and his angels constitute the kingdom of evil which wages war continually against God and his faithful. *Matt.* xii. 26. They, therefore, tempt men upon earth, and seek to injure them in every way, as far as God permits them, in order that after a sufficient trial, they may one day be fit to occupy the places in heaven forfeited by the rebel angels. However, the common enemy of God and man has no power to injure any one, either in his body or his temporal goods, nor to hurt any one's soul by temptation, except in as far as God permits him; unless man, of his own free will, yields to his evil suggestions. "Be sober, and watch," says St. Peter, "because your adversary the devil, as a roaring lion, goeth about, seeking whom he may devour; whom resist ye, strong in faith." *St. Peter*, v. 8. And St. James: "Be subject, therefore, to God; but resist the devil, and he will fly from you." *James*, iv. 7.

St. Augustine, speaking of this, expresses himself very strongly: "The devil can bark, says he, as a dog in chains; he can tempt; but he can bite only those who are willing to be bitten; for he does not harm by forcing, but by persuading us to evil; he cannot force us to consent to evil, but he entices us to do so." Now, as Satan excites man to sin, chiefly by means of the goods and pleasures of this world, Christ and His Apostles call him: "The prince of this world;" *John* xii. 31; *Ephes.* ii. 2, "to whom, therefore all those belong, who thirst after worldly enjoyments, and transgress the commandments of God. For, "He that commiteth sin is of the devil." 1 *St. John*, iii. 8.

Practice.—Praise the Lord who created by His omnipotence such a multitude of heavenly spirits, in whose nature and powers His image shines forth so brilliantly. Rejoice that you are called to be a citizen of the heavenly Jerusalem, enjoying for ever their happy company, and that your human nature has been exalted by Jesus Christ above the greatness and dignity of the holy angels. But walk also in a manner worthy of this your calling, and follow the example of those blessed spirits in the struggle of life, exciting and encouraging yourself by the war-cry of victory: "Who is as God?" Follow their example; imitate their purity of heart, walking constantly in the presence of God, united to Him by prayer; ardently desiring to do His will, and full of zeal for His glory: be always ready to assist your neighbor in his wants, temporal as well as spiritual. But let the remembrance of the fall of so many angels be to you a powerful warning to humble yourself, and to inspire you with a salutary horror of even the shadow of sin. He who found guilt in the angels, and spared none of them, will one day be your judge. Resist the tempter, therefore, in the beginning, manfully and entirely; then let all hell raise against you, it can do you no harm. Honor, in a special manner, the Archangel St. Michael as the patron of the Church militant; the Archangel Gabriel as the messenger sent by God to announce the joyous tidings of our Redemption; the guardian angels of the places where you are living, and those of the souls with whom you converse; but show particular respect to your own guardian angel.

Q. What is man?

A. Man is the most noble being in the visible world, composed of a body by nature mortal, and of a soul by nature immortal, and created after the image and likeness of God.

Q. What were the privileges that God gave to man when He first created him?

A. Man came forth from the hand of God endowed with the most magnificent gifts of nature and grace; and we call this first state of man the state of *exalted nature* or that *of primitive justice.*

But there are seven gifts which particularly characterise that state of man before his fall, namely:

1st. Grace itself, by means of which our first parents, in the state of primitive justice, were in the friendship of God, and children of God by adoption.

2d. A clear knowledge of all things that could contribute to their temporal welfare and their eternal salvation, in order to do good and avoid evil.

3d. The harmony of the powers of both soul and body, in consequence of which they were free from the rebellion of concupiscence; the flesh being subject to the spirit.

4th. A great willingness to do good, and a facility in doing good and avoiding evil.

5th. The immunity from all cares, troubles, and fears; for their wants were abundantly supplied, and there was no danger which threatened them from without.

6th. Immortality—even of their body—if they should not sin.

7th. The eternal happiness promised them, on which they were to enter, not by death, but by transition, enjoying the blissful sight of God, in the company of the heavenly spirits.

Q. Did human nature always remain in this happy state of primitive justice.

A. No, for our first parents, Adam and Eve transgressed the commandment which God had given to them, in order to try what use they would make of their free-will. Satan, under the form of a serpent, seduced Eve. She ate first of the forbidden fruit, and offered it to Adam, who, seduced by Eve, also ate of it. Thus both of them committed a sin of ingratitude and disobedience of the blackest dye, believing the devil rather than God; and they thus forfeited both for themselves and for us their descendants, all those promised gifts and graces, together with the inheritance of heaven. And, besides, they plunged themselves and us into the greatest temporal misery, and, at the same time, into eternal perdition, had we not been redeemed therefrom.

Q. What is this sin of our first parents called?

A. This sin is called *original* sin, because by the fallen nature of man it passed to all the descendants of Adam.

Q. Are all men born with this sin?

A. Yes.

"By one man sin entered into this world, and by sin death: and so death passed unto all men—by Adam—in whom all have sinned." *Rom.* v. 12. This fact is an article of faith, as St. Augustine expressly remarks, when he upbraids the heretics of his time, saying: "It is not I who invented original sin, which was always a point of the Catholic faith, but you who deny it, are without doubt a new heretic." *Lib. de Nupt.*

Moreover, the Council of Trent declares and decides: "If any man say that the sin of Adam harmed only himself, but not his posterity, and that the original sanctity and justice bestowed upon him by God, was lost for himself only and not for us; or that Adam, defiled by the sin of disobedience, drew bodily death and punishment upon the entire human race, but not the sin itself which is the death of the soul, let him be cut off from the communion of the Church, since he contradicts the Apostle who says: 'By one man,'" etc. *Sess.* v. *Can.* 2. And again: "If any man deny, that the first man Adam, after having transgressed the commandment of God in paradise, lost that very instant the original sanctity and justice in which he was constituted, and drew upon him by this crime the anger and aversion of God, and, on that account, became subject to death, and with death fell into captivity under the power of him who then held the dominion of death, i. e., of the devil; and that the whole Adam was brought by the guilt of this crime to a worse condition both in regard to body and soul: let him be cut off from the communion of the Church." *Can.* i.

Q. What is original sin in our regard?

A. Original sin in our regard is a state in which we are deprived of sanctifying grace; and this state we inherit from Adam and Eve by propagation. Original sin, therefore, subsists in us as our own, until we have been regenerated in the salutary waters of Baptism.

Q. What are the effects of original sin.

A. The effects of this deplorable state in us are: In respect to the soul, regarding the intellect, ignorance, and darkness spread over the light of the understanding; and with regard to the will, a certain weakness connected with the evil concupiscence, which, according to the apostle, is a law within us, "fighting against the law of the mind." *Rom.* iii. 23.

But the effects with regard to the body, are a multitude of

the bodily infirmities and hardships of this life, and finally death itself. And with regard to eternity, the loss of heaven, which, for a being originally created for heaven, is the punishment of eternal reprobation.

Besides, concupiscence as a consequence of original sin is a powerful incentive to, and a fruitful source of innumerable, grievous, and personal sins in the adult.

Q. Can we fully understand the mystery of original sin?

A. No, for all that we call sin or consequence of sin is, in its ultimate relation, no object of our understanding, since sin in reference to God takes the proportion of something infinite, which is no longer subject to the judgment of reason alone.

Q. Why, therefore, do we believe in original sin?

A. Because the Word of God expressly teaches it, and because the state of man in his spiritual and bodily miseries here below, sufficiently indicates such a fall on the part of our first parents.

Q. Does not the mystery of original sin involve contradiction?

A. No. For, since Adam revolted against God, it was a just punishment, that the exterior world and the body itself should not any longer obey the spirit of man, and that hence man should lapse into a state in which God did not unite himself to him, any further, by means of sanctifying grace. Now, the want of this in a being originally destined for a supernatural end, is what we call the essence of sin. For sin is the turning away from God to creatures, and this is what happens in man in consequence of his corrupt nature, robbed of sanctifying grace through the guilt of Adam: in it concupiscence wars against the law of the spirit, and prompts man to turn away from God to creatures, in an inordinate manner.

But Adam could give no other nature to his posterity than this very degraded and revolted nature, which, after the fall, was his own and Eve's, and through which we enter into this world, in a state of separation and aversion from God. This state, therefore, is the state of sin, inherent by nature itself, from and through Adam, in every one that is a descendant of him.

Q. Have none of the descendants of Adam and Eve been preserved from the stain of original sin?

A. Yes, one; Mary, the Mother of our Redeemer.

Q. Whence do we know this?

A. From the whole economy of salvation, but particularly from the express word of revelation—to wit: from Holy Scripture, from the testimony of the holy Fathers, and finally from the solemn declaration and decision by the head of our holy Church.

Q. How do we conclude this from the entire order of salvation?

A. Christ was to be the new heavenly Adam, and Mary, His blessed Mother, as it were, a second Eve in the order of grace. When Christ was about expiring on the Cross, he gave us to her as a Mother, in the person of St. John. Now, from this, reason, enlightened by faith, rightly concludes: What was becoming for Christ and His Mother, God did in her regard; but it became Christ and Mary, that she should, from the very instant of her conception, be preserved, immaculate, and free from the curse of sin; therefore, God did so. This was the Sylogism of the celebrated Duns Scotus, at the university of Paris, for maintaining that prerogative of Mary.

How, indeed, could it be that Jesus Christ should take His flesh and blood of a soil which at any time bore the curse of sin? This was not becoming for Him. The body of the first Adam was taken from a pure soil. It was not, therefore, proper that the body of the heavenly Adam, Jesus Christ, should be taken from a soil stained by sin, and that His Mother should have been, even for a moment, under the sway of Satan. The disgrace of the Mother sullies the honor of the Son, who took from her His body and first nourishment. This most intimate union of the Holiest and the Purest demanded, too, the most perfect purity in the Mother that gave Him birth. This immaculate purity was also due to her dignity. She, indeed, the Eve of the new covenant, the Mother of the Son of God incarnate, she, the chosen bride of God, and destined to be the Queen of Heaven, and of all the angels, should not be wanting in any prerogative, gift, or grace, bestowed upon any other creature by the Almighty. But the whole of this visible universe came into existence without a spot of guilt: also fallen Eve was created without a stain of sin; she came forth from the hand of God pure and immaculate. Even there is no devil in hell who was not, when he first passed into existence, a pure and spotless angel. Now, is it probable that Mary, the most noble of all God's creatures—Mary, who was "full of grace," that she should have been deprived of that privilege, and been at the moment of her entering existence an object of divine displeasure, and a captive of the devil? This is contrary to reason enlightened by faith, and contrary to the dignity to which God the Creator called Mary from all eternity. And reason will more easily assent to this truth in that the Church applies those places of Holy Scripture which speak of the wisdom and goodness of the Creator, particularly to Mary, as to the most perfect creature next to the humanity of Christ our Lord and Redeemer.

Q. How is this conclusion of reason confirmed by the Holy Scriptures?

A. In the very beginning, when God's mercy promised to the fallen race of man a Redeemer, we find also the glorious promise which announces the full victory of Mary over sin and hell: "I will put enmities between thee and the woman, and thy seed and her seed: she shall crush thy head." *Gen.* iii. 15. Now, if Mary had been conceived in sin, it would have been Satan that crushed her head, and not she that crushed his. This crushing imports an entire destruction of the satanic power.

In unison with this promise, other texts of Holy Writ have also a special application to Mary, and to her exemption from the curse of sin. And thence she is called the "lily among thorns," the only one chosen, who is all fair and without spot; a sealed fountain of life; a tower which is built with bulwarks, and terrible (to Satan) as an army set in array. *Cant. of Cant.* ii. 4-6. But more particularly yet does the salutation of the Angels prove this prerogative of Mary: "Hail! full of grace." *Luke,* i. 28. Now, how could Mary be called full of grace if the first and most excellent of graces had been wanting to her, namely: that of being immaculate in the sight of God, and pleasing to Him; of having never been separated from Him, but always united with Him in charity and grace? Certainly, had Mary been permitted to choose, she would have preferred the grace of being immaculate even to the dignity of Mother of God.

Q. How does tradition confirm this prerogative of Mary?

A. Relying on those arguments of reason, the tradition of the Church, and those texts from Holy Scripture cited above, the holy Fathers, too, have asserted this prerogative of Mary ever since the days of the Apostles.

Thus we read in the Epistle of the clergy of Patros on the martyrdom of St. Andrew, that that Apostle, when in the presence of the proconsul and the faithful of Patros, making a profession of his faith, and a comparison between the Redemption and the Creation, said: "In the same manner as the first Adam was made of earth immaculate and not cursed, so was also the new Adam formed of earth new and pure, of the body of a virgin, pure and immaculate." *Martyr S. And. Apost. apud Moricelti.* St. Ambrose in his treatise on Ps. 118, calls the Blessed Virgin Mary, "free from every stain of sin." St. Jerome calls her, "light without any spot of darkness."

St. Augustine says: "We do not concede to Satan any part in Mary on account of her birth; its common law was suspended in her regard by the grace of regeneration." *Contra Tul.* iv.

"In Mary, Christ found an abode worthy of him, not on account of the body, but on account of original grace which was in her." Thus St. Maximus of Turin. *Op. S. Maximi Taurinensis ed. Rom.* 1784.

St. Peter Chrysologus says in one of his sermons: "The Virgin was wedded to Christ even in her mother's womb, at the instant of her creation." *De Annunt. B. V. M. Serm.* 140.

St. John Damascene gives the reason why Mary was born of parents barren and old; he says: "Nature thereby ceded to the operation of grace; a virgin Mother of God was to be born of Ann; therefore nature is not permitted to prevent grace; it waits till the fruit of grace ripens." In *Mat. B. V. f., Hom.* 1.

"If Mary had not been always holy and pure," writes the learned Saint Paschasius Radbert, "her flesh would have been a flesh of sin; and if her flesh was of the mass corrupted by original sin, how then was it possible that Christ, the Word made flesh, could remain immaculate, since he would have been made of flesh infected by sin?"

In the following century, John, the Geometrician, sings to the honor of Mary, thus:

>Hail heaven allied! hail best of human kind!
> Untouched by aught of sin! hail Virgin blessed!
>God thee from all eternity designed
> To bear His Son within thy hallowed breast.
>Rejoice, dear Mother, from every stain most free,
>For Adam's guilt has never sullied thee.

"Mary, being entirely immaculate and free from every sin, gave birth to the Holy of Holies." Thus the venerable Hildebert of Tours, in the tenth century. *Ven. Hildebert Tour*, p. 537.

The strictly orthodox St. Peter Damian teaches, in the eleventh century: "The flesh of the Virgin, though derived from Adam, yet remained free from the stain through Adam." *Serm. in Assumpt. B. V. S.* ii.

The liturgical books of divine service, of the eastern as well as of the western church, bear witness to the same thing: introducing by means of the prayers and hymns in honor of the Immaculate Conception, this profession of holy faith in divine service. And more than this, we find since the ninth century, that a proper feast of Mary's conception was celebrated in many places in the Greek and Latin Church. Now, a conception in sin can certainly be no subject for a proper festival; and do you think the Church would have remained silent if that festival had not accorded with her own belief?

After the eleventh century, the profession of this article of faith appeared gradually in a fuller light in the holy Church of God: which believing always the same, yet, by the particular guidance of the Holy Ghost, under particular circumstances, proclaims and professes this or that article of faith more or less openly and solemnly.

It was then that entire universities arose, who made the defence of this mystery of faith a condition of their charter, and conferred no degrees in theology unless the promise was made to defend this prerogative of Mary. Moreover, special confraternities, under the title of the Immaculate Conception of Mary, were established, until finally, in the plenitude of time, the holy Father, Pius the IXth. felt himself particularly impelled by the power of the Divine Spirit, to decide and to define, that this prerogative of Mary, was, henceforth, to be regarded as an article of faith, and to be acknowledged as such by the whole Christian world. He sent a circular letter to all the bishops of the Catholic world, and in the answers of six hundred and fifty bishops there was not found even a single one against this mystery of faith, nay, six hundred of the bishops besought the holy Father to give his decision and define it as an article of faith, which he did accordingly, after invoking the Holy Ghost, on the 8th of December, 1854, in the cathedral of St. Peter at Rome, surrounded by two hundred bishops. The entire Catholic world rejoiced in this exaltation of Mary, the Immaculate Mother of Jesus.

Q. Was Mary not redeemed, then, through Jesus, because she was conceived without sin?

A. Yes, she was; for she owed this exemption from sin alone to the redemption which came to the human race through Jesus, as St. Anselm remarks in some of his writings, saying: "The redeeming power of Christ did embrace not only those that lived after Him, but reached also those that were before Him, so that, hence, He could free her in whose womb He was to assume flesh and blood, from all sin, by way of anticipation. The purity of His divine nature demanded that a mother equally pure should conceive Him.

Q. Who was it that freed us children of Adam, born in sin, from this stain, and from the pernicious consequences of original sin?

A. The same incarnate Son of God, as we solemnly profess in the second article of faith.

Practice.—Thank God, that He cleansed you from the stain of original sin by baptism, and for making you the restored image of God: preserve now with the utmost solicitude that sanctifying grace, and endeavor to become more and more like unto God by the constant practise of virtue. But be sure you also keep up that lasting struggle against the concupiscence of the flesh; and the temporal adversities and sufferings of life you will turn to your advantage for an increase of merit and your eternal joy. Do not give the devil the pleasure of depriving you a second time of heaven, and hurrying you into eternal perdition.

The Second Article of Faith.

Q. What is it that the second article of faith teaches us?
A. It teaches us concerning the Second Person of the most Holy Trinity, the Son of God and our Redeemer.
Q. Why do we say: and in Jesus Christ?
A. Because that is the name of the Son of God, made man.
Q. What does the name, "Jesus," signify?
A. It signifies Saviour: "For," said the angel to Joseph, "He shall save his people from their sins." *Matt.* i. 21.
Q. Why do we incline our head, or bend our knee, when

we pronounce the name, "Jesus," when we do not do so on hearing or speaking the other divine names?

A. Because it is this very name that reminds us of the greatest of the blessings of God, our Creator and Redeemer; for, as the Church says: "To have been born would have availed us nothing, if we had not been also redeemed."

Then, because this name puts us particularly in mind of the humiliation of the Son of God, whom the Father, on that account, exalted, in order that, at the name of Jesus, every knee should bend in heaven, upon earth, and under the earth. We bend our knees adoring with the holy angels, and also the evil spirits do it, because they are vanquished and prostrated by the power of this heavenly name.

Q. How great is the power of the most holy name of Jesus?

A. By means of the most holy name of Jesus we are enabled to obtain all heavenly graces and to defend ourselves against all evil, as far as it is conducive to our salvation.

Q. When should we pronounce this holy name?

A. 1. Whenever we wish to address God in prayer, and to strengthen our confidence in God.

2. Whenever the evil spirit assails us; especially, by temptations against purity, which are effectually repelled by virtue of this most holy name.

3. Whenever we are in any other danger of body or soul, to the end that we may be preserved by the power of this name from all misfortune.

4. In the evening, when we go to bed, let the most holy names of Jesus and Mary be our last words, and in the morning our first thought be of them. Only beware lest you do it out of mere habit or with levity.

5. And finally, at the hour of death, let this name of salvation be in our hearts and on our dying lips, to the last breath we draw—remembering the words of the prince of the Apostles: "For there is no other name under heaven given to men whereby we must be saved." *Acts*, iv. 12.

To this particular veneration of the most holy name of Jesus we are also induced, by the treasures of grace, or indulgences, which the Popes have granted to those who honor devoutly this holy name in life, and by the plenary indulgence granted to them at the hour of death.

Wherefore, let us also, very often and confidently, say and sigh: " O Jesus! O most amiable Jesus! O most sweet Jesus!

O most ardently desired Jesus! O Jesus! through the love and reverence wherewith thy most beloved mother called Thee thus, I beg of Thee to be merciful to me now and at the hour of my death! Jesus, for Thee I live, for Thee I die; into Thy hands I commend my spirit!" Make frequent use likewise of the beautiful and consoling salutation: "Praised be Jesus Christ, for ever and ever. Amen."

Q. Why do we add "Christ?"

A. Because Christ means *anointed*, which is a name of dignity and office; for instance—

Priests, prophets, and kings, were anointed with holy oil. Jesus is the eternal high-priest, "who, reconciling the world to His Father with his own blood on the altar of the cross, ascended into heaven, having obtained eternal redemption. There he is interceding for us with His Father, offering to Him his merits, and pouring forth upon us His graces and benedictions." *Heb.* ix. 12.

Jesus is also the light of the world, whose spirit enlightened the Prophets of old, and through whose word the world received the full knowledge of the true God. It is He whom all the prophets predicted, and of whom Isaiah in particular testified: "The Spirit of the Lord is upon me, because the Lord hath anointed me: He hath sent me to preach to the meek." *Is.* lxi. 1.

Jesus is, moreover, that King of kings and Lord of lords, of whom the angel spoke to Mary: "And of His kingdom there shall be no end." *Luke*, i. 33. And who appeared to St. John from heaven, with the inscription: "The King of kings and the Lord of lords." To him the Father delivered not only the kingdom of His Church on earth, but all power in heaven and on earth, over the whole world, whose principalities and powers shall all be subject to Him at the end of time." 1 *Cor.* xv. 28.

Jesus is also called Christ, in order to indicate by this name that eminently high dignity, to which the human nature of the incarnate Son of God was exalted, surpassing all other creatures in heavenly glory; because in it there dwells the plenitude of the real Deity, according to the Apostle: "God, thy God, hath anointed thee with the oil of gladness above them that are partakers with thee." *Heb.* i. 9.

Q. Whence do we know that Jesus Christ is the promised Messi

A. Because in him was fulfilled all that the Prophets had predicted concerning the Messiah, as may be seen from the life of Christ.

Q. Which are the things that the Prophets predicted, concerning the Messiah?

A. 1. The time of his coming, the circumstances of his birth, of his life, of his sufferings, and of his death.

2. His resurrection from the dead and ascension into heaven, and the sending of the Holy Ghost.

3. The destruction of Jerusalem, which was to take place after his death, the rejection of the Jews, and the conversion of the Gentiles.

4. The founding, the spreading, and the eternal duration of his Church.

Q. How did the Prophets point out the time of his coming?

A. The Patriarch Jacob prophesied that the Messiah would come at that time when the sceptre should have been taken from the tribe of Judah. The Prophet Daniel more clearly indicated that time: he prophesied that from the time of the mandate, issued for the rebuilding of Jerusalem, till the death of the Messiah, there would elapse nearly seventy weeks of seven years each; *i. e.*, nearly four hundred and ninety years. And Aggaeus said: That at the coming of the Messiah, the second Temple would yet stand, and that the whole world would be in great expectation. Now, all this was fulfilled in Jesus, with the greatest accuracy, as both Gospel and history prove.

Q. What did the Prophets say, concerning the birth of the Messiah?

A. That he was to be born in Bethlehem, of a Virgin of the tribe of Juda, and of the family of David; that he should be worshipped and adored by kings coming from the East. *Ph.* vii. 11, xi. 1, and lx. 6; *Mich.* v. 2; *Ps.* lxxi. 10. All this was accurately fulfilled in regard to Jesus.

Q. How do the Prophets describe the life of the Messiah?

A. They prophesy his return out of Egypt, his public teaching, his wonderful cures, his forbearing love and mildness, his public entry into Jerusalem. *Is.* lxi. and xxxv. 3; *Zach.* ix. 9. All this, too, was fulfilled in Jesus.

Q. What do the Prophets say of the sufferings and death of the Messiah?

A. They predict nearly all the circumstances attending it, namely : that he should be sold for thirty pieces of silver—that he should be bound, brought before judges, outraged, and spat upon—that they would pluck out his hair, whip him, give him vinegar and gall to drink, nail him to a cross, and mock him whilst he hung thereon ;' and wagging their heads, cry out : " He has hoped in the Lord, let the Lord help him "—that they would divide his clothes, and cast lots for his upper-garment, and that they would break no bone of his body. *Zach.* xi. 12, 18 ; *Is.* l. 6 ; *Ps.* xxi. 4, lxviii. 24. All this, too, was done unto Jesus.

Q. What do the Prophets announce concerning the works of the Messiah, and their effect after his death ?

A. That his tomb should be glorious, that his body should be free from corruption ; that he would raise himself to life again, ascend into heaven, and pour forth his spirit into the hearts of the children of men. *Ps.* iii. 10, lxvii. 19–34 ; *Is.* xi. 10 ; *Joel*, ii. 28, 29. This was likewise fulfilled in Jesus.

Q. What do the Prophets say of the fate that was to befall the city of Jerusalem and the Jewish people after they had killed the Messiah ?

A. They say, that a strange people would come, together with their rulers, to destroy Jerusalem and the Temple, and that this destruction should last till the end of time. Further, that the Jews themselves should be blinded and rejected, dispersed among all nations, and live without a Temple ; but that they should last till the end of the world, and finally be converted to the true faith.

Now, Jerusalem was destroyed, and the Temple burnt down, by the Romans, seventy years after the birth of Christ. One million one hundred thousand Jews lost their lives, and the rest were driven into exile, and scattered over the whole earth, to be living witnesses of the divine punishment inflicted upon them for the murder of the Redeemer, and as such they are miraculously preserved among the nations even to the present day.

Q. What do the Prophets say concerning the conversion of the nations, and the Church of God, as the kingdom to be founded by the Messiah ?

A. All that we see realized since the descent of the Holy Ghost upon the Apostles during one thousand eight hundred years ; namely, they announced that the Messiah should be the light of the Gentiles, and that all nations should be blessed in Him. *Wis.* xxii. 18; *Ps.* lxxi.; *Is.* xlii. 5.

That He would institute a new sacrifice, a new priesthood, and, therefore, a new covenant, a new kingdom of God, *i. e.*, establish His Church; which kingdom should reach from sea to sea to the boundaries of the earth, and last for all eternity. *Mat.* i. 11; *Is.* lxvi. 21; *Jer.* iii. 15; *Zach.* ix. 10; *Dan.* ii. 44, and xvii. 14. And so it has come to pass; the Church is really established upon earth, victorious and unshaken amid storms and turmoils, as the teacher of nations enlightened from above: sending her missionaries throughout the world, ever since the times of the Apostles.

Q. Were these prophecies known to the world before the coming of Christ?

A. Yes; even in paradise, immediately after the fall of the human race in the person of Adam and Eve, there was promised to them the future redemption and the rescue from the power of Satan. The promise is this: "I will put enmities between thee and the woman, and thy seed and her seed: she shall crush thy head, and thou shalt lie in wait for her heel." *Gen.* iii. 15.

This promise was often repeated in after times, and confirmed, and rendered still more clear, especially to those and through those, whom the Lord had chosen, by a particular favor, to be special instruments in the order of salvation. To this connection belongs especially the celebrated promise made to Abraham the noble patriarch of the faithful: "Because thou hast done this thing, and hast not spared thy only begotten son for my sake: I will bless thee, and I will multiply thy seed as the stars of heaven, and as the sand that is by the sea shore: and in thy seed shall all the nations of the earth be blessed." *Gen.* xxii. 16–18. Christ, the Saviour, was to be a descendant of Abraham according to the flesh, and to bring salvation to all that love of His coming.

Soon after, the Lord confirmed this promise to Jacob, the grandson of Abraham. For when in a dream, he saw a ladder which reached from earth to heaven, and upon which the angels of the Lord were ascending and descending, he heard the voice of the Lord from above assuring him: "In thy seed all the tribes of the earth shall be blessed." *Gen.* xxviii. 4. And so it came to pass.

For this promise was afterwards more and more confirmed

by the election of the people of Israel, by the legislation of Moses, by all the types and emblems of the Old Testament, both in its religious institutions and political relations.

The whole of the Old Testament was, according to the express remark of St. Paul in his *Epistle to the Hebrews*, x. 4, a foreshadowing of the church, as the reign of the coming Messiah. About this reign of God upon earth, and the person of the Messiah, the Prophets, enlightened by the Spirit of God, announced, moreover, the most important events in a manner which gives the most conclusive testimony of the Divinity for the authenticity of the Saviour of the world and His holy Church. For they predicted, as we have seen above, the birth of the Redeemer, the events of His life, His passion, His death, His Resurrection, His ascension, and the fate of the Church which He established, down till the day of general judgment.

The primitive tradition of a Saviour to come was kept up, to a certain extent, even among the heathens themselves, as may be shown from the works of a Suetonius, Tacitus, and other pagan authors of antiquity.

Suetonius in his life of the Emperor Vespasian, writes thus: "It was an old and constant opinion throughout the entire East, that by an indubitably certain decree, at that time descendants of the Jews should attain the highest power." *Vita Vesp.* c. iv. Namely, through the reign of the Church, which, established through Christ by the Apostles, soon actually overspread all the kingdoms of the world.

Tacitus speaks in almost the same terms—he says: "Many persons were firmly persuaded, it being contained in the old writings of the priests, that at the same time the East should become powerful, and that the descendants of the Jews should attain the highest power."

Moreover, in the works of the most celebrated poets of classical antiquity, are found allusions to this primitive tradition, and to a universal expectation of the nations for an event that would tend towards the amelioration, happiness, and sanctification of man.

Virgil sings in his fourth Eclogue, thus:—

> "The last great age, foretold by sacred rhymes,
> Renews its finished course; Saturnian times
> Roll round again; and mighty years, begun
> From their first orb in radiant circles run.

> The base deger. ate Iron offspring ends;
> A golden progeny from heaven descends.
> O chaste Lucina! speed the mother's pains;
> And haste the glorious birth!—
> The father banish'd virtue shall restore;
> And crimes shall threat the guilty world ro more."

Also the celebrated books of the Sibyls bear testimony of this expectation of the nations, and this primitive tradition of a Saviour that was to come, though it was often disfigured by human additions. Justin appeals to them thus against the pagans themselves: "Believe," says he, "the primeval Sibyl, whose books are spread over the whole world ... when predicted clearly and evidently the coming of our Redeemer Jesus Christ." *Graec. Cohert.* i. 25.

We read also in *Tobias* distinctly enough, that the very dispersion of the Jews among the nations greatly contributed to the revival and preservation of this expectation.

Q. Did Christ declare himself as the Messiah, and, in order to prove His declaration, point to those prophecies.

A. Yes, He did. "Search the Scriptures," says Jesus to the Jews, "for the same are they that give testimony of me." *John*, v. 39. At another time, He opened the Scriptures, and quoted a passage from the Prophet *Isaias:* "Now this prophecy begins to be fulfilled in me." Besides, we often read that Jesus said: This or that happens, "that the words of the Prophets might be fulfilled." And when the Samaritan woman at the well said: "We know that when the Messiah comes, He will teach all things;" Jesus said plainly: "I who speak to thee, I am He." In like manner did Jesus, after His resurrection, point to predictions of the Prophets, which had been fulfilled by His life, passion, and death.

Q. Did the Apostles believe and teach the same?

A. Certainly, they did. For, in the very first address St. Peter made to the people, after the descent of the Holy Ghost, he proved that Jesus was the Messiah promised in the Old Testament. The Evangelists, too, constantly refer to the Prophets, when they relate the life of Christ. And the Epistles of all the Apostles everywhere renew this assertion, especially those of St. Paul.

Q. Why does the Church add the words: "His only begotten Son?"

A. Because Jesus, the promised Messiah, is God—namely the Second Person of the Divinity.

Q. Whence do we know that Jesus Christ is true God?

A. 1. From the predictions of the Prophets. They distinctly speak of the promised Redeemer, as God. "God himself will come, and will save us." *Is.* xxxv. 4. "His name shall be Emanual—God with us." And *Jeremias:* "This is the name by which He shall be called: The Lord, Jehovah, our Trust." "Behold I send my angel before me," says the Prophet Malachias, where God, the Lord, speaks of the precursor of the Messiah. *Malach.* iii. And the Prophet Aggaeus asserts, that the Lord would show himself as Saviour and Prince of Peace in the second Temple." *Ag.* ii.

2. Jesus Christ is true God. This is manifest from the Salutation of the angel to Mary. He says: "The power of the Most High shall overshadow thee; and, therefore, also, the Holy One which shall be born of thee, shall be called the Son of God." *Luke,* i. 35.

3. Jesus Christ is true God. The testimony of the Father from heaven shows this clearly. For, at the Baptism, and at the Transfiguration of our Lord on Thabor, a voice was heard from heaven, which said: "This is my beloved Son, in whom I am well pleased." *Matt.* iii. 17, xvii. 5.

4. Jesus Christ is true God. This is clear from the confession which Jesus made of himself as well as from the testimony by which he confirmed the same through his miracles, his prophecies, his doctrine, his life, death, and resurrection.

For Jesus Christ positively asserted, that he had the same nature with the Father, and the same divine power, that he performed divine works, and that he was from eternity, and, by nature, the Son of God. Here are the words of Scripture: "I and the Father are one. Believe that the Father is in me, and I in the Father." *John,* x. 38. "He that seeth me, seeth the Father also." *John,* xiv. 9. "All things whatsoever the Father hath, are mine." *John,* xvi. 15. "What things soever the Father doeth, these the Son also doeth in like manner. For, as the Father raiseth up the dead, and giveth, so the Son giveth also life to whom he will; that all men may honor the Son, as they honor the Father." *John,* v. 19, xxi. 23. "Amen, amen, I say unto you, before Abraham was made, I am." "Dost thou believe in the Son of God?"—So Jesus asked the man born blind. "Who is the Lord?" said he, "that I may believe in him?" And Jesus said to him: "Thou hast seen him, and it is he who talketh with thee." And the man said: "I believe, Lord." And falling down, he adored him. And Jesus permitted him to do so, and thus professed himself to be God.

Q. How did Jesus confirm this testimony of his Divinity?

A. In the first place, by his miracles, of which very many are recorded in the Gospel, and which were so manifest that even his most bitter enemies could not deny them. To these Jesus appealed as an undeniable testimony of his divinity. Thus, when Jesus said: "I and the Father are one," the Jews took up stones, to stone him. And when Jesus asked them on account of which of his works they intended to stone him, the Jews answered: "For a good work we stone thee not, but for blasphemy; and because that thou, being a man, makest thyself God." Then Jesus replied: "If I do not the works of my Father, believe me not; but if I do, though you will not believe me, believe the works, that you may know and believe that the Father is in me, and I in the Father." *John*, x. 30, 31, 32, 37, 38.

Secondly, Jesus confirmed this testimony by his prophecies, especially by those concerning his death and his resurrection by his own power. "I have power to lay down my life and to take it up again." *John*, x. 18.

Thirdly, Jesus confirmned this testimony by his doctrine and by the sanctity of his life. Jesus preached the most pure doctrine, regarding the worship and adoration of God. He taught men the most holy duties to God, in a manner that every one understood and acknowledged: "Never has any man thus spoken!" And he corroborated this doctrine by the example of so holy a life, that he could ask his most bitter enemies themselves: "Which of you shall convince me of sin?" Now, if Jesus were not God, he would have committed the greatest of crimes, and been guilty of the most shocking blasphemy, and have led men into more heinous idolatry than man had ever done before. But this disagrees with his holy teaching, and the example of his holy and virtuous life, especially as Jesus did not derive any temporal advantage from it, but, on the contrary, had to suffer only persecution, torments, and the most ignominious death, as man.

Fourthly. Jesus confirmed the profession of His Divinity by His death, for it was the real cause of His crucifixion.

For Jesus Christ was thus asked by the high-priest: "I adjure Thee by the living God, that Thou tell us, if Thou be the Christ, the Son of God." And Jesus said to him: "Thou hast said *it.*" Then the high-priest rent his garments, and saying: "He hath blasphemed: what further need have we of witnesses? Behold, now you have heard the blasphemy: what think you? But they answering, said: He is guilty of death." *Matt.* xxvi. 63–66. And it was this crime, of which they accused Jesus before Pilate, as a certain ground for His condemnation. "We have a law," said the Jews; "and according to the law He ought to die; because He made himself the Son of God." *John,* xix. 7. Even whilst He was hanging on the cross they mocked Him, saying, "If thou be the Son of God, come down from the cross."—*Matt.* xxvii. 40.

Finally, Jesus proved His divinity by His *resurrection,* which is the seal of the truth for the whole and entire faith, as He himself taught it, and the Apostles preached it. But they believed and taught, that Jesus is the Son of God, and therefore true God.

Q. What is the doctrine of the Apostles concerning the divinity of Christ?

A. The Apostles expressly confess: 1. That Jesus Christ is true God, and the Son of God. 2. That He possesses the whole plenitude of the divinity and the infinite perfections of God. 3. That on this account He is entitled to the homage of all creatures.

"Thou art Christ," answered St. Peter, "the Son of the living God." *Matt.* xvi. 16. "We know that the Son of God is come. This is the true God, and eternal life." 1 *John,* v. 20. "Christ . . . who is over all things, God blessed for ever. Amen." St. Paul to the *Romans,* ix. 5. "In Christ dwelleth all the fullness of the Godhead corporally." The same Apostle to the *Colossians,* ii. 9. And St. John testifies of Christ the Son of God: "In the beginning was the Word, and the Word was with God, and the Word was God. The same was in the beginning with God. All things were made by Him: and without Him was made nothing that was made —and the Word was made flesh, and dwelt among us: and we saw His glory, the glory as of the only begotten of the Father, full of grace and truth." *John,* i. 1–4, 14.

"In Him (in Christ) were all things created in heaven and

on earth, visible and invisible, whether thrones or dominations, principalities or powers: all things were created by Him and in Him. And He is before all, and by Him all things consist." Thus St. Paul to the *Colossi ins*, i. 16, 17. The same Apostle commences his Epistle to tne Hebrews with the following illustrious and all-embracing confession of the dignity of the Messiah, and of the proper divine nature of Christ: "God having spoken on divers occasions, and many ways, in time past, to the fathers by the prophets; last of all, in these days hath spoken to us by His Son, whom He hath appointed heir of all things, by whom also He made the world: who is the splendor of His glory and the figure of His substance." *Heb.* i. 1–3.

Whence St. Paul assures us, that it is written of Jesus in the Psalms: " Let all the angels of God adore Him." *Heb.* i. 6. And again: "That in the name of Jesus every knee should bow of those that are in heaven, on earth, and in hell." *Philip.* ii. 10. Now, according to the doctrine of Jesus himself, adoration is due to God alone; but this adoration is due to Jesus, therefore Jesus is God.

The Apostles also confirmed this faith by their doctrine, by their holy lives, by the innumerable miracles they wrought, by their martyrdom and death, and by the wonder of wonders, the conversion of the whole world.

But regarding the faith of the primitive Christians, this faith is attested, not only by the acts of the martyrs, but also, and more especially by the Creed of the Church, drawn up by the Fathers of the first Œcumenical Council of Nice, and in which the Church solemnly professes her belief in the holy Sacrifice of the Mass, "that Jesus Christ is real God and consubstantial with the Father, God from God, Light from Light, true God from the true God, born of Him, not created, by whom all things were made."

This faith, also, the holy martyrs so often confirmed and sealed with their own blood.

Q. Having considered the arguments for the dignity of the Messiah and the Godhead of Jesus; what are we to think of the Jews, and of the stupidity of the so-called free-thinkers, who say that Jesus was only a wise and eminently just man?

A. Both, indeed, excite our astonishment and pity; but both, too, are a striking proof of the blindness of man, if he voluntarily closes his eyes to the light of faith. As regards the Jews, it is well known that they anathematized any one who should attempt to interpret the prophecy of Daniel, over the preservation of which they themselves watched most carefully, and which would lead them directly to Christ; and yet they do not believe, but purposely closing their eyes, they seek the sun whose rays fall burning on their head. This their blindness is at the same time a punishment of God, for having murdered the Redeemer; but yet, on that account, none of the Jews who is of good will, must necessarily perish. God permits that this veil of darkness should remain on the eyes of this unhappy people, in order that they, as the most bitter enemies of Christianity, may be unimpeachable witnesses of the foundation of the prophecies. In this manner, their historical certainty is established beyond a doubt even before the eyes of infidels, for it is recorded by the testimony of the bitterest enemies of the Christian name, with an accuracy which made them count every letter of every book of the Holy Scriptures so as even to know which is the first, the middle, and the last letter, and how often every one of them occurs. Nevertheless, every Jew has the grace for his conversion, provided he will make use of it; and this many of them do during their life, and, as we hope, many more at the hour of death. Innumerable examples confirm this hope, especially in Galicia and Poland, where the greatest number of them are gathered together, and where it is known, that Jews on their death-bed not unfrequently desire baptism, and thus die with the baptism of desire.

But as for the blinded free-thinkers, who losing their faith in the midst of Christianity, look upon Jesus only as a wise man and the greatest teacher of virtue; this senseless infatuation too, excites in us astonishment and pity. For what wisdom, or what virtue is there in this, that a mere man should pretend to be a God, and thus lead others into idolatry? But this is the very thing which Jesus did, if he is not in reality the second person of the Deity, and he has deluded the human race far more than Mahomet, who made himself only a prophet of the most High, but never laid any claim to the divine nature and substance, or suffered himself to be adored.

He who fancies himself to be a God, is a fool; and he who induces others to believe in him as really so, is a criminal, no hero of virtue, no sage, but the son of perdition, who shall one day come pretending to be God, as St. Paul says; namely, Antichrist. Thus then it comes also to pass here, what the Psalmist said of old : " Malice has belied itself."

Q. In what sense is it that Angels and we ourselves are called the sons and children of God ?

A. In the figurative sense, namely, according to grace, and in as far as we together with the Angels have been created after the image of God, and are like unto Him by the sanctification of grace.

Q. Why are the words " Our Lord " added ?

A. 1. Because Jesus Christ, by His divinity, is our Lord, as is the Father and the Holy Ghost.

2. Because as man He is also our Lord, since he freed us by His death from death eternal, and placed us in the liberty of the children of God; on which account the Father has given to Him all power in heaven and on earth. He is therefore in the true sense of the word our Lord, because He bought us with His own blood, as the Apostle expressly reminds us, saying : " You are bought with a great price." 1 *Cor.* vi. 20.

Practice.—Bear a great love to Jesus, being mindful of His natural dignity and majesty ; and considering in His person, being both God and man, the king of Angels, whom the Father in heaven has crowned with the diadem of power and glory. Consider also what Jesus has done for you and still does; He became your Redeemer, your Father, your friend and your brother ; and think of the mercy, the liberality and the love with which He imparts to you, as the child of His Church, the graces of redemption. Make good use of every opportunity to increase in the knowledge and love of Jesus, and do all you can, to make Him known and revered by all mankind, as their incarnate Redeemer.

The Third Article of Faith.

Q. What does the third article of faith teach us ?

A. It teaches that the same Jesus Christ our Lord, the Son of God, became flesh in a miraculous and supernatural manner, that is to say, He assumed our human nature, in the womb of the Virgin Mary, and was born of that virginal mother, in order to appear among us as the Saviour of the world, and to redeem the fallen race of man by His infinite merits.

We profess, therefore, by this article of faith, that Jesus Christ the only begotten Son of God, took upon Himself our human nature in the material womb of Mary, in a manner altogether beyond the power and order of nature, and was conceived and made man by the power of the Holy Ghost, so that the same person remaining God from all eternity, united to Himself the nature of man, in time. This is the solemn declaration of St. John, the Evangelist. He who resting on the bosom of the Lord, drank in the profoundest knowledge of this ineffable mystery, announces it to us in the following terms: "In the beginning was the Word, and the Word was with God, and the Word was God." "And the Word was made flesh and dwelt among us: and we saw His glory, the glory as of the only begotten of the Father." *John*, i. 1, and 14. The divine Word, namely, which subsists in the Godhead as a person, appropriated human nature to itself forming one person, whence followed that wonderful union of the two natures, by which each of them preserves its properties uneffaced, yet so that the human nature was elevated and ennobled to an infinite extent by this union, according to the remark of Pope Leo the Great, both beautiful and correct in its bearing.

Q. What means, therefore, the expression: "Conceived?"

A. It means that the body of Christ was formed of the human blood of the Virgin Mary by the Omnipotence of God.

Q. What is this mystery called?

A. The Incarnation of Christ the Son of God.

Q. In what does the wonder of this Incarnation of the Son of God consist?

A. It consists in this, that, as soon as Mary had spoken the words of consent: "Behold the handmaid of the Lord: be it done to me according to Thy word;" at that very moment the body of Christ was formed in her womb by the power of God, and the soul of Christ united with it, and both the body and the soul, with the Divinity through the second divine person, in an unspeakable and undefinable manner, so that the whole humanity of Christ remains united to the person of the Son of God, and, consequently, the Deity dwells bodily in Christ, on whom the ever blessed Trinity pours out grace in such overflowing abundance, "tha. of His fullness we all have received." *John*, i. 16.

Q. Why do we say: "Who was conceived by the Holy Ghost;" did not the Father and the Son, too, participate in effecting this wonder of the conception of Christ?

A. Certainly; for each person in the Deity effects in union with the other all the operations of God that are external to Him, and, because all three persons are but one in essence and nature; but, on account of the relation of the Divine persons to each other, the works of might are nominally ascribed to the Father, those of wisdom to the Son, and those of love to the Holy Ghost. Now, since the Incarnation of the Son of God was preeminantly a work of love, the conception of Christ is nominally ascribed to the Holy Ghost.

Q. How many different natures, therefore, are found in Christ?

A. Two; the divine and the human nature.

Q. Are there also two wills in Christ?

A. Yes, the divine and the human, but these ever agree in the most perfect manner, as Christ himself testifies. "Father, not mine, but Thy will be done." But also: "I do always what is pleasing to my Father."

Q. How many persons are in Christ?

A. There is but one, namely, the second divine person.

Q. In what sense is Mary the mother of Christ?

A. In this, that Christ as man, took His body of her.

Q. In what sense is Mary the mother of God?

A. In this sense, that He who was born of her, is according to His person—God.

Q. Who was Joseph in regard to Jesus?

A. He was His foster-father. "Jesus Christ being (as it was supposed) the son of Joseph." Thus, *St. Luke*, iii. 23.

Q. What follows from this article of faith with regard to the manner in which we are to speak of Jesus?

A. That, in speaking of Him, we are never to confound the natures, nor to separate the person; but that, on account of the union of the two natures into one person, there are predicated of course in Christ *human* things of God, and *divine* things of the man, but which are always to be understood in the sense just stated above, namely, without confounding the natures, or separating the person. Thus the Scriptures speak of Christ, thus the holy fathers also, and thus Christ speaks of himself, as for instance: "The Father is greater than I." This holds good of Christ in respect to His human nature; whereas, when the same Jesus says of himself: "I and the Father are one;" He says so in reference to His divine nature. In this there is no contradiction.

Q. Why do we add in this article of faith: Born of the Virgin Mary?

A. Because we profess, by means of this addition, our belief in the maternity of the Virgin Mary, who was before, in, and after her delivery a virgin, and at the same time truly the mother of God, and must be called so, because the one whom she, in accordance with the prophecy of Isaias, conceived and bore, herself a virgin, is in reality true God and true man.

The words of the Angel themselves point clearly to this. "Behold, thou shalt conceive in thy womb, and shalt bring forth a Son; and thou shalt call His name Jesus. He shall be great, and shall be called the Son of the Most High." *Luke,* i. 31, 32.

It was becoming that this wonder of the wonders of God, this pledge of the divine power and love, should be prefigured and declared by signs, and be honored by anticipation long before it was to happen. This was typified according to the unanimous interpretation of the doctors of Holy Writ, by that east gate of the sanctuary, which the Prophet Ezechial saw ever shut. It was also prefigured by that stone mentioned by Daniel, which "was cut out of a mountain without hands," and then "became a great mountain and filled the earth." So, too, with the rod of Aaron, which alone budded, bloomed, and brought forth fruit among the rods of the princes of Israel; so, too, in fine with that bush which Moses saw on fire, but which was not burnt. *Ezech.* xliv. 2; *Dan.* ii. 34, viii. 35; *Num.* xvii. 8; *Exod.* iii.

This most auspicious birth took place at Bethlehem, as the prophet Michaeas had foretold: "And thou Bethlehem, Ephrata, art a little one among the thousands of Juda: cut of thee shall come forth unto me that is to be the Ruler in Israel." *Mich.* v. 2. But we are admonished by the words of the angel, with what joys and exultation we should celebrate the memory of this blissful mystery of our redemption; we are admonished by his words when he announced the tidinigs of joy to the world at the birth of the Redeemer, saying: "Behold, I bring you tidings of great joy, that shall be unto all people; for this day is born to you a Saviour, who is Christ the Lord, in the city of David." *Luke*, ii. 10–11. And suddenly there appeared with the angel a multitude of the heavenly host, praising God: "Glory be to God in the highest, and on earth peace to men of good will." *Ibid.* 13, 14. Now how far should our joy exceed that of the angels, since the Lord did not redeem them, but us. The holy Fathers, moreover, justly remark, that in this work of the redemption by Christ, the most holy Virgin Mary being the Eve of the new Covenant and the mother of the children of God according to the spirit, was in a similar manner to Him the heavenly Adam, what the earthly Eve was to the earthly Adam. Even the apostle often compares Christ with Adam, calling Him the heavenly Adam. 1 *Cor.* xv. 22–45. As namely, in the order of nature, Adam is the head of the human family, so, in the order of grace, in the order of regeneration for heaven, Christ is our head as children of God. And if on the one hand the earthly Adam brought death upon us all, so Christ on the other hand, brought to all of us life. In a similar manner, discerning the prerogatives of Mary, we are allowed to compare her with Eve in paradise. For through Eve who proffered Adam the forbidden fruit, we came to be born children of wrath: through Mary, we received Jesus the blessed fruit of life, and by Him are born again in the charity of God for heaven.

Eve believed the fallen angel, Satan: Mary believed the angel of light. Fallen Eve exalts herself: Mary full of grace, humbles herself to the lowest.

Eve, in punishment of her disobedience, was to bring forth her children in sorrow: Mary, in recompense for her obedience, gave birth to Jesus the Son of God, in exultation of spirit, and remaining a virgin. O would to God, that following the humility, the obedience, and purity of Mary, we were always worthy to be called the children of such a mother; in order that we, too, might be like unto Jesus, and share in abundance the fruits of that redemption which Christ effected by His bitter passion and death.

To that end you will often consider the lives of Jesus and Mary as they are set before us in the pages of the holy Gospel.

The Fourth Article of Faith.

Q. What does the fourth Article of Faith teach us?
A. It teaches us that Christ, after having labored for our salvation during a space of thirty-three years by His example, by His doctrine, and by His miracles, finally redeemed us by His passion and death on the cross, from death, sin, and hell.

Q. Was no other being capable of saving fallen man, except Jesus?
A. No, for none but a being personally united with God was able to oppose merits of infinite value to the infinite justice of God, in order to atone for the guilt of sin committed against Him.

Q. Why did Christ suffer for us?
A. First, In order to free us from the guilt and punishment of sin.

Christ, indeed, could have redeemed a numberless multitude of worlds even by a single prayer or supplication, since every action of His being that of a God-man, was of infinite value; yet He choose to suffer, in order to prove the greatness of His love for us, and thereby to excite us the more powerfully to subdue ourselves, and to persevere in virtue till the end; even if it should require the greatest sufferings on our part, nay, death itself.

Secondly, Christ suffered, in order to regain for us grace and the state of children of God, which we lost by sin, as well as the means of grace and of salvation, and finally eternal life, in greater abundance and with greater efficacy.

Thirdly, in order to teach us by his own example those principal virtues which we are to practise, and by which we are to serve God here upon earth, if we wish to be saved through Christ.

These virtues are: Humility, Obedience, Patience, and perfect Charity, towards God and man. Nothing, indeed, teaches us these virtues so expressly, or calls upon us so powerfully, to practise them faithfully, as the example and model of the suffering Saviour. According to the admonition of the prince of the Apostles, St. Peter: "Christ suffered for us, leaving you an example, that you should follow his steps. Who, when He was reviled, did not revile. Who, his own self, bore our sins in his body upon the tree (of the cross), that we, being dead to sin, should live to justice." 1 *Peter*, ii. 21–24. And St. Paul exhorts us, in these words: "Let mind be in you, which was also in Christ Jesus; who, being in the form of God, thought it no robbery himself to be equal to God; but debased himself, becoming obedient unto death, even unto the death of the cross." St. Paul to the *Philippians*, ii. 5–8. "Nowhere," writes St. Augustine, "have I found such an efficacious remedy, as the wounds of Christ."

Q_1 How did Christ suffer, and how could He suffer, since He was the true Son of God?

A. Christ suffered in those powers of His person, capable of suffering; for, by means of His humanity, He could truly and really suffer in body and soul; but, according to His Divinity, He, of course, could not suffer, and neither did He suffer, according to His Divinity, though He suffered as God, since, according to His person, He was as man, also the Son of God, as already stated many times.

Q. Why do we particularly add, "crucified?"

A. Because Christ finished His sufferings and the work of Redemption, by His death on the cross. But Christ wished to accomplish the work of Redemption in this manner, because this kind of death was preëminently fitted for appropriating to us the greatness of His love until the end of time. The sight of the Redeemer nailed to a cross, with His arms expanded, His sacred heart pierced through for our sake—these are, indeed, the visible expression of this love, offering itself for those who are His, faithfully, until death, panting, as it were, after our salvation. A sight which constantly cries out to us in the words of the Prophet: "He was offered, because it was His own will." *Is*. liii. 7. Christ himself confirms it, saying: "And I, if I be lifted up from the earth, will draw all things to myself." *John*, xii. 32. And again: "No man taketh it (life) away from me; but I lay it down of myself, and I have power to lay it down." *Ibid*, x. 18.

Moreover, Christ chose the death of the cross, because, by the wood of the tree of the forbidden fruit, temptation to sin entered this world. Just, therefore, as Satan made use of wood, to cause the fall of man, in the same manner did Christ choose to gain the victory over him by the wood of the holy cross; delivering man, by that victory, from the power of the devil and from hell. Besides, this mystery was also prefigured in the Old Testament. Types of the bloody sacrifice of Christ on the cross were the offering of Isaac, who carried to the mountain the wood, upon which He himself was to die; the killing of the paschal lamb and its preparation, and particularly the brazen serpent set up in the desert. *Gen.* xxii. ; *Exod.* xii. ; *Num.* xxi.

Q. Why do we add, " who died ?"

A. First, that we may be the more impressed with the great truth that it was the death of Christ which freed us from eternal death. Second, that Christ wished to offer himself to His heavenly Father for us, in a very particular manner, in the sacrifice of love which was typified by all the sacrifices of the Old Law. Third, that Christ sealed, by His death, the New Law, and the promises of eternal life; for, " Being consummated, He became the cause of eternal salvation to all that obey him." *Heb.* v. 9.

Q. Why do we add, " buried ?"

A. It was the will of Christ to be buried, and to remain till the third day, in the grave.

First, in order to place it beyond doubt that he had truly died.

Second, to give a clearer proof of, and an increase of glory to His Resurrection, on the third day.

Q. Since Christ redeemed all men by His passion and death, why is it that all are not saved ?

A. Christ, indeed, redeemed all men by a superabundant edemption; but in order to appropriate to ourselves the ruits of redemption, and to be saved by it, it is necessary, that, on our part, we should offer no impediment to the divine grace, but cöoperate with it, by professing the holy faith, and by a diligent practice of good works. But in this many are negligent and deficient, and hence it is, that they remain the enemies of God and are lost; but lost through their own fault. For whosoever is truly of good will, avoids evil with the help of God's grace, as well as he can; does good in life or in death, and will surely attain, by the grace of Christ, to the knowledge of the holy faith, as far as it is necessary for his salvation.

Q. What should we do when we look at an image of our crucified Redeemer ?

A. We should return our warmest thanks to our Saviour

for the immense benefit of our redemption, and then endeavor to excite ourselves powerfully, to follow Him by the perfect exercise of the virtues mentioned above, and also to avoid every shadow of sin. But is it possible, that a Christian could wish to wound and to crucify his Saviour anew by new sins, the Saviour whom he already sees offered for him on the cross, offered a victim of love? Moreover, we should implore the mercy of God to pardon the sins already committed, and we should love to exclaim with St. Francis Xavier; "O Jesus, my crucified love!" How pleasing this kind of veneration is to the Saviour, he indicated one day in a particular manner to St. Gertrude, saying: "As often as any one looks devoutly upon me on the cross, so often is he benignly looked upon by God's mercy." *Blos. Man. Spir.* c. i., *Pass. Christi.* Certainly, the passion and death of Christ imparts consolation to the sinner; grace, strength and life to all; "for," as St. Paul says, "if we have suffered with Christ, we shall also be glorified with Christ."

The Fifth Article of Faith.

Q. What are we taught by the fifth Article?

A. That Christ, having died on the cross, His soul descended into the lower regions, partly in order to appear as conqueror in hell, partly in order to liberate thence the souls of the patriarchs and the just who awaited His coming in Limbo. According to His body, Christ remained in the tomb, from which He, by His own power, rose on the third day to the life of immortality and glory.

Q. By whose power did Christ descend to the lower regions?

A. By His own power.

Christ did not descend thither, carried or necessitated, but with great glory, might, and splendor, converting, by His mere presence, the darkness of that abode of expectation into a paradise of consolation, in accordance with the words which Jesus spoke to the penitent thief who was crucified with Him: "This day thou shalt be with me in paradise." *Luke*, xxiii. 43.

Q. Whither did Jesus descend?

A. Into the lower regions, where three places are to be distinguished. The first is the real Hell. That is the place where the damned suffer eternal punishment.

The second place is Purgatory, *i. e.*, a place where those souls are who departed this life in the grace of God, but stand as yet in need of being cleansed, on account of sins which they committed upon earth, for the temporal punishment of which they did not make satisfaction in the flesh.

The third place is Limbo, or that place which received the souls of the just who died before Christ, hoping in the Saviour, and in that hope serving God, saved themselves.

It was to this latter place that Christ descended in the quality of deliverer, in order to take with Him, on His ascension into heaven, the just of past ages. "Thou also," says the Prophet Zacharias, " by the blood of Thy testament, hast sent forth Thy prisoners out of the pit wherein is no water." *Zach.* ix. 11. "He was put to death, indeed, in the flesh, but brought to life by the spirit, in which also He came and preached to those spirits which were in prison." 1 *Pet.* iii. 18, 19. But Christ showed himself, too, in other places of the lower world, to the terror of the evil spirits, whose power He had vanquished and destroyed; to the horror of the damned, who saw in Him the judge that was one day to pronounce sentence upon them; but also for the consolation and deliverance of the souls who were suffering in the flames of purgatory.

Q. If only the soul of Christ descended, why then do we say positively: Christ descended into hell, and not, the soul of Christ descended?

A. Because the person of Christ remained inseparably united to His soul, as well as to His most holy body in the tomb. We say, therefore, with justice: Christ was in the sepulchre, and Christ descended into hell.

For the rest, as the holy fathers remark, according to the indication of St. Peter, there is a good deal of obscurity about that which Christ during those days did in the nether world, namely, as to how He applied the fruits of the redemption just effected. This obscurity it is impossible for us to penetrate, but it is also unnecessary. The day of judgment will reveal the secret.

Q. How may we prove that Christ rose from the dead on the third day, though the time intervening between His burial which was on Friday evening, and His resurrection which happened on Sunday morning, is not three, but only two entire days?

A. We do not assert, that Christ rose from the dead after three full days; neither did Christ do so, but only, "after three days, or on the third day." But this is really so; for Friday was the first day on which he rested in the grave, Saturday the second, and the time from midnight of Easter-Sunday belongs of course to the third day.

Moreover, if any one pays his debt or fulfils his promise before the appointed time, he certainly keeps his word. It might be a question, if the appointed time had expired.

Q. Why do we say of Christ: He rose from the dead; whereas we say of Lazarus and others, He was raised from the dead?

A. Because Christ the Son of God rose by His own power from the dead, whereas the others who returned to life again, were resuscitated by the power of God. In the same manner shall we also be one day raised from the dead, and thus come to life again. If, therefore, at times we hear it said, that Christ was resuscitated, we are to understand this manner of speaking only of Christ's human nature, which of course was restored to immortal life by His divine nature.

Q. Is there not another difference to be noted, between the resurrection of Christ and that of others?

A. Yes, there is this difference, that Christ did not again cease to live—whereas the rest who were recalled to life, did again separate from their bodies, and subsequently died once more.

Q. Whence do we know that Jesus Christ really rose from the dead?

A. First, from the testimony of His Apostles and disciples, to whom, as St. Luke tells us, "He showed himself alive after His death, making Himself known to them by many demonstrations; for they saw Him after His resurrection, during a space of forty days, they touched Him, they sat at table with Him, they spoke and conversed with Him, and announced His resurrection everywhere before the people and the Council of the Elders, solemnly and openly, joyfully suffering for this testimony, all manner of hardships and torments, nay even death itself."

Secondly, from the fruitless endeavors of the enemies of Christ, who denied His resurrection, giving money to the soldiers who guarded His sepulchre, that they should say His disciples had come and stolen His body, whilst they were asleep. But if they were actually sleeping, how could they have seen the disciples? And even if they did, what was it that gave courage to the timid disciples, to attempt a thing of the kind; and what profit could they derive from it? On the contrary, the disciples would have been the more hated, and would have only gained by it persecution and martyrdom. Moreover, why were not the guards who were thus forgetful of their duty, punished, instead of receiving money for it?

Thirdly, From the conversion of those who crucified Jesus, and that of His enemies in Jerusalem themselves. For immediately after the first sermon of St. Peter, who bore witness to the resurrection of Christ, on the day of Pentecost before the people in Jerusalem, three thousand of them were converted to the faith, and among them were even many priests of the Old Law, receiving the faith of Christ, in spite of the growing persecution. "And the word of the Lord increased; and the number of the disciples was multiplied very much in Jerusalem: a great multitude also of the priests obeyed the faith." *Acts*, vi. 7. Now, how could this have happened, if the testimony of the Apostles and disciples had not been perfectly plain and incontestable?

Fourthly, From the conversion of the heathens to the faith. If the resurrection of Christ had not been incontestably proved, never would the Roman people have adored a crucified Jew, and acknowledged Him the God and Saviour of the world.

The resurrection of the Lord is, therefore, the surest pledge of our faith, that, firmly believing in Christ, we quit vice for virtue, and awake from the death of sin to the life of grace, and, finally, from the death of the body to the life of immortality. "He who raised up Jesus, will raise up us also with Jesus." Thus the Apostle, 2 *Cor.* iv. 14. But in order that our resurrection be a glorious one, it is necessary that it be preceded by the resurrection to the life of the spirit in this world, *i. e.*, the resurrection from the death of sin to the life of justice, in which we shall continue to live, with the assistance of God, without ever again losing His friendship. "Christ rising again from the dead, dieth now no more." *Rom.* vi. 9. This is the Easter-joy to him who is truly risen in Christ, and this is the application to our life of virtue: A new life in the imitation of Christ without relapsing into the evil of sin.

The Sixth Article of Faith.

Q. What does the sixth article of faith teach us?

A. That Jesus, after effecting the work of redemption, appeared at several different times to those that were His, and confirmed by many proofs the truth of His resurrection; moreover, that He ascended into heaven on the fortieth day after His resurrection, in order to take possession of the kingdom of glory, as the man-God, exalted above all in the heavens, and to offer to His heavenly Father His merits for us as our Mediator, pointing to His radient wounds as the glorious conqueror of hell, and the author of our redemption.

Q. How did Christ ascend into heaven?

A. 1. Christ ascended into heaven by His own power in the same manner as He rose by His own power from the dead.

2. In the triumph of victory, surrounded by the souls which He carried with Him from limbo to heaven, and hailed by all the choirs of the holy angels; in that triumph which the royal prophet foresaw in exultation of spirit: "Lift up your gates, O ye princes, and be ye lifted up, O eternal gates: and the King of glory shall enter in. Who is this King of glory? The Lord of hosts is the King of glory." *Ps.* xxiii. 9, 10. And again: "O clap your hands, all ye nations: shout unto God with voices of joy: God is ascended with jubilee." *Ps.* xlvi. 126. "Thou hast ascended on high, Thou hast led captivity captive." *Ps.* lxvii. 19.

Q. Why is it said of Christ, that He sitteth in heaven?

A. 1. By the "sitting" is pointed out the perfect possession which He took of the heavenly kingdom, and of which nobody ever can deprive Him. 2. It is indicative of the repose which Christ enjoys eternally in the delights of heaven. This expression, therefore, is a figurative one, since the blessed in heaven stand in need of no repose in their glorified immortal bodies, as we do.

Q. What means the expression: *At the right hand* of God the Father Almighty?

A. This expression, too, is to be understood in its figurative sense; it signifies the glory of Christ, His majesty and His power in heaven and on earth being equal to that of the Father; for he who sits at the side of another, sits neither higher nor lower, but on a level with the other. God is a pure spirit; He has, therefore, no body, and consequently neither a right nor left side; the Holy Scriptures simply make use of this figurative expression, in order to speak in a manner palpable to our human perception.

Q. What practical benefit can we derive from the consideration of this article of faith?

A. Just as the resurrection of Christ is the pledge of our faith, so is His ascension the pledge of our hope, since by it we are powerfully excited to direct all our endeavors and desires to that end which Christ our head pointed out to us, saying: "I go to prepare a place for you." *John,* xiv. 2. But in order that we may actually go thither one day, we are told to elevate our minds to heaven, whilst living here upon earth, obedient to the call of the Apostle: "If you be risen with Christ, seek the things that are above; where Christ is sitting at the right hand of God." *Coloss.* iii. 1. By these words the Apostle puts us in mind, that only those are truly risen with Christ to a new life of grace, who expect their goods, their repose, their glory, and their life eternally there, where Christ has taken up His lasting abode. But by the addition: "Seek the things that are above, not those that are below," the Apostle points out the mark by which we may know whether in reality we possess those qualities which the spiritual resurrection with Christ requires of us. For, as the state of the appetite is indicative of the health and condition of the body, so are the demands and inclinations of man demonstrative with regard to the state of his soul. He who rejoices in things that pass away, who longs only for them and their enjoyment, forgets, indeed, what is above where Christ is; to him, then, Christ is not life, nor is death his gain. Whereas, he who, being filled with a desire for heaven, longs only for that which is true, lawful, just, and holy, which is in heaven, and he lives in Christ and Christ in him; for him death has no terrors, for he longs to be dissolved and to be with Christ.

Wherefore, place yourself often in spirit on the mountain of Olives, abiding in company with the Apostles and disciples near your Saviour, who ascends thence into heaven, to prepare a place for you in His kingdom, and you shall be enabled to bear with joy the hardships and trials of this life, which very soon will be changed into triumphant and everlasting delight. Yes, we shall be glorified with Him, if we have suffered with Him.

The Seventh Article of Faith.

Q. What do we profess by the seventh article of faith?

A. We profess by this article, that Jesus Christ will come again on the last day, to judge the world, *i. e.*, all men, both the good and the wicked, in the presence of all the angels, all men, and all the spirits of hell.

Q. When shall Christ come to judge us?

A. "Of that day and hour no one knoweth" but this we know, that it shall be the last day, the day, when time shall be no more. *Matt.* xxiii. 36.

Q. Shall any signs precede the day of this judgment?

A. Yes; many and terrible signs.

First, The perversion of a multitude of men by Antichrist, and a dreadful persecution of the Church over the whole earth through him, the son of perdition and malice, and through those who are his adherents.

This Antichrist will be a man, who, embodying within himself all the malice of Satan, shall lay claim to the worship of God, personating, as it were, the Redeemer of the world; but whom Christ, appearing from heaven, will destroy. For thus, St. Paul, the Apostle of the Gentiles, assures us, writing to the Thessalonians: "The coming of our Lord Jesus Christ shall not be at hand, till there come first a revolt, and the man of sin be revealed, the son of perdition, who opposeth, and is lifted up above all that is called God, or that is worshipped, so that he sitteth in the temple of God, showing himself as if he were God. Whose coming is according to the working of Satan, in all power, and signs, and lying wonders, and all seduction of iniquity to them that perish, whom the Lord Jesus shall kill with the spirit of His mouth." 2 *Thess.* ii. 1–10.

And St. John writes: "You have heard that Antichrist cometh." 1 *John*, ii. 18.

But the last day shall be preceded by terrible signs from heaven; for, "immediately after the tribulations of those days, the sun shall be darkened, and the moon shall not give her light; and the stars shall fall from heaven; and the powers of the heavens shall be moved;" and the whole world shall pass into flame, "and heaven and earth shall pass away," because they shall be changed into a new heaven and a new earth. *St. Matt.* xxiv. 29, 35.

"But," says St. Peter, (2 *Peter*, iii. 10, 13,) "the day of the Lord shall come as a thief, in which the heavens shall pass away with great violence; and the elements shall be dissolved with heat; and the earth, and the works that are in it, shall be burnt up." "But we look for new heavens and a new earth, according to His promise." St. Jerome commenting on this text, says: "The form of this earth shall pass away, but not its essence." For St. Peter does not say: "We shall see another heaven and another earth, but those which now exist shall be changed into others new and glorious." *St. Hier. Com.* in Is. 65. And St. Cyril of Jerusalem, says: "This world shall pass away, in order that a more beautiful world may be formed of it."

"Then Christ shall send His angels with a trumpet, and a great voice; and they shall gather together His elect from the four winds, from the farthest parts of the heavens, to the utmost bounds of them. And all nations shall be gathered together before Him: and He shall separate them one from another, as the shepherd separateth the sheep from the goats, *i. e.*, the good from the wicked; and then shall appear the sign of the Son of man in the heavens, to the great consolation of the good, but to the terror of the wicked." "For as the lightning, that lighteneth from under heaven, shineth unto the parts that are under heaven, so shall the Son of man be in His day, "as the terrible judge from heaven, and then his judgment shall begin." *Matt.* xxiv., xxv.; *Mark* xiii.; *Luke* xvii.

Q. How shall Christ come to judgment?

A. Christ shall come with great majesty and power, and all the angels with Him, and He shall sit upon the seat of His majesty, in order to enforce the solemn acknowledgment and attestation, that He is, in truth, the Son of God and the Lord and King of all. He shall come to judge as the God-man, because as such He is the Redeemer; and though the power to judge is proper originally to the Deity, yet the administration of this judgment and the execution of this divine power are committed conjointly to Christ as man. *Matt.* xxv.; *John*, v. 22.

Q. How shall Christ judge the world?

A. A wonderful light shall pervade the consciences of all, so that every thing, even the most secret thoughts of the heart of man shall be revealed and laid open to all the world, because "Christ will bring to light the hidden things of darkness, and will make manifest the counsels of the heart." 1 *Cor.* iv. 5.

St. John bears witness to this in the Apocalypse; he says: "And I saw the dead, great and small, standing before the throne; and the dead were judged by those things which were written in the books, according to their works." *Apoc.* xx. 12.

At that moment, when all the deeds, omissions, thoughts, words, and desires shall be laid open, the sentence of every individual shall also become manifest to all, which, then, Christ himself shall pronounce against the good and the wicked. Then shall He say to them that shall be on His right hand: "Come, ye blessed of my Father, possess the kingdom prepared for you from the foundation of the world." But then shall He say to them also that shall be on His left hand: "Depart from me, ye cursed, into everlasting fire, which was prepared for the devil and his angels." *Matt.* xxv. 34, 41.

Q. Shall man be judged, for the first time, on the last day, at the general judgment of all?

A. No, all men are judged by Christ immediately after death, in the particular judgment, according to the Apostle: "It is appointed for men once to die, and after this the judgment." *Heb.* ix. 27. This particular judgment of the soul is followed immediately by the reward or punishment of the soul till the last judgment; so that the saints and the souls already purified go immediately to heaven; but those who die in the state of venial sin, or have yet to satisfy for the temporal punishment due to the sins which they committed whilst on earth, go to purgatory; finally, those who quit this life infected with mortal sin, are hurled immediately into hell. The Council of Florence teaches expressly, that the souls which are perfectly clean when parting this life, go instantly up to heaven and are there admitted to the beatific vision of the Triune God, in a degree more or less perfect according to their works and merits. But on the other hand, that the souls of those who died in mortal sin, are sent straight to hell, to undergo their eternal chastisement of woe.

Q. But why, then, shall a general judgment take place?

A. First, the wisdom, the goodness, and the justice of God themselves require this satisfaction. For, since it often happens before the eyes of the world that, here below, the wicked live in prosperity, whilst the good and virtuous suffer want and misery, it is just and right that it also should be manifested to all the world why God permitted this and so ordained it; namely, in order to show that every good action will be rewarded, and every bad one punished, here and hereafter.

Secondly, The respect and authority of Christ, likewise, demand this satisfaction of an universal judgment. For it is just and right, that he should now himself appear as the judge of all, who, innocent as He was, was judged and condemned by the wicked, for the salvation of all.

Thirdly, The full requital of the just, too, demands that satisfaction. For, since, in the world, the wicked often persecuted, derided, calumniated, and condemned the virtues of the just, it is fitting that their justification should also be laid open to the whole world, before the very face of the wicked.

Fourthly, It is equally just that the hypocrisy and specious sanctimony of so many wicked persons, who, like the Pharisees, make clean the outside of the cup and platter, but are, in their hearts, full of rapine and iniquity, should be unmasked before all the world.

Fifthly, Since man is essentially a compound of body and soul, and his deeds and actions, generally, are connected with consequences tending to the salvation or ruin of others, it is just and proper that he should be judged with body and soul, and in common with all mankind.

Q. Why is it said: Jesus shall "judge the living and the dead?"

A. Because those standing before the tribunal are either good or bad. Now, by the living are understood the good, and by the dead the wicked—*i. e.*, those who are dead as to the life of grace. But we may take the phrase also in its literal meaning—namely, we may understand by the living those who are in the flesh when the signs of the judgment of the world appear, then also these shall die in the dissolution of the world; but since the signs of the judgment meet them whilst yet alive, they are styled "the living."

Q. What impression should this truth make upon us regarding our conduct in this life?

A. First, this truth should induce us to lead a life the more holy since we well know that soon we shall have to appear before our Judge, who is Omniscient, and to whose eye everything is clear as noon-day, and who, one day, shall pass sentence on all our thoughts, words, desires, works, and omissions.

Secondly, By bearing constantly in mind that terrible judgment to come, we are powerfully supported in the hour of temptation, and prevented from yielding to it. In this let every one of us imitate, as far as he can, the example of St. Jerome, who, at every action of his, thought of the sound of the trumpet on the day of judgment: "Arise, ye dead, and come to judgment."

Thirdly, If one has sinned, the remembrance of this judgment is an efficacious means of rousing the sinner to repentance, and especially of bringing him to a sincere and full confession of his sins, and to a firm purpose of amending his life, mindful of the threats of St. Peter: "If the just man shall scarcely be saved, where shall the wicked and the sinner appear?" 1 *Peter*, iv. 18.

And it is on this account, as St. Gregory the Great wisely remarks, that the Lord kept concealed from us the day of our death and that of the judgment: in order that we should live so as to be always ready to appear before the tribunal of the Divine Judge." We should especially endeavor to walk constantly in the Divine presence, and to act so, as if He, who shall one day come to judge us on all our actions, were to see us, as He really does, He who will judge everything in that judgment, upon which our eternal happiness or misery is dependent.

The Eighth Article of Faith.

Q. What does the eighth article of faith teach us?

A. It teaches us expressly to profess our belief in the Third Person of the Blessed Trinity—namely, in the Holy Ghost, who proceeds from both the Father and the Son, and who is to be adored and glorified with both as true God, being consubstantial and co-eternal with them.

Q. How can we prove that the Holy Ghost is true God, equal to the Father and the Son, and that he proceeds from both in common?

A. 1. From the words prescribed by Christ the Lord, in the administration of the sacrament of Baptism—namely: "Go ye, therefore, and teach all nations; baptizing them in the name of the Father, and of the Son, and of the Holy Ghost." *Matt.* xxviii. 19. If the Holy Ghost were not God, Christ would not have required that we should be dedicated by the tie of religion to the Holy Ghost, as we are to the Father and to the Son. But that Christ mentions the Holy Ghost after the Father and the Son, indicates his procession from both.

2. The same acknowledgment appears from the words of St. Peter to Ananias: "Why hath Satan tempted thy heart, that thou shouldst lie to the Holy Ghost; thou hast not lied to men, but to God." *Acts*, v. 3–7. The same Apostle calls the Holy Ghost, also, the "Spirit of Christ." 1 *Peter*, i. 11. But this could not be said if the Holy Ghost did not proceed in the same manner from the Son as from the Father.

The holy Fathers confirm what has been said, and point out many more texts of Holy Scripture that prove the same. Thus St. Epiphanius says, in his book, *Ancorato*, 67: "Since Christ, as faith teaches us, is of the Father—God of God, and the Spirit from Christ, or from both, as Christ assures us in these words: 'Who proceeds from the Father, and shall take of *mine*.'" The same holy Father, on the occasion of refuting the heresy of Sabellius, expresses himself just as positively—he says: "The Holy Ghost is not separate from the Father and the Son, but is of the same Deity, of the Father and the Son; He subsists with the Father and the Son, as Holy Ghost." And Clement of Alexandria writes: "Let us praise the one Father and Son, with the Holy Ghost, who is one in All—in whom all, through whom all—to whom honor now and in all eternity. Amen." *Lib.* iii., *Strom.* c. vi. The fourth Council of Lateran has declared this doctrine solemnly against the error of the schismatic Greeks, who denied the common procession of the Holy Ghost from the Son.

The self-contradiction of this error is plain to every one that believes and thinks. For, if one denies this procession of the Holy Ghost from the Son, he renders himself incapable of discerning or defining any difference between the Son and the Holy Ghost, since besides the procession of the one Person from the other, in the most Holy Trinity, there can be no difference assigned, as was remarked already by St. Anselm, writing against the Greeks, which remark of his they could not refute.

Q. Why is the Third Person of the most Holy Trinity called the Holy Ghost?

A. 1. Because He is sanctity itself, and the author and source of all sanctity. 2. Because He imparts to us the graces of Redemption in the Church militant here upon earth, and, hereafter, in the beatific vision of God, He being the substantial Love of the Father and of the Son, unites us with himself, the Father and the Son, by the indissoluble ties of love.

Q. Why is this name, Holy Ghost, only applied to the Third Person; are not the Father and the Son, then, also, a spirit, and essentially holy?

A. Certainly; the Father and the Son are also a spirit, and holy, since the Divine nature itself is the most pure spirit, and most holy; but this name, Holy Ghost, is given to the Third Person, on this account especially, that by this nominal mark the Third Divine Person is most aptly pointed out and distinguished in his relations to the two others. Because this name indicates the one nature of God, who is the most pure spirit, and in which it is only with respect to the procession of the Persons that any distinction is made, as has been already stated more than once. But, since the spirit is essentially understanding and will, this procession is also, in God, but two-fold—namely, that of the Son from the Father by cognition, and that of the Holy Ghost from the Father and the Son in common, by the Divine will, which is in God essentially love and sanctity.

Q. Why is the Holy Ghost represented in the form of a dove?

A. 1. Though the Holy Ghost has no body, any more than the Father, yet, in the same manner as the Father is represented under the form of an aged man—because he appeared under that form to Daniel—so is the Holy Ghost, if materially exhibited, represented under the form of a dove, because, under this form, He appeared at the Baptism of Christ. 2. The Holy Ghost is also represented under the figure of a dove for this reason: the effects which the Holy Ghost produces in the just, by His grace, are, in a certain sense, similar to the properties of a dove. These effects and properties in the just are, therefore, entirely characteristic: innocence, meekness, and harmless simplicity of the heart, according to the maxim of Christ himself: " Be ye simple, like the dove." *Matt.* x. 16.

Q. Did the Holy Ghost appear under any other visible form ?

A. Yes; on the day of Pentecost, at the consecration of the Apostles, for their apostolic function, He appeared in the shape of fiery tongues. This symbol is indicative of the gift of languages, of wisdom and charity : namely, the tongue signifies the gift of languages ; the light, wisdom ; the fire, charity.

Q. How is this to be understood, that the Holy Ghost came down upon the disciples, and has also been imparted to us, since as God, He is indeed present everywhere ?

A. By this is indicated, that He communicated special graces to the Apostles and disciples of the Lord upon that day of Pentecost, and that He also protects, by His divine assistance, the Church of God, and favors and sanctifies, more and more, each one of her children. In this sense the Holy Ghost abides with the whole Church, teaches, governs, and sanctifies it, by communicating to the same the graces, which, on account of the merits of Christ, are constantly administered to souls therein.

Q. What fruit are we specially to gather from this article of faith, for the conduct of our life ?

A. Since the Holy Ghost proceeds proximately from the will in God, who is essential love, it evidently follows that those effects, which are specially ascribed to the Holy Ghost, are also specially the property of God's love towards us. But we should esteem and value more than all other gifts of grace, that of justification, by which we are rendered just in the sight of the Lord, and stamped with the mark of election for the eternal inheritance of salvation. For, by justification our soul is united to God by the tie of His love; whence, springs up in us an earnest desire of walking thus in the path of renewed life, that, being made participants of the Divine nature, we are called and really are, the children of God, sanctified temples of the Holy Ghost, who, as it were, dwells in us by the effects of His grace and love, as the Apostle tells us.

But let us take heed not to defile this sanctuary by sin, particularly not to pollute it by the vice of unchastity, and other lusts of the flesh, and never to banish the Holy Ghost, in this manner, from our hearts, or to grieve Him, as the Apostle says, by tepidity and the perpetration of venial sin. But, on the contrary, the true children of God follow "with fervor His inspirations, and are led by the Holy Ghost." *Rom.* viii. 14.

The Ninth Article of Faith.

Q. What does the ninth article of faith teach us?

A. The second part of the Apostles' Creed commences with the ninth article of faith. The first part treats directly of the Deity and the three Divine Persons; but this second treats of the Church. As we believe that there is in God but one divine nature and three distinct persons, so do we confess that the Church is but one in essence, yet comprises within herself three different relations, of which the *first* regards the soul, namely, the remission of sins; the *second*, the body, namely, its resurrection; the *third*, the soul and the body together, namely, the eternal bliss of the just in the life to come, as will be seen from the following article of faith.

Q. What is the Church?

A. The Church is the visible kingdom of God upon earth, that is to say, the society of all the faithful, who, by the use of the same means of salvation united, live in the communion of faith, hope and charity, under a visible head, the Pope, who is the successor of St. Peter, and the vicegerent of Christ.

Q. Of how many parts does the Church consist?

A. Of three.

1. The church militant upon earth, to which belong all the faithful who live in her communion here on earth; she is called the militant church, because those that belong to her, are yet at war with the world, the devil, and the flesh.

2. The church suffering, to which the souls in pugatory belong.

3. The church triumphant in heaven, namely, the communion of the angels and saints in heaven.

Q. Who is the founder of the Church?

A. Jesus Christ.

Q. How many churches did Jesus Christ establish?

A. Only one. "Thou art Peter, and upon this rock I will build my Church; and the gates of hell shall not prevail against it." *Matt.* xviii.

To which, in a wider sense, the Jewish Church of the Old

Testament also belongs; for the Church of the Old Law, before the coming of Christ, prepared the human race for the reception of the Gospel by its types and prophecies.

Of the Marks of the Holy Church.

Q. By what marks may we discern the true Church of Christ?

A. By the very marks by which Christ our Lord wished to point out His Church, in order that it might be known from all other temporal or spiritual institutions, and recognized as such by the whole world.

Q. Which are these marks of the true Church of Christ?

A. They are—Unity, Sanctity, Universality, Apostolicity or Apostolic institution. In other words: the Church of Christ is one, holy, catholic, and apostolic.

Q. What do we understand by each of these marks?

A. First, that the attribute, which is expressed by each mark, is in reality a property given to His Church by Christ.

And secondly, that this essential attribute or distinguishing mark belongs exclusively to the Catholic Church, and that consequently she only is the *true* Church of Christ.

Q. What means the Church is one?

A. It means that the Church of Christ is by her internal and external unity, but one visible kingdom of God upon earth.

Q. In what consists the internal, and in what the external unity of the Church?

A. The internal unity consists in the preserving and professing one and the same doctrine of salvation, which Christ revealed through himself and His Apostles.

The external unity consists in the connection of all the members of the Church by subordination to their superiors, the bishops and priests, under one and the same head, the vicegerent of Christ, the successor of St. Peter, the Pope of Rome.

Q. How can this mark of the Church be proved from Holy Scripture?

A. Regarding the internal unity, Christ expressly demands the unity of faith, since He says: "He that believeth not shall be condemned." *Mark*, xvi. 16. He required the same unity in regard to the recognition of duties, for He says: "Teach them to observe all things, whatsoever I have commanded you." *Matt.* xxviii. 20. He demands of all the same hope and charity, promising to all the same inheritance of salvation, and requiring of all the same love with which He loved us." *John*, xiii.

Regarding the external unity, it is evident both from the manner in which He sent His Apostles, and the power He gave them; namely: "As the Father hath sent me, I also send you." *John*, xx. 21. "If he will not hear the Church, let him be to thee as the heathen and the publican." *Matt.* xviii. 17.

But this will of Christ appears in a particular manner, from the institution of the Primacy in the person of St. Peter, who presides, in each of his successors, over the members of the Church, and unites all in perfect union as the one supreme shepherd.

The Apostles also teach the same thing, being the true interpreters of the will of Christ, and the messengers of the Holy Ghost. Concerning the proof of this, we find a beautiful text in the Epistle to the Ephesians, where the Apostle writes thus: "Be careful to keep the unity of the spirit in the bond of peace." "One body, and one spirit; as you are called in one hope of your vocation; one Lord, one faith, one baptism. One God and Father of all, who is above all, and through all, and in us all." *Ephes.* iv. 3–6. St. Paul could not, indeed, have expressed himself more clearly and more positively regarding the necessity of the *internal* unity of the Church, which stands upon the foundation of one and the same faith. He inculcates the same thing in his *Epistle to the Philippians*, ii. 12; to the *Galatians*, i. 6; to the *Romans*, xvi. 17; and 1 *Cor.* i. 10. The same Apostle insists no less forcibly on the preservation of the *external* unity; he says: "The chalice of benediction which we bless, is it not the communion of the blood of Christ? And the bread which we break, is it not the partaking of the body of the Lord? For we being many, are one bread, one body, all who partake of one bread." 1 *Cor.* x. 16, 17.

In these words, the Apostle points to the external communion of all the faithful in Christ Jesus and His holy Church, sanctified by the partaking of one and the same sacrament of the bodily presence of Christ in the most holy sacrament of the altar. But, that finally Peter is the uniting link, Christ himself declares, saying: "Thou art Peter, and upon this rock I will build my Church." And again: "Feed my lambs, feed my sheep." *Matt.* xvi. 16; *John*, xxi.

Besides, all the figures under which the Church is represented by Christ and His Apostles, go to demonstrate this union. For the Church is compared to a building, to a people, to an inheritance, to a flock of sheep, to a kingdom, to a city, to a body, to an army: symbols which all of them express the idea of the unity of many. The Church is also called the one spouse of Christ.

Add to this the historical proof, which includes within itself the authority of tradition. For all the heretics, sectarians, and schismatics, were, since the beginning of the Church, cut off from it by the chief pastors of the Church, and of course numbered no more amongst the members of the true Church, which on account of her truth is one.

Moreover, reason itself shows the necessity of this mark of the true Church, for two parties contradicting each other, can never be the true Church established by one and the same Founder, whence it necessarily follows, that the true Church of Christ must of necessity have the mark of unity.

Q. Why is the Church called holy?

A. 1. Because Christ, the head of the Church, is most holy.

2. Because all that enter the Church are sanctified by the Sacrament of Baptism.

3. Because she has the most holy sacrifice, together with holy laws, sacraments, and ceremonies; further, because she promotes every virtue, condemns every vice, and contains within herself nothing, or approves nothing, which is not, as far as it belongs to her, good and holy.

4. Because the Holy Ghost protects the Church according to the promise and assurance of Christ.

Q. How can this mark of the Church be proved from Scripture and tradition?

A. That Christ willed His Church to be holy, is proved, in the first place, by the very character of Christ, and by His will, which was to sanctify all men, according to these words in which He prayed to His Father: "Sanctify them in truth." *John*, xvii. 17. And His express command is: "Be ye perfect, as also your heavenly Father is perfect." *Matt.* v. 48. And the whole of the Gospel breathes nothing but sanctity. The Apostles everywhere assert the same thing by their precepts, admonitions, institutions, and by the counsels given in their missionary Epistles. St. Paul especially, in his Epistle to the Ephesians, makes use of words, which prove this assertion in a remarkable manner; he writes: "Christ loved His Church, and delivered himself up for it, that He might sanctify it, cleansing it in the laver of water in the word of life; that He might present it to himself a glorious Church, not having spot or wrinkle, nor any such thing; but that it should be holy and without blemish." *Ephes.* v. 25-27.

The same thing is corroborated by the authority of tradition, which shows how earnestly the holy Fathers of the Church and all her zealous pastors were, at all times, intent on advancing by word or deed, orally and in writing, the sanctification of the faithful in the holy Church; recognizing only those as living members of the Church, who, gifted with supernatural life by means of sanctifying grace, lived in the holy Church as children of God.

Q. Why is the Church called universal or *Catholic?*
A. Because Christ willed His Church to be universal in regard to time, place, and persons; that is to say, He willed her a Church of all times, of all tribes, and of all nations.

Q. How can we prove this mark of the Church?
A. That Christ willed His Church to be universal from the beginning, in regard to time, is plain from the words of Christ himself: "I am not come to destroy the law, but to fulfill it."

The Church of Christ, therefore, commenced in the beginning with the very first revelation of God to man; and even before Christ, this Church which stands in connection with Christ the Promised One, exercised its power and influence over the whole human race, in order to keep alive amongst men the expectation of the coming Redeemer. But that Christ had in view all people and all times, is manifest from these words: "Go ye," says He, "and teach all nations, baptizing them . . . . behold, I am with you all days, even to the consummation of the world. *Matt.* xviii.

The decisions and actions of the Apostles, as well as the entire history of the Church, tend to the corroboration of the same thing in their arguments, concerning the spread and propagation of the Christian religion. *Acts*, x. 10, xii. 7-10; *Ephs.* ii. 14; 1 *Cor.* xv. 24.

Reason itself demands such an universal Church, since the wants of men which render a church, instituted by Divine authority, necessary, are common to all men. Consequently, if God has instituted such a church, reason justly concludes, from his goodness and wisdom, that God instituted the same for the entire human race.

Q. Why is the Church of Christ called Apostolic?

A. Because Christ our Lord chose the Apostles as the first proclaimers of the Gospel, and because He subsequently established the Church through them. It must, therefore, be possible to trace back to them the true Church of Christ, by means of the uninterrupted succession of its chiefs, in order to point it out as the first, before the eyes of all the world, the Apostolic, and therefore the true Church of Christ. Any congregation which is unable to do this, cannot be the true Church of Christ, since it wants that mark which the Apostle specially points out, writing: " Now, therefore, you are no more strangers and foreigners; but you are fellow-citizens with the saints and the domestics of God: built upon the foundation of the Apostles." *Ephes.* ii. 10, 20.

The characteristic marks of the true Church of Christ are, therefore: " Unity, Sanctity, Universality or Catholicity, and Apostolicity or Apostolic Institution."

Q. Have these attributes of the Church really the characteristic marks of the Church of Christ?

A. Certainly; for, a characteristic mark is that by which we know an object as such, and distinguish it from every other of a similar kind. From this it follows—first, that a characteristic mark must be more easily understood than the object itself which it designates; second, that it is proper to the object which it distinguishes; and third, that it can be easily observed. Now, the marks in question have all these properties, in relation to the Church of Christ.

They are, in the first place clear and easily understood; for, what can be more easily understood than that which all members of a society openly profess, and openly do; what the manner of its administration is; who governs it; how long it publicly exists, and how far it extends.

Second, They are proper,—*i. e.*, belong exclusively to the Church of Christ; for, they appertain essentially to the primitive formation and institution of the Church, and admit of no reference to any other society besides the Church.

Third, They can be easily observed; for, they subsist in external things, which are plain to behold, and everywhere known to all people; and their proof can be obtained from innumerable documents, both historical and otherwise, without any great trouble. And this kind of proof, since it does not so much consist in philosophic discussion, as in establishing evident facts, is the most simple, and, at the same time, the most efficacious and suitable for every individual. The truth of what has been advanced shines forth particularly in the mark of Apostolicity, *i. e.*, the succession of the Apostles in the bishops of the churches founded by the Apostles, and preëminently in the closely linked chain of the successors of Peter, the Primate of the Apostles, in the persons of the Popes of Rome. They, as the highest power, unite into one body all the members of the Church: so that every faithful Christian, being allied to the head of the Church by his immediate or mediate spiritual superiors, has also, on that very account, the certainty of being a branch of that great tree, to which Christ compares His Church, which overtops all others, with so great vigor and magnificence, in the successors of him, whom Christ appointed as His Vicar upon earth, and whose successors, as history proves beyond a doubt, are the Bishops of Rome. All the faithful, therefore, are entitled to exclaim with St. Ambrose: "Where Peter is, there is the Church."

Q. But which of those churches that call themselves Christian, is marked with this sign of the true Church of Christ, and consequently the only true one?

A. The *Roman Catholic* Church only.

Q. How may this be proved, and first that the Roman Catholic Church is *one?*

A. The Roman Catholic Church is *one* in respect to its origin; for, it knows of no other author or founder than the Lord Jesus Christ.

Secondly, It is one in respect to its doctrine; for, all the children of the Roman Catholic Church profess, in reality, one and the same faith. Regarding this, we appeal to the Creeds which the Church publicly professes, to the Decrees of the Councils, and the Catechisms which are authorized by the Church.

The Roman Catholic Church is one in regard to worship and divine service. For the principal object of worship is essentially the same, because the Sacrifice of the New Covenant—namely, that of the Mass, to which all other ceremonies of the Church are subordinate—is, throughout the whole Roman Catholic Church, the same.

Finally, the unity of the members of this church is plainly evident, as before observed, from the intimate union of the ecclesiastical connection, through the one principal head, the Pope, the true successor of St. Peter and Vicar of Christ.

The saying of St. Optatus of Milevi, in his letter to Parmenianus, forcibly reminds us of this. Hear his glowing words: "You cannot deny, for you know it well, how the first episcopal chair was erected by Peter, in the city of Rome—the only one in which the unity of the Church should be sustained."

Q. Is it not so with the non-Catholic sects?

A. No; they are principally divided into Protestants and the Schismatics of the Oriental church. About the latter we shall say as much as is necessary in a particular remark further on.

As to Protestants, they have no unity of origin; for they are not from Christ, nor from one, but from many different persons, such as Luther, Zuinglius, Calvin, &c.

Hence they are without unity of doctrine, of worship, or of members. From the very beginning, the Protestant sects have been divided in this regard. None of their bodies ever adhered constantly to one and the same doctrine, as becomes evident by comparing the creeds which they brought forward at different times, and which cannot be denied by the Protestants themselves. In fact, nothing else could be excted; for, as St. Hilarius justly remarks: "Since every resy has its root in some novelty, it must end in some her novelty, so as to prove itself true to its spirit, and of kindred birth."

Tertullian writes: "They differ from each other, because every one changes at pleasure what he has received, just as he who advanced the error, fabricated it as he pleased. Or, why should not the Valentinians have been permitted to do what Valentine did, and the Marcionites to act as Marcion acted—namely, to change, in their belief, whatever they pleased." Protestants are more particularly deserving of this reproach, since they expressly claim for every one the right of private judgment in matters of faith—a thing which we do not find in any of the early heretics.

To external unity, Protestants can lay no claim since they have no common head. Private interpretation, or the civil power of each country, is the only recognized rule of their belief. The several churches of the state, therefore, are in no necessary connection whatever, and consequently form no *one* external church.

Q. How do we prove the Roman Catholic Church to be holy?

A. It is holy in its origin; for its founder is no other than Jesus Christ himself, through his Apostles. Otherwise our opponents must tell us who else founded it?

It is holy in its doctrine; for, the entire doctrine of the Roman Catholic Church tends to the sanctification of our lives by means of faith and virtue. And our opponents are not able to point out a single doctrine of the Church, which does not mediately or immediately tend to this end.

It is holy in its worship or divine service, which breathes only sanctity, is in the highest degree worthy of God, and surpasses all other religions in majesty. Our very opponents concede this, and admire our worship.

It is holy in its members. For, to it belong all the innumerable saints, according to their different choirs—namely, all the holy martyrs, bishops, confessors, widows, and virgins, which is a fact acknowledged by the whole world; and the Church never ceases to show forth new models of sanctity, whose greatness in virtue God declares and glorifies by irrefutable miracles and gifts of graces.

Even Leibnitz himself writes of our holy Church: "Nothing is trifling that is recommended by that church, which alone has retained the name and the marks of the true Church, in which alone we behold heroic virtue, and see it everywhere exhibiting and forming eminent examples of perfection." This is also proved in a very particular manner, from those of her children, whom the Church solemnly ranks among the number of saints, whose virtues God attested by supernatural signs. How severely and how cautiously the Church proceeds in the ratification of the virtues and miracles, in the process, for the canonization of a saint, is acknowledged even by impartial Protestants.

The Protestant objection to the Church's sanctity, founded on the dissoluteness of those Catholics who lead a bad life, we answer as did St. Augustine: "I would have you cease to reproach the Catholic Church, for you censure the morals of those men, whom the Church itself condemns, and whom, bad children as they are, she daily tries to correct. But you—why do you chafe? Why do you suffer a party spirit to blind you? Why do you stoop so far in defence of error? Seek the fruits in the field, the corn in the barn— they are easily seen, and comfort those who look for them." The Church, indeed, cannot be defiled by the sins of those children, whose vices it condemns, and endeavors to correct in every possible way, after the example of the holy and meek Lord Jesus.

Non-catholics have no claim to this attribute of the Church. The community of their churches is not holy in its origin. The founders of the Protestant churches were by no means men of eminent virtue, nor did they even show themselves lovers of truth; but, on the contrary, they proved themselves men of an impure, a dissolute, and a fanatic spirit, who, given to the pleasures of this world, did not seek what was Christ's. Their writings, yet extant, furnish ample proof of our assertion, for in them they accuse each other in turn of fraud, of lying, and other hideous vices.

Just as little have they sanctity of doctrine. For the doctrine of justification, as originally set up and determined by Protestants in their creeds, is, that faith alone will save us, without good works; that God does not *impute* to man *any sin* at all, if He has predestined him to eternal life; that on the contrary, some men are destined before hand to be damned for all eternity. These and the like doctrines can lead, indeed, to nothing else but the extinction of every sentiment of efficacious and practical piety, to paralyze all zeal for good, and throw open door and gate to licentiousness in morals. Add to this, that the innovators set aside and rejected all the difficult means of virtue, in order to bring over the populace to their party; as for instance, fasting, external mortification, holy confession and others.

Such is the doctrine of the so-called real Protestants or orthodox Lutherans, Calvinists, etc. By other Protestants, who call themselves simply Protestants or Lutherans, and on that account believe what they please, how can any question about sanctity of doctrine be raised?

Furthermore, they have not sanctity of worship, for the worship of the Protestant churches is cold and inadequate to satisfy the cravings of a devout heart. Besides, they have only imperfect means of salvation, since, besides baptism, they have no other sacrament and no sacrifice at all. Their so-called Lord's Supper is no sacrament, because they have no priesthood and acknowledge none. The other sacraments as well as the sacrifice of the Mass are rejected by them.

Finally, these churches are not holy in their members, for no sect of non-catholics can point to any saint of theirs. There are among them no examples of heroic virtues, which God was pleased to attest by miracles and supernatural signs, nay, they do not even aspire to this honor, but rather ridicule and calumniate the veneration of saints, although they are often necessitated to assume as Christian names the names of saints who lived in the Catholic Church (even after the time of the so-called Reformation), or are otherwise forced to choose for themselves the names of pagans and Jews of the Old Testament.

Q. How do we prove that the Roman Catholic Church is universal?

A. It is universal. 1. In its origin, for when at Jerusalem the Holy Ghost came down upon the Apostles and disciples of Christ, there were men gathered together at Jerusalem from all quarters of the then known world. The great day of Pentecost is the birth-day and anniversary-feast of our holy Church. *Acts*, ii. 9–11.

How this Church of Christ reaches back to the Old Testament, and through the times of the Patriarchs, to the very origin of the human race, has been already stated above.

2. The Church is universal in its extent and duration. Regarding its extent, it began, as we remarked a little while ago, with the conversion of persons from the most distant parts of the earth; and, as soon as the Apostles preached God's word, it resounded throughout the universe. Neither did the Church ever cease to be universal, or to be spread more and more among pagans and gentiles. All the nations that ever received Christianity, were converted to the faith by its missionaries alone. Numerous storms, indeed, have since assailed it with fury, but always in vain; the more they raged, the more gloriously was it fortified against them by the most benign, wise, and powerful providence of the Lord. For a space of one thousand eight hundred years has He brought His Church victoriously out of all

its combats, and thereby revealed to the whole world, at least to all who do not close their eyes and hearts to the evidence of truth, that *it* is the Church which He built upon the Rock, that there it stands *unshaken*, and that the powers of hell never can prevail, nor ever shall prevail, until the end of time.

3. The Church is universal in its doctrine. For it never admitted, in the least, of any innovation in articles of faith, but that which was always, and everywhere held as divinely revealed, that is its faith; and he who denies this and remains obstinate in his denial, is cut off from her communion.

4. The Church is universal in reference to its worship. The essence of its worship is, in all countries of the world, one and the same sacrifice, and the same holy sacraments: a worship which was already prefigured in the Old Testament; nay, even in the age of the Patriarchs indicated and announced.

5. The Church is universal in its members. This follows of itself from the first point.

6. Finally, the Church is also universal regarding its name. For Catholic signifies the same as *universal*. Never would this name have been conceded to it exclusively, if it had not been, in fact, the one universal Church.

O that all of us who are conscious of belonging to the only true and universal Church, would appropriate to ourselves that saying of St. Pacianus: "*Christian* is my name, *Catholic* my surname; by this appellation our people are distinguished from the heterodox." Hence, St. Augustine writes in his book of the true religion, c. vii. "Whether heretics and adherents of schismatics will it or will it not, if they speak with others beyond their own communion, the word *Catholic* means nothing else than the Catholic Church. They could not be understood, if they did not designate her by this name, being the one by which that Church is known throughout the whole world."

Whereas, the non-catholics have no universality of origin. They came to light only after one thousand five hundred years and more had rolled by since the institution of the Christian Church, and then they sought for invisible ancestors, since they could find no visible ones; and in doing so, they have been changing ever since, and are now completely divided and dismembered among themselves. Never have

Protestant missionaries converted any pagan nation; but in the words of an ancient Father: "Heretics are able, indeed, to make believers non-believers, but they cannot make Christians of pagans." They are able to pervert, but not to convert. A few persons bought or talked into their religion from paganism form no nation. They want, therefore, Catholicity of origin, extension of doctrine, of worship, and of members.

But, indeed, the fact, itself, that every one of them has his own principle of faith, deprives them of the mark of universality. For their principle of faith is this: "Let every one believe, what, according to the dictates of his reason, he considers as scriptural or necessary to be believed." Every one, of course, has his own personal faith, and thus universal faith is wanting; consequently, too, the universality of the Church. In the strict sense, there are with them as many religions and precepts of faith as there are heads, a thing diametrically opposed to the idea of the unity and universality of the Church.

Q. How do we prove that the Roman Catholic Church is really *Apostolic?*

A. Its duration, its doctrine, its worship, and its pastors reach back as far as the times of the Apostles; it is, therefore, really apostolic. As to its existence, it is an historical fact, that it is the oldest, and, therefore, the first Church, and the one which was founded by Christ and His Apostles themselves.

As to its doctrine and worship, it professes no other doctrine than that which was delivered to it in the course of ages by the Fathers after the Apostles.

The same holds good with regard to its essential worship.

As to its succession, its pastors, *i. e.*, the ecclesiastical hierarchy, even that alone places its apostolicity beyond all doubt, and, consequently, proves the truth of the Catholic Church being the first and the only true Church.

For, regarding the primacy of the principal head of the Church, there is no other Church in the world besides the Roman Catholic, which, by the succession of its supreme rulers, the Roman Pontiffs, dates from the days of Peter, whom Christ appointed in His own stead as head of all, and upon whom He so solemnly founded His Church, which was to endure till the end of time.

The prerogatives which Christ bestowed upon Peter, were, since Peter was not immortal, necessarily to pass to his successors, and with them the true Church was to be inseparably connected, whence it evidently follows, that only that Church can be the true one, with which Peter abides in the person of his successors, according to the axiom of St. Ambrose: "Where Peter is, there is the Church." But since the successors of Peter in the person of the Roman Popes Linus, Clement, etc., in uninterrupted succession down to Pius IX., belong to our Church, it becomes evident and incontestable, that that Church is Catholic in the true sense of the word, and the first and the only true Church of Christ. Violent interruptions of this succession of Popes, which happened from time to time, detract as little from this perfect unity and the rights of the apostolic chair as the interruption of the line of a dynasty lawfully established in a realm.

But in the bishops who are in ecclesiastical communion with the succession of the prince of the Apostles, the Church acknowledges the successors of the other Apostles, whose apostolic descent is also confirmed by their titles.

This last, however, is not always necessary, for it suffices for the apostolic mission, that the bishop of a single church has his mission directly or indirectly from Rome.

For by this he becomes ingrafted and already grows as a branch on that great tree of the world, the trunk of which reaches in the succession of the Roman Pontiffs as successors of Peter, up to Christ himself.

How strongly convinced of this relation were the bishops of ancient times, appears from the solicitude with which they endeavored to prove the succession of the Roman Popes, and they showed greater solicitude in this than in authenticating the succession of their own predecessors in their episcopal sees. Thus Irenæus does not record the succession of the bishops of Lyons, nor Eusebius that of Cesaræa, nor Epiphanius that of the Salaminian bishops, nor Optatus that of Milevi, nor Augustine that of Hyppo; but all of them assert, with one voice, the succession of the bishops of Rome. It was enough for them to be able to show the apostolicity of that Church of which they gloried in being members, and from which the sacerdotal unity of the whole Church is derived.

The Roman Catholic Church possesses in like manner the

Order of priests and deacons instituted by Christ through His Apostles, with the functions in the church proper to them, because it alone has bishops possessed of the apostolic mission, which proceeds from the head, and is only to be found in this Church.

The non-catholic communities can show nothing of all this. They can not show the apostolicity or the duration of their church and of its doctrine; for how can they prove that their churches and their doctrines are apostolic, when they were unknown in the Church of God for a space of one thousand five hundred years? Will Scripture bear witness for them? But whence will they prove the apostolicity of the Holy Scriptures themselves without the testimony of the Roman Catholic Church? Perhaps by tradition? But that they do not accept. To say nothing of their maxim: "To whom the country belongs, to him also belongs the church," that is to say, he is also head of the church.

All the churches of the East which have separated from that of Rome, likewise lack this characteristic mark. They are set adrift from Peter, and therefore from the Rock upon which Christ founded His Church. And it is on that account they want all the other above-mentioned marks of the true Church of Christ. The Greek schismatic church, together with its sects, can not be called *one*, because it fails in internal and external unity. It lost the external unity because it lost the head, which Christ had placed in His stead over His Church upon earth, namely, Peter, in the person of his successors, the Roman Pontiffs. But even on that account, it is no longer the one faith which Christ gave to us through His Apostles; for the primacy in the person of his successors is an article of faith, which the Greek church itself at one time professed. It differs, moreover, from this unity of faith in respect to the article of belief regarding the procession of the divine persons in the most Holy Trinity, since it denies the simultaneous procession of the Holy Ghost from the Father and the Son, and which, as we have already proved, is an article of faith asserted also by the oldest Greek Fathers.

The Greek schismatic church, together with its sects, can not be called *holy*, since it is known by what intrigues and infamous doings it began to tear itself loose from the unity of the Church, and bowed so shamefully beneath the yoke of worldly power. Besides, it, too, is wanting in the sanctity of its members, since it, like the Protestant churches, lacks perfect examples of holiness. This church, once so rich and fertile in saints, cannot show forth a single saint since its separation.

Finally, that church can not be styled universal, which did not exist always, but first appeared under the form of a distinct church upon earth about nine hundred years ago. Neither is it apostolic, inasmuch as it tore itself away from the successors of the prince of the Apostles, and thus wants, too, the valid apostolic mission for the members of the other ecclesiastical hierarchy.

The Roman Catholic Church, therefore, is alone that true Church of Christ, which we profess in the Apostles' Creed, saying: " I believe in the Holy Catholic Church."

Q. Can the Church ever cease to be ?

A. No, for Christ promised His Church everlasting duration.

"Blessed art thou, Simon Bar-Jona: because flesh and blood hath not revealed it to thee, but my Father who is in heaven. And I say to thee: That thou art Peter, (*i. e.*, a rock) and upon this rock I will build my Church; and the gates of hell shall not prevail against it." *Matt.* xvi. 17, 18. And at His ascension into heaven, bidding farewell to His disciples, He gave them this admonition: "Go ye and teach all nations: baptizing them in the name of the Father, and of the Son, and of the Holy Ghost; teaching them to observe all things whatsoever I have commanded you; and, behold, I am with you all days, even to the consummation of the world." *Matt.* xxviii. 19, 20.

The same thing is confirmed by the holy Fathers in express terms: "The Church is built on Peter," writes St. Jerome, "no thunderstorm can shake it, no raging of the tempest overthrow it." *Comment. in cap.* 16 *Mt.* And St. Alexander, bishop of Alexandria, writes to Alexander of Constantinople: "We acknowledge but one Church, the Catholic and Apostolic, which, as it can never be vanquished, though the whole world should storm against it, so on the contrary, it conquers and destroys every malicious attack of heretics."

Q. With what gift did Christ endow His Church, so that it can never fail ?

A. With the gift of infallibility in matters of faith and morals. If the Church could fail in these points, it would be the very thing by which it should fall and cease to be the true Church of Christ.

Q. How can we prove the infallibility of the Church from Holy Scripture and tradition?

A. "I will ask the Father," says Christ our Lord in St. John, "and He shall give you another Paraclete, that he may abide with you for ever, the spirit of truth." *John,* xiv. 16, 17. "The Spirit of truth shall come, he will teach you all truth." *John,* xvi. 13. And in St. Matthew, our Lord gives the assurance: "If any one will not hear the Church, let him be to thee as the heathen and the publican." *Matt.* xviii. 17.

This infallibility of the Church is also attested by the Apostle in his Epistle to Timothy, wherein he says: "These things I write to thee .... that thou mayest know how thou oughtest to behave thyself in the house of God, which is the Church of the living God, the pillar and ground of the truth." 1 *Tim.* iii. 14, 15.

And all the Apostles, gathered together in the Council of Jerusalem, make known their judgment in these words: "It hath seemed good to the Holy Ghost and to us." *Acts,* xv. 28.

This article of faith is also confirmed by tradition with innumerable testimonies. Hear only and consider, what St. Augustine says in this regard: "I would not myself believe the Gospel, if the authority of the Church did not move me." *Lib. cont. Epist. fund.* Because, if we deny the infallibility of the Church, we have, indeed, no infallible testimony as to the divinity of the Gospel. The same belief is expressed by St. Jerome, who writes thus: "It is said to the Church, rise, be filled with light. . . . . that it may have no shadow of error." *In. Com. ad cap. 60 Isai.* And St. Isidore writes: "The divine saying means by 'the gates of hell' the society of the wicked and the slanders of the heretics, all of which the Church of God resists, and crushes and destroys, but can never be vanquished by them."

Practice. — Thank God at every breath you draw, for the unmerited, inestimable happiness of being a child of the true, unshaken, and infallible Church, but show also by the whole of your life, that you are a child of the true Church of Christ, and worthy of calling her your mother, and that she may have no reason to be ashamed of you, but rather cause to rejoice over you as a mother. As the Church is One, Holy, Universal, and Apostolic, so also should your life show forth these marks by your peace with God, with yourself and your neighbor through unity of faith and charity; by efficacious endeavors to attain to true sanctity and perfection of life, at all times, in every place, on every occasion, after the example set by Apostolic Christianity. Hold firmly to the doctrine of the holy Church, and instruct yourself as carefully as possible, in order that you may remain free from error in matters of religion, and be able to render an account of your faith whenever an occasion requires it.

Of the Government of the Holy Church.

Q. To whom did Christ commit the teaching of His doctrine and the government of His Church?

A. To the Apostles and their successors—namely, the bishops and priests, and their coadjutors.

The Apostles were chosen by Christ our Lord himself, as the Holy Scriptures expressly record, and the Lord attests in these words: "It is not you that have chosen me, but it is I that have chosen you." But that Christ also chose their successors, in their persons, and willed this succession to be lasting, we see from the election of the Apostle Matthias, by the Apostles themselves, and from the instructions which St. Paul gives in his letters to the bishops appointed by himself, respecting the ordination of other bishops, priests, and deacons.

Q. What do we call this body of persons appointed for the administration of the Church and its doctrine?

A. In regard to the doctrine, it is called, the *teaching Church*; in regard to the government of the Church, it is called, the ecclesiastical Hierarchy.

That portion of the faithful not consecrated to the service of the Church, is called the Laity.

Q. Whom did Christ make the head of the whole Church, and His vicegerent upon earth?

A. St. Peter. This appointment is solemnly and expressly attested by the very words of Christ, as recorded by the holy Evangelists, Matthew and John. How Christ accosted St. Peter, as related by St. Matthew, has been already repeated. He calls him a Rock, upon which He would build His Church, and delivers to him the keys of heaven; and these words mean nothing else than the very highest power over the whole Church. Our Lord, after His resurrection, confirmed this in the most positive terms, saying three times to Peter, in presence of the other Apostles: "Simon, son of John, lovest thou me more than these?" He saith to Him: "Yea, Lord, thou knowest that I love thee." He saith to him: "Feed my lambs".... He saith to him again: "Feed my lambs".... He saith to him the third time: "Feed my sheep." *John*, xxi. And so in every other part of Holy Scripture, where mention is made of the Apostles, Peter is always mentioned *first* before the others.

The same thing is taught and professed by entire Tradition. St. Ambrose writes thus: "The Primacy was not given to Andrew, but to Peter." *Cap.* 12, *Epist.* 2 *Cor.*

St. Cyril writes: "He (Peter) shines forth before the others, the prince and head of the rest." *Lib.* 12 *in Joan.*

St. Augustine: "In the Holy Scriptures we learn to know Peter, in whom the Primacy is so eminently conspicuous." *Lib.* 2, *de Bap.* c. 2.

And Eucherius, of Lyons, writes: "The Lord commits to Peter, first the lambs, then the sheep; for, He made him not only a shepherd, but shepherd of the shepherds." *Homil. in Vig. S. Pet.*

Q. Who is the successor of Peter and the vicegerent of Christ?

A. The *Pope of Rome*, because he succeeds Peter in his Episcopal See, who governed the Church of Rome, as bishop, and there suffered the death of a martyr. This is a historical fact, so indubitably established, that none enjoys a greater historical certainty. The entire Church has thus acknowledged and professed it; since the time of the Apostles.

St. Irenæus, a bishop, who lived in the sub-apostolic age, writes thus concerning the Roman Church: "We will establish the Tradition of the greatest and most ancient Church, which is acknowledged by all, founded and confirmed by St. Peter and St. Paul, the most trustworthy of the Apostles. Every other church—*i. e.*, the body of the faithful—must necessarily agree with this Church on account of its supreme power." *Lib.* 3, *adv. haeres.*

St. Optatus writes: "You cannot deny, that, you know the first episcopal doctrinal chair was erected in the city of Rome, by St. Peter, upon which he, the head of the Apostles sat . . . . . . whom Linus succeeded, Clement," &c. *Cont. Parmen.*

St. Cyprian writes to Pope Cornelius: "They venture to ascend the chair of Peter, and enter the first Church, from which ecclesiastical unity has its origin." *Epist.* 55.

St. Jerome writes to Pope Damasus: "I rejoice in the ecclesiastical union with your Holiness — *i. e.*, with the doctrinal chair of Peter; I know that upon this Rock the Church is built." *Ep.* 14, *ad Dam.*

St. Augustine attests: "The supreme power of the Apostolic See always proved itself to be in the Roman Church.' *Ep.* 43.

This profession was made by all the General Councils, from the first, at Nice, till the last at Trent.

Q. Which are the principal *rights* of the Pope of Rome, as head of the whole Church?

A. 1. The Pope of Rome is, as successor of Peter and vicegerent of Christ, the supreme *Judge* in matters of faith. This appears preëminently from those well-defined words of our Lord, by the Evangelist St. Luke: "Simon, Simon, I have prayed for thee, that thy faith fail not; and thou being once converted, confirm thy brethren." *Luke*, xxii. 32. The same thing is proved by those words of Christ to St. Peter, so often quoted: "Thou art Peter (a rock), and upon this rock I will build my Church, and the gates of hell shall not prevail against it." Where the foundation of a building is tottering and falling, there also totters and falls the building itself. Peter, therefore, as the foundation of the Church in faith, was to be immovable. But the successors of St. Peter enter upon all the rights of St. Peter, as head of the Church and vicegerent of Christ, since our Lord did not grant these rights to His disciples for their own sake, but for the sake of His Church. For the successors of the Apostles stand more in need of being strengthened than the Apostles themselves.

This was acknowledged, at all times, by the entire Church; and this acknowledgment appears, too, from innumerable texts and testimonies of the holy Fathers, and the General Councils of the Church.

Thus St. Peter Chrysologus writes to Eutyches, in the following terms: "We admonish thee, brother, to listen obediently to all that was written by his Holiness, the Pope of Rome; for St. Peter, who lives and presides in his chair, gives to those that ask, the truth of faith for answer." *Epis. ad Eutych.*

St. Basil writes to the Pope, in his own name and in that of the whole Synod of Alexandria: "That which the Lord has granted your Holiness, is well deserving of that most praiseworthy voice which called you happy, because you discern what is false from the genuine and true, and announce the faith of the Fathers without any blemish."

St. Maximan, Patriarch of Constantinople, professes, in his letter addressed to the entire East: "All the boundaries of the globe, all confessors of the true faith, look up to the dignity and authority of the Pope of Rome, as to the sun. The Creator of the world chose him from among the rest of mortals on the surface of the earth; He yielded up to hir , by preference, the office of instructor; and conferred upon him this right for ever, that whosoever wishes to know divine and hidden things, must have recourse to this oracle of science and doctrine."

"We must, therefore, permit ourselves to be thence instructed in regard to what we are to believe, to think, and to hold." Thus St. Cyril to Pope Celestine.

"All controversy is at an end," St. Augustine cries out, as soon as he knew that a decision emanated from Rome. And he esteemed it of greater value to have such a decision against his opponent, in order to convince him of his error, than all the books of argument which he had written against him.

"By the letters of Innocent," says he, "every doubt in this matter is taken away." *Lib. 2, c. 3, cont. 3 ep. Pelag.* And he again asserts: "The Catholic faith is, in the profession of the Apostolic chair, so ancient and firmly grounded, so sure and clear, that it would be a crime to doubt the same. It is the Rock against which the gates of hell cannot prevail." *Epist. 157 et in Psalm, cont. Don. part.*

This belief is also that of the *General Councils* of the Church: "Peter has spoken through Leo." So the Fathers of the Council of Chalcedon exclaim, "cursed be he that does not believe thus!"

In a similar manner did the Fathers of the Sixth General Council exclaim when they read the Apostolical letters of Pope Agatho: "It seemed to be paper and ink, yet through Agatho, Peter has spoken." And in their letter to the Pope, the Fathers of the same Council write: "To thee, being the

Primate of the Universal Church, we refer the decision of what is to be done, since thou standest on the rock of faith." No less decided and solemn is the language of all the other General Councils of the Church.

Second, The Pope of Rome, as the successor of St. Peter and the vicegerent of Christ, *governs* the entire Church with Apostolic and plenipotentiary power.

This power is indicated and proved by the words of our Lord to Peter: "I will give to thee the keys of the kingdom of heaven; and whatsoever thou shalt bind upon earth, it shall be bound also in heaven; and whatsoever thou shalt loose upon earth, it shall be loosed also in heaven." *Matth.* xvi. 18, 19. And those words: "Feed my lambs—my sheep." For, all of these expressions signify, according to the language used in Holy Scripture, the highest power.

The same thing is professed and confirmed by Tradition.

No doubt, the whole East and West profess most solemnly, from the beginning of the Church, this Apostolic plenipotentiary power of the Popes of Rome, as the successors of St. Peter and the vicegerents of Christ. As a proof of this, let us only hear the belief of the Oriental church at the time of St. Cyril, who, in his writings, already quoted, makes his profession thus: " We must honor him—the Bishop of Rome —we must ask him before all, because it is his province alone to reprove, to correct, to command, to ordain, to bind, to loose, in His stead, who placed him, and who has given to no one else all that is His, save to him alone, before whom all bow their heads, according to divine right, and whom all the pastors of the Church obey as they would Jesus Christ."

Let us listen to the voice of the West in this regard, namely, that of St. Bernard, who, closing the series of the Fathers, takes their belief into his profession, and most solemnly acknowledges the same fullness of Peter's power in his successors—the Popes of Rome. He writes to Pope Eugene, who was once his disciple, in these words: "Let us first examine who thou art, whose person thou representest in the Church of God. Who art thou? Thou art the high-priest and supreme bishop. Thou art the prince of the bishops, the heir of the Apostles. As to the primateship, thou art Abel; as to the guidance, Noah; as to the patriarchate Abraham; as to the order, Melchisadech; as to the dignity, Aaron; as to the authority, Moses; as to the power, Peter; as to the anointment, CHRIST. Thou art the one to whom the keys of heaven were given. The others, indeed, are also pastors and shepherds of flocks, but thou art so the more gloriously, the more different the name is which thou didst receive above the others. They also have, indeed, their particular flocks; but to thee all are entrusted, to one—'the one flock.' Not only for the sheep, but also for the shepherds art thou ONE, the shepherd of all. For to what other, I do not say among the bishops, but even among the Apostles, are so unreservedly entrusted all the sheep? Which sheep? Perhaps this or that people, of this city or that country? 'My sheep,' said the Lord. Ah! who is there that does not plainly understand that Christ did mean, not some but all? St. James, who was a pillar of the Church, was content with one Jerusalem, leaving to Peter the entire world. If thus the brother of the Lord did yield, who else, I ask, would dare to dispute the primacy with Peter? Others, therefore, are entrusted with a part of the care, but Thou with the fullness of the power. The power of the others is reduced to certain limits, but thine extends even to those who received power over others. Thus, therefore, stands thy prerogative, unshaken, as well in regard to the keys given thee, as the sheep entrusted to thy care."

And this is also the belief and profession of the General Councils of the Church in innumerable and most solemn testimonies.

Thus the Fathers of the eighth General Council of Constantinople signed the following profession of faith:

"The saying of the Lord can not remain unfulfilled; and he has said: 'Thou art Peter, and upon this rock I will build my Church.' What was here said, is confirmed by fact, for upon the apostolic chair the Catholic religion was always preserved unadulterated, and the holy doctrine taken care of."
"Wherefore, following in all things the apostolic chair, and holding its dispositions; we hope to merit being in that communion of yours, announced by the apostolic chair, in which the Christian religion has its full, true, and firm foundation."

The Council of Florence solemnly gave the following decision of faith: "We declare it to be an article of faith, that the Apostolic See and the Pope of Rome has the primacy, the highest dignity of the Church in the whole world, and that the same Pope of Rome, the successor of St. Peter, the prince of the Apostles, and the true Vicar of Christ, is the head of the whole Church, and that he is the Father and teacher of all Christians, and that Jesus Christ our Lord, has given to him in St. Peter the full power to feed, govern, and lead the whole Church, as it is also contained in the transactions of the general councils, and in the holy canons."

Q. How is this authority of the Pope usually styled?

A. The Apostolic plenipotentiary power because it passes from St. Peter, the prince of the Apostles, to all his successors orderly and without division, on which account the Roman Episcopal See received also the epithet "the Apostolic chair."

Q. How does the Pope of Rome exercise this apostolic authority in ruling the holy Church?

A. The Pope usually rules the Church by those who, though entrusted with power in the Church, are yet subordinate to him, to wit: the Cardinals, Patriarchs, Primates, Archbishops, Bishops, &c., who, dispersed throughout the Church over the whole earth, unite the entire body of the faithful with the Apostolic chair.

However, it does not follow that the Episcopal power is merely a succedaneous one, on the contrary, it is likewise a proper power instituted by God, but subordinate to that of the Head of the Church; by which power the Bishops are constituted true shepherds with proper authority to feed the flocks intrusted to them by God, through the Apostolic See. The entire body of the Church, united in this manner with the head, by means of an immediate Pastor, and spread over the face of the earth, is called in familiar language: "the dispersed Church." But if the Pope call together the chiefs of the Church, the Bishops and Doctors, to any particular place, such an assembly is styled a General Council of the Church, or simply, a Council.

But the power of the Pope is by no means lessened by such an assembly; for it is he who convokes the Councils, presides over them, either personally or by his legates, and ratifies their decrees, without which ratification they have no force, and no general value in the Church. The Pope, therefore, is, and remains, whether in a Council, or out of it, the head of the whole Church by divine institution as vicegerent of Christ and successor of Peter.

ON FAITH.

Q. Who belongs to this true Church of Christ, whose head is the Pope of Rome?

A. Every one who has been received into the Church of Christ by holy Baptism, and has not been excluded again from its fold?

Pagans, Jews, Heretics, Schismatics, and excommunicated persons are therefore by no means members of the holy Church. Not the Pagans nor the Jews, because they never entered the Church. Not the Heretics, &c., because they were separated again from the Church. He is called a heretic who obstinately contradicts and denies an article of faith solemnly declared by the Church. Whereas that one is called a Schismatic who renounces the communion of the Church, and refuses obedience to his lawful sovereign pastor by throwing off the ecclesiastical authority.

Finally, an excommunicated person is he who by virtue of ecclesiastical judgment is separated from the communion of the Church by a spiritual ban in consequence of a crime.

Practice. — Study to have a particular reverence, love, and obedience for the authority of the Church, and that of its ministers, instituted by Christ; but especially nourish always within you the most profound respect for the Pope, as being the chief head of the Church, and the visible vicar of Christ. "He that honors you, honors me," says Jesus Christ, "and he that despises you despises me;" Even if it happens that some priests have faults, honor them nevertheless, and remember that if they were not precisely faults of priests, they would, perhaps, not appear so great to the eyes of the world, but remain unnoticed. But, in particular, the faults which they impute to some Popes, are for the greater part mere calumnies, as is proved even by Protestant writers themselves. Nay, there is no other succession of men, in any other dignity and administration, who are so prominent for sanctity, learning, and benefits conferred on the human race, as that of the Popes.

On the Communion of the Members of the Church.

Q. What do you understand by the expression: The communion of saints?

A. By the communion of saints we understand the spiritual connection which embraces all the members of the militant, suffering, and triumphant Church, and unites them into one Church, the family of God.

Q. Why is this connection called the communion of saints?

A. Because all who belong on earth to this communion, are called to sanctity of life by the profession of the Christian faith, and are sanctified by baptism, and the reception of the other sacraments. The souls in purgatory, and the blessed in heaven, are all of them in the state of sanctifying grace, and confirmed in it for ever, to all eternity.

Q. By what means are the members of the militant Church upon earth connected with each other?

A. By the participation of the same sacraments, and the spiritual goods of the Church, and by sharing the prayers and good works which the faithful on earth perform. There exists, therefore, among the members of the Church upon earth a union similar to that of the members of the human body; that is, they mutually support one another, for the welfare of the whole body, according to the Apostle in his Epistle to the Romans, chap. xii. 4-5, and to the Ephesians, chapter iv. 3; where he says: "Be careful to keep the unity of the Spirit in the bond of peace, one body, and one Spirit, as you are, called in one hope of your salvation." And again: "That we may in all things grow up in Him who is the head, Christ: from whom the whole body, cemented and firmly joined together, by what every joint supplieth, according to the operation in the measure of every part, maketh increase of the body, unto the edifying of itself in charity." *Ephes.* iv. 15, 16.

Q. How is the Church militant in communion with the Church *suffering?*

A. The souls in purgatory are helped by the prayers of the faithful and their good works; and they, themselves, pray to the Lord in return for the faithful upon earth.

Q. What is purgatory, and how do you prove that there exits a communion with the souls that are there?

A. Purgatory is that place and intermediate state in the other life, in which souls are purified that are not as yet perfectly cleansed from all imperfections, and who departed this life in the state of venial sin, or are yet to satisfy for the temporal punishment due to the sins which they had committed, after the guilt of them was forgiven.

The punishments in purgatory are two-fold; first, the punishment of delay in regard to heavenly glory; and then the punishment of pain especially by fire.

That there is a purgatory, was already revealed to man in the Old Testament. Thus we read in the Second Book of the Machabees, chapter xii. verse, 43: "That Judas, making a gathering, sent twelve thousand drachms of silver to Jerusalem for sacrifice, to be offered for the sins of the dead."

In the New Testament, Christ our Lord points to this place of purification, assuring us, by St. Luke, speaking of the prison of pain: "I say to thee thou shalt not go out thence, until thou payest the very last farthing." *Luke*, xii. 59.

But that the pain of purgatory is a pain of fire, is indicated by St. Paul, who states in his Epistle to the Corinthians: "The fire shall try every man's work, of what sort it is. . . . . If any man's work burn, he shall suffer loss; but he himself shall be saved, yet so as by fire." 1 *Cor.* i. 13–15.

Reason itself, enlightened by faith, concludes, from most obvious and most powerful motives, the existence of such a place of purification. For all men do not die entirely pure, and without a stain of sin, although they may die not infected with mortal sin. It is, therefore, fitting that there should be, in the other life, a place in which souls may be purified from their stains, before entering heaven.

But as far as this corresponds with the justice of God, so far is it also in accordance with His goodness and mercy that the suffering should be helped by the intercession of the living, because by it charity is exercised, and man the more powerfully reminded and admonished to live here a life most pure, and to do penance, in order to avoid the torments of Purgatory. Holy Writ confirms this advantage which the divine wisdom thereby intends for us and the dead, in express terms: "It is a holy and wholesome thought to pray for the dead, that they may be loosed from their sins."

Moreover, the living among themselves can pray for each other efficaciously, according to St. James the Apostle: "Pray for one another, that you may be saved." *St. James*, v. 16. Why, then, should not we be able to pray also with efficacy for the dead, especially since the souls in purgatory departed this life in the state of grace and holy love, the bond of which is "not torn by death, but remains," as the Apostle tells us in his 1st Epistle to the Corinthians, chap.

xiii. ? St. Augustine in his book, of the care which we should have for the dead, bears witness to the belief of the Church in these words: "There is no doubt that the dead receive succor from the prayers of the Church, and the holy sacrifice, and the alms-deeds, which are offered up for their souls. For according to the tradition received from the Fathers, this is observed by the whole Church, that prayers are made for those who died in the communion of the body and blood of Christ, when mention is made of them in the holy sacrifice (of the Mass) in its place, and that it is also offered up for them. But if works of mercy are wrought in their behalf, who can doubt that they are benefited by them, for the Lord is not besought in vain? There is, indeed, no doubt at all, that all these things profit the dead; but only those are benefited by them who lived such a life before their death, that these works can be of service to them after their death." *Lib. de cura pro mortuis gerenda* c. 1.

St. Cyril, of Jerusalem, teaches thus: "Finally, we pray for all those who have departed from among us, believing, that thereby the greatest hope is afforded to them for whom the propitiation of that holy and efficacious sacrifice is offered upon the altar." *Catech. Myst.* v.

That the pain of purgatory is fire, is attested by Cyprian, who, agreeing with the teaching of the Church in his time, says, "It is one thing to be purged from sin by protracted tortures of pain, and another to be cleansed by fire." *Ep.* xxii.

St. Clement, of Alexandria, writes: "We say that the fire does not sanctify the flesh, but the souls defiled with sin." *Lib. Strom.* 7.

Q. What are the principal works by which the souls in purgatory are assisted?

A. Prayer, Alms-deeds, Fasts, Pilgrimages, and all other works of penance, and exercises of virtue. Also, indulgences, which may be applied to them in an intercessory manner, and most particularly by the offering up of the holy sacrifice of the Mass. That the souls in purgatory, intercede with God for us, is equally certain. For they are in the bond of holy love, and, therefore, incited by gratitude and mutual charity to pray for us, if we do so for them. Moreover, there are on record so many instances, in which help was obtained from God, through the intercession of the souls in purgatory, that an attempt to deny all of them would be as foolish as presumptuous.

Q. How is the Church militant in communion with the Church *triumphant?*

A. By the veneration, invocation, and intercession of the saints. Namely, the faithful upon earth venerate the saints in heaven, on account of their eminent sanctity, and their intercession with God. The saints in heaven, again, pray for the whole Church, and in a special manner for those who call for their mediation with the Almighty. But in the widest sense, we understand by the saints, all the blessed inhabitants of heaven, both angels and men.

The latter, however, are particularly those of whom we treat, because they are more closely connected with us by their nature, and there is a most powerful motive for us to imitate them in our lives.

Q. How do you call this veneration and invocation of saints?

A. The worship of saints, or the veneration of saints. For to venerate is simply to esteem highly, and to give signs of this veneration founded on high esteem.

Q. How do you call this worship in order to distinguish it from that which we give to God?

A. It is called worship or service, and the homage of *veneration*, whereas the worship which we render to God is termed the worship and homage of *adoration*. We adore God alone for his own sake; we only honor the saints, and that, indeed, for God's sake, who made them holy.

Q. Which is the principal ground for this veneration of saints?

A. It is the acknowledgment of the virtues and merits of the saints, and the pious respect which hence is due to them. I say pious, that is to say, respect which is, as it were, due to them from a religious, and not a mere natural motive.

Certainly, if virtue upon earth is a just object of our esteem and veneration, and if we properly and profitably call upon the faithful and virtuous upon earth, to pray to God and intercede with him for us, why then should we not honor the virtues of the saints in heaven, seeing that they are already crowned and glorified by God, and ask them for their intercession with Him, whom they now behold face to face, since they now reign with Christ in heaven? Moreover, this worship of the saints is well adapted to remind us efficaciously of them, and induce us to follow in their footsteps.

And this, too, is the very reason why the Divine Wisdom would have the intercession of the saints efficacious in our regard, in order that the bond of charity might link closer together all the members of the Church militant, suffering, and triumphant, and lead them to virtue and to God by mutual help and encouragement.

Q. Do Scripture and tradition both approve of and confirm the veneration of the saints?

A. Certainly. For we read in Holy Scripture, that, from a motive of religion, a particular veneration was shown to the angels and saints. Thus Isaias venerated the angel who appeared to him, by prostrating himself upon the ground. *Isa.* c. 5. The same thing was done by the disciples of the prophets before Eliseus. *4th Book of Kings,* ch. ii. King Nebuchodonosor himself wished to honor the sanctity of Daniel, by prostrating himself in the dust before him; and Holy Scripture praises the king for it in the narrative by Daniel, ch. ii. Now all this is still more applicable in regard to the veneration of these servants of God, who are already with God in heaven, and united to Him by the indissoluble ties of glory.

But that the saints pray efficaciously for us, is likewise confirmed in the Old as well as in the New Testament.

Thus, we read, in the second book of Machabees, concerning Jeremias, who had already passed to the other life: "This is a lover of his brethren, and of the people of Israel; this is he that prayeth much for the people and for all the holy city, Jeremias, the Prophet of God." 2 *Mach.* xv. 14. Similar things are recorded of Moses and of Samuel, by Jeremias himself: *Jer.* c. 15. And in the *Book of Job,* xlii. 8, the Lord himself says: "And my servant Job shall pray for you; his face I will accept." And St. John, in his Apocalypse, speaks thus of his vision: "The four-and-twenty ancients fell down before the Lamb, having every one of them harps and golden vials full of odors, which are the prayers of the saints." *Apoc.* v. 8.

This belief of the whole Church, from its very origin, is recorded also by the holy Fathers.

In the first place, St. Augustine writes thus: " We honor

the martyrs with the worship of charity and of communion, with which we likewise honor the holy servants of God upon earth, whose hearts we perceive ready to encounter the same sufferings for the truth of the Gospel. But we honor these with greater devotion, because they are safer, since they have fought the good fight, and come forth victorious from the struggle, as we also bestow more solemn praise upon those who have already entered upon the life of bliss, than on those who are as yet engaged in the combat here below. But we bestow upon none, that worship, which, in the Greek, is called λατρεια, and which can hardly be expressed in Latin by one word, since it signifies a worship proper to the Deity alone, nor do we teach any one to bestow it upon any other save God alone." *Lib. 20, contra Faust.*

And St. Jerome, in his book against Vigilantius, writes to this effect : "If the Apostles and martyrs, yet living in mortal flesh, could pray for others, whilst they had still to watch over themselves, how much more are they now able to do so, after gaining the crown, bearing off the palm of victory, and being enthroned in triumph? Or, do you think that they are now less able to do so, because they have commenced to reign with Christ?" *Lib. adv. Vigil.*

And St. Basil writes : " I do, in consequence of the genuine Christian faith, which we have received from God, believe in one God Almighty, the Father, Son, and Holy Ghost. I receive also the holy Apostles, and prophets, and martyrs, for intercessors with God ; I call upon them, that through them, *i. e.*, through their intercession, God, the merciful Lord, may be propitious to me."

Q. In what manner is the veneration of saints principally practised ?

A. We yearly celebrate their feasts on certain days ; altars and churches are erected and dedicated in their honor to God, and the holy sacrifice of the Mass is offered up to God for their special glorification. The faithful are also wont to bind themselves, by vows or promises, before the Lord, to works of piety and virtue in their honor, as also to venerate, with religious devotion, their pictures and relics. We say with religious devotion, in as far, namely, as the motive for this veneration is no temporal and political one, but one founded on religion.

St. Augustine writes thus, on this subject, against Faustus:

"The Christian people celebrate the memory of the martyrs with religious solemnity, partly in order to excite a desire of imitation, partly in order to participate in their merits, and to receive succor through their intercession; yet so, that if altars are erected, they are never erected to a martyr, but to the God of the martyrs himself, though they are erected to the memory of the martyrs. For, where can any prelate of the Church be found, who, whilst standing at the altar, in those places dedicated to the veneration of the saints, said, at any time: 'We offer (sacrifice) to thee Peter, or Paul, or Cyprian?' But what is offered up, is offered to God who crowned the martyrs, in places associated with the remembrance of those whom He did crown."

Eusebius writes in a similar manner: "We, the champions of true piety, honor the friends of God, and approach their tombs, making vows to them, on account of their sanctity, through whose intercession with God, we are, as we confess, greatly supported." *Lib.* viii. *Praep. Evang. c.* 7.

The Council of Gangra, held in the fourth century, thus defines: "Whosoever does not confess that all the saints of the New and Old Testaments are to be venerated . . . let him be excluded from the communion of the Church, according to the ecclesiastical Tradition."

Very remarkable, too, is the testimony of Theodoret, who, proving this veneration of the saints of old, as it is at present exercised, speaks thus: "But that those who make a vow are rendered participants of their wishes, is clearly proved by their votive gifts, which indicate healing. For some offer images of eyes, others of feet, others of hands, and some, indeed, of gold, others of brass, and so on."

Behold then, how, even the primitive Christians as well as we, were wont to express their gratitude to God and the saints.

Q. Was it also the custom to pay a due tribute of respect to the images of the saints in the Church?

A. Certainly, it was; for this is proved from the most ancient Fathers, and from the decrees of the Councils.

Thus, St. Basil writes: "That the use of images in the Church was universal, and derived from Apostolic Tradition." *S. Basil, Epis.* 360.

St. Chrysostom and Theodoret bear witness that the likenesses of St. Simon Stylites were painted, for the sake of protection, not only in the Churches, but also in the houses and workshops of the faithful." *St. Chrys. orat. de S. Meletio, Theod. in vita Sim. Styl.*

The second Council of Nice declares solemnly, in its seventh session: "We decide with all certitude and care, that holy images are to be erected . . . in the churches of God, in houses, and on the way-sides, and traced upon the holy vases. For the respect which we show to the images, passes to the object of which they are representations . . . Thus, the doctrine of our Fathers stands firm, *i. e.*, the Tradition of the Catholic Church."

By these words, the Councils also point out the reason of this veneration: "We, by no means, venerate the image, not that which is painted, but the object represented by it, *i. e.*, the person whose image it is."

That in pictures this reference of the image to the person represented by it is to be regarded, is plain even to the most unlearned, as is also manifest from the use of images in common and civil life.

St. Ambrose aptly appeals to this practice, writing as follows, "He who crowns the image of the Emperor, certainly honors him whose image he crowns; and he who dishonors the image of the Emperor, is looked upon as if he had dishonored the Emperor himself, though he insulted only his image." *In Psalm*, cxviii. This purely natural reason also incites men to honor with due respect the images of their parents, friends, and acquaintances.

Q. Is this use of the images of saints commendable and useful for any other reasons?

A. No doubt it is; first, because images are well calculated for the instruction of the uneducated, as was said by St. Gregory the Great. "The image on the wall instructs more than the Scripture in the hand, which is not understood."

Second, Because the images of the saints very often powerfully exhort us to follow them in their actions. Justly, therefore, did the poet sing: "The mind is less impressed with what the ear hears, than with what the eye beholds."

Third, Because images preserve in us the memory of Christ and his saints, in the midst of other occupations, and admonish us to whom we must have recourse.

Q. What is meant by the term, "Relics," and is the veneration of relics allowable and salutary?

A. By the word "relics," in a stricter sense, is meant the remains of the bodies of saints. But, in a wider sense, we understand by relics all objects of which the saints made use, whilst living, or whatever had any connection with them—to wit: their clothing, their handwriting, the instruments of their martyrdom. Now, these relics are, indeed, on account of their relation to saints, an object of lawful, religious veneration, because that veneration proceeds from a purely religious motive.

That, in this sense, the veneration of relics is both just and laudable, is confirmed in the first place by Holy Scripture.

Thus we read in the fourth book of Kings, xiii. 21: "Some that were burying a man, saw the rovers, and cast the body into the sepulchre of Eliseus. And when it had touched the bones of Eliseus, the man came to life, and stood upon his feet." If, therefore, the mere touching of the relics of the prophet, without any intention of veneration, even restored the dead to life, how salutary must be the actual veneration of holy relics?

In the Acts of the Apostles we likewise read, that "many sick have been healed by the mere shadow of St. Peter falling upon them." *Acts*, v. 15.

Speaking of this, St. Augustine justly remarks: "If even the *shadow* of one passing by had such an effect, what effect may not be produced by the *body* of him who is already reigning with Christ?"

Moreover, we thus read in the same Acts of the Apostles concerning the relics of St. Paul: "God wrought special miracles by the hand of Paul, so that even there were brought from his body to the sick, handkerchiefs and aprons, and the diseases departed from them, and the wicked spirits went out of them." *Acts*, xix. 11, 12.

According to the testimony of history, and of the holy Fathers in all ages, God always favored the veneration of holy relics with many and great miracles.

Thus St. Ambrose has left a record of the many and great miracles which the Lord wrought by means of the relics of SS. Gervasius and Protasius; and St. Augustine, of those wrought by means of the bones of St. Stephen. St. Chrysostom, speaking of relics in general, writes thus: "Thou sawest how great the power of the saints is! for not only their works, but even their clothes are worthy of veneration from all creatures."

"The cloak of Elias divides the Jordan. The shoes of the three youths in the furnace trod on its fire. The wood of Eliseus changed the nature of the waters. . . . The garments of St. Paul expel evil spirits." The Church, therefore, has justly honored relics ever since the first centuries, as is also found written in the Acts of the Martyr Saint Ignatius, dating from the apostolic times,"that the faithful of Smyrna valued his bones more than jewels and gold, and guarded them devoutly." St. Jerome, particularly, in his book against Vigilantius, gives an explicit and very strong testimony regarding this uninterrupted public worship of holy relics in the Church of God. "The holy relics," he writes, "are carried everywhere in golden vases, with solemn pomp, by the bishops themselves." And he testifies the same thing in a letter written to St. Marcella: "We everywhere honor the tombs of the martyrs, and touch our eyes with the holy ashes, and we also kiss the same where we can do so." *Epist.* 17, *ad Marc.* Behold here the proof, that the very kind and manner of this veneration has been from the earliest times of Christianity, identical with the present. We will add, moreover, the words of St. Augustine, spoken in reference to the relics of St. Stephen: "A little dust has gathered such a multitude of people! The dust is concealed, the favors of grace are manifest. Weigh and consider, beloved! what the Lord may reserve for us in the land of the living, since He imparts to us so much good from the dust of the departed."

The second Council of Nice declares as follows, in its second session: "Christ our Saviour has left to us the relics of the saints, to be fountains of salvation, whence He causes to issue a multitude of favors and graces for the needy, since He is dwelling in them." The Council of Trent has collected in a few solemn words, the whole of this doctrine: " The sacred bodies of the martyrs and others who live with as the Church has already condemned them of old, and does so still." *Sess.* xxv.

The general disposition of the mind of man is such that our love is greater in proportion to the qualities of those we love; why should not this bear application to the saints? Moreover, we are, by the veneration of relics, forcibly reminded of the lives and actions of Saints, and incited to imitate them. These relics also place before our eyes very plainly the dignity of our bodies sanctified by Christ.

Q. Which of the saints does the Church honor beyond all others, and in a particular manner?

A. Mary, the most blessed Virgin and Mother of our Lord, who on account of her dignity is so far elevated above angels and men. The kind of veneration with which we honor her above the other saints, is hence also designated by a special term. The worship, namely, with which we honor her, is called not as that of the saints, "*Cultus duliæ,*" but "*Hyperduliæ.*" In English we might call the "*Cultus duliæ*" the worship of veneration, and that of "*Hyperduliæ*" the worship of superior veneration. There remains, however, between this superior veneration of the most blessed Mother of God and the worship of adoration by which we do homage to God alone, an infinite difference. Beautifully and energetically, therefore did Epiphanius set down in writing, in accordance with the universal belief of all the faithful of his day: "Let Mary be venerated by us, but the Father, the Son, and the Holy Ghost alone adored." *Hæres.* 79.

Q. To whom is the worship referred, with which we venerate and adore the holy cross?

A. To Christ our Lord, who chose it and redeemed us by it.

Q. What are we to think, therefore, of those who, neglecting all that has just been said, upbraid Catholics with idolatry, as if they adored the saints or their images and relics, and as if, by this worship of veneration, we encroached upon the worship of adoration which we owe to God?

A. As for those persons, we can only pity their ignorance and their infatuation if they do not perceive the essential and the infinite difference which exists between veneration and adoration, a difference which, with us, even the smallest children and the newly-converted, even of the most barbarous nations, do immediately, and with ease, understand. But if our adversaries do understand that which we believe and teach, then we cannot sufficiently condemn the *malice* with which they, as enemies of the Church and of truth, upbraid us in spite of their better knowledge and convictions, with a vice of which they declare us guilty, and thus show themselves more malicious than even the blinded pagans. "Who ever adored a martyr?" exclaims St. Jerome, in just indignation against the heretic and slanderer Vigilantius.

Moreover, if we honor and glorify the saints, we honor and extol in them only the gifts of God. How, therefore, can this veneration paid to the servants of the Lord encroach upon his honor; for God is glorified by this veneration, since we acknowledge that it is His grace and goodness which made them holy?

And it is upon this ground, that the same St. Jerome also writes to Riparius: "We honor the servants, in order that the honor of the servant may fall back upon the Lord." *Epist. ad Rip.*

This worship diminishes just as little the honor which we owe to Christ, and our confidence in His mediation with the Father. For we know no merits and no dignity in the saints, but through the merits and the grace of Christ, nor do we know their intercession to be efficacious otherwise than through Jesus Christ. Listen to St. Ambrose: "Whosoever," he says, "honors the martyrs, honors Christ, and whosoever despises the saints, despises Christ." *Serm.* 6. And St. Jerome, citing the words of St. Paul to Philemon: "I give thanks to my God, always making a remembrance of thee in my prayers, hearing of thy charity and faith, which thou hast in the Lord Jesus, and towards all the saints," adds: "Charity and confidence in God is, therefore, not full, if it be diminished by hatred and faithlessness towards His servants." *S. Hier. in S. Pauli ad Philem.* Heretics act in this manner, who show themselves averse to the veneration of the saints by their calumny and derision, unmindful of the confession of faith which they make in the Apostoles' Creed: "I believe in the communion of saints." But it is different with the orthodox and those children of the true Church who live according to their faith;- their actions are in accordance with their confession of faith, and they thereby follow the example and the type of the primitive, apostolic Christians.

Practice. — You live in the communion of saints on

earth. Show the influence of this communion upon your life by the zeal with which you make use of every occasion offered you by the holy Church, for participating in its means of grace, especially by the reception of the holy sacraments, and by common prayer. But also by the sympathy which your heart feels for the joys and sorrows of the Church of God, after the example of the Apostle of the nations, who could say in truth: "Who is weak and I am not weak? who is scandalized that I do not burn?" 2 *Cor.* xi. 29. So it ought to be with members of the same body. Show, too, this life of the Church within you by the zeal with which you care for the corporal, and especially the spiritual welfare of your neighbor, by a burning zeal for souls, endeavoring by prayer, word and deed, to save and sanctify your brethren in Christ.

You live in the communion of the Church suffering. What do you do for the consolation and help of the souls in purgatory? Ah! with what care would you try to avoid the least shadow of venial sin, if you were often to think of the inevitable punishment which awaits it in purgatory; if you have succored the souls in purgatory during your life, the prayers of the faithful shall likewise succor you when your turn comes to undergo those purging flames.

You live in communion with the Church triumphant in heaven. Think often of where the saints now are, and where they were one day, and read frequently the lives of the saints, and you shall feel within you the power of that exhortation of St. Augustine: "If they were able, why should not I be able also?" Have a special reverence for the saints of your name, for St. Joseph, and above all for Mary, the Queen of Saints.

Q. What follows from the article of faith, concerning the Church and the communion of saints, with respect to eternal salvation?

A. Resting on the truths of faith just cited and explained, we believe and confess that all who are not members of the true Church, that is, of the Roman Catholic Church, are not in the way of salvation; or, in other words, we believe and confess that the Roman Catholic Church, being the only true Church of Christ, is also the *only one* in which man *can be saved*.

Q. How do you prove this?

A. The proof follows clearly and incontestably from what has been already shown.

For there is no salvation but through Jesus Christ who deposited the means of salvation in his Church, and said absolutely: "Let him who does not hear the Church, be to thee as a heathen and a publican," and again: "He that does not believe, shall be condemned." But since this Church of Christ is, and can be, and shall remain but *one*, and according to what has been proved above, the holy Roman Catholic Church can alone be this one, it is manifest that it is the only one in which man can be saved.

None of the other Christian sects are, as we proved, the Church of Christ, and since salvation can be obtained only through Christ, it is plain that those sectarian churches, founded by man, can never lead to salvation, nor can it be said that they do so.

Granted even, that many things are believed in them which Christ did reveal; if one does not believe all, but only some things, he has offended against all, according to the Apostle: "Whosoever shall keep the whole law, but offend in one *point,* is become guilty of all." *St. James*, ii. 10.

The reason of this assertion is manifest. For the one and undivided authority of God, who founded the Church, contends for one article of faith as much as for all. To deny and attack this authority of God in itself or in his Church in one point, is as much as to endeavor to destroy it in all.

This, too, is the unanimous doctrine of the holy Fathers.

Thus St. Ignatius, the martyr, the disciple of St. Polycarp, who was a disciple of the Apostles, writes in his circular to the Magnesians: "Do not err, my brethren, if any one follow a schismatic, he cannot attain to the inheritance of God; if any one walks in the path of strange doctrine, he cannot become a partaker of God's inheritance."

St. Cyprian, in his book on the Unity of the Church, says: "He cannot have God for his Father, who has not the Church for his Mother."

St. Augustine teaches: "Whosoever is separated from this Catholic Church, shall not have life, but the anger of God remains upon him, on account of this crime that he is torn from the unity of Christ, though he may appear to lead a life ever so praiseworthy." *Ad. pop. fact. Dan.* c. 141.

St. Fulgentius teaches likewise: "Believe it firmly and do not doubt it in the least, that not only the pagans, but also the Jews, and all the heretics and schismatics, who terminate their present life out of the communion of the Catholic Church, go into everlasting fire." *Lib. de Fide*, c. 38.

Finally, St. Gregory the Great asserts: "The Holy Universal Church teaches, that no one out of her communion can ever really be saved." *Lib. mor.* 14.

But this is to be understood of those who, through their own fault, adhere to an error in faith, and who, consequently defend the error with obstinacy. For such it is impossible to be in the way of salvation, since, by the very fact of their sinfully rising up against the authority of God and His Church, they certainly sin grievously, and go on, therefore, to eternal perdition, unless they return to God whilst time is granted them. Indeed, if even he who disobeys and dishonors his earthly parents in matters of consequence, thereby becomes guilty of grievous sin and incurs eternal chastisement, how should he who despises his heavenly Father and his holy mother, the Church, remain free from mortal sin, or escape the judgment?

It is different, with those who are born among heretics, and, as it were, without a suspicion of being wrong, suck in the error as with their mother's milk, and do not obstinately confess the same; who only exteriorly adhere to the same from guiltless ignorance, but interiorly have a desire after truth, and as soon as it dawns upon them, are ready to confess the same as freely. The number of such persons amongst the common people, in countries inhabited by heretics and unbelievers is not small; if these were validly baptized, they are really members of the Church; but if they are not baptized, they are, by their desire after the truth which is Christ, invisibly incorporated in the Church, and will, if they keep themselves otherwise free from mortal sin, be saved in an extraordinary manner—but still as children of the one true Church to which they invisibly belong. But who are in such a position, no man can decide but God to whom alone it belongs to judge, whether or not the error is culpable, and whether or not any one persevered to the end in his error without any fault of his.

There is, therefore, but one only road to heaven, namely the Catholic Church, as being the only true Church of Christ.

But there are more roads than one to the Church, namely, as many as there are manifest and hidden *decrees* of God, by which His providence leads those who are of good will to the knowledge of the truth of salvation, even though there be exteriorly no opportunity for all to enter the Church as visible members by baptism, or the confession of faith, yet they enter it by means of the baptism of desire.

But never, in any case, do we judge any individual, since the judgment of persons can never be passed with certainty by men, as stated above, but is reserved for God alone. We condemn the error, indeed, at all times, but we love the erring in Christian charity, and seek to bring them back, with charity, into the road of truth and of salvation.

The article of faith, and the doctrine according to which there is but One only Church that leads to salvation, is, therefore, by no means incompatible with the peace and the welfare of civil society. For not only do the duties of common charity towards our neighbor bind us to every man, according to the express command of Christ, but we are, even by the desire of saving our neighbor, impelled to exercise those duties of charity towards him, and with particular solicitude towards such as have erred, on every occasion, in order to gain their good will, and to win them, in this manner, the more easily and efficaciously to the truth.

But if the morals of those who are wandering in error be such that proximity to and intercourse with those persons might be dangerous to the orthodox, then, as a matter of course, they are to be avoided. Yet to judge of this does not so much belong to a single person, but rather to the public, ecclesiastical and civil authority, which then disposes what is just and profitable for society.

Q. What is the application of this article of faith to our life?

A. If we consider well and take to heart all that has been hitherto said about the Church, how fervent should be our desire to return thanks to God, that He, the Lord and Creator, our God and Redeemer, has called us, in His mercy, to this His Church, which is the only true one, having salvation; and we, therefore, exult with the Psalmist: "How lovely are Thy tabernacles, O Lord of hosts! my soul longeth and fainteth for the courts of the Lord," "Blessed are they that dwell in Thy house." *Ps.* lxxxiii. 2, 5. Let us, therefore, love the

Church, our Holy Mother; let us show ourselves everywhere and at all times as her children, and prove this our love and fidelity towards her, by the zealous and faithful observance of her commands and precepts. We shall have occasion to speak more at large touching this observance in the course of this book: "In order that every one may know how he ought to behave himself in the house of God, which is the Church of the living God, the pillar and ground of the truth, and the sure harbor of salvation." 1 *Tim.* iii. 15.

The Tenth Article of Faith.

Q. What is proposed to our belief in the tenth article of faith?

A. The highest and most important benefit bestowed upon the human race by God's infinite mercy, to wit: "the forgiveness of sin," which is obtained in the Church solely and exclusively; this by the Sacrament of Baptism for those that enter the Church; and by the Sacrament of Penance for those that sinned after having received Baptism. In this article, therefore, and in the following articles of faith, is laid before us, as it were, the whole operation of that grace which God will impart to us by His Church in the communion of Saints, namely: The supernatural life of the *soul* by the forgiveness of sin, which is the death of the soul, and by the conferring of sanctifying grace. And, moreover, also, the immortal and glorious life of the *body* by the resurrection from the dead; and finally the eternal life of *happiness* in heaven, which is prepared for those children of the militant Church upon earth, who died in the state of grace and in the filial friendship of God, according to the words of our Saviour himself: "I am come that they may have life, and may have it more abundantly." *John*, x. 10.

Q. Who are they in the Church that have power to forgive sins?

A. All those priests empowered by their ordinaries; namely, by the holy power of the keys, which Christ gave to St. Peter and his successors first of all, and who then, by conferring the ecclesiastical jurisdiction or mission, impart the necessary authority to the subordinate pastors and priests of the Church for exercising this power, in order that, by the administration of the Sacrament of Penance to the faithful their sins may be forgiven.

Q. Is any sin so great that it cannot be forgiven?

A. No; for Christ says without restriction: "Receive ye the Holy Ghost: whose sins you shall forgive they are forgiven them," (*John*, xx. 23), provided that the sinner himself do not place any obstacle, but with due preparation confess his sins, sincerely purposing to sin no more. We shall say more on this subject in the treatise on the Sacraments.

Q. Is this forgiveness of sins something great and wonderful?

A. Certainly; and, indeed, so much so that upon earth there can be nothing greater or more important for us. For listen to the testimony of St. Augustine, who says, "that the conversion of a sinner from evil to virtue is to be considered a greater work than even the creation of the world out of nothing. For if the creation could be effected only by means of an infinite power, it necessarily follows that the forgiveness of sins must be still more a work of infinite power." For a creature which is endowed with free will, and has fallen, can resist the will of God, but this a creature cannot do at the moment of its creation.

Q. What does this truth of faith demand of us?

A. That we should return infinite thanks to God for this most important of all His benefits; moreover, that we should use it with the greatest diligence for our salvation. Indeed, if even the remedies for recovering our bodily health, and saving our temporal life are of importance for us, and their success a cause of rejoicing, how much more important and welcome must be to us those remedial agents which the wisdom of God has prepared for the salvation of souls and the purchase of eternal life; especially since the latter, unlike the former, are sure to cure us, provided only that we make use of them as we ought. What we have to guard against most carefully is, that we do not become eventually ungrateful towards the Holy Ghost, and careless in regard to sin, because we have the means of obtaining pardon for it. Such a disposition would render us incapable of obtaining even the forgiveness of our sins, and throw us into a still more pitiful state of dereliction on the part of God. *Conc. Trid. Sess. VI.*

The Eleventh Article of Faith.

Q. What does the eleventh article of faith teach us?
A. The future resurrection from the dead.

Q. Who shall rise again?
A. All men, without exception; not all, however, in a like manner; for the good shall rise to glory, but the wicked to torment; wherefore the resurrection to a true life of happiness is promised only to the good.

Q. Shall we rise again with the same bodies in which we now are?
A. Yes, we shall. For it would be no real resurrection if we were not to receive again the same body; nay, this resurrection is, moreover, to take place, that man may be rewarded or punished both in soul and body, according as his body has served him as an instrument of good or of evil. Another body would neither be deserving of the glory nor the punishment; we shall, therefore, reassume the same body, although transformed.

Q. But how is it possible, that a body burnt to ashes or otherwise dissolved should revive again?
A. In the natural course of things, this is certainly impossible, but possible, beyond doubt, through the omnipotence of God, of which omnipotence we already treated in the first article of faith.

Certainly, if we consider how God the Lord created heaven and earth out of nothing, we shall find no difficulty in believing that this omnipotent God is also able to raise a dissolved body to life again. Is there any thing hard or impossible to the Almighty? Moreover, according to the doctrine of the Apostle of nations, God even implanted in nature types and emblems of this future resurrection from the dead, and of the transformation of mouldering bodies. You that doubt, listen to the words of the Apostle himself: "Senseless man, that which thou sowest, is not quickened, except it die first. And that which thou sowest, thou sowest not the body that shall be, but bare grain, as of wheat, or of some of the rest. But God giveth it a body as He will." 1 *Cor.* xv. 36–38.

The holy Fathers speak in the same manner.

We will cite the beautiful saying of Minutuis Felix; he

speaks thus: "Behold, I pray, how the whole of nature typifies our future resurrection for our comfort and hope; the sun sets and rises again; the stars disappear beneath the horizon, and appear again; the flowers wither and revive ... a springtime of the body is also awaiting us." In *Octavio*.

Q. What will be the nature of the bodies of the just after the resurrection?

A. The bodies of the just, after the resurrection, shall be glorified bodies, and in this condition, have principally four properties, namely: impassibility, brightness, agility, subtility.

Q. Who teaches us this, and what does each of these gifts of the glorified body comprehend?

A. That the bodies of the just shall be of that nature after the resurrection, is taught by St. Paul, in his Epistle to the Corinthians, and by the unanimous tradition of the holy Fathers.

But the nature of these gifts is the following:

Impassibility is that gift, by virtue of which the bodies of the just shall be free, after the resurrection, from every pain or affliction, and also indestructible—consequently immortal. The Apostle writes: "It is sown in corruption: it shall rise in incorruption." 1 *Cor.* xv. 42.

Brightness is that gift, in consequence of which the bodies of the blessed surrounded with the splendor of light, shall be more dazzling and more glorious than the sun. The words of Christ in St. Matthew, point to this quality: "The just shall shine as the sun in the kingdom of their Father." *Matth.* xiii. 43. Our Lord had confirmed this future state of glorified bodies by the emblem of His own transfiguration. *Matth.* xvii. 2. The Apostle calls this quality, now brightness, now glory. "He will reform the body of our lowness, made like to the body of His glory.' *Philip.* iii. 21. "It is sown in dishonor, it shall rise in glory." 1 *Cor.* xv. 43. But this quality is not common to all in the same degree, but according to the degree of election in the kingdom of God, and the glory of the brightness shall also be greater according to the greatness and value of the merits. To this also the Apostle bears testimony, writing: "One is the glory of the sun; another, the glory of the moon; another, the glory of the stars, for star differeth from star in glory: so also, is the resurrection of the dead." 1 *Cor.* xv. 41, 42.

Agility is that gift by which the body of the blessed shall be freed from the burden that now presses it down; and shall acquire a capability of moving with the utmost facility and lightness wherever the soul pleases.

Thus St. Augustine teaches in his book on the city of God, and St. Jerome on *Isaias*, c. xl. To this quality also the Apostle points in these words: "It is sown in weakness, it shall rise in power." 1 *Cor.* 43.

Finally, *Subtility*, a quality which subjects the body to the absolute dominion of the soul, so that no other bodies shall be capable of impeding or opposing it in its progress, but it shall penetrate everywhere even as the glorified body of Christ penetrated the doors of the dining hall in Jerusalem. The Apostle also points out this quality, saying: "It is sown a natural body, it shall rise a spiritual body." 1 *Cor.* xv. 44.

None of all these glorious gifts shall be proper to the risen bodies of the damned, but they shall be more shocking and more abominable than any thing that we can imagine; for they shall be bodies raised by Divine justice to be so many dwellings for the damned souls in the eternal pains of hell.

Q. What influence should this article of faith have on us?

A. The lively faith in the resurrection of the dead affords us the sweetest consolation in all the sufferings and tribulations of this life. For listen to Job, that man so grievously afflicted, who, in all his trials, fortified himself in this confidence with these words: "I shall be clothed again with my skin, and in my flesh I shall see my God. This my hope is laid up in my bosom." *Job*, xix. 26. This remembrance of the resurrection also powerfully incites us to the diligent practice of virtue, and strengthens us in it; for as the Apostle reminds us: "We all must appear before the judgment-seat of Christ, that every one may receive the proper things of the body according as he hath done, whether it be good or evil." 2 *Cor.* v. 8. And, on the other hand, this remembrance forcibly deters men from indulging in vice. For the wicked, too, shall rise one day, but for judgment, and to be punished in the everlasting torments of hell.

The Twelfth Article of Faith.

Q. What does the twelfth article of faith teach us?

A. Life everlasting. By life everlasting we understand that eternal happiness which is prepared for the good in heaven, and which is called in Holy Scripture by different names according to the principal fountains of eternal bliss in the realm of God.

Namely, the state of the just in eternal life is called in the first place, the kingdom of heaven, because there all the blessed are crowned with glory.

2d. *The kingdom of God and of Christ;* because there God displays eternally His might and the beauty of His glory in a particular manner, and because Christ has acquired this kingdom for us by His own merits, and is glorified there in all the fullness of His splendor.

3d. *Paradise;* on account of the wonders of creation, which the Lord has prepared for His elect to complete their eternal happiness in the enjoyment of creatures.

4th. *The Holy City;* because all the blessed are there united together most intimately and most inseparably, by the bonds of charity.

5th. *The Joy of the Lord;* because God himself is there our reward, our love and happiness.

6th. *The Repose of the Lord;* because in that blessed place there is no labor or toil, or hardship any more.

7th. *Eternal Life;* because this state is immutable, that is to say, without end, accompanied by the fullest consciousness of happiness which is there enjoyed.

Q. Which are those goods of eternal life, that are specially promised to us there?

A. They are *twofold;* namely, essential and accidental ones.

Q. In what do the *essential* goods and joys of heaven consist?

A. In the *vision* and *blissful fruition* of God.

For thus teaches the Apostle and disciple of love, St. John, in his 1st. Epistle, chapter iii.; " Dearly beloved, we are now the sons of God: and it hath not yet appeared what we shall be. We know, that when He shall appear, we shall be like to Him, because we shall see Him as He is." The Apostle, then, makes here two things especially manifest in the state of happiness, namely, the *seeing* of God and the becoming like to God. That is that those, who there see God, shall by that very act be rendered similar to God. The reason why this happens is this, that whatever shall be known in itself, becomes known either in His essence or from its being similar to Him. Wherefore no one can see God in His essence, unless God raises the creature in a supernatural manner to a degree of similarity with himself by this, that He unites it in a supernatural and divine manner with His essence. Now, this is what happens with respect to the blessed in heaven. "We see now," says the Apostle, "through a glass in an obscure manner; but then face to face." 1 *Cor.* xiii. 14.

The medium through which this is accomplished is the light of glory, wherewith being surrounded, we see God, the light, in the light, according to the Psalmist: "In Thy light we shall see light." *Ps.* xxxv. 10.

But how this is really done, no understanding here below can conceive; yet we can represent this future deification (through the vision of God) in a sensible manner, though the representation is but a faint image of the reality. Namely, as iron when placed in the fire becomes glowing, and, although it remains iron, yet appears as if it were fire: just so shall the blessed see God in the light of glory, and united with God, become deified, *i. e.* transformed into God, without ceasing, however, to be what they are, namely creatures, and as such infinitely different from God. Thus the Roman Catechism.

In a word, then, the essence of our happiness, shall be God himself, the possession of Him and His love in the fruition of that happiness, which makes Him happy himself from eternity to eternity, as we read in these words: "Thou shalt make them drink of the torrent of Thy pleasure." *Ps.* xxxv. 9. And again: "I am Thy reward exceeding great." *Gen.* xv 1. What more could the Lord give us, than himself?

But to the accidental or non-essential joys of heaven belong all those excellencies, goods and enjoyments which shall one day be imparted to the just in heaven by creatures in the communion of saints. Moreover, these goods and pleasures shall be so great, that the Apostle writes with justice concerning them: "The eye hath not seen, nor ear heard, neither hath it entered into the heart of man, what things God hath prepared for them that love Him." 1 *Cor.* ii. 9. A joy, indeed, of which the Psalmist sings with exultation: "A thousand years in Thy sight are as yesterday, which is past." *Ps.* lxxxv. 4.

Q. Shall there be a difference in the happiness of eternal life?

A. Yes, in the sense of which mention was made above; namely, that the degree of happiness shall be in proportion to the degree of election and of merit; but it must not be supposed on that account, that there shall be even one blessed soul in heaven whose happiness will not be complete. All shall be perfectly happy, *i. e.* they shall be so replenished with overflowing bliss, that none of the blessed, according to his capacity, shall be able, to harbor within himself a greater measure, though the measure itself shall be different. One example will render this clear and intelligible. Namely, it is possible to have many drinking-glasses of different capacities placed upon a table. Now if all are filled to overflowing, it is plain that each glass is as full as it can be, and is incapable of receiving more, yet the quantity of liquid contained in each is not the same, because the glasses themselves are of different size and capacity.

Let us therefore strive, that by our diligence in doing good works, we may render ourselves capable of the greatest possible glory and happiness according to the saying of the Apostle: "He who soweth in blessings, shall also reap of blessings." 2 *Cor.* ix. 6.

Q. Why is this celestial glory called eternal life? Shall not the damned also live for ever?

A. The true life, presupposes, in a higher sense of the word, and is also self-dependent activity. The state of the blessed, therefore, is in a more special signification called the life, and indeed the eternal life, because the blessed shall be in a state in which, without any impediment, they do and enjoy all things according to their own wishes; consequently, they live truly, in the higher sense of the word, and, indeed, the more so, because they are substantially united to Him who is essentially the life. *St. John*, xiv. 6; v. 26. But, on the contrary, the damned shall be in a state, in which they exist, act, and suffer eternally but all that against their will. This, therefore, is a state of eternal necessitation, and consequently a death of the faculties of the soul, so that it may rather be styled a state of eternal death for the damned, notwithstanding their eternal existence as to person, and their incapability of being ever annihilated by their pains. The state of the blessed excludes every mixture of adversity, woe, or suffering, and is, therefore, substantially life. On the contrary, the state of the damned excludes all that affords even a shadow of contentment, and is consequently, in truth, the most painful, spiritual death for an endless eternity.

Q. Why is this article of faith placed at the conclusion of the Apostles' Creed?

A. Because this eternal life being the possession of God is the very end for which we are created.

Q. Are all men created for the attainment of this end.

A. Yes, all; for God wills not, that any man should perish, but that all should be saved, as the Apostle positively teaches; 1 *Tim.* ii. 4, and, because Christ himself assures us of it by the Evangelist, *St. John*, iii. 17.

Q. Are all men, then, really saved?

A. No; because all men do not do on their part, what they can do, and what they are bound to do; or, in other words, because all men do not make good use of the means of salvation which God gives them, in order to save themselves.

Q. What are these means?

A. They are faith, and the living according to faith, by keeping the commandments of God and of His holy Church, and making good use of the Sacraments, which are the means of grace in the New Law. This appears from the clear and positive words of Christ and His Apostles, as proved by all the texts which we have cited, where there was question of the Catholic Church as the only one in which salvation is found.

Q. To what place do those go, who knowingly deny the faith, and die in mortal sin?

A. They go to *hell.*

Q. What is hell, and how may one prove that there is such a place as hell?

A. Hell is that dismal place of torment, in which the damned suffer pain in the flames of everlasting fire.

That there is such a place as hell, is an article of faith, which Holy Scripture and tradition both teach in the most positive manner, so that there is no other truth of faith, which is more plainly and more explicitly taught in those sacred records, than this very one, in order, doubtless, that we might take the greater care to avoid such a woful eternity of torment. We shall prove this presently more at large, by citing what Holy Scripture and tradition teach concerning the greatness and eternity of the punishments of hell.

Q. Are the punishments of hell great?

A. Yes; and greater than it is possible for men on earth to imagine, according to the joint assertion of the holy Fathers; which is also indicated by the very names by which Holy Scripture designates this place of torments.

For the state of the damned is styled in Holy Scripture; "Damnation;" *Rom.* xiii. 2. "Destruction;" *Matt.* vii. 13. "Everlasting punishment;" *Matt.* xxv. 46. "Everlasting fire;" *Matt.* xxv. 41. "The fire of hell;" *Matt.* v. 22. "Exterior darkness;" *Matt.* viii. 12. "Where there shall be weeping and gnashing of teeth;" *ibid.* "The fire that cannot be quenched, where the worm dieth not;" *Mark*, ix. 42. "A place of torments;" *St. Luke*, xvi. 28. "A flame of fire, giving vengeance;" 2 *Thess.* i. 8. "A pool burning with fire and brimstone;" *Apoc.* xxi. 8. Certainly, whoever seriously reflects on these expressions of Holy Writ, must admit, that the highest degree of torment and misery is expressed by them.

Q. In what do the torments of hell principally consist?

A. 1. In the first place, the damned are deprived for ever of the *vision* of God, as well as of the joys of heaven, which punishment is called the punishment or pain of loss. This is pointed out by the parable which Christ himself proposes to us, concerning the man who had come to the wedding, without having on a wedding garment, and who on that account was sent away from the king's presence, and cast into exterior darkness, "where there shall be weeping and gnashing of teeth." *Matt.* xxii. 13.

Second, The worm of conscience shall torment the damned without intermission, calling out to them continually and for ever: "Ah! you yourself are the cause of this dismal doom"—"you could save yourself, but you would not." "Their worm dieth not," says Christ, meaning the worm of conscience. *Mark*, ix. 42.

Third, The damned shall be covered with shame and confusion, and their portion shall be hopeless despair. The phrase: "They shall say to the mountains and the rocks, 'Fall upon us,'" has reference to this pain, *Apoc.* vi. 16.

Fourth, Another particular punishment of the damned will be the company of so many of the reprobate. "Then," says Christ, "shall the King say to those on his left: 'Depart from me, ye cursed, into everlasting fire, which was prepared for the devil and his angels.'" *Matt.* xxv. 41.

Fifth, But it is principally the pain of fire, which torments the damned, in proportion to the measure of their guilt, and of which mention is made in so many places of Holy Writ, as already shown, which texts the holy Fathers understand, not in a figurative but in a literal sense.

St. Cyprian writes thus: "The place of pain, which is called hell, sends forth, through the awful night of massy darkness, ever raging fire in steaming flames. There are, in that dire abode, various kinds of torments, where the pain returns into itself, which is caused by the devouring flame of the heat that issues in streams." *Lib. de laud. martyrii,* c. 12.

St. Augustine says: "There the bodiless spirits shall adhere to the material fire, to suffer pain." *Lib.* 21, *de civit. Dei.* And that this is possible and contains in itself no contradiction, St. Gregory the Great proves in the following words: "Certainly if the devil and his angels, though they have no body, yet suffer pain in a real fire, what wonder that the damned souls, before resuming their bodies, should suffer the pain of the body?" *Lib.* 4, *Dialog.* c. 29. The body without the soul has not even the power of sensation; it is, therefore, in reality only the soul that suffers, as long as man is living here on earth, and not the body in itself; for, as soon as the soul leaves the body, it is dead and senseless.

Q. Is it known what kind of fire it is?

A. No; but we know enough, if we know what the pain of fire is.

Q. Are the pains of hell eternal?

A. Yes.

Q. Shall they, therefore, never have an end?

A. Never; for Christ says positively: "And these shall go into everlasting punishment; but the just, into life everlasting." *Matth.* xxv. 46. This antithesis plainly shows, in what sense the word "eternal" is to be accepted. For, since no one can doubt that, concerning the just, the word "eternal" is to be accepted in the strict sense, it follows necessarily, according to the laws of contrast, that the word "eternal," as regards the reprobate, must be also taken in the strict sense. And this follows the more necessarily, as Christ, in other places of Holy Scripture, as already shown, also speaks of the pain of hell as *eternal*, and because the Apostles, too, are unanimous in calling the pains of hell eternal. The disciple of love, St. John, writes thus: " They shall be tormented day and night, for ever and ever." *Apoc.* xx. 10. And St. Paul, in his second Epistle to the Thessalonians, asserts : " They shall suffer eternal pains in destruction." 2 *Thess.* 1–9. The unanimous doctrine of the holy Fathers, and the solemnly declared belief of the Church, are of precisely the same tenor.

St. Justin writes in this manner: " They shall, according to the just sentence, suffer pain in everlasting fire, for their transgressions." *Apol.* 2. And St. Irenæus: " But they to whom He shall say, 'depart from me,' &c., shall be damned for ever." *Adv. haeres.* 5–47.

St. Basil: " If the eternal punishment shall one day have an end, so then eternal life shall also have an end. But if, in regard to (eternal) life, the words of the Gospel are not so accepted, what reason can there be for supposing that the eternal punishment shall have an end ?" *Interogat.* 267, *in Comp. Reg.*

Further, St. Cyril, of Jerusalem : " But he who is a sinner, shall receive an immortal body, capable of suffering the punishments of sin, so that although he is burning in an everlasting fire, yet he shall never be consumed." *Cath.* 18.

And St. Chrysostom: " That hell shall have no end, Christ asserts, saying: 'Their fire cannot be quenched, and their worm dieth not.'" *Hom.* 9, *in* 1, *ad. Corinth.*

And St. Augustine: " That which God hath spoken by his prophet regarding the eternal punishment, shall be fulfilled, yes, indeed, it shall come to pass, their worm shall not die, and their fire not be extinguished." *De civ. Dei.* 21, *c.* 9.

Moreover, the Church has solemnly declared this truth of faith in many of her Councils, as, for instance, in the fourth of Lateran, in the second of Lyons; as also in the Councils of Florence and Trent, the latter of which teaches expressly the eternity of the pains of hell. *Sessions*, vi. and xiv. The Church proclaims the same faith in the Athanasian Creed, of which she makes public use, saying: " Those who have done good, shall enter into eternal life, but those who have done evil, into everlasting fire."

Q. Is not this article of faith in contradiction with reason?

A. By no means. Infidels, indeed, alleging the infinite mercy of God, fancy themselves in a position to prove the contrary. But we ask in the first place, why do not such persons rather remember the infinite justice of God, when mention is made of the divine punishments, in order to infer from the nature of this infinite justice the eternal duration of the punishment, especially since the question turns on punishing sin, which is an offence against the infinite majesty of God? Certainly, God is infinitely good, but He is, at the same time, no less infinitely just. He rewards the good with good eternal, because He is infinitely good, and no one thinks of complaining, or finding fault, though such a reward far surpasses the merit. But He punishes the wicked with the everlasting punishment due to an offence committed against God, because He is also infinitely just. This is a tremendous truth to the wicked, and they will try to throw doubts upon it in order that they may continue to sin with less remorse and greater liberty.

Moreover, reason understands well that, where there is question of punishing sin, it is not her province to pronounce the final sentence, since the nature of this subject lies far above her reach, and that she is, consequently, to receive as indubitably certain that which the truth proved by miracles and prophesies to be divine revelation, teaches us concerning this matter. But reason submits herself to this doctrine of faith with all the greater facility, since whatever she knows of the nature of sin, points out the very same consequence. For mortal sin, as an offence against God, accompanied by an entire turning away from Him, is something which, in reference to an infinite God, may be called infinite. But the punishment must be determined by divine justice, so as to correspond with the guilt of the offence, and since man, as a finite being, is incapable of suffering a punishment infinite in intensity, he is to suffer one infinite in duration. A second reason for the eternity of punishment is given by St. Gregory the Great, who writes: "It is proper to the sentence of the judge, that they should never be free from punishment, whose souls, in this life, were never free from sin, and that the punishment of a reprobate should never have an end, because, whilst living, he placed no bounds to his malice." *Lib.* 34, *mor. c.* 19. Alas! how many are so disposed, that, if they were to live eternally, and at liberty, they would also sin eternally! A third reason is the infinite authority of the divine law, to which a punishment of infinite importance must correspond, so that, in any case, the punishment is sufficient to deter a man from transgression. But this can have no possible reference unless where the punishment is endless. And even then man, as experience testifies, transgresses the law of God, and abuses his liberty. Now, if this be so, what would happen, if there were no eternity of punishment, and if all might one day be happy in heaven, no matter how they lived while on earth? The threat of the punishment would then bear no proportion to the dignity of the law, and would, therefore, be contemptible.

Nay, what would be the entire order of salvation, as faith places it before our eyes, if there were no eternity of punishment? St. Jerome: says with justice: "It would be a mere farce!" Who could imagine, for a moment, that Christ and Lucifer, Mary and the devils, St. Peter and Judas, should be ever united in mutual love and happiness? No!—light and darkness are for ever separated. Reason enlightened by faith understands this—requires this! Moreover, it is a remarkable fact, that even men who live in heathenism, though scarcely able to know God, yet believe in punishments, and, indeed, in eternal punishments, after death. This points to a common source of knowledge, which is our reason, united with that which the first tradition taught man concerning the everlasting duration of the pains of hell.

And no less significant is that secret fear which pervades the consciences of all men, even of the most impudent deriders of our holy religion: "That hell might not be a mere fable." Hence their anger, if they hear hell spoken of.

Finally, we ask: Is there not capital punishment, aye, and endless punishment, too, even in this world; and yet, under certain circumstances, we undoubtedly consider it equitable and just, and at the same time necessary. The same holds good for the other world, concerning eternal death or the punishment of hell, and, indeed, for reasons far weightier, as we have shown a little before. He who enters eternity infected with mortal sin, leaves himself, for eternity, in the state of sin, and deserves, therefore, an eternity of punishment. So far, reason itself can comprehend. But what kind of punishment it shall be, is, of course, manifested to us only by the voice of Revelation, and that only as far as is requisite for us, to be warned of the dreadful consequences of sin.

Q. What influence should the consideration of this article of faith exert upon the conduct of our lives?

A. To make us do carefully all that we are able to do with the help of God, in order to gain the everlasting bliss of heaven, and in order to increase, by our zeal and sanctity of life, the happiness to be enjoyed there for ever. But also, to avoid every species of sin, in order to escape the awful punishment of eternal perdition.

Q. Does the Apostles' Creed contain all the articles of faith, so that there is nothing to be believed beyond what it contains?

A. No; it contains only the principal points of the Christian faith, which include, indeed, all the rest; but do not state them all expressly. But the Apostles' Creed includes all of them, because in it we profess our belief in the Church; consequently in everything which the Church proposes to us, whether it be written or not.

Q. How are these truths of faith called, which every man must know, in order to be saved, and which are they?

A. The truths of faith which every man must know and believe, in order to be saved, are those which are necessary as *means* of salvation. They are:

1. That there is one God, one in essence and triune in person.
2. That the Second Divine Person became man, in order to redeem us from sin and its punishment, and to make us eternally happy.
3. That the soul of man is immortal.
4. That without the help of God's grace it is impossible to do good, and obtain salvation.
5. That God is a just judge, who rewards the good and punishes the wicked.

These truths of faith are necessary for salvation, because, without knowing them, it is impossible to live according to God's law. But, in how far a mediate belief in Christ and the most Holy Trinity can save man, was already indicated above in treating of the members of the Church.

Q. What other truths of faith is every Christian bound to

believe, and to know expressly, under pain of mortal sin, by virtue of the existing law?

A. 1. The Apostles's Creed;

2. The Lord's Prayer;

3. The Commandments of God and of the Church;

4. The holy Sacraments of Baptism, of Penance, and of the Altar.

The others, when he is about to receive them.

Q. Why do we pronounce the word "Amen" at the end of the Apostles' Creed?

A. The word "Amen" signifies as much as, "be it so"—"such is my belief"—"so it is." It is a protestation of our firm and unshaken belief in all that we have professed, and also of our firm resolution to live according to the demands of this holy faith, so as to be made partakers of its blessings here on earth, and its happy fruition in the world to come.

Take courage, then, Christian soul! Walk in this way of salvation, which the light of faith points out to you, and illuminates, with its saving beams, the way that leads to the Author of the faith, and to the crown of eternal life; keep in your heart, and consider often the short but mighty watchword:

Oh happy eternity! O eternal happiness! What must I do to possess thee?—what must I avoid, that I may not lose thee?

CHAPTER II.

ON HOPE.

In the last article of faith we treated of eternal life as our last end, towards which, therefore, all our actions are to tend. Now, it is hope which inspires us to expect with confidence this our last end. Regarding this divine virtue, as also the truths subordinate to it, we shall explain the doctrine of the Church in the present chapter.

Q. What is hope?

A. Hope is a divine virtue infused by God, in consequence of which we confidently expect from Him, through Jesus

Christ, eternal salvation and all the means necessary for obtaining it.

Q. On what is Christian hope founded?

A. On the infinite goodness and fidelity of God, who has promised to all that keep His commandments and cöoperate with His grace, eternal life, through the merits of Jesus Christ.

"Let us hold fast the confession of our hope without wavering; for he is faithful that hath promised;" thus St. Paul in his Epistle to the *Hebrews*, x. 23. And St. James: "Blessed is the man that endureth temptation: for when he hath been proved, he shall receive the crown of life, which God hath promised to them that love him." *James*, i. 12.

Q. To what goods does Christian hope refer?

A. In a particular manner to the goods of heaven, which renders man happy throughout all eternity. It has also reference to all those goods which can anywise assist man in this life in attaining to his last end. Hence we justly pray to God for these.

Q. By what means may we increase this virtue of hope within us?

A. 1. By frequent and devout prayer to God.

2. By the daily consideration of the goodness and the blessings of God, and of what he has already done for the salvation of the world, as attested by sacred history, the lives of the saints, and the vicissitudes of the entire Church.

3. By considering those favors which the Lord has already bestowed upon ourselves.

4. By purity of conscience and the diligent practice of good works, and especially by patience in suffering.

"Trust in the Lord," sings the royal prophet, "and do good." *Ps.* xxxvi. 3.

Q. What exercise is especially proper to Christian hope?

A. Prayer; for it enlivens, strengthens, and increases our hope.

On Prayer.

Q. What is prayer?

A. Prayer is the raising of our minds to God. By it we either praise and thank God, or beg Him to avert evil from, and to bestow favors upon ourselves or others. Whence also we justly distinguish prayer as of three kinds, viz.: praise, thanksgiving, and supplication. This distinction was made by St. John Damascene. St. Gregory of Nyssa expresses himself still more briefly, defining prayer to be "an intercourse and a conversation with God." *Lib. de Oratione*, c. 1.

Q. Is prayer good in every place?

A. Certainly. For thus our reason tells us, agreeing with the assurance of the Apostle, 1 *Tim.* ii. 8: "I will, therefore, that men pray in every place."

Q. Why then do we go to church to pray?

A. Because churches are built and consecrated for the very purpose; to serve for the exercise of devotion and to promote piety amongst the faithful. Further, because in Church Christ is always present in the most holy Sacrament of the altar; and because the united prayer of the faithful assembled together in the church ascends more powerfully to the throne of God.

Q. Can we pray at all times?

A. Yes, we can, and we are bound to do so; according to the express words of Jesus Christ, who says: "that we ought always to pray, and not to faint." *Luke,* xviii. 1.

Q. But how can this be done?

A. Either in praising God by word of mouth, or by work, and thus raising our hearts to Him.

Q. How do we pray by works?

A. If we refer all our actions to God. He who at the commencement of his every action invokes the assistance of God, and does all in His honor, practises a continual prayer.

Q. What should be the posture of our body whilst we are praying?

A. Though no precept is given us regarding the posture of the body during prayer, yet it is the custom for Christians during prayer, as far as it can be done, to kneel and pray with joined hands.

Q. Why do we pray in this attitude?

A. In order to humble ourselves before God, and to show in this manner, that we are poor sinners who implore Him for the assistance of His grace.

Q. Is it an ancient custom to pray kneeling?

A. Yes; for mention is made of it both in the Old and the New Testament. Thus we read in the 3d book of *Kings,*

viii. 54: "And it came to pass, when Solomon had made an end of praying all this prayer and supplication to the Lord, that he rose from before the altar of the Lord: for he had fixed both knees on the ground." St. Peter also went on his knees to pray before he raised to life the deceased Tabitha. *Acts*, ix. 40. The same thing we read of St. Paul. *Eph.* iii. 14. And finally, Christ himself, whose words and actions should be our model, prayed kneeling in the garden of Olives. *St. Luke*, xxii. 44. Nay, as St. Matthew tells us, (xxvi. 29), He postrated Himself with His face on the ground and prayed.

Q. Why did our Saviour pray in this manner?

A. In order to show the greater reverence for His Father. Moreover, in order to present himself before Him, as it were, laden with our guilt, and to offer himself entirely for our propitiation. Why, then, should not we also prostrate ourselves upon our knees, or rather upon our faces, we who have so often offended God by our own sins? If we pray for any length of time, we should at least begin and conclude our prayer kneeling. We should also devoutly bend our knees at Mass at least during the consecration and the blessing of the priest.

Q. Why do we strike our breast when we are at prayer?

A. The striking of our breast is a sign of penance and of a contrite heart. Thus the Evangelist St. Luke tells us, that the publican struck his breast, saying: "O God, be merciful to me a sinner." *Luke*, xviii. 13.

Q. Why do Christians, and particularly the clergy in the choir, pray standing on Sundays and during the whole of the Paschal time?

A. It is done in memory of our Lord's Resurrection, of which a particular commemoration is made at that time. And this is the reason why St. Augustine says, *Ep.* 119, cap. 15: "We pray standing, to rejoice in the resurrection of the Lord, seeking the things that are above, and not those that are below."

Q. Is every prayer pleasing to God?

A. No; only that which has the following conditions: *First*, that we pray to God as children of God; this requires purity of conscience. Thus we are taught by St. John, who writes: 'If our heart do not reprehend us, we have confidence towards

God: and whatsoever we shall ask we shall receive of him." 1 *John*, iii. 21.

Nay, Christ himself assures us: "If you abide in me, and my words abide in you, you shall ask whatever you will, and it shall be done unto you. *John*, xv. 7.

Q. But, then, if a prayer made by one who is in the state of sin is displeasing to God, would it not be right to say that such a one had better not pray at all?

A. Not so. For prayer is the very means by which we may obtain grace to purify the conscience by true repentance.

Q. What other conditions must prayer have in order to be pleasing to God?

A. The *second* condition of a prayer pleasing to God, is *confidence*, a disposition of mind by which we firmly hope that God will hear our prayer, and as children of a loving Father, that he will grant our petition. This confidence is also expressly recommended by our Divine Saviour in the following words: "All things whatsoever you ask when ye pray, believe that you shall receive: and they shall come unto you." *Mark*, xi. 24. The same thing is inculcated by St. James: "If any ask, let him ask in faith, nothing wavering." *James*, i. 6.

Q. Upon what must this our confidence be founded?

A. Upon the mercy and goodness of God, by virtue of which He is ready and able to grant us more than we ask. For even as the sun puts forth his rays, the fire its heat, and the fountain its water, so is the goodness of God communicated to us when we approach Him in prayer. Such a confidence had that woman in the gospel, who accosted Christ the Lord saying within herself: "If I shall touch only His garment I shall be healed." *Matth.* ix. 21.

The *third* condition is, that we pray in the proper order, namely: in the first place, for that which concerns the welfare of our soul. Hence, Christ said: "If you ask the Father any thing in my *name*." *John* xvi. 23. But Jesus means: Salvation and Saviour. St. Augustine, therefore, says with justice: "We may pray for any thing whatsoever, yet if we ask any thing that is injurious to the welfare of our soul, we do not ask it in the name of Jesus." And for this reason, if we petition for any temporal favor which is neither good nor bad, as, for instance, health, riches, honors, etc., we should not ask it but only in so far as it may be conducive to the greater honor of God and the salvation of our soul.

The *fourth* condition of a prayer pleasing to God is *perseverance*. That this condition is requisite, our Divine Saviour specially declares in the parable of the man who asked his friend for three loaves of bread, and obtained them at last because of his persevering in asking. *St. Luke*, xi. A beautiful example of perseverance in prayer was given us by the woman of Canaan, who, though she was repeatedly repulsed by Christ, yet persisted in her request, and at length obtained the health of her daughter. *Matth*. xv. A prayer, endowed with the above named qualities, as it were, forces God, and is sure to be heard.

Such was the prayer by which Moses vanquished the enemies of the people of God, and reconciled God himself to His fallen people. *Exod*. iii. 17. Such, too, was the prayer by which the Prophet Jeremias averted the punishments of God; on which account also the Lord said to him: "Do not thou pray for this people .... and do not withstand me." *Jer*. vii. 16. Such also was the prayer by which Josua caused the sun to stand still. *Jos*. x. The prayer of the Prophet Isaias, too, was of this kind, when in order to show that the life of king Ezechias had been really prolonged, he caused the sun to move back in the heavens for the space of ten hours. *Judges*, iv. King Ezechias himself recovered from his malady by virtue of such a prayer, obtaining a prolongation of his life for fifteen years. Numberless examples of such powerful prayers are found in the New Testament, and also in the lives of the saints.

Q. How many kinds of prayer are there?

A. Two. *Oral* and *mental* prayer, according as one merely thinks of God and of the truths of faith, and excites the corresponding affections and forms resolutions, or at the same time praises and prays God by word of mouth, and thus unites himself to God.

Q. Which is the most excellent of all oral prayers?

A. The most excellent of all oral prayers is the Lord's prayer, which Christ the Lord himself taught us.

Q. How do you say the Lord's prayer?

A. "Our Father, who art in heaven,
 "Hallowed be thy name,
 "Thy kingdom come;
 "Thy will be done on earth, as it is in heaven,
 "Give us this day our daily bread,

"And forgive us our trespasses, as we forgive those who trespass against us,

"And lead us not into temptation,

"But deliver us from evil. Amen."

Q. Why is the Lord's prayer to be preferred before all other prayers?

A. 1st. Because, as said above, Christ himself, the Son of God, the Eternal Wisdom taught it to us.

2d. Because it contains all things which we can and should ask of God.

3d. Because it is the most powerful of all prayers, for by it we ask in the words of Him who is at the same time our intercessor; and who, on that account, also knows best how and for what we must pray, if we wish to be heard.

Q. Of what does the Lord's prayer principally consist?

A. It consists of such petitions as include all kinds and species of prayer, namely, the prayer of praise, of thanksgiving, of supplication, and of propitiation, according as we wish to praise, to thank, to petition, or to propitiate God by our prayer.

Q. What do the first words: "Our Father, who art in heaven," signify?

A. These words are a short introduction or preparation to the prayer. For if we call God our *Father*, we enliven our hope and our confidence: God will listen to us as His children. And if we say: "Who art in heaven," we remind ourselves that we should approach God only with great reverence and humility, since He is not an earthly, but a heavenly and Divine Father. We remember at the same time, that God is Almighty, and that we are heirs of heaven. But we remember, too, that we have not as yet taken possession of our heavenly inheritance, but are, like pilgrims and strangers, travelling on perilous roads, and standing much in need of the protection of God.

Q. Why do we say: "*Our* Father and not *my* Father?

A. We say Our Father, in order to indicate thereby, that we are all *brethren*, and should love one another as such, being children of one Father. We say also *Our* Father, in order to show, that a common prayer is possessed of a particular power. For if all say: Our Father, every single one prays for all, and all pray for every one in particular.

Q. Why do we say: "Who art in heaven;" is not God present everywhere?

A. If we say: "Who art in heaven," we by no means intend to say that God is not present everywhere, but wish only to indicate thereby, that heaven is that particular part of the creation in which God manifests in a particular manner His majesty, power, wisdom, and glory, and where the angels and the saints behold Him face to face, participating in His infinite happiness.

The First Petition.

"Hallowed be Thy name."

Q. What is the meaning of this petition?

A. If we pray that the name of God be hallowed, we petition for nothing else, but that the presence, majesty, power, wisdom, and goodness of God and all the other attributes of the Divine nature may be known and praised in every part of creation; that He, the Creator and the Redeemer of mankind, may everywhere be known, honored, adored, revered, and loved. The name of God, therefore, means here the knowledge of God, just as we are accustomed to say of him who is favorably known to many: He has a great name. But because there are so many infidels in the world, who do not know God, and so many bad Christians, who do not serve God, but offend Him; hence it is that those who are the children of God, and inflamed with zeal for the honor of their Father, pray with intense desire that His name may be kept holy.

Q. Why do we begin the Lord's prayer with the petition: "Hallowed be thy name?"

A. Because we are bound to love God above all things, even more than ourselves, wherefore our first and chief desire must be to promote the honor of God, for the end for which we were created, and endowed with reason, is that we might know, love, and praise God, and do His most holy will. In this also consists our last end, and our future happiness.

The Second Petition.

" Thy kingdom come."

Q. What is the meaning of this petition?

A. In saying: "Thy kingdom come," we mean to ask, in the first place, for God's glorification, and then to beg of Him our own salvation.

Q. What do you understand by the kingdom of God?

A. The kingdom of God can be taken in a threefold sense, to wit: the kingdom of *nature*, the kingdom of *grace*, and the kingdom of *glory*.

The kingdom of *nature* is that by which God as a creator guides and governs all creatures as the absolute Lord and master of all things.

Although the wicked go on committing sin, and do not observe the law of God, yet God continues to govern them: for if He deems it proper, He defeats their intentions, frustrates their resolutions, and if He permits them to do the evil which they will, He turns it to the advantage of the good, but He punishes the sinner according to His justice, so that no one is able to withstand His will.

The kingdom of *grace* is that operation of God, by which He leads and rules the hearts and souls of the good, giving them grace and spiritual life, that they may know Him, love Him, and serve Him, and seek His honor before all and in all things.

Finally, the kingdom of *glory* shall be first completed and fully manifested in the life to come after the day of general judgment. For there the wicked spirits and bad men shall be deprived by God of all their power, and cast into hell to burn for ever; then there shall be an end to the corruption and the temptations of the world and the flesh which now try the servants of God; so that this kingdom shall be, and remain a kingdom of peace for ever, making all true servants and children of God happy in the secure possession of a perfect and an everlasting happiness.

Q. Which of the three kingdoms is meant in this petition?

A. Not the first; for that is come already. The second, indeed, but not principally, for of it mention was made already in the first petition, and it is also come, even now, for the greater part. The third, therefore, chiefly and above all, viz:

the kingdom of eternal glory, which is yet to come, and is so ardently desired by those who are fully acquainted with the miseries of this present life, because such persons love God with their whole heart.

The Third Petition.

" Thy will be done on earth as it is in heaven."

Q. What is the object of this petition?

A. In this petition, we beg God for grace, to keep his commandments.

For, since in the second petition we ask for eternal life, which is the final aim of man; it is fitting and proper that we should also pray for the principal means of obtaining this final object, which means consist in the very observance of the commandments, according to the testimony of our Divine Saviour himself, who says: "If thou wilt enter into life, keep the commandments." *Matth.* xix. 17. But because we are of ourselves by no means capable of keeping all the commandments, as we are bound to do, we, therefore, pray to God that His will may be done in us: *i. e.*, that he would give us grace, to do his will, and to obey in all things his holy law.

Q. If God sends us tribulations, must we even then conform our will to His?

A. We certainly must, esteeming nothing more just and meritorious, than to subject ourselves willingly and entirely to the divine will, in prosperity as well as adversity, denying our will, which is corrupted by the fall of Adam and inclined to evil, and seeking solely to rest in the good pleasure of God, who is able to turn all to our advantage, even what may appear to us hard and difficult. But we are bound in a special manner not to murmur, nor to complain against divine providence. For whatsoever He sends upon us, or causes to befall us, always happens in accordance with His will either for our greater merit, if we are good, or if we are bad, for our punishment and correction.

Q. But, then, are we not allowed to pray for deliverance from sickness, distress and adversity?

A. We are, indeed, allowed to do that, but only inasfar as it is pleasing to the divine will, and profitable to our salvation. Our Divine Saviour himself has given us an example of this, when praying in the garden, He besought His Father that the bitter chalice might pass away from Him. *Matt.* xxvi. 39. For he added to his prayer: "Nevertheless not as I will, but as Thou *wilt.*"

Q. Why do we subjoin to this petition the words: On earth as it is in heaven?

A. In order to show that we must be just as ready to obey God and feel as much pleasure in keeping his commandments as do the holy Angels, who are never guilty of any, even the slightest infringement on the commandments of God.

The Fourth Petition.

" Give us this day our daily bread."

Q. What is the meaning of this petition?

A. We humbly beg of God, the author and fountain of all good, whatever is necessary for us, both in this life and that which is to come.

But, in asking for this, we very appropriately make use of the term *bread;* for he that begins to live, craves food first of all, in order to preserve life. But it is to be remarked, that, in the petition, we first of all pray for the spiritual bread, which is the nourishment of the soul, and then for the material bread, which is the nourishment of the body. By the spiritual food we understand the most Holy Sacrament of the Altar, which is a heavenly and divine bread, wonderfully maintaining and increasing the life of our soul. Further, we understand by it the word of God, whether announced to us by the mouth of his ministers or read in the pages of spiritual books, which last affords not a little nourishment to our souls. Finally, we understand by it the divine inspirations, prayer and all those things which contribute to the preservation and increase of grace, in which the life of the soul has its subsistence. But by the material or bodily food, we understand all that is necessary for the maintenance of our body, of which the soul makes use as the instrument of her good works.

Q. Why do we call this bread *" our* bread?

A. It is not without reason that we call it *our* bread. For, if we speak of the most Holy Sacrament of the Altar, that is certainly *our* bread; because it is offered on our altars by Christ, the eternal High Priest, by the hands of his ministers, for our salvation. Moreover, we call it *our* bread, because it belongs exclusively to the children of God; and because we are not permitted to give it to unbelievers, or to such as are publicly known to be in the state of mortal sin.

But if we speak of doctrine, we also ask for *our* bread; that is to say, we ask for that doctrine which the priests and sacred orators of the holy Church of God communicate to the faithful, and not for strange, foreign bread, which the heretics proffer to their adherents, and which contains no substantial nourishment, but rather conceals within it the poison of falsehood.

And, finally, if we speak of the material bread, we pray that God may give us *our* bread, but not the bread of others; that is to say, we ask God to assist us in our lawful occupations, to bless our temporal goods and labors, so that being freed from the dangers of an oppressive poverty, we may be able to satisfy our natural wants.

Q. Why do we call this bread the *daily* bread?

A. We call it the *daily* bread, because we ask for that of which we stand in need every day; for we ask neither for any thing superfluous, nor for any thing costly, but for that which is sufficient for the simple maintenance of the body, and that because we know that in this life we are but pilgrims and strangers.

Q. Why do we say: Give us?

A. In order to indicate thereby, that though we exert ourselves ever so much to earn our spiritual and corporal bread, yet all our exertions are fruitless, unless God assist and protect us by his grace and providence. We pray, moreover, that God would *give* our bread, that is to say, that he not only would aid us, by procuring it for us, but also by sanctifying and blessing it, when we are taking it, that it may be good for our salvation.

Q. Why do we add: This day?

A. We pray to God that he would give us this bread to-day, because we do not wish to be solicitous about the next day, since we do not know whether we shall live till then. For Christ himself has taught us, that "sufficient for the day is the evil thereof." *Matt.* vi. 34. Let us, therefore, ask to-day for the bread which is necessary for to-day, and to-morrow for that which is necessary for to-morrow. But the phrase "this day" signifies also the whole time of our temporal life.

And it is on this account that we ask God to nourish us with spiritual and corporal bread during the whole time of our earthly pilgrimage, until we reach our final abode in heaven. For there we shall require no more Sacraments, no more instructions, far much less food for the body.

If, however, our Saviour admonishes us that we should be solicitous only for the present day, he thereby means nothing else than to free us from unprofitable cares, which keep us from praying and from many other things which are necessary for eternal life.

If, then, solicitude for the future is not superfluous, but rather necessary, as it really is, it is not wrong to occupy one's self in procuring such things for the future. Nay, such a solicitude may be even called a solicitude for the present day; for if we were to put off every thing till the morrow, we should seldom, indeed, have our necessaries for the supply of our present wants. God requires of us nothing unreasonable, but he will suffer no arrogant presumption.

The Fifth Petition.

"*And forgive us our trespasses, as we forgive those who trespass against us.*"

Q. What is the meaning of this petition?

A. In the four first petitions we asked of God all good things, both temporal and eternal. But in the three following we ask that God would deliver us from all past, present and future *evil*.

We pray, therefore, in the first place, that God would free us from past evil, that is to say, from the sins we have committed. For when Christ, our Saviour, taught his Apostles this prayer, he declared to them, that by these *trespasses* they were to understand *sin*. *Matth.* vi. 16.

Q. Why are sins called trespasses?

A. They are called so for a threefold reason.

1st. Because every man offends God by his sins, and thus becomes a trespasser against him, *i. e.*, becomes guilty in his sight, and bound to atone for the offence thus committed.

2d. Because he who sins, transgresses the law of God; and because those who transgress it, are threatened with punishment; every transgressor of this law is therefore a debtor, as regards this punishment.

3d. And, finally, because every man is bound to cultivate the vineyard of his soul, and to restore to God the fruits of his good works. We owe that return to God for the faculties and graces which he has bestowed upon us precisely for that end. But because all of us offend often in many things, doing that which we should not, and omitting that which we ought to do, it is fair that we should daily beg of God, with great humility, to pardon our transgressions.

Q. Why do we add, "as *we* forgive those who trespass against us?"

A. Because it is absolutely necessary, that we too should forgive others their offences against us, if we wish to obtain from God the forgiveness of our sins. For what would be more unjust, than to desire that God, whom we offended, after receiving from him so many and so great benefits, should pardon us, if we were unwilling to pardon those who offended us; especially since the offense offered to a man, compared with that against God, is as nothing. For this reason the Holy Ghost admonishes us by the mouth of the wise man: "Man to man reserveth anger, and doth he seek remedy of God? He hath no mercy on a man like himself, and doth he entreat for his own sins? He that is but flesh, nourisheth anger, and doth he ask forgiveness of God? who shall obtain pardon for his sin?" *Ecclus.* xxviii. 3–5. Truly, he who does not wish to forgive, deprives himself of the means of obtaining forgiveness, and walks on a road that does not lead to life everlasting. For thus Holy Scripture tells us in many places. Justly, therefore, does St. Augustine remind us: "Perhaps some one has offended you? Forgive him, lest, if you close the door of mercy upon your brother, you also close the door of pardon between you and your heavenly Father." And again: "Truth cannot lie: unless you forgive, the Father shall not forgive you. He that is not roused by these words of thunder, is not merely asleep, but dead." *Serm.* 158 *de temp. et in Ench. c.* 74. The Holy Fathers and doctors, moreover, remark with justice, that the prayer of him who asks forgiveness with an unforgiving heart, is not only useless, but that he even demands his own condemnation, having the audacity to say: Forgive us our trespasses, as we forgive those who trespass against us; which means, indeed, nothing less than: "Lord, I do not forgive,—neither do thou, therefore, forgive me, but cast me away from thy face."

Q. To whom, then, does he the most harm, who does not forgive others?

A. To himself; for he calls down the avenging justice of God upon himself, asking that evil may be returned him for evil. Christ confirms this in a remarkable manner in the parable of that cruel servant, who, after his master had remitted him so many talents, demanded of his fellow-servant, sternly and without mercy, the few pence which he owed him. The master cast him into prison for such conduct, until he should pay all the debt. "So also," says Christ, "shall my heavenly Father do to you, if you forgive not every one his brother from your hearts." *St. Matt.* xviii. 35.

Q. But some may perhaps say: This man has so grievously offended me that I cannot possibly forgive him, he does not deserve it of me?

A. But did not you likewise grievously offend God, and that how often? Do you deserve that He should pardon you? And even granted, that your neighbor does not deserve it, does not God deserve it, and He requires that you obey him? Does not Christ deserve it—Christ for whose sake you forgive, who so ardently desires it, and rewards you for it so abundantly? Most people are familiar with the example of St. John Gualbert. It happened that he met the murderer of his brother in a narrow street, on Good Friday. John was armed, the other was not. John drew his sword; but the wretch threw himself on his knees before him, and, signing himself with the sign of the cross, said, "John, for the love of Christ, who on this day shed his blood for thee and for me: pardon—pardon me!" The love of Jesus was victorious in John. He embraces the wretch, and goes in haste to the Church of Minatus. There he threw himself on his knees before an image of our crucified Redeemer, and behold the divine image bowed its head towards him, and his heart was inundated with such an abundant flow of grace, that immediately after he entered the cloister, and there after begging admission at the feet of the Abbot, and obtaining it, he lived and died a Saint. Do thou for the love of Jesus forgive! and be assured that He will be as merciful to you, as he was to St. John Gualbert, for the salvation and sanctification of your needy soul.

Q. But suppose I say: "He offends me over and over again?"

A. No man ever offended you as often as you have offended God, and yet you ask and desire that God should forgive you? Why do not you act in the same manner towards those who offend you? Meditate on the words of our Lord to St. Peter, when he asked him: "Lord, how often shall my brother offend against me, and I forgive him till seven times? Jesus saith to him: I say not to thee, till seven times; but till seventy times seven times!" *St. Matth.* xviii. 21, 22. That is, forgive him, as often as he shall offend against thee. Thus you shall be a true child of God—thus you shall obtain a secure pledge of reconciliation with God, and thus also your deliverance on the day of judgment; if you really forgive every one, as you wish, that God should forgive you. But, alas! how few forgive in this manner?

The Sixth Petition.

"*Lead us not into temptation.*

Q. What is the meaning of this petition?

A. By this question we ask for help against evils to come, namely, against the *temptations* which are indeed the only road to real evil, that is, to sin. We pray, therefore, by this petition, that God may not permit us to fall, when temptations weigh heavy upon us. But, since, indeed, the danger, in which we are at the time of temptation, is very great, we beg of the Lord that He may save us from temptation, inasfar as that is conducive to our salvation. This reminds us of the very consoling truth: that the devil is not only unable to harm us, but cannot even as much as tempt us, unless God suffer him to do so, for our trial and for our advantage.

Q. How, then, are the words of this petition to be understood in reference to God?

A. In the figurative sense. That is, we entreat God, that He may not permit us to be assailed by temptations fatal to us, in punishment of our negligence and infidelity in his holy service.

Q. Who, therefore, is it that really tempts man?

A. The *devil*, who, according to St. Peter, " goeth about as a roaring lion, seeking whom he may devour." 1 *Peter,*

v. 8. Moreover, the world, too, tempts us; for it surrounds us everywhere, and especially in the conversation and example of its sinful children, who live for nothing else than the goods and pleasures of this world. Finally, our own flesh or our wicked desires tempt us, whence the law of concupisence resisting the law of the spirit.

Q. Whom does the devil tempt?

A. All men. He tempts the wicked, and alas! but too often in accordance with their own will and desire, so that they themselves even love and seek the temptations, and are scarcely aware that they are tempted. Nay, for the very reason that they yield without the least resistance to the temptation, they do not at all feel the struggle. But the prophet assures us: that "there is no peace to the wicked." This false peace which the wicked enjoy, consists in their complete overthrow and subjection to the power of the devil. *Is.* lvii.

But the virtuous are tempted by the devil with yet greater fury, and they feel the weight of his assaults, and the great danger in the struggle; but they encourage themselves by their confidence in God, who never suffers us to be tempted above our strength, remembering, at the same time, the crown of eternal life promised to him that conquers. Hence the Holy Ghost reminds us by the mouth of the wise man: "Son, when thou comest to the service of God, stand in justice and in fear, and prepare thy soul for temptation." *Ecclesias.* ii. 1.

Q. In how many ways does the devil tempt men?

A. He tempts us either by *himself*, as he did Eve and Christ our Lord; or, he does it by means of *others*, as he tempted Adam by means of Eve. And in these temptations he either excites the imagination of man by bad influences upon the mind directly, or he excites the passion of concupiscence by bad influences upon the senses. Or he makes use of other circumstances in order to retard us in the service of God, or to withdraw us from it, and to bring us over to the service of the flesh and of the world, which are: the bad example of others, their advice, their allurements, and their threats. Besides, he tries to exhibit vice without its blackness, and, if possible, even to veil it in a cloak of virtue; so that man may deem avarice prudence, anger justice, licentiousness necessity, and sloth modesty, etc. But, on the contrary, he frequently endeavors to make him regard virtue as weakness, imprudence, self-will or exaggeration.

Q. Which are the principal means that help us to gain the victory in the combat against temptation?

A. The *first* means is, prayer. "Watch ye, and pray that ye enter not into temptation;" thus Christ himself reminds us. *St. Matth.* xxvi. 41. Truly if it is our duty at all times, and on every occasion, to have recourse to God, it is particularly so in the time of temptation, in order to seek protection from Him, who is our helper in every necessity and every affliction, and united with whom we become invincible. "He that dwelleth in the aid of the Most High, shall abide under the protection of the God of Jacob. He shall say to the Lord: Thou art my protector, and my refuge: my God, in Him I will trust. . . . . A thousand shall fall at thy side, and ten thousand at thy right hand, but it shall not come nigh thee. . . . . Thou shalt walk upon the asp and the basilisk : and thou shalt trample under foot the lion and the dragon. Because he hoped in me I will deliver him. I will protect him because he hath known my name. He shall cry to me and I will hear him: I am with him in tribulation, I will deliver him, and I will glorify him." *Ps.* xc. Of this our Lord assures us by the mouth of the royal prophet. In temptation especially we should instantly place ourselves in the presence of God, and call upon the holy name of Jesus, with a firm confidence in his assistance. It is the name of Him who gloriously vanquished the power of the devil for ever. You should also sign yourself with the sign of the holy cross. Satan knows the weapon by which he was conquered, and he dares not resist its power.

The *second* means is : devotion and recourse to Mary. Next to God and the Redeemer, Mary is the most powerful protectress in temptation, being that woman of whom it is said in holy writ, that she crushed the serpent's head : she is the heavenly Judith who was victorious over the Holofernes of hell. St. Bernard justly salutes Mary as the star of the sea, to whom we should look up, and in whom we should place all our trust in time of temptation, that we may not perish in the storm. Innumerable examples confirm the truth of what we here advance. Especially powerful in the combat against temptation is the devotion to and invocation of Mary through the prerogative of the *Immaculate Concep tion*, by which mystery of grace she crushed the head of Satan. Say every morning and evening three Hail Mary's in honor of the Immaculate Conception, and Mary will obtain grace for you either to escape temptation, or to overcome it. Say often, too, with the same intention, the short prayer of praise: "Hallowed and praised be the holy and Immaculate Conception of the Blessed Virgin Mary." And again: "Through thy Immaculate Conception and thy undefiled Virginity, purify my heart, body and soul, in the name ✠ of the Father, and ✠ of the Son, and ✠ of the Holy Ghost. Amen." To these salutations and invocations there is also an indulgence attached.

The *third* means is: The consideration of our last end. "In all thy works remember thy last end, and thou shalt never sin." Thus speaks the Holy Ghost himself by the mouth of the wise man. *Eccles.* vii. 40. This remembrance of death, judgment, hell, and eternity, instills into our heart that salutary fear which fastens us, as it were, with nails to the cross, so that we cling to it in time of temptation. "Pierce thou my flesh with thy fear: for I am afraid of thy judgments." *Ps.* cxviii. 120. This recollection deprives temptation of its allurements. Especially if it be an avaricious desire of earthly possessions which tempts you, think on death, and how soon you and all that you call yours, must part company for ever.

If it be the concupiscence of the flesh, think of the *fire* of hell, and the words of St. Gregory the Great: "*Short* is the pleasure, but *eternal* the pain." If it be human respect that tempts you, think of the judgment, which you are one day to undergo at the tribunal of divine justice, before, and in common with, all mankind. If you think of this, what will you care for the opinion of men? But particularly, consider yourself lying on your death-bed, about to breathe your last, and what you would then wish to have done, and you will have no difficulty in saying when assailed by temptation: "Begone, Satan!"

The *fourth* means is: The frequent and worthy reception of the Sacraments.

The reason is: because the Holy Sacraments confer graces upon men in such abundance, that by virtue thereof we are enabled to do all good and withstand every temptation. Besides, the reception of the Sacrament of Penance offers to us, by means of holy confession, the occasion of laying open our whole soul to our spiritual Father and guide, which is the very best means of bringing to light the hidden snares of Satan, and putting the tempter to flight. This is what the enemy fears, for he ever acts as a seducer who tries to keep nis evil desires as secret as possible. Now holy confession defeats precisely this cunning device of Satan, and saves the humble penitent from the snares of temptation.

As regards Holy Communion: the holy Church teaches in the Council of Trent, that one special effect which it produces is this, that it weakens in us the power of concupiscence; moreover, that it unites us personally with Christ, and transforms us into himself.

And thus we become, as St. Chrysostam remarks, like lions spitting fire against the dragon of hell, and are nourished and strengthened in the combat against him, that we may not grow weary, or faint, or be overcome. This operation of the Eucharistic Bread, which is indeed the most Holy Sacrament, was prefigured by that bread in the Old Testament, by taking which Elias was strengthened and rendered able to travel for forty days, without nourishment and without fatigue, all the way up to the mountain of Horeb. 3 *Kings*, xix. With justice, too, do we refer to the taking of this bread the words of the Psalmist: "Thou hast prepared a table before me, against them that afflict me." *Ps.* xxii. 5. Wherefore, approach this table often, and worthily, and the enemy shall have no power to hurt you. It is that table of grace, "the corn of the elect, and the wine," of which the prophet Zachary tells us, that it "springeth forth virgins," *i. e.*, imparting to the souls, who often and devoutly partake of it, purity of heart, preserving it in them, and administering to our sanctification in the practice of Christian perfection, by uniting us with Christ himself.

The *fifth* means is: Full and prompt resistance in the first moment of temptation. Yes, in the first moment, and entirely; this is the victorious war-cry in every temptation. "Do not play with the serpent," says St. Jerome, "but crush its head," *i. e.*, resist immediately and completely. *In cap.* 9, *Eccl.* We may also very appropriately compare the evil suggestion of the temptation to a spark of fire upon a heap of flax. If we do not immediately extinguish the spark, the whole will speedily catch fire. And just so it will be, in a spiritual sense, with regard to him who does not quench immediately the spark of temptation which falls upon the passionate cravings of his heart, concupiscence will be inflamed.

The *sixth* means is: To avoid the occasion of sin. Great is the power of occasion, and alas! it has already precipitated many who seemed to stand firm as a rock into the abyss of sin. Strong indeed was David, a man according to God's own heart; yet the occasion which offered itself to him through the sight of a woman, caused him to fall. Pleasing in the sight of God was Solomon, the wisest of men; yet through the occasion of his intercourse with pagan wives he went so far as to become an idolater himself. Hence St. Jerome says, whilst admonishing us to fly the occasion of sin: "Thou art no stronger than Samson, no wiser than Solomon." And the Holy Ghost answers us by the mouth of the wise man: "He that loveth danger shall perish in it." *Eccls.* iii. 27. Innumerable persons have already experienced the truth of this to their own temporal and eternal ruin. Take care, lest you be taught, but too late, by your own experience, and fly the occasion of sin!

Q. Do we ask God in this petition to deliver us from every temptation?

A. No; for, according to the all-wise intentions of God, our life here on earth shall never be entirely free from temptation; but rather it shall serve as a trial of our virtue, and to increase our merits; hence holy Job calls "the life of man upon earth a warfare." *Job*, vii. 1.

Wherefore, we pray not in this petition that we may not be tempted at all, but only that God would not permit us to fall in the temptation. Further, we pray that God would crush the power and wrath of the devil, and heal our imperfections, that we may not ourselves present to the evil one the arms for our destruction. Finally, we pray that God may not suffer us to be tempted, when there is a particular danger of our yielding to the temptation. If God guards us against this, temptations will become even salutary for us; for in them we are taught our own weakness, and have an opportunity of humbling ourselves. We also increase our merits, if we resolutely struggle against them. In this manner, God "will make also with temptation issue (*i. e.*, a way to escape) that we may be able to bear it," according to the Apostle. 1 *Cor.* x. 13.

The Seventh Petition.

"*But deliver us from evil.*"

Q. What is the meaning of this petition?

A. This last petition confirms on the one hand the preceding petition; but on the other, it adds thereto a new one, and on this account we say, "but deliver us from evil," *i. e.* we do not only ask that God would pardon us all the sins which we formerly committed, and keep us from falling into new ones, but we also pray that He would free us from any present evil which was but the consequence of sin. Let us remark here how wisely our Divine Master taught us, to petition in general only for deliverance from evil, without descending to particulars, as, for instance, that we might be delivered from poverty, from sickness, from persecutions, etc. For it frequently happens that we fancy something to be good for us, whereas God already foresees that it would injure us; and on the contrary, we frequently look upon a thing as hurtful, which would be profitable for us. Let us, therefore, ask in accordance with the words of Christ, that he would free us from those things, which he knows will do us harm.

For the rest, whether these things be pleasing or displeasing to us, let us ask Him to take them from us, that our soul may not suffer damage. For in reality, there is but one evil, and that is sin.

Q. What is the meaning of the word "Amen?"

A. Amen is a Hebrew word, and as already remarked, means "let it be done," or "be it so." Just as the word "Amen" at the end of the Creed means, "So it is," "This I believe most firmly;" so it means at the end of the Lord's prayer, "Thus may it be done," "Thus I desire and pray that it be done," "This I hope most confidently."

On the Patronage and the Invocation of the Blessed Virgin Mary.

Q. After Christ, in whom are we to place our hope?

A. In the patronage and invocation of the Blessed Virgin Mary.

Q. Why so?

A. Because she is the mother of Jesus and our mother, the intercessor and mediatrix with her Divine Son.

Justly does the holy Church apply to Mary those words of Scripture: "I am the mother of fair love, and of fear, and of knowledge, and of holy hope." *Eccl.* xxiv. 24. Though this and other texts of Holy Writ are to be understood first of all in reference to the Eternal Wisdom who was made man for us, yet the Church, guided by the Holy Ghost, applies them, in the canonical hours, to the most Blessed Virgin Mary, because she is the mother of Christ and our mediatrix with him.

The same is unanimously taught by the holy fathers. St. Bernard, one of their number, expresses himself thus: "Let us honor Mary with all our heart, and with the plenitude of our minds, because such is the will of Him who willed that we should obtain all through Mary. You are afraid of going to the Father; behold, He has given you Jesus as your Mediator. And what is there for you to think of, which such a Son could not obtain for you from such a Father? Perhaps you fear, too, the Son. O do not; he is your brother, and has assumed your flesh, tried in all except sin, in order that he should be taught to have mercy. Mary has given to you this brother; and if you should dread Him on account of his divine majesty, fly to Mary. The Son will listen to the mother, and the Father to the Son. Behold, children, this is the ladder of salvation for sinners. This is my greatest trust, this the whole ground-work of my hope." *Serm. de Nativ. B. V. M.*

This Mother is the hope of the *just* and of *sinners*. She is the hope of the just, because all children and ranks of the Church are sheltered by her special protection, in order to enable them to struggle against Satan, the world, and the flesh. But she is also the hope of sinners, because they are brought back to life by her intercession, so that we may justly apply to her those words of the Wise Man: "My children, behold the generations of men: and know ye that no one hath hoped in her, and hath been confounded."— *Eccles.* ii. 11.

Full of this confidence in the assistance of Mary, St. Bernard exclaims: " Never was it known that any one who fled to thy protection, implored thy help and thy intercession, was left unaided." *Serm. de Assumpt.* It is plain that this is to be understood with the proviso, if that for which we asked her was really conducive to our salvation.

Q. In what manner can we make ourselves most sure of the protection of Mary?

A. By *true* and *constant* devotion to her. That will assuredly save you.

Q. Why?

A. Because, if you are truly a child of Mary, you belong also to the number of the children of God. You will be a true child of Mary, if you honor her with a childlike, true and constant devotion. In it then, of course, you have a most consolatory mark of your pre-election, as the doctors of the Catholic Church with justice assert. Yes, the Church herself applies in the Canonical Hours, the following text to Mary: "Blessed is the man that heareth me, and that watcheth daily at my gates, and waiteth at the posts of my doors. He that shall find me, shall find life, and shall have salvation from the Lord." *Prov.* viii. 34, 35. From these and many other texts of Scripture do the doctors of the Church draw their proof how powerful and efficacious is the protection of the most Blessed Virgin for obtaining eternal salvation. Among the rest, St. Bonaventure does not hesitate to say: "Just as any one, who despises thee, O most holy Virgin, and turns his back upon thee, must perish; so it is also impossible that any one who has recourse to thee and is received into thy protection should perish." *Lib.* 1. *Pharet.* c. 5.

Q. You will perhaps ask: "Am I then certain of my salvation, if I honor the most Blessed Virgin and say every day some prayers in her honor?"

A. By no means; you must also imitate her virtues. Neglecting this, our devotion to Mary profits us nothing, for it is a false devotion; nay, it cannot be called a devotion at all.

Q. Which are particularly the virtues in which a servant of Mary should imitate her?

A. Purity of conscience, humility, chastity, patience, and love of God and our neighbor. These and all other virtues of the Blessed Virgin, a true servant of her's must imitate, as condition and circumstances require, if he wishes that his devotion should be pleasing to Mary; and hopes to enjoy her particular protection. But vain would be every external devotion to Mary if we were wanting in those virtues, or were perhaps even to go so far as to wound her most holy and pure heart by the commission of sin. But pride, lust, impatience, and hatred, are the vices which render us particularly displeasing in the eyes of Mary and unworthy of her protection.

Q. Do you know of any prayer by which Mary is honored in a special manner?

A. Yes; by the salutation with which the angel Gabriel saluted her, which St. Elizabeth repeated, and to which the Church also added a petition.

Q. How do we call this prayer of salutation?

A. The "Ave Maria" or "Hail Mary."

Q. Say the "Hail Mary."

A. "Hail, Mary, full of grace, the Lord is with thee: blessed art thou amongst women; and blessed is the fruit of thy womb, Jesus. Holy Mary, Mother of God, pray for us sinners, now, and at the hour of our death. Amen."

Q. Which are the principal parts of this prayer of salutation?

A. First: The words with which the archangel Gabriel, sent by God, saluted Mary: "Hail, full of grace, the Lord is with thee."

Second: The words with which St. Elizabeth, filled with the Holy Ghost, saluted Mary: "Blessed art thou amongst women, and blessed is the fruit of thy womb."

Third: The words which the Church, guided by the Holy Ghost further added: "Jesus, Holy Mary, mother of God, pray for us sinners, now, and at the hour of our death." On this very account is this prayer of salutation the most pleasing to Mary, the mother of Graces, as she herself once revealed to her servant, St. Mechtildis.

Q. In what sense do we say, "Hail, Mary?"

A. We congratulate Mary on the sublimity of her election, as the chosen daughter of the heavenly Father, the mother of His eternal Son, the spouse of the Holy Ghost, and as the Eve of the New Covenant side by side with Jesus, the heavenly Adam.

We salute Mary thus, and rejoice at the same time in having the happiness of saluting her, as the Mother of God, and our Mother. We salute her, too, in the salutation of joy and thanks, and in remembrance of all that we have already received from God in virtue of her intercession.

Q. What is the meaning of the words, "Full of grace?"

A. They are the *first* praise which we bestow upon Mary, saluting her with the salutation of the Angel.

Q. Of what nature is the operation of grace?

A. The operation of grace is threefold.
1. It blots out the stain of sin.
2. It adorns the soul with spiritual beauty.
3. It renders the soul capable of meritorious works in the supernatural order, and fills it with heavenly treasures.

But then, Mary is full of grace, being entirely free also from the stain of original sin. "No spot is in thee," thus the Holy Ghost assures us of Mary. She is full of grace, because she also received a greater measure of sanctifying grace than all Angels and Saints together. The holy Fathers call her, on that account, "an ocean of grace;" and the Holy Ghost himself says of her: "Thou art chosen like the sun." She is finally full of grace, because she co-operated with every actual grace more diligently and in a manner more meritorious, than any Angel or Saint ever did, namely, by uniting with and wholly conforming her will to, the most holy will of God. "Many daughters have gathered together riches; thou hast surpassed them all." Thus it stands written of Mary, as the holy Church herself applies these words of the Holy Ghost to her. *Prov.* xxxi. 29.

Q. What do we mean by saying, "The Lord is with thee?"

A. These words contain the *second* praise of Mary; namely, at she not only received such a plenitude of grace, but that ae also preserved the same most faithfully and without diminishing it in the least, nay, increasing it continually from the instant of her conception till the last moment of her most holy life. But these words refer directly to her, because she is the mother of the Incarnate Word of God.

Q. What do the words signify: "Blessed art thou amongst women?"

A. They contain the *third* praise of Mary; namely, that she is the only one of all the daughters of Eve, who was, by a miracle, at the same time a *Mother* and a *Virgin*—the one chosen mother of our Lord and Redeemer.

But, moreover, she is also in the order of Grace the mother of all the children of God, the true Eve, the mother of life and of the living.

Q. What do these words signify: "And blessed is the fruit of thy womb, Jesus?"

A. They contain the *fourth* praise of Mary; namely, that she was adorned and gifted with such high prerogatives not only in herself, but also in that the glory of the blessed humanity of Christ shone upon her, since she is His mother. But since Jesus, because His humanity is united to the person of the Son of God, is elevated not only above all men, but even above all the Angels, being their King and Lord, this, too, is the prerogative and glorification of His blessed mother Mary.

Thus, then, the salutation of the "Hail, Mary," includes the *praise* of all the prerogatives of Mary, both in the order of nature and of grace. The conclusion embraces in like manner, every petition that can be addressed to Mary.

Q. What is the sense of the petition in the "Hail, Mary," which the Church added to this salutation?

A. The Church once more reminding us of the dignity of Mary as Mother of God, admonishes her children to have recourse to Her, with an unlimited confidence, in every concern of body and soul, in life and in death, because *she*, as the mother of our Lord, is also on that account the mother of Grace, and the most powerful intercessor at the throne of her divine Son for all those who, as her true children, seek shelter in her protection. But if we stand in need of her protection and her intercession all through life, we do so more particularly at the hour of death.

Q. By what form of prayer do we specially honor Mary?

A. By the holy Rosary and the Angelical Salutation repeated three times every day.

Q. What is the Rosary?

A. The Rosary is a manner of praying by which we often repeat the "Hail, Mary," united with the consideration of the most important mysteries of the life, suffering and death, and also of the glorification of Jesus and of Mary, in due order.

Q. Why is this method of prayer called the Rosary?

A. Because on account of the regular recurrence of salutation and petition, united with the above recollection concerning Jesus and Mary, and on account of the above-mentioned mysteries of faith, this prayer forms, as it were, garden of fragrant roses of true devotion.

Q. But does not the frequent repetition of the same salutation disturb devotion?

A. By no means; on the contrary, if it is done in the right manner, it increases the ardor and efficacy of the prayer. For have we not in the 135th Psalm, the one verse: "His mercy endureth for ever" repeated twenty-seven times? And we read of Christ our Lord himself, that He offered up three successive times, the same prayer to His heavenly Father. *Mark*, xiv. 39.

Q. Why is the signal given three times every day, *i. e.*, morning, noon, and night, for the prayer called the Angelus?

A. In order to put us in mind, that every day and at every hour of the day, we are exposed to the loss of our salvation, and have need to implore the assistance of Mary; and that it is not enough, to begin daily and with new fervor every work of our calling in the service of God under her care and protection, we must also, with the same fervor, continue and end it. Besides, the Church wishes to call to our memory, by means of this sign repeated three times daily, the three most important mysteries of our redemption, namely: the incarnation, the passion, and the resurrection of Jesus Christ, our Lord and Saviour.

Q. Say the Angelus.

A. The angel of the Lord declared unto Mary; and she conceived of the Holy Ghost. Hail, Mary, &c.

Behold the handmaid of the Lord; may it be done unto me according to thy word. Hail, Mary, &c.

And the word was made flesh, and dwelt among us. Hail, Mary, &c.

Prayer.—Pour forth, we beseech thee, O Lord, Thy grace into our hearts, that we, to whom the Incarnation of Christ, Thy Son, was made known by the message of an angel, may by His passion and cross be brought to the glory of His resurrection, through the same Christ our Lord. Amen. At night we add one *Our Father*, and one *Hail Mary*, for the faithful departed.

Q. When should we pray particularly?

A. Every morning, and every evening, and before and after meals. At the morning prayer the principal thing is to make a *good resolution* for doing good and avoiding evil during the ensuing day. But at the evening prayer—the examination of *conscience* and an act of *contrition* must be made. Accustom yourself also, to make a brief examination at noon, and to practice faithfully the particular examination of conscience for the extirpation of a particular fault, or for the acquirement of a particular virtue. More particular instruction on this matter you can ask of your spiritual father.

Practice.—Love and practice prayer with all possible fervor. Let it be to you as regards your soul, what food and respiration are for your body; namely, a necessity; the consolation and the delight of your life through your communion with God. Such was prayer to the Saints, and so should it also be to you. But this will only be the case, if you pray often and properly, in proportion to your state and calling, and particularly, if you practice the interior prayer of contemplation, and a familiar intercourse with Christ in the most holy Sacrament of the Altar. Procure for yourself the prayer-books, which give you special directions on this subject, and lay out for yourself a fixed time for contemplation and oral prayer, observing that time conscientiously; prepare yourself well for holy Communion, and make your thanksgiving with the greatest care, and the Lord will most certainly be merciful to you; you shall taste how sweet the Lord is to them that come near him, and he will fill you with the gift of prayer. You shall pray *well*, and on that account also live *well*, as St. Augustine assures us. Besides, nourish in yourself a most intimate and childlike devotion to Mary, and try to propagate it wherever you can.

Q. What sins are opposed to the holy virtue of hope.

A. Despair and presumption, according as man hopes too little or too much.

Q. When does man sin through despair?

A. When a man, tormented and alarmed by the consciousness of the sins which he has committed, puts away from himself all thoughts of conversion, because he believes that it is impossible for him to be converted, and that his sins are too great to be forgiven.

Q. Is the sin of despair a great sin?

A. Yes; it is a very great one, and the seal of condemnation.

Q. To which attributes of God is the sin of despair particularly opposed?

A. 1st. To the Omnipotence of God, of whom it is written,

"that He is able even of stones to raise up children to Abraham." *Math*. iii. 9.

2d. To the veracity of God. For the Lord expressly assures us by Ezechiel: "In the hour, when the sinner shall return to me, all his iniquity shall be remembered no more." And again: "As I live," says the Lord God, "I will not the death of the sinner, but that he be converted and live!"

And Christ himself assures of this, saying: "Receive ye the Holy Ghost; whose sins you shall forgive, they are forgiven." *John*, xx. 23.

3d. To the goodness and mercy of God, with the commendation and praise of which the entire Holy Scriptures are filled, and to which the examples of innumerable penitents, both of the Old and New Testaments bear witness, who, no matter how grievously they had sinned, were received again into favor by God, if sincerely repenting they returned to Him like David.

We read in the works of Blasius (in *Man. Sp. c.* 4.) that one day God revealed to St. Catharine of Sienna, that He was more offended by the final despair of a sinner, than by all the sins which he committed in his whole life.

Q. When does a man sin by presumption?

A. He does so, if he expects that God will be merciful to him, even if he should continue to sin blindly, and despise His threats and His judgments.

Q. Is presumption a grievous sin?

A. A very grievous, and most dangerous sin. It is very grievous, because it is an open sin against the Holy Ghost, and a most culpable contempt of the menaces and chastisements of God, which ought justly to fill us with fear and trembling.

It is at the same time a most dangerous sin; for this disposition of presumption makes the sinner careless and indifferent, so that he is ready to run thoughtlessly into the danger of perdition, and to think but little of the necessity of doing penance. In this way, the sinner becomes more and more negligent and cold, sinks into the depths of indifference, and completes his ruin by final impenitence. "God is good, therefore I live badly." This is the language of the presumptuous man; certainly, he deserves that God should cast him away.

Not in vain, therefore, says St. Peter in his 2d Epistle:

"Brethren, labor the more, that by good works you make sure your vocation and election." 2 *Peter*, i. 10.

And St. Paul admonishes all: "Work your salvation with fear and trembling," as such who are one day to render an account to the Lord. *Philip.* ii. 12.

Of course, the presumptuous man thinks, that he has yet time enough for repentance, but he deceives himself. Nowhere has God promised the sinner a certain time for repentance, and experience teaches that it is very often the presumptuous sinner who is carried off by a sudden death, and dies either without his senses, or without the assistance of a priest.

Wherefore, think often on the beautiful saying of St. Augustine: "Meek and just is the Lord. Love, because He is meek, and fear, because He is just. Being meekness, He says: I am silent; but being justice, He cries out: Shall I remain silent for ever? He is merciful and compassionate, still fear, for He is also truthful. To those who are assailed by the temptations of despair, He points out the harbor of forgiveness, yet He has left uncertain the hour of death, for the warning of those that hope presumptuously." *Aug. tract* 33. *in Joan.*

Practice.—Make often an act of Christian hope, and animate and fortify within you a great desire of trusting in the providence of God. This disposition and this resignation of ourselves to the Divine Providence, is one of the consoling marks of predilection, and of being on the way to heaven.

CHAPTER III.

ON CHARITY.

"AND now," says the Apostle, "there remain, faith, hope and charity, these three, but the greatest of these is charity." 1 *Cor.* xiii.

Great indeed is the power of faith, which, as Christ himself tells us, is able to move mountains, and to work miracles.

Great, too, is the power of hope, which protects us as a

helmet, and serves as an anchor, by means of which we hold ourselves fast in the promises of faith, and, expecting, are filled with great consolation and strengthened in the combat. Yet greater is the power of charity, which is the root and consummation of every meritorious virtue, and without which all the power of faith and of hope is as nothing, whilst it proves itself stronger than death and hell. "We know that we have passed from death to life, because we love the brethren. He that loveth not abideth in death." Thus St. John tells us, 1 *John*, iii. 14; presupposing, of course, that this charity is really a true and tried one. We shall now propose the most necessary and most important things concerning this holy charity as a means of salvation.

Q. What is charity as a divine virtue?

A. Charity is a virtue infused by God, by which we love God above all things, and our neighbor as ourselves.

Q. What means: To love God above all things?

A. It means to esteem God higher than any thing in the world, so that we wish rather to lose every thing, even life itself, than offend God.

It also means to nourish an inclination of the heart to God, by which we prefer God to all other objects of love.

It means, finally, to love God for himself alone, and all others only for His sake and in Him, because, and as God wills it, and because it is He from whom every thing good and every thing worthy of love or esteem proceeds as from its source.

Q. Why should we love God?

A. Because He is of himself the most perfect good, and alone worthy of our love.

Q. What disposition of heart does this act of love include?

A. First: The estimation of God above all things, so that we immeasurably prefer God and the possession of him to all created things, and are willing to lose all things rather than God, or to displease Him.

Second: Affection; namely, that we endeavor to preserve a greater inclination of the heart for God, than for any other created being, even although this inclination does not always manifest itself so sensibly as the inclination for other beings and things.

Third: The disposition of benevolence; namely, that we wish God, with all our heart, to possess every good, whether this belongs to Him essentially in virtue of the perfections of His divine nature itself, or in virtue of His external glory, desiring to increase the latter as much as possible.

Fourth: An act of friendship and communion, by which we offer ourselves to God with all that we are and have, and desire to be made one with God himself, and to receive in return from God the communication of His gifts, and the union with Him here below through sanctifying grace, and in heaven above by the light of glory. 1 *Cor.* viii.

Q. When is this love towards God perfect?

A. If we love God principally and first for His own sake as the supreme and most perfect good. But if the motive of our love towards God is first of all, because he is good to us, then this love is imperfect.

Q. By what means is the love of God augmented in us.

A. 1. By a great purity of conscience.

2. By a fervent practice of virtues and good works.

3. By prayer, especially that of contemplation.

4. By the reception of the Holy Sacraments, and by intercourse with Jesus in the most Holy Sacrament of the Altar.

5. By the remembrance of the benefits received from God, especially of the benefit of redemption, and of being called to the true faith, and by constantly walking in the presence of God.

Q. What is particularly contrary to the love of God?

A. The love of the world. "If any man love the world, the charity of the Father is not in him." 1 *John*, ii. 15.

Q. What are we to understand here by the expression: "the world?"

A. The desire of enjoying the goods of the world, inducing the neglect of our last aim and end, which is to serve God,—so that a man directs all his thoughts and endeavors solely to this, how he may attain to the enjoyment of the riches, honors, and pleasures of this world.

Q. Which is the second commandment of charity?

A. To love our neighbor. "Love thy neighbor as thyself."

Q. What do you mean by the term "neighbor?"

A. In general all rational beings that are called to the possession of eternal happiness, or are already happy in God, namely, the blessed in Heaven, the souls in purgatory, and men on earth.

But more particularly the latter, that is to say, all mankind living with us upon earth.

Q. Why must we love our neighbor?

A. Because he is the creature and the image of God, and our brother in Adam and in Christ, and because God commands us to do so.

Q. What must be the qualities of the love of our neighbor?

A. It must be first: sincere, *i. e.*, we must love our neighbor not from a motive of mere self-interest, and not show him this love, that he may be favorably disposed towards us, and that we may obtain some temporal advantage.

Second: It must be *active*, according to the maxim inculcated by Christ our Lord: "All things whatsoever you would that men should do to you, do you also to them." *Matth.* viii. 12. And St. John writes: "My little children, let us not love in word, nor in tongue, but in deed, and in truth." 1 *John*, iii. 18.

Third: It must be universal; namely, without excepting even our bitterest enemies, as we have heard and proved already in treating of the Lord's prayer.

Q. What persons are particularly recommended to our charity in Holy Scripture.

A. Our parents, the poor, the widows and the orphans, both as regards their temporal and spiritual welfare.*

Q. Are we also bound to love ourselves?

A. Undoubtedly we are; the commandment itself reminds us of that, because Christ says and ordains that we are to love our neighbor *as ourselves.*

Q. When do we love ourselves?

A. When we regard ourselves as the image of God, and esteem our every faculty and all that we have, as God's gift, and do all in our power to work out our salvation.

Q. What is directly opposed to the love of ourselves?

A. Selfishness, which consists in seeking in all things but one's own temporal advantage, and thinking of nothing else but that alone.

---

* We shall have an opportunity when we interpret the Commandments of God, and in the third part, where we shall speak on the practice of the Christian virtues, to show in particular how we are to fulfil those duties, in accordance with the demands of this second precept of charity.

Q. In what does the love of God and our neighbor particularly show itself.

A. In the keeping of the commandments. 1 *John,* v. 3.

Practice.—O that we all of us would take to heart and understand what it is, to be allowed to love God, in order to unite ourselves one day with Him in His infinite beauty and happiness, He who is, essentially, love itself! That we might love all other things only in God and for God, especially our neighbor, in order that he also may know and love God and be one day united with Him for ever. Thus did St. Ignatius, in particular, love God, and hence he lived entirely for God; and hence it was, too, that he was heard to sigh so frequently: "O God, that men would know and love thee!" Whence he was wont to send his subjects into all parts of the world, with this injunction: "Go, inflame the whole world!" namely, with the fire of this true love for God, the true mark of which is, the accomplishment of the divine will by keeping the commandments.

On the Commandments of God.

St. John writes: "This is the charity of God, that we keep His commandments." 1 *John,* v. 3. And again: "But whosoever keepeth His word, the charity of God is truly perfect in him: and by this we know that we are in Him." 1 *John,* ii. 5. Christ himself teaches: "If you love me, keep my commandments." "He that hath my commandments, and keepeth them; he it is that loveth me. And he that loveth me, shall be loved by my Father: and I will love him, and will manifest myself to him." "He that loveth me not, keepeth not my words." *John,* xiv. 15; xxi. 24.

Q. Which are the principal commandments of God?

A. The *ten* commandments which the Lord gave through Moses to the people of Israel on the mountain of Sinai, and which Christ through himself and His Apostles commanded the children of God, in the New Testament, to keep in their full perfection.

Q. Which are the ten commandments?

A. 1. I am the Lord thy God. Thou shalt not have strange gods before me. Thou shalt not make to thyself a graven thing and adore the same.

2. Thou shalt not take the name of the Lord thy God in vain.

3. Remember that thou keep holy the Sabbath day.

4. Honor thy father and thy mother, that thou mayest be long lived upon the earth.

5. Thou shalt not kill.

6. Thou shalt not commit adultery.

7. Thou shalt not steal.

8. Thou shalt not bear false witness against thy neighbor.

9. Thou shalt not covet thy neighbor's wife.

10. Thou shalt not covet thy neighbor's house, nor his field, nor his servant, nor his handmaid, nor his ox, nor his ass, nor any thing that is his.

Q. Are there any other commandments of God besides these.

A. Yes, there are many others; just as many, indeed, as there are duties for man to accomplish, and all of them are included in the one principal commandment of the natural law: Do good and avoid evil.

Q. But why, then, are these ten commandments called the commandments of God, and their observance particularly commanded.

A. First: Because they explain the law of nature in its nearest relation to God and our neighbor in the clearest and most concise manner.

Secondly: Because the Lord has planted them himself in our conscience as the law of nature, whence they bind all men without exception.

Thirdly: because the Lord announced them again with such great solemnity to man on Mount Sinai, amid thunder and lightning, and the sound of Angels' trumpets. *Exod.* xx.

Fourthly: Because any grievous transgression of these commandments excludes us from the kingdom of God.

Fifthly: Because they are in such intimate and inseparable connection with the law of charity towards God and our neighbor.

Q. Which is the sum and substance of these ten commandments?

A. The very law of charity towards God and our neighbor.

For this reason the law itself was given to the people of God on two tables of stone. Upon one of them were graven the three principal commandments relating to God; upon the other, the remaining seven, which relate to our fellow-men, binding us to do good to them, especially to those who are most closely connected with ourselves, and forbidding us to injure them, either in regard to their person, their honor, or their possessions, and this neither in word or deed, in thought or in desire.

Q. What do these words of introduction mean: "I am the Lord thy God?"

A. By this solemn introduction we are reminded of the majesty and supreme dominion of God who commands us to keep these commandments, and are thereby filled with reverence and forcibly exhorted to observe what is so solemnly ordained in these commandments of God, either to be done or to be avoided. But it is not the majesty of God alone, which moves us to this zeal for the fulfillment of the law, but also the greatness of the promised reward, and the assistance of God for the observance of these commands. For listen to the Prophet: "I will put my spirit in the midst of you; and I will cause you to walk in my commandments, and to keep my judgments, and do them." *Ezech.* xxxvi. 27. And to Christ himself, who teaches us the perfection of these commandments, saying: "My yoke is sweet, and my burden light;" that is to say, from the strength and power given to us by his *love*. *Matth*. xi. 30.

The First Commandment.

Q. What is *ordained* by this commandment?

A. That we adore one only God, and serve Him for His own sake.

Q. In what consists the act of adoration?

A. In the expression of that homage, whereby we render to God our acknowledgment of His supreme dominion, and our full dependance and subjection.

Q. Why do we owe God this adoration and homage?

A. Because He is the Creator and Preserver of the whole world, and our Redeemer, self-existing, infinite, and most perfect.

Q. How do we show our adoration?

A. Either internally, by the dispositions of our heart and the prayer of the mind; or externally, by words, and by the attitude of the body, in kneeling down or prostrating ourselves upon the ground. But especially by offering up the Holy Sacrifice of the Mass.

Q. In what does the service of God, which the act of adoration requires of us, consist?

A. In the performance of God's most holy will, by faith, hope and charity, in the manner taught us by that religion revealed by God himself. He who thus believes, hopes, and loves, is a true servant of God, fulfils His holy will, and walks in the way of salvation.

Q. What is *forbidden* by the first commandment?

A. Unbelief, idolatry, heresy, voluntary doubts in matters of faith, indifference in things of religion, fortune-telling, sorcery, witchcraft, superstition, tempting God, diffidence in God, despair, presumption, hatred of God, sacrilege, and simony, or spiritual usury.

Q. What do you understand by those different sins?

A. Unbelief is that perverse inclination of the mind, by which man refuses assent to the revealed truths of faith. The mere want of knowledge of the true religion, without positive resistance, is called want of faith, or paganism.

Idolatry is that blindness of man in which he pays divine homage to an image or any other creature. If this homage be directed towards animals, it is called *fetichism*.

Heresy is that perverseness, by which a man obstinately adheres to his false doctrine, against the judgment and solemn declaration of the Church in matters of faith.

Doubts of faith is that disposition of mind, by which a man voluntarily and deliberately doubts concerning those things which the Church proposes to us to be believed. Mere transient doubts, which a man wills not, but rather rejects, are no sin, but only temptations.

Indifference in matters of religion we call that destructive condition of the heart in which a man finds himself if he is not at all concerned to know whether he has the true religion or not, and has no regard for what that true religion requires of him; a condition in which, therefore, religion itself is to him no more than a mere name, a peculiar custom, or human prejudice.

Fortune-telling is the attempt to inquire or predict from arbitrary means things future, or otherwise unknown, with an express or tacit invocation of the devil. To this sin belong:

consulting the spirits of the dead, or necromany; interpretation of dreams (or oneiromancy), divining from marks or signs in the hands (chiromancy), or in the body; from the elements, or motions of animals, or of the stars, from the flight of birds, from cards, from drawing lots, and from the use of magic; or if one knows, or endeavors to know, distant or secret things by the coöperation of the devil.

It may happen, indeed, that God might indicate by a dream, by lots, or some other natural means a future event, for assuming such a thing, however, a supernatural authority is required. But to infer directly, and especially with certainty, from natural signs, events which depend on the freewill of man, is a sin against the first commandment.

If this kind of sin is committed, the devil is *tacitly* invoked thereby, for this reason, that the natural powers of the means are insufficient for effecting such things.

Sorcery is the attempt to effect wonderful things by the aid of the devil.

Witchcraft is the attempt to do harm to others by the help of the devil, either in their person, their cattle, or other property.

Superstition is the entertaining of the false belief that a special service is rendered to God by some one arbitrary arrangement of exterior things and prayers, and that God has imparted to them particular healing virtue, if they are recited in a certain form and order, and applied for particular purposes. To this belongs the so called cure by sympathy.

We may, of course, pray for health, recovery from sickness, and other such blessings, for ourselves and others, but we are never allowed to believe that there is virtue in charms or spells, or in a particular prayer said at times and in certain words. All this is superstition and sin. To this class belong, nominally, all superstitious preventatives, such as the spiritual shield, Our Lady's Dream, and many other small pamphlets, bearing the words: " Printed in this year," by means of which we may obtain a certain favor in life, or be saved from a sudden death, &c. All of this is superstition, contradictory to the word of God, and to the doctrine of the Holy Church.

Tempting God is the attempt to find out in any matter, whether God can do all things, and know all things; or to ask Him on any occasion to perform a miracle, or to render us some extraordinary assistance, and neglect what we ought ourselves to do.

When speaking of the virtue of hope, we already explained more fully what is meant by *despair* and *diffidence* in God. He who despairs thinks that God does not help him any more. He who only doubts in this, rather sins by *diffidence*.

Hatred of God would be the sin of one who should fall so deep into the abyss of wickedness, as to feel anger and aversion toward God, instead of the love which we owe him above all things. Alas! that there are such devils amongst men upon earth.

Sacrilege is the profanation of persons, things and places that are holy, or consecrated to God; for instance, laying violent hands on a Priest; receiving the Holy Sacrament unworthily; violating a church, or profaning the sacred vessels.

Simony or spiritual usury is committed, if one buys, sells, or exchanges spiritual things, offices and the like, for money or an equivalent, so that he compares, as Simon the magician did, the spiritual with money.

All of these sins are, by their nature, mortal sins, and can only be venial where there is ignorance, or only an imperfect transgression in lesser things.

Q. Which means are we to use against witchcraft and other external influences of the evil spirits?

A. First: We are to purify our consciences by a good confession.

Secondly: We are to receive holy communion frequently and worthily.

Thirdly: We are to make use of holy water and other blessed objects.

Fourthly: We are to make use of the sign of the cross.

Fifthly: We are to pray, to invoke the most holy name of Jesus, and to have a great devotion to Mary.

Sixthly: We are to make use of the exorcisms of the holy Catholic Church. But there is no reason, why any one should be troubled or perplexed in his mind, if he fancies himself, or any thing that is his exposed to such influences. For neither a sorcerer nor Satan himself has any power, even so much as to bend but a hair of our head, unless God permits him, and this happens only when it is for our greater good, if we are otherwise of good will.

Q. But they who practice the black art (or magic), and

have made themselves over to the devil by writing; can they yet be converted and obtain salvation?

A. Certainly, if they are sincerely sorry for their sins, confess them, and do penance for them. For there is no sin too great to be forgiven through the blood and merits of Christ, who conquered Satan completely, tore up the deed of sin which was written against us, and nailed it to the cross. This is the assurance of the Apostle of the nations. *Coloss.* ii.

Q. Does the first commandment forbid the use of images, and the veneration of Saints in general?

A. By no means. It only forbids idolatry and the worship of images, from which the veneration of the Saints and their images differs entirely, as shown in the explanation of the Apostles' creed.

Practice.—Show your faith in God specially by a lively remembrance of Him, in all that you do, and by renouncing all that is not God, and does not promote His glory, so that the motive of your life and actions may be to accomplish the most holy will of God, so that you may say before God in all sincerity of heart: To be rich or poor, honored or despised, healthy or sick, to live a short life or a long one, is entirely the same to me; the will of God be done. Let me only serve Him, as He wills it, and be saved.

Thus the Saints taught, and thus they lived. O that the images which you have of them might remind you of this! But do not suffer in your house any image or picture, even the least offensive to modesty, not even though it should be the representation of a holy object. Be not credulous when you hear of witchcraft and the like, but neither must you believe that the influence of the evil one is a mere fable. Guard yourself against superstition of any kind, and with a powerful confidence in God, expect all aid from Him alone, in whatever may serve for *His* glory and *your* salvation.

THE SECOND COMMANDMENT.

Q. What does the second commandment enjoin, and what does it forbid?

A. It *enjoins* the glorification of the Divine Name. It *forbids* the profanation of that name by words.

Both the command and the prohibition contain each four

principal points, for in a fourfold manner is the name of God particularly honored, or, on the contrary, profaned by word, namely:

First: It is honored, if we utter the holy name with due reverence. But it is profaned, if we pronounce that holy name lightly, inconsiderately and without devotion.

Secondly: It is honored, if in reverence and in truth, we call upon God as a witness, by means of an oath, where there is a necessity for doing so. But it is profaned by *perjury*, and by rash, frivolous swearing.

Thirdly: It is honored, if we make a *vow* to God. But it is profaned, if we vow something bad, or do not *keep* a lawful vow, and violate our word given to God.

Fourthly: It is honored by calling upon and praising that holy name. But is profaned by cursing and blaspheming, and by scoffing at religion.

Q. What particulars are to be remarked in each of these relations?

A. As regards the naming of the Divine Name, as also those of the Saints and the Holy Sacraments, and things consecrated particularly to God, we are to attend, not so much to how often it is done, as to the disposition of the heart, with which we do it. A heart that loves God, thinks always of God and divine things, and loves to speak of them. This is not taking the name of God in vain. It happens only, then, when one pronounces the name of God and of holy things without devotion, from mere custom, and on every occasion; and this is also the case, when one abuses, in this manner, the words of Holy Scripture, making use of them in a light or jesting way.

Q. What is it to take an oath?

A. To take an oath is to call upon God as witness, that something we have said is true, or that we will fulfil a promise which we have made, whether we name the majesty of God itself, or something else in which it shines forth particularly.

Q. Are we allowed to swear?

A. Certainly, we are; with three conditions which render an oath lawful and praiseworthy.

Q. Which are these three conditions?

A. The *first* condition is, that that which we promise or assert is *true*. He who asserts a falsehood on oath as a truth, or promises something with an oath which he is not willing to fulfil, swears, in the language of Scripture, with "deceit," *Ps.* xiv., and thereby commits a mortal sin of the blackest die. Woe to him, who knowing the untruth, becomes guilty of an oath! God punishes this crime very often in this world.

The *second* condition is, justice; that is to say, one must have also the *right* of confirming his assertion by oath, or of promising this or that thing. He who should confirm a calumny by an oath, would commit a great sin; and so also, he who would bind himself by an oath to do that which he could not do without committing sin.

The *third* condition is, *prudence* and *necessity*; namely, that before an oath is made, we consider and examine the circumstance whether the thing is really so important as to render an oath necessary or advisable, and whether people do not believe otherwise. He who does not consider this, exposes himself, moreover, to the danger of swearing falsely at one time or another, and shows by this frivolous levity itself, that he has but little reverence for God.

Q. Is perjury, *i. e.*, swearing falsely, or to a thing the truth of which is doubtful, a great sin?

A. It is one of the greatest sins, especially if it be committed in a court of justice; because he that does so, in the first place, derides, as it were, the omniscience, justice and sanctity of God. Secondly, he destroys the last means of preserving fidelity and trust amongst men. Thirdly, he, as it were, solemnly renounces God, and calls down upon himself his awful vengeance.

The prophet Zachary writes thus upon this subject: "And he (the Lord) said to me: This is the curse that goeth forth over the face of the earth: every one that sweareth shall be judged by it. I will bring it forth, saith the Lord of hosts: and it shall come to the house of him that sweareth falsely by my name: and it shall remain in the midst of his house, and shall consume it with the timber thereof, and the stone thereof." *Zach.* v. 3, 4.

Q. Does the custom of swearing free one from sin?

A. No, on the contrary, it aggravates the guilt; for the greater such custom is, the greater is the profanation of God's name by the oath. "A man that sweareth much, shall be filled with iniquity." *Eccles.* xxiii. 12. But it would be otherwise, if a man, earnestly endeavoring to break himself of this evil custom, should fall thoughtlessly, on account of that custom, and utter an oath, without full deliberation, repenting immediately and correcting himself seriously. In that case, the old custom would certainly lessen the guilt of such a course.

Q. What is a *vow?*

A. A deliberate promise made to God, to do something that is pleasing to Him.

Q. What are we particularly to remark regarding the vow?

A. 1. That a vow is a *promise;* therefore, not a mere purpose or a mere desire, but an express, holy promise, made to God with the heart or with the mouth, to do, or to avoid something under obligation of sin.

2. That this promise is made to *God*, for his glory and to honor him more perfectly. If, therefore, we vow something in honor of the most holy Virgin or of the saints, it is still to be understood in this way, that the vow, if valid, is made not so much to the saints, as to God himself in honor of a saint.

3. That a vow can never have for its object any thing but what is good and pleasing to God. Consequently, vowing to do something bad, or something which would prevent you from doing good or a greater good, would render the act invalid and make it a sin, and generally a great sin. The same thing holds, if you do not fulfil the vow which you made, or if you do not fulfil it at the time specified, especially if the matter be of importance.

"When thou hast made a vow to the Lord thy God, thou shalt not delay to pay it: because the Lord thy God will require it. And if thou delay, it shall be imputed to thee for a sin." *Deut.* xxiii. 21. And again: "If thou hast vowed any thing to God, defer not to pay it: for an unfaithful and foolish promise displeaseth him: but whatsoever thou hast vowed, pay it: and it is much better not to vow, than after a vow, not to perform the things promised." *Eccls.* v. 3.

Q. What reasons do specially invite us to praise God?

A. His internal and infinite perfections. His noble achievements without by the wonders of creation, preservation and redemption, particularly the consideration of those graces and operations of Divine Providence, which takes care of our personal welfare and salvation throughout our whole lifetime.

Q. What is blasphemy?

A. A word or oath, injurious or insulting to God or His Saints, by which we have the insolence to impute some fault to God, or deny some of His perfections.

It is a great sin. "He that blasphemeth the name of the Lord, dying let him die: all the multitude shall stone him." *Levit.* xxiv. 10. The grievousness of the crime is manifest from the greatness of the punishment. In the book of Tobias we read: "When King Sennacherib was come back fleeing from Judea by reason of the slaughter that God had made about him for his blasphemy." *Tob.* i. 21

Q. What is cursing?

A. Cursing is uttering imprecations and evil prayers against ourselves or our neighbors, whereby the curser usually calls upon Him frivolously, or names things otherwise holy, and pronounces their name irreverently. This sin is the greater, because it is generally accompanied by anger and by insult towards our neighbor. Moreover, since cursing and blaspheming is peculiarly the language of the devils, how careful should we be of contracting a vice which reminds us so powerfully and so awfully that we are the children of the devil, if we make use of his language.

Q. When do we sin by *scoffing at religion*?

A. If we speak lightly or contemptuously about religion, priests, ecclesiastical rites and ceremonies, or make a jest of them.

Practice.—Never utter the name of God without particular respect; and speak always with the greatest reverence of God and divine things. Never swear, therefore, but in extreme necessity. Make no vows without the counsel and consent of your spiritual guide. Let no curse or word of imprecation ever fall from your lips. Love trials and tribulations as precious gifts from the hand of God, and you shall dwell in peace. On the contrary, accustom yourself to have in readiness a short sentence in praise of God, as often as any trials befall you; for instance: "Thanks and praise be to God." "For the love of God, I will bear, suffer, or do this." They will animate and protect you, and make you acquire great merit.

The Third Commandment.

Q. What does this commandment *ordain?*

A. That we spend devoutly the time destined for the service of God; especially the Lord's day, which was in the Old Testament the *Sabbath*, but is now in the new dispensation the *Sunday*.

Q. Why did God, in the Old Testament, command the Sabbath to be kept.

A. 1. As a memorial of the Creation which was completed in six days.

"In six days the Lord made heaven and earth, and the sea, and all things that are in them, and he rested on the seventh day: therefore the Lord blessed the seventh, and sanctified it." *Exod.* xx. 11.

2. That servants and laborers, nay, even the beast, might enjoy rest and recreation, in order to remind us the more of the eternal rest and peace of heaven, as the last aim and end of man.

Q. Why is the *Sunday* now kept instead of the Sabbath?

A. The reasons are many and weighty. The work of *Creation* began on Sunday, which day has also been sanctified by the principal mysteries of the work of Redemption far more than the Saturday by the close of the Creation; as the Church justly sings on Easter Day: "What would it profit us to have been created, if we had not been redeemed?" Christ was born on a Sunday, as tradition proves; on a Sunday he rose from the dead; on a Sunday he sent down the Holy Ghost, and through him established his holy Church and manifested the same to the world. The Sabbath, moreover, typified the rest of the fathers in limbo; the Sunday is a type of the rest of the blessed in heaven.

But that the Church has instituted the Sunday as the Lord's day, instead of the Sabbath, and determined it as the day to be specially employed adoring and worshipping God, shows forth the great *power* which she solemnly received from Christ.

Christ affirms of himself: "The Son of Man is also the Lord of the Sabbath;" the Church, invested with His power, ordained that the Sunday should be kept holy instead of the Sabbath, by which ordinance she declared and confirmed.

openly and freely, before all the world, the close of the Old dispensation and the institution of the New at one and the same time.

Q. To what does the celebration of the Sunday oblige us?

A. That we are to assist at the divine service, particularly at the holy sacrifice of the Mass, with becoming devotion, and to sanctify the day in a special manner by the exercise of works of Christian devotion and of charity towards our neighbor.

Q. What does the celebration of the Sunday *forbid?*

A. Servile work and every thing else which in any way disturb the santification of this day.

The particular acts prescribed by the holy Church for the observance of the Lord's day by the faithful, will be explained more at large, when we come to expound the commandments of the Church.

Practice.—Be always conscientious in celebrating the Lord's day, particularly in this country, where the rest of the Sabbath is almost, as it were, the only vestige of religion that remains. Labor not without extreme necessity. There is no temporal advantage from such gain, as experience has often proved, and it is a great scandal in this country, and even in some degree an obstacle to the conversion of those who are not of the Catholic faith, to see Catholics do away with the observance of the Sunday. Avoid also, as far as possible, all buying and selling on Sunday. Let not either sloth or the desire of amusement, influence you to neglect the evening services of the Church, commonly called Vespers, and be careful to abstain from drinking in public houses. To take refreshment, if necessity requires it, and then to pass on again, is one thing; but it is another thing to gather together for the sake of drinking and gambling, and thereby giving grievous scandal. Upon the true santification of the Sunday as the first day of the week, generally depends also the santification of the whole ensuing week, and thence that of our whole life. A certain Saint was accustomed to say: "Tell me how you prayed this morning, and I will tell you how you spent the day." The same might be said with regard to the Sunday and the whole week.

The Fourth Commandment.

Q. Why do the commandments of the second table begin with this one?

A. Because it places before our eyes in a particular manner the duty of loving our neighbor; and of all mankind, none are nearer to us than the *Father* and the *Mother* through whom we entered life.

Q. What are we commanded, what forbidden by this commandment?

A. We are *commanded* by it, to show our parents reverence, love and obedience, and to support them in necessity.

We are *forbidden* by it, to show them any disrespect, aversion, or disobedience, or to abandon them in their necessity.

Q. What reverence do we owe our parents?

A. We owe them interior and exterior reverence; namely, we are to esteem them in our hearts as the deputies of God in our regard, and also to show to them this esteem exteriorly, in words, and by exterior signs of reverence, by salutation, politeness, respect in conversation, and by bearing with patience the frailties that may afflict them.

"Honor thy father, in work and word, and all patience." *Eccls.* iii. 9.

We also read a beautiful example of filial reverence in the book of Solomon, who, though he was king, respectfully arose to meet his mother, causing her to be seated upon a throne on his right hand. 3 *Book of Kings,* ii. 19. And the Wise Man gives this admonition: "Son, support the old age of thy father; and grieve him not in his life. *Eccls.* iii. 14.

Q. What kind of love do children owe to their parents?

A. An inward, active and true love coming from the heart. God himself has planted, by natural instinct, this love in the heart of every child, and the parents deserve it the more they have suffered and done for the welfare and salvation of the child. With justice, therefore, did the aged Tobias inculcate the performance of this duty when, at the point of death, he gave his last instructions to his son, saying: "My son! when God shall take my soul, thou shalt bury my body: and thou shalt honor thy mother all the days of her life; for thou must be mindful what and how great perils she suffered for thee in her womb." *Tob.* iv. 2–5.

Children must particularly show this love to their parents by the cordial affection which they manifest for them on every occasion; moreover, they must thank them for the benefits received, be a cause of joy to them by leading a good life, treat them kindly, and support them in sickness and in want.

Q. How are children to *obey* their parents?

A. They are to obey them in all things regarding education, the regulation of the house, and the affairs of salvation.

"My son, hear the instruction of thy father, and forsake not the law of thy mother." *Prov.* xii. 18.

Children prove this obedience by the promptness and fidelity with which they execute the commands of their parents in all allowable things, and by the humble submission with which they receive their counsels and admonitions.

"Children, obey your parents in the Lord; for this is just." *St. Paul to the Ephes.*, chap. vi. 1. But should parents will or command any thing that is sinful, or which withdraws us from the service of God, and does not tend towards our salvation, then of course we are not allowed to obey them; but we must then rather admonish them, with love and respect, saying why we do not yield them obedience in such a thing, according to the Apostle: "We ought to obey God rather than men." *Acts* v. 29.

Q. What support do children owe to their parents?

A. A temporal and spiritual support; that is, children are to assist their parents in all temporal wants as far as it is in their power, and necessity requires it; but they are especially to do this in regard to their spiritual wants and distresses. Children comply with this duty, by praying for their parents, and by endeavoring to procure for them, if poor, the necessaries of life at home and abroad. Moreover, should their needy parents be so unhappy as to degenerate, or have not the happiness of belonging to the true faith, they are to do all they can, to make them return from their evil ways, and to bring them to the knowledge of the true and holy faith. But children are to assist their parents particularly at the point of death, and to afford them every bodily and spiritual comfort, and when they are dead, to take care that they have assistance in purgatory for the comfort and deliverance of their souls.

Q. What is promised to children who carefully fulfil this duty towards their parents?

A. They are promised particular blessings from God, as evident from the words of the commandment itself.

The first blessing is that of a longer life, and, consequently, if they are of good will, a more meritorious one. For, since they honor those from whom they received life, God rewards them for it, provided they are otherwise diligent in keeping the commandments, by prolonging their lives; unless, perhaps, God foresees that a shorter life is more profitable for their salvation.

The second blessing is that of rewarding them in their own children. "He that honoreth his father shall have joy in *his own* children." *Eccls.* iii. 6. Ephraim and Manasses treated their father Joseph most kindly, because he himself had loved and honored his father Jacob.

The third blessing is welfare of body and soul; for St. Paul says: ,'that it may be well with thee." *Ephes.* vi. 3. And Ecclesiasticus: "He that honoreth his mother is as one that layeth up a treasure, and he that honoreth his father shall be heard in the day of his prayer." *Chap.* iii. 5 and 6. "Honor thy father, that a blessing may come upon thee from him, and his blessing may remain in the latter end." *Verse* 10.

Q. How do children sin against the reverence which they owe to their parents?

A. They sin against it, if they contemn and deride them, if they scoff at their commands, are ashamed of them, speak ill of them, treat them harshly and unkindly, if they affront them, or above all, raise their hand to strike them. "The eye that mocketh at his father, and that despiseth the labor of his mother in bearing him, let the ravens of the brooks pick it out, and the young eagles eat it." *Prov.* xxx. 17. "He that striketh his father, or mother, shall be put to death;" "he that curseth them, shall die the death." *Exod.* xxi. 15 and 17.

Q. How do children sin against the love which they owe to their parents?

A. They sin against it, if they treat their parents with cold indifference, and give them no sign of sympathy or affection; if, on the contrary, they rather shew aversion for them, nay, wish in their hearts that evil may befall them, perhaps even death, in order to come the sooner into the possession of their fortune. The sin is still greater perhaps if they go so far as to express this in words, and grieve and afflict them by their ill conduct. Finally, and most grievous of all, if they really hate them in their hearts, and openly show this hatred by words and actions.

Q. How do children sin against the obedience which they owe to their parents?

A. They sin against it, if they do not fulfil what parents have the right of commanding them to do, either not at all or not as they ought; if they are obstinate and murmur against them, refuse to obey them, abuse, insult, or curse them, or even do the very opposite of what their parents have commanded them to do in matters relating to domestic order or to the duty of leading a Christian life; as, for instance, if parents forbid them to go out or to remain out at night, to frequent balls, taverns, and bad company, or if they bid them go to church or say their prayers at home.

God has already commanded in the Old Testament the most severe punishments to be inflicted upon those who sin against the obedience due to parents. We read thus: "If a man have a stubborn and unruly son, who will not hear the commandments of his father or mother, and being corrected, slighteth obedience, they shall take him and bring him to the ancients of his city, and to the gate of judgment, and shall say to them: "This our son is rebellious and stubborn; he slighteth hearing our admonitions; he giveth himself to revelling, and to debauchery and banquetings: the people of the city shall stone him; and he shall die, that you may take away the evil out of the midst of you, and all Israel hearing it may be afraid." *Deut.* xxi. 18–21.

Q. How do children sin in not supporting their parents?

A. They sin, if they abandon their parents in their temporal wants, or if they withhold the maintenance for which their parents expressly stipulated on yielding up their property to them; and they thus wrong them by becoming unfaithful to their promise; perhaps causing their parents thereby to suffer misery and hunger. In reference to the spiritual support which is due to parents, children sin, if they do not pray for them, and do not care for the welfare of their souls, should the parents be unhappy enough to lead a sinful life, or to walk in the way of heresy and unbelief; furthermore they sin, if they neglect to procure for their parents the assistance of the priest at the hour of death.

Q. What are children to expect who thus violate in a grievous manner the duties which they owe their parents?

A. They reap the curse of God, and also ignominy and disgrace in this world, and should they die impenitent, eternal damnation in the other.

"Cursed be he that honoreth not his father and mother; and all the people shall say: Amen." *Deuter.* xxvii. 16. "Remember thy father and they mother, ... lest God forget thee in their sight, and thou wish thou hadst not been born, and curse the day of thy nativity." *Eccles.* xxiii. 18–19.

Q. Does the fourth commandment refer to any other persons besides the natural parents?

A. Yes, it does; it refers also to those who hold the place of parents in regard to children; namely, to foster-parents and guardians; it has reference, moreover, to our spiritual and temporal superiors.

Q. Who are our spiritual Superiors?

A. The Pope as head of the Church, and the Bishops and Priests of the Church.

Q. What do the people owe them?

A. They owe them reverence, love and obedience. For they hold the place of Christ in our regard, and exercise the sacred ministry. St. Ignatius, the martyr, writes thus: "The priesthood is the highest dignity among men; he who dishonors it, dishonors God and our Lord Jesus Christ." *Ep. ad Smyrn.* And we read in the Old Testament: "With all thy soul fear the Lord, and reverence His priests." *Eccles.* vii. 31. But also: "He that will be proud, and refuse to obey the commandment of the priest . . . . that man shall die." *Deuter.* xvii. 12. Now, if this was true respecting the priests of the Old Law, how much the more must it hold good in the New Law, where the priests, whose right to due reverence and submission is violated, are in the place of Christ who said: "He that honoreth you, honoreth me, and he that despiseth you, despiseth me." Besides, the Priests of the Lord are our spiritual fathers in Christ, who lead us on in the way of salvation and are to render an account of our souls in the life to come. "Obey your prelates, and be subject to them. For they watch as being to render an account of your souls, that they may do this with joy, and not with grief." *Hebr.* xiii. 17.

Q. How does one sin against this reverence due to priests?

A. He sins by want of respect, of charity, and of obedience.

By *want of respect,* if he refuse to honor them with that mark of distinction outwardly due to them, or even dishonors them openly by jests and caricatures, songs, mockery, &c.

By *want of charity,* if he interprets their actions as evil, if he mentions their faults in public, without necessity, to the scandal of others, or exaggerates the same, even adding malicious and false insinuations.

By *want of obedience,* if he resist their just commands, and deprive them of succor and subsistence.

Q. What are the punishments of God in regard to those who despise and contemn the priests?

A. His punishments in their regard are temporal, spiritual and eternal. "Woe to them, for they have gone in the way of Cain, and have perished in the gainsaying of Core." *Jude,* 11. As Cain, therefore, became a fugitive and a vagabond, and Core, Datan, and Abiron were swallowed up by the earth, and went alive to hell, so it often happens that men who rise in revolt, are smitten by the avenging hand of the Lord. The curse that fell upon Cham, who mocked his father, awaits them in reference to the soul. Those very men who scorned the priests of the Lord during their life-time, are often deprived of their aid at the hour of death; and that even when they ardently desire their assistance.

Those, on the contrary, who zealously honor the priests of the Lord, love and assist them, not unfrequently enjoy particular blessings in this world, and obtain their aid when they are about to enter eternity.

Q. Who are they whom we call temporal superiors?

A. They are the civil rulers, masters and mistresses; for subjects are bound to show to the civil authorities reverence and obedience in all things that are not forbidden, and come under the direction of those authorities. "He that resisteth power, resisteth the ordinance of God." *Rom.* xiii. 2.

Subjects ought, therefore, to pray for their temporal superiors, render to them due respect, assist them, and pay conscientiously the lawful duties and taxes. In the same manner do servants and apprentices owe to their masters reverence and obedience in all obligatory things. "Servants, obey your masters." *Ephes.* vi. 5.

Q. How does one sin against those authorities?

A. One sins, if he despise them, speak ill of them, blame them unjustly, and refuse to comply with their lawful ordinations; but the more so, if he resist them and rise against them in revolt contrary to law and justice. The Apostle, speaking of those who revile those authorities, says: "These are murmurers, full of complaints, walking according to their own desires: and their mouth speaketh proud things, admiring persons for gain's sake. *Jude*, xvi.

Q. How does one sin against his masters?

A. By slighting them, and by not observing their regulations concerning the order of the house; further, by speaking ill of them in other families or elsewhere, by opposing their commands or obeying them with reluctance, &c.

Q. Are subjects allowed to execute the orders and regulations of their masters and rulers, even if they are unjust?

A. By no means; "for we must obey God before man." Servants sin, therefore, against this, if they assist their masters in their sinful plans, by helping them to wrong their neighbor, or by participating in their sins in any other way, particularly by message-bearing or rendering assistance in matters against the sixth commandment, and by wounding the reputation and violating the property of others.

Q. To whom besides has the fourth commandment reference?

A. To teachers, tutors, and old persons. For scholars are to show to their masters and tutors respect, love, and obedience, and reverence to old age.

Children sin against this commandment by irreverence, ridicule, and disobedience, and by insult, deriding or abusing persons who are old.

Q. Does the fourth commandment include any relative duties?

A. Yes, it includes the duties of parents, priests, superiors, and teachers towards children and subjects.

Q. Which are the duties of parents towards their children?

A. They are—love, support, correction, and education.

Regarding this love. God himself imprinted it in the hearts of the parents by the bond of natural affection. But, in Christian parents, this love should be still heightened and sanctified by motives of faith.

For children are souls, which God specially intrusted to them. Regarding the temporal support, parents are bound to nourish and sustain their children as long as they are under age and incapable of supporting themselves, and induce and keep them to labor, that they may become fit for maintaining themselves afterwards.

As to correction and education, parents should not only look to it, that their children learn and observe the rules of politeness in social intercourse, but also that they are brought up to be one day good and fit citizens; and by being well instructed in regard to morals and religion, rendered dutiful children of the Church and future heirs of heaven. " Fathers, ... bring your children up in the discipline and correction of the Lord." *St. Paul to the Ephes.* vi. 4.

Parents should, therefore, take the greatest care to have their children baptized as soon as possible; and they should afterwards offer them frequently to God, with an ardent and sincere desire of educating them in the manner most pleasing to his goodness; imitating the mother of St. Elzear. She took him in her hands as soon as he was born, and offered him to God, saying: " Grant, O Lord, to Thy servant the grace of bringing up this child in piety, according to Thy good will and pleasure. But should he one day prove disobedient to Thee, O then take him to thyself now that he is baptized." *Surius*, 3.

After baptism they should sign them frequently with the sign of the holy cross, and bless them with holy water morning and evening.

Then, as the children grow up, the parents should zealously endeavor to instill into their minds, from their very infancy, the spirit of piety and the fear of the Lord. Moreover, as soon as the children begin to speak, parents should teach them the most Holy Names of Jesus and Mary, and how to sign themselves with the sign of the holy cross.: following the example of the mother of St. Francis Borgia (as related by father Ribadeneira in his life of the Saint). Furthermore, parents should teach their children some short prayer, but particularly, how to say the Lord's Prayer, the Apostle's Creed, the Ten Commandments, the Commandments of the Church, and the Hail Mary. They should be, moreover, very solicitous that their children say, morning and evening, and also before and after meals, a short but devout prayer, and they should try to imbue them with a great horror of every shadow of sin and offence against God. If, however, they do sin, then, of course, parents are to correct them in earnest and even severely; but that the correction may prove salutary, they should say a short prayer together, both before and after the correction, to put the children in mind that they are punished not from anger, but from duty and necessity, and from the love of God and their salvation. "The child that is left to his own will bringeth his mother shame." *Prov.* xxix. 15. "Withhold not correction from a child: for if thou strike him with the rod, he shall not die; thou shalt beat him with the rod, and deliver his soul from hell." *Prov.* xxiii. 13, 14.

A beautiful example of such parental care is found in the Scriptures of the Old Testament in the book of Tobias, who said, "Hear, my son, the words of my mouth, and lay them as the foundation in thy heart. . . . All the days of thy life, have God in thy mind, and take heed thou never consent to sin, nor transgress the commandment of the Lord our God. . . . We lead indeed a poor life; but we shall have many good things if we fear God, and depart from all sin, and do that which is good." *Tob.* iv. 2, 6, 23.

As an example taken from the Lives of the Saints in the New Law, and particularly instructive in this regard, may be cited that of Blanche; she often said to her son, "My child, I would rather see you dead, than in the state of mortal sin." The fruit of this admonition, so often repeated, was the holy life of St. Louis, her son.

After children have reached the age for frequenting school, the parents should be careful to send them to good Catholic schools; and to make them attend regularly. They should co-operate with the exertions of the teachers by causing their children to prepare their lessons at home which they are to recite. They should prevent them from running about the streets in the company of bad and ill-mannered children, and see that the children do not spend their time in idleness or useless plays, or otherwise degenerate, but that they grow up in discipline, and good morals.

Besides, it is the strict duty of parents to watch that their children go to church on Sundays and all other days of obligation, and there behave themselves with piety and edification, assisting at the whole of the divine service, not leaving it when they please.

It is further the duty of parents to clothe their children decently, but not extravagantly, and so to regulate their exterior conduct towards them that they may be kind and gentle, but not too indulgent.

Moreover, when the time is approaching, for the children to make their first Communion, then should parents do all in their power to prepare them for it, so that being well prepared they may reap from it the greatest fruit for their souls. But still more are parents bound to see that their children afterwards frequent the holy sacraments of penance and of the altar, once a month, if possible, but with piety and devotion.

Furthermore, there comes a time when children are to chose a state of life. And it is then that parents should ask of God particular grace and light, to be able, by their counsels to direct and assist them in their choice; permitting them to continue their studies, or causing them to adopt some trade or profession, as they shall deem it fitting in the Lord. Should a youth feel himself called to the priesthood or to enter in a Religious order, then should parents by no means place obstacles in his way to hinder him from following such a vocation, but rather offer every possible means of assistance for obeying that call, deeming themselves happy, that the Lord favors their child so highly.

There still remains something to which parents are seriously to attend, namely, that as long as the children continue to reside in their house, they make it a point of the strictest duty not to allow them to be out at night, to frequent public ball-rooms, theatres, and taverns, or other dangerous or suspicious places. This relates especially to the acquaintances of their daughters. Parents should also make sure that their children attend to their religious duties, when away from home, and thus be saved from the shipwreck of their faith.

Parents, indeed, should love their children, and prove their love towards them, yet it should be no blind or merely carnal love they bear them, but one purified and rendered holy by the light of faith.

Finally, they should zealously endeavor to confirm by their own example what they teach their children, and see that they serve them in all things as an excellent model for imitation. They should take care, therefore, that they do not scandalize them by bad example, especially by cursing, drinking, anger, quarrelling, theft, or injustice. Alas! how few parents do their duty in this regard; nay, how many of them neglect it altogether, bringing thereby upon themselves the greatest responsibility before God.

Q. What do foster-parents owe to their foster-children?

A. The same obligations mentioned above, for they hold the place of the parents in their regard. The duties of priests towards their people and congregations are treated in moral theology.

Q. What do the civil authorities owe to their subjects?

A. Their duty towards their subjects is to discharge conscientiously the duties of their office, to promote the common welfare, as far as it is consistent with that power with which they are entrusted; they are to guard particularly against endangering the salvation of those over whom they rule, for the sake of filthy lucre, or to arrogate to themselves any undue power in spiritual things.

Q. What do lords and masters owe to their subjects?

A. They owe them love, solicitude, correction, justice, and good example. Against this all those lords and masters sin who treat their subjects and domestics harshly, who care not for the necessities of their servants when they fall sick, who do not correct them for their faults, nor cause them to attend to their religious duties; who unjustly withhold from them their wages, abuse them before others, and even scandalize them by their own bad example, particularly by cursing, immorality and intemperance.

" Masters, do to your servants that which is just and equal; knowing that also you have a master in heaven." *Coloss.* iv, 1. . . . " For if any man have not care of his own, and especially of those of his house, he hath denied the faith, and is worse than an infidel." *Tim.* v, 8.

Practice. Listen to your parents, pastors, teachers, masters, and superiors; esteem, love, honor, and obey them, lest the complaint of Scripture should be fulfilled in you : " Why have I hated instruction, and my heart consented not to reproof; and have not heard the voice of them that taught me, and have not inclined my ear to masters?" *Prov.* v, 12, 13, and thus the curse of the commandment, instead of its blessing falls upon you.

But if you are a father, a master, mistress or superior, you will watch carefully over your own children and all those who are intrusted to your care, and endeavor particularly to give a good example to all around you in the virtues of humility, meekness, wisdom, moderation, true love, and charity; doing this, you will neither be wanting in patience or fortitude, in order that you may be able to render an account to the Lord concerning the care and direction of the souls which you had in charge. Regarding parents in particular; if they have discharged their duty in educating their children well and faithfully, the blessing, " that thou mayest be long lived upon the land," promised to the children in the fourth commandment, shall also be theirs. For there is nothing which consoles and gladdens the heart of a parent more than good children; and by the joy and consolation they afford him, his life is even prolonged. On the contrary, there is nothing which grieves the heart of a parent more, and carries him sooner to the grave, than the sorrow and affliction which a degenerate child brings upon him.

THE FIFTH COMMANDMENT.

Q. What does this commandment enjoin, and what does it forbid?

A. It *enjoins* meekness, affability, kindness, clemency, beneficence, and forbearance; so that we are ready for God's sake to forget and forgive injuries, as we would that God should forgive us.

It *forbids* murder and every injury to our neighbors' health and life, also anger, hatred, animosity and ill-will, revenge, and all other uncharitable feelings against our neighbor: " Whoever shall shed man's blood, his blood shall be shed." *Gen.* ix. 6. " Whoever hateth his brother is a murderer." 1 *John*, iii. 15.

Q. When is it forbidden to kill one's neighbor?
A. As often as killing him is unjust.
Q. When is it allowable to kill one's neighbor?
A. 1. If lawful authority ordains it for the punishment of great crimes.
2. In a just war.
3. In self-defence, in order to save one's own life, or that of somebody else.

Q. Is it lawful to commit suicide?

A. Never; for suicide is a grievous sin against nature. Moreover, suicide is an offence against the Divine Majesty, which alone has power over life and death; the self-murderer voluntarily renders himself guilty of eternal damnation, and exposes his relatives to the greatest shame and affliction. The Church, therefore justly refuses Christian burial to the self-murderer, as a just punishment for his crime.

Q. Are we allowed to do any thing else that tends directly to the destruction of our life or health?

A. No; and this is the sin of all those who by debauchery, excess, and dissipation destroy their health.

Q. May we wish for death?

A. Not if we do it from impatience; but we may if it proceeds from a desire of being freed from the calamities of the world, and the dangers of our salvation, in order to be with God.

Q. Are we allowed to permit death, or injury to our health?

A. Certainly, if the higher duties of the love of God and our neighbor demand it. We have examples of this in the holy martyrs, who delivered themselves up to certain death often of their own accord.

Q. Is it lawful to fight a duel?

A. No; except by lawful command in time of war. But a duel, undertaken by one's own authority is always a grievous sin; for by it we expose both our antagonist and ourselves to the danger of death, and of incurring eternal damnation, and also to the penalty of excommunication.

Q. But is not one's honor a sufficient excuse?

A. By no means; for the duel has nothing to do with honor, on the contrary, by duelling a man rather loses his honor, since he shows himself in the light of one who loves revenge and cares not whether he makes himself and others unhappy in time and in eternity. But, should a man be unjustly attacked by another, he may then show his courage by defending himself manfully against his aggressor for this is *self-defence* and no duel; or he may warn the challenger, and tell him that, in the case of an attack, he shall know how to defend himself; and this is sufficient, even for a soldier, to save his honor and his reputation for courage.

Q. Is it allowed to be present at a duel, to act as second, etc.?

A. No; for all those who do so incur excommunication, because, by their aid and presence they directly confirm the duelists in their wicked undertaking, which is highly sinful.

Q. Who else sins against the fifth commandment?

A. All those who wish death or temporal injury to others, or inflict either upon them; particularly mothers who endanger the lives of their children before they are born, or expose the same to the danger of suffocation by having them sleep with them during the first months; and husbands who strike their wives while pregnant, thereby exposing the child to the danger of perishing without the sacrament of baptism.

Q. Is any thing else relating to morality forbidden by this commandment?

A. Yes; spiritual murder or the ruin of souls by scandal, namely, if any one by his word or example, excite others to, or cause them to fall into sin. To this class belong all those who, by ungodly discourse, obscene songs or jests, indecent dresses, bad books, immodest pictures or statues, etc., lead others into sin; and those who harbor in their houses thieves, drunkards, gamblers, and other wicked people; for carrying on wicked designs and sinful courses; and also those authorities and superiors who give bad example and permit scandal, though their duty requires them to prevent it. Finally, all those who make it their business to induce to sin by any means whatsoever.

Q. Is it a great sin to give scandal?

A. Certainly it is, and indeed one of the greatest, as is plain from the words of Christ, our supreme judge; he says, "He that shall scandalize one of these little ones that believe in me, it were better for him that a mill-stone were hanged about his neck, and that he were drowned in the depth of the sea." "Woe to the world because of scandals." And "woe to that man by whom the scandal cometh." *Matth.* xviii. 6, 7.

He that scandalizes another, deserves this curse: for he does in reality the work of the devil, who has been a tempter from the beginning, and robs the Lord of the souls who were bought by Him, at the price of His precious blood on the altar of the cross. "He (the devil) was a murderer from the beginning." *St. John*, viii. 44. "Destroy not him (thy brother) with thy meat, for whom Christ died." *Rom.* xiv. 15.

He that gives scandal commits in one such sin innumerable others, because by it he becomes the cause of a multitude of sins in his fellow-men, perhaps even till the end of time; for he first sowed the seed of evil in them, who, after having been seduced themselves, again seduce others, who then continue to give scandal and to corrupt others, even after he himself has been converted, and perhaps long after he has been carried to the grave.

Surely, he that reflects upon this must feel himself strongly moved by these admonitions, to exercise the utmost vigilance in avoiding scandal, that he may not charge himself with so great a responsibility, and be the cause that a soul may, perhaps, curse him for all eternity, and accuse him, on the day of judgment, before his God and Judge.

Q. What must we do, if we have injured our neighbor in body or soul?

A. We must be sorry for our sin and confess it, and make compensation for the evil we have done to him, as far as we are able.

Practice. Avoid carefully inflicting injury, causing grief, or giving offence to your neighbor, but especially giving scandal, that you may never become guilty of killing the soul of your brother by any sinful word or deed. Resist every tempter with courage, without any regard to who he may be, and defeat his efforts with the full determination rather to die than to yield to his wicked designs.

Sixth Commandment.

Q. What is ordained and what forbidden by this commandment?

A. This commandment *ordains* that married people should be mutually faithful, and bids be chaste in body and mind, by preserving the purity of heart which becomes their state. It *forbids* adultery, and every inordinate, sensual, and impure lust in thought, word, desire, or action.

Q. Why does this commandment expressly and above all forbid adultery?

A. Because the ten commandments specially inculcate the law of justice towards our neighbor; and adultery is at the same time a sin of injustice.

Q. Is adultery a grievous sin?

A. Certainly; for the adulterer profanes the sacrament of

matrimony most shamefully, he wounds the heart of the husband most deeply, gives often the most frightful scandal, and causes the most dreadful consequences for entire families.

How abominable this crime is in the sight of God, also appears from the severe penalties and curses pronounced against it in Holy Scripture. In the Old Law, this crime was to be punished with death. All the people were to stone the criminal. The New Law threatens the adulterer with eternal death and damnation. "Adulterers shall not possess the kingdom of God." 1 *Cor.* vi. 9.

Even the ancient pagans decreed the most sensible and most shameful punishments against adultery; as, for instance, the Egyptians, the Romans, and the ancient Germans.

Q. Is any thing else forbidden by this commandment?

A. All occasions that lead to sins of this kind, as, inconsiderate curiosity of the eyes; frivolous words and songs; scandalous jests, dances, comedies; idleness; intemperance; the reading of bad books; a too familiar intercourse with persons of the other sex, particularly being alone with them without necessity.

"But . . . *all uncleanness* . . . let it not so much as be named among you, as it becometh saints, nor obscenity, nor foolish talking, nor scurrility, which is to no purpose." *Ephes.* v. 3, 4.

Should you doubt whether this or that be a sin against the virtue of purity, ask the counsel and instruction of your confessor.

Practice. "Oh how beautiful is the chaste generation with glory! for the memory thereof is immortal, because it is known both with God and with man. . . . It triumpheth crowned for ever, winning the reward of undefiled conflicts." *Wisd.* iv. 1, 2.

Yes! "Blessed are the clean of heart." *St. Matth.* v. 8.

On the contrary how unhappy are they who have fallen by the opposite vice into the power of the devil, and become the slaves to the lusts of the flesh. The very contrary may be said here: "O how abominable is the unchaste generation with reproach, the memory thereof is death, infamy and shame before God and before men. Everlasting fire will chastise their bodies and souls; they shall be tormented according to the measure they have filled with iniquity." "As much as she hath been in delicacies, so much torment and sorrow give unto her." *Apoc.* xviii. 17. May God guard you against the least shadow of this vice, especially against any violation of conjugal fidelity. In conclusion: fly and resist the first appearance of any temptation against this heavenly virtue; resist not in part, but wholly.

THE SEVENTH COMMANDMENT.

Q. What does this commandment *enjoin* what does it *forbid?*

A. It *enjoins* and requires that we observe equity and justice in buying and selling, and to promote our neighbor's advantage on every occasion.

It *forbids* stealing, fraud, usury, and every other unjust violation of the rights and property of our neighbor.

How much these sins are opposed to Christian charity, appears from the saying of the Apostle: "Thieves shall not possess the kingdom of God." 1 *Cor.* vi.

Q. Who sins by stealing?

A. He who secretly appropriates the property of his neighbor against his will. He who does so in the presence of the owner by violence, commits robbery.

Q. Who sins by fraud?

A. He who defrauds his neighbor in trade and business, in buying and selling, namely, if he sells him spoiled goods, gives him false weight or measure, or false money; if he takes unjust pay for his labor, or does not labor in accordance with the contract he has made; if he counterfeits documents, or bribes judges, that they may decide a lawsuit in his favor to the prejudice of his neighbor.

Q. Who sins by usury?

A. He who takes a higher percentage than is permitted by law; who hoards up or monopolizes grain or goods, in order to raise the price; in general, he who abuses the want and ignorance of his neighbor to his neighbor's loss and his own profit.

Q. Who else sins against the seventh commandment by causing damage?

A. The functionaries of the state who use for their own advantage the public revenues of the commonwealth. All those who carry on unjust lawsuits; and all attornies or lawyers who knowingly sustain such suits.

Judges who decide a cause against justice and law; parents who unjustly prefer and favor *one* child before the others, and bestow upon him a portion to the detriment of their other children.

Children, who after receiving the patrimony of their parents, do not support them, in as far as they are bound in duty, or who do not fulfil the last will of their parents, defrauding thereby their brothers and sisters.

Servants who distribute or give away food or other articles belonging to the house, without the will or consent of their masters and mistresses.

Merchants who declare themselves insolvent or unable to pay, and thereby take the money or property of others secretly to themselves, and apply it to their own use.

Mechanics, who do their work badly, so that it will not last any time. Also those who slander and calumniate other mechanics, for the purpose of drawing to themselves a greater run of custom.

Neighbors who move the landmarks on their fields so as to make them larger. Millers and tradesmen generally who retain part of the goods belonging to others. Counterfeiters of coin who make false money.

All those who damage trees on another's premises, or cause any other damage in forests. Persons who do not pay tithe, if custom require it of them, or, who do not comply with the obligation contracted by them towards the Church. To these, especially in America, belong those, who, without paying their pew-rent leave the congregation, and consequently defraud it.

Smugglers, who make it their particular business to smuggle goods into the country against the express prohibition of the civil authority. Grant, if you will, that such persons do not always sin against justice, yet the nature of their occupation is such that it exposes them to frequent occasions of sin by fraud and lying, and becomes thus more or less dishonest.

Debtors, who neglect to pay their debts.

All persons who buy stolen goods, or take them into their keeping, or assist thieves in their evil courses.

Finally, all those who keep articles which they have found, after finding out the owner.

Q. Which is the principal cause that seduces men into those violations of another's property?

A. 1. The evil inclinations of the heart, which tempt many from their very youth to commit theft and fraud. Experience furnishes the most remarkable proof of this.

2. The bad example of others. St. Austin relates of himself that he, in his youth, was induced by bad example to steal. *S. Augustinus, l.* 2. *confess. c.* viii.

3. Bad company united to licentious and unbridled conduct. They lead young persons into the occasion of gambling, dancing, and company that makes them lose their money, and subsequently induces them to steal, in order to keep up their wicked courses.

4. The ambitious desire of leading a life above their rank and means. Parents should, therefore, as soon as they discover in their children an inclination to stealing, use their utmost endeavors, to eradicate, immediately, such an ungodly propensity, by severe chastisement, and leave nothing undone to withdraw their children from bad company, and to induce them to live a simple and frugal life, as regards their food, dwelling, dress, and other necessaries of life. But, alas! many parents do not act thus; and there are even some who, by their words and examples positively induce their children to steal and to carry home what they have stolen. Such parents, however, receive in return, often even in this life, the curse of their children, and carry it with them to the grave, because God frequently permits that sins of the kind against justice, are punished and chastised, even in this world, according to their just desert. Parents who are so forgetful of their duty, should call to mind the fact related by St. Bernardine of Sienna, of a youth, who, when being led to the gallows, called for his father to embrace him, as it was thought, for the last time. However, it was not so; instead of that, he bit a piece out of his father's cheek, to thank him for the fatal indulgence he had shown him in regard to the thefts committed in his early youth, saying, "Your cruel indulgence has brought me to the gallows, from which your chastisement might have saved me."

Q. What are they bound to do who sin against the seventh commandment?

A. They are bound to make restitution. "Without restitution," says St. Augustine, "the sin is not forgiven." Alas! but few seem to think of this in good earnest, nay, many, on the contrary make even a bad confession, because they neglect this duty, and God alone knows how many are, on that account, eternally lost.

Q. Who is to make restitution?

A. In the first place, he who caused the damage mediately or immediately, or who possesses the unjustly acquired goods or their value. Secondly: should that person not repair the damage, then they are bound to do it, who participated in the sin by counsel or deed, or they who did not prevent the damage, if they could do so, and were bound to do so by contract or duty.

Q. To whom must restitution be made?

A. To the owner or his heirs; and should this be impossible, it must be made to the poor, or for other pious purposes.

Q. How much must be restored?

A. If a man has wilfully and unjustly taken possession of another's property, then he must repair all the damage arising therefrom to the owner. But if the damage was done without his knowledge and consent, then he must restore as much of the ill-gotten goods as there is yet remaining, and as much as he has injured the other in his gains, to this he is, however, only bound, if he has grown richer by possessing the ill-gotten goods. But in both cases restitution is made with deduction of the expenses which the owner would have to incur himself.

Q. When must restitution be made?

A. Without delay.

Q. But what is he to do who is not able to make restitution?

A. He must have the sincere desire of making it, as soon as possible, and must endeavor to render himself capable of complying with this duty. But in order to do this, he should ask and follow the counsel and decision of an enlightened confessor, and not constitute himself his own judge, so that he may act more safely and prudently.

Q. What is one to do, if he find things belonging to another person?

A. He must take care that the owner may learn where he can recover that which he has lost. Should this not be done, and it be afterwards unknown who is the owner, then the thing found or the value of it is to be given to the poor, or to be employed in other pious purposes. But should one have been unable to find the owner, in that case he can keep the thing found for himself.

He that finds a treasure, is to observe the same rule, unless the laws of the country determine otherwise.

Q. What kind of theft is most detestable?

A. That of sacrilege, namely, if one steals things dedicated to God, and things that are holy, or any thing else out of a holy place.

Q. For what reasons should we particularly abstain from any theft or injury of another's property?

A. *First:* on account of the constant gnawing of conscience, by which theft is followed. *Second:* on account of the necessity of restoring every thing that we steal, if we ever intend to obtain pardon from God. Why therefore should we steal, if in any case, we are to restore? *Third:* on account of the certainty of death, which will so soon take every thing away from us. *Fourthly:* on account of the consequences attending theft in eternity, either in purgatory or, perhaps, even in hell.

Practise. Be honest even in the smallest thing, and never take the least thing which does not belong to you. Be content with what you have; you do not live for the sake of this world; remember that you remain here below but for a short time. Guard yourself against idleness, intemperance, gaming for money; against pride and vanity, and love of pleasure; for all these things induce to fraud, theft and injustice. But if you have been so unfortunate as to injure your neighbor in his property, then do all you can to repair the injustice without delay; or else penance will be in vain, and the salvation of your soul in the greatest danger.

The Eighth Commandment.

Q. What are we commanded to do, and what forbidden by this commandment?

A. We are *commanded* to speak well of our neighbor, and to defend his honor as far as we can.

We are *forbidden* to injure our neighbor's honor by false witness, backbiting, calumny, slander, detraction, rash judgment, suspicion, tale-bearing, and disgracing our neighbor; finally we are forbidden to tell lies, to be hypocrites or pretended saints.

Q. What do you mean by false witness?

A. False witness is, " saying something against any one that is not true, especially in a court of justice, or concealing intentionally what is true, to the injury of the person whom it concerns.

False witness is generally a great sin against God, against our neighbors, and against human society, the welfare of which is universally endangered by false witness.

Q. What is it that generally induces men to bear false witness?

A. 1. Money, if one suffers himself to be bribed by others.

2. Any other advantage.
3. The inordinate love of one's relations and friends.
4. Aversion and hatred against others.
5. Human respect.

It often happens that God punishes false witness by special chastisement even in this world, particularly if it be combined with false oaths.

Q. What is calumny?

A. Calumny is imputing faults to others of which they are not guilty, and divulging them as if they were true. "If a serpent bite in silence, he is nothing better that backbiteth secretly." *Eccls.* x. 11.

Calumny is, therefore, a sin either mortal or venial, according as the good name of our neighbor is thereby wounded more or less grievously.

To determine the grievousness of the sin in a particular case we must not only regard the thing which was spoken, but also the person of whom it was said, since the character of a person may render the injury done to his honor the greater. For it is a greater sin to calumniate a priest and a superior, than if persons less esteemed and of less influence are calumniated.

Moreover, the sin is the greater the greater the injury is which flows from the calumny; the greater the number of persons injured by it, and the more malicious the intention with which it was uttered.

The same is said of detraction.

Q. What is detraction?

A. Detraction is publishing the actual faults of others, when one has no right to do so. "The detractor is the abomination of men." *Prov.* xxiv. 9. "Detractors are hateful to God." *Rom.* i. 30.

The reason is that the detractor wounds charity in its most tender part, since he injures the good name of a man, which, according to Holy Scripture, is far above the value of any other thing that can be possessed. "A good name is better than great riches; as good favor is above silver and gold." *Prov.* xxii. 1.

The detractor, moreover, becomes often the cause of numerous quarrels, enmities and great scandals.

Q. When is it lawful to speak of the faults of our neighbor?

A. 1. When the object is to correct our neighbor.
2. To warn others.
3. To protect or defend one's self.

Q. Is it a sin to listen to a calumny, or detraction?

A. Yes; 1. If by listening or by speaking to the detractor we encourage him in his detraction or calumny.

2. If we inwardly rejoice that the good name of our neighbor is attacked, even though we should not have given rise to the detraction or calumny. "It is difficult," says St. Bernard, "to decide which is more damnable, to listen to the detraction or to the detractor." *Lib.* 2. *de Consid.*

Q. What should we, therefore do if we hear that the good name of our neighbor is injured?

A. 1. We should interrupt the detractor, or if we have any authority over him we should tell him to be silent.

2. If we have no authority over him, we should then manifest our displeasure at such discourse by a severe look, by sudden silence, or any other exterior sign, and endeavor, if possible, to turn the conversation to something else, or otherwise to excuse the fault as much as possible; in a word, we should observe how dangerous it is to believe what people say when it concerns the faults of our neighbor; or if we cannot stop the evil conversation, we should go away.

"Hedge in thy ears with thorns; hear not a wicked tongue." *Eccles.* xxviii. 28.

"The north wind driveth away rain, as doth a sad countenance a backbiting tongue." *Prov.* xxv. 23.

Q. What is he bound to do who has injured his neighbor's reputation?

A. He must restore the reputation of his neighbor. Surely if one is bound to repair the damage which he does to his neighbor in his material property, he is much more bound to do so, when he has injured a much greater good, namely, the good name of his neighbor.

Should the neighbor sustain temporal damage from the injury done to his good name, he that caused it must repair the damage.

Q. How is one to restore his neighbor's good name?

A. If he did calumniate his neighbor, he must recall the calumny, and justify his neighbor in the opinion of all those who listened to the calumny.

But if he merely detracted the person, *i. e.*, spoken of actual but as yet unknown faults, then he is to remove the impression he made on others, as far as he possibly can, by excusing his neighbor, bestowing praise which he otherwise merited, &c. And he must take care to do this to every one who heard the detraction. He who seriously reflects on this great duty of recalling the detraction, will certainly guard himself against committing this sin; for, to restore the good name of which a person was robbed, is found to be attended with the greatest difficulty, so much so, indeed, as to make one feel that it is hardly ever done. And yet how many sin with the greatest levity by the vice of detraction, from childhood even to old age. Children who speak ill of their parents and teachers, and school-fellows, and calumniate them; servants who slander their masters, and masters their servants, one tradesman the other, subjects their spiritual and temporal superiors, and the latter their subjects: all these sin against this commandment.

Add to this the detractions caused by the impulse of so many vehement passions, such as aversion, hatred, envy, anger, vengeance, garrulity, and drunkenness.

And yet, how few are there, that think of restoring the good name, of which they robbed their neighbor!

Q. Are there any reasons that excuse us, in part, from restoring the good name of our neighbor?

A. Yes. 1. Impossibility; namely, if we cannot find out what influence the detraction has had.

2. The just fear that to mention again the reputation of the neighbor would, perhaps, expose it to new injury. In this case, we are partly excused, especially if the people already begin gradually to forget the detraction, or are inclined to be-

lieve the evil rather than the good, we are telling. Therefore, if no duty command us to speak, where a fault of our neighbor is concerned, then follow rather the counsel of the Wise Man: "Tell not thy mind to friend or foe, and if there be a sin with thee, disclose it not." *Eccles.* xix. 8.

Q. What is backbiting?

A. It is censuring the absent, by speaking of their known faults without necessity. This is often sinful, either because charity is wounded thereby, or because it is useless, and may yet give occasion to temptation or detraction. Truly, it is a beautiful sign of Christian charity and perfection, if one never sins against his neighbor by speaking ill of him. On the contrary, there is no vice, by which a pious soul is more easily cast into grievous sin, than that of an unbridled tongue, if the character of his neighbor is at stake.

Q. When do we sin by rash judgment?

A. When, without sufficient reason, we form within ourselves the opinion that another has committed this or that sin.

Q. Is judging rashly sometimes a grievous sin?

A. Yes; if, for very light reasons, we form a certain opinion that our neighbor has committed a mortal sin, especially if he be otherwise a very virtuous person.

Q. When is judging thus rashly more particularly to be condemned?

A. When one goes so far as rashly to pronounce another's intention as bad, where he cannot condemn the action. This shows a great want of charity.

Q. Why should we avoid this sin more particularly?

A. Because it is so often committed, and so diametrically opposite to the love of our neighbor; and because Christ our Lord solemnly forbids us to judge others, promising, on the contrary, a propitious sentence to him who keeps himself free from this vice: "Judge not, that you may not be judged." *Math.* vii. 1. Finally, because we are very easily deceived in judging of our neighbor by exterior signs, for although they seem to be certain, they may be so only in appearance.

Think of Joseph and Susanna. Would you not have supposed, that perhaps Joseph did render himself guilty of the crime of which his wicked mistress accused him, if you had seen the cloak in her hands, which she showed to her husband Putiphar, in proof of her criminal accusation? And yet he was innocent, and so was Susanna, though she was accused by two of the most respected judges of the people. St. John the Baptist and our Lord himself were falsely judged, and this too by the scribes and doctors of the law. The lives of the saints prove the same thing. How many of them were unjustly and falsely condemned, and very often this was not known until after their death. Therefore, let us not judge, but leave the judgment to Him who searches the heart—God!

Q. How does it happen that men are so prone to judge rashly?

A. 1. On account of man's natural propensity to evil, and the consciousness of the real malice and faultiness. "Yea and the fool when he walketh in the way, whereas he himself is a fool, esteemeth all men fools." *Eccles.* x. 3.

2. On account of hatred and envy. For he who sincerely loves any one, interprets the actions of the same favorably, whereas he who dislikes another, or perhaps even hates him, censures every thing that person may do.

3. On account of pride, which is always pleased to see the neighbor humbled.

Q. How may we cure our proneness to judging rashly?

A. The first means is an humble acknowledgment of our own baseness. "He that is without sin among you," says Christ, "first cast a stone at her." *St. John,* viii. 7. And St. Ambrose: "Let him judge the fault of his neighbor, who has not in his own heart what he should condemn." *S. Ambr. super. Ps.* cx. The ancient poets sang of a woman, called Lamia, who, as often as she went out put in her eyes, but kept them locked up at home, and was there of course blind. Those who judge others, act in a similar way, they use their eyes to see and judge the faults of others, but are blind as to their own. "Why seest thou a mote in thy brother's eye, and seest not a beam in thy own eye? Thou hypocrite, cast out first the beam out of thy own eye, and then shalt thou see to cast out the mote out of thy brother's eye." *St. Matth.* vii. 3–5.

The second means is to remember often the words of Christ: "Judge not, that you may not be judged. For with what judgment you have judged, you shall be judged." *St. Matth.* vii. 1, 2. And the great merit of charity is, that it covers a multitude of sins.

The third is to call to mind the examples of the saints, especially that of St. Augustine, St. Bernard, and St. Ignatius, who are such bright examples in the practice of this virtue, and who exhort us so earnestly to imitation.

Q. What do you mean by false suspicion?

A. We have false suspicion if without a sufficient reason we suspect something bad of our neighbor, but yet are not firmly settled in our opinion. This sin is ordinarily venial; but it leads to rash judgment, and hence all that we have said above regarding rash judgment, is also, in a certain manner, true of false suspicion, though in a less degree.

Q. What is tale-bearing?

A. Tale-bearing is telling without necessity to another, what this or that one has said of him, the ordinary consequence of which is enmity and hatred. "The whisperer and the double-tongued is accursed: for he has troubled many that were at peace." *Eccles.* xxviii. 15. And again: "Six things there are which the Lord hateth, and the seventh his soul detesteth —him that soweth discord among brethren." *Prov.* vi. 16.; vii. 19.

Q. How do we sin by disgracing our neighbor?

A. By rendering our neighbor contemptible, by means of exterior signs, such as derision, sneers, cursing, or by caricatures and unjust libels. How grievous and dangerous this sin frequently is, appears from the threats of Christ: "Whoever shall say, Thou fool, shall be guilty of hell fire." *St. Math.* 5. 22. "The stroke of a whip maketh a blue mark: but the stroke of the tongue will break the bones." *Eccles.* xxviii. 21.

Q. What is a lie?

A. A lie is a falsehood told intentionally to deceive another. There are four kinds of lies:

1. The ordinary lie, if one knowingly tells a falsehood without any further intention.

2. The pernicious lie, if one tells a lie in order to injure another.

3. The jocose lie, if one tells a falsehood in jest.

4. The officious lie, *i. e.*, if one tells a lie in order to avert from himself or another any evil.

Q. Is it allowed to tell a lie?

A. No; for we are never allowed to do any thing repugnant to the perfections of God; and God is essentially true.

Q. Who is the author of lies?

A. The devil. Holy Scripture calls him, "a liar and the

father thereof." *John,* viii. 44. In heaven he seduced the angels, so that they fell off from God, and in paradise he seduced Eve by his false promise: "No, you shall not die the death, you shall be as gods." *Gen.* iii. 4. St. Ambrose therefore says justly: "Brethren, take heed against lies, for all that lie, are children of the devil, not by their pedigree, but their crime."

Q. Are we always bound to tell every one the truth?

A. No; we may also remain silent, or conceal the truth by a fitting answer, but without a lie; this is allowable if an evil might follow, in case our neighbor should come to learn the truth.

Q. Is there any other way of lying than by words?

A. Yes; by hypocrisy and dissimulation, namely, if from a desire of pleasing others, we try to appear better and more pious, than we really are. "Woe to you, scribes and pharisees, hypocrites; because you are like whited sepulchres, which outwardly appear to men beautiful, but within are full of dead men's bones, and of all filthiness. So you also outwardly indeed appear to men just, but within you are full of hypocrisy and iniquity." *St. Matth.* xxiii. 27, 28.

Q. Is it a duty to take care of one's good name?

A. Yes; we are to do so by leading a pious and righteous life, and by avoiding even the shadow of evil, according to the admonition of the Apostle: "From all appearance of evil refrain yourselves." 1 *Thess.* v. 22. The reason is the obligation of giving a good example, and the preservation of the necessary authority and influence for the welfare and salvation of our neighbor. "Let your light so shine before men, that they may see your good works, and glorify your Father who is in heaven." *St. Matth.* v. 16. And St. Bernard says: "You owe your good conscience to God, but your good name to your neighbor."

Q. What are we to do if our good name is attacked by calumny?

A. We should defend it in humility and with moderation, if the honor of God and our souls' salvation require it so, but if not, then should we bear it in silence after the example of Christ, and suffer the persecution patiently.

"For we foresee what may be good not only before God, but also before men." *Cor.* viii. 21.

But also: "If you be reproached for the name of Christ, you shall be happy." 1 *Pet.* iv. 14.

Practice. Love the truth, speak the truth; hate, abhor, fly from falsehood; to lie is the mark of the children of satan, for he was a liar from the beginning. Guard, too, against exaggeration and avoid vehement speech. Above all, never speak uncharitably of others, or of their faults, save when necessity requires it: but love to speak of their virtues; be rather silent concerning thyself, true humility and modesty being therein thy guides.

The Ninth and Tenth Commandments.

Q. What is ordained by these two commandments?

A. Sincerity of heart and benevolence towards all, so that we wish others well from the bottom of our hearts.

Q. What is forbidden by these two commandments?

A. Every unlawful *desire* after other persons or the property of other persons.

Q. Why are we even forbidden to covet the property of another?

A. 1. Because it is inordinate and unjust to desire what we cannot lawfully possess.

2. Because such desires include within themselves the seed of and the impulse to unjust actions.

"The lust thereof shall be under thee, and thou shalt have dominion over it," were the words of God to Cain, who was the first that sinned in this manner. *Gen.* iv. 7.

Q. Do we sin by the mere thoughts, without the desire of executing them?

A. Certainly we do, if we dwell upon them deliberately, for the reason just stated above. Such thoughts have reference to something bad, and are apt to excite in us unlawful desires.

Q. What are we to do, if evil thoughts and desires insinuate themselves into our heart against our will?

A. We are not to lose courage, nor grow faint-hearted, but we are to resist their attacks with constancy, and from the beginning; the tempter will fly, and the victory gained will bring us each time a new reward. Blessed is the man that endureth temptation; for when he hath been proved, he shall receive the crown of life, which God hath promised to those who love him. *St. James*, i. 12.

Practice.—Suffer not thyself to be vexed by the temptations of evil desires. Resist them at the beginning and entirely, and endeavor to fill your heart rather with a great desire for the fulfilment of the law as it is described by the Apostle. Charity is patient, is kind; charity envieth not, dealeth not perversely, is not puffed up, is not ambitious, seeketh not her own, is not provoked to anger, thinketh no evil, rejoiceth not in iniquity, but rejoiceth with the truth, beareth all things, believeth all things, hopeth all things, endureth all things; charity never faileth." 1 *Cor.* xiii. 4–8. Examine yourself often upon these marks of the true love of God and your neighbor. If this love be within you, envy and ill-will will have no place in your heart; you will fulfil the commandments of the Lord with ease, and live in and with God, who is a God of love and charity.

On the Commandments of the Church.

Q. Are Christians bound to observe any other commandments besides the ten commandments of God?

A. Certainly; the commandments of the Church.

Q. From whom has the Church received power to give us commandments?

A. From our Lord Jesus Christ, the founder of the Church, who said to his Apostles in explicit terms: "As the Father hath sent me, I also send you." "He that heareth you, heareth me." "Whatsoever ye shall bind upon earth, shall be bound in heaven." *St. Luke* x. 16; *St. Matthew* xviii. 18. And: "If he will not hear the Church, let him be to thee as the heathen and publican." *St. Matth.* xviii. 17. Read how St. Chrysostom, Theophilus, and Euthymius, interpret those words of St. Matthew in his 18th chap. Listen also to the words of St. Paul: "And he went through Syria," says he, "and Cilicia, confirming the churches; commanding them to keep the precepts of the Apostles and the ancients." *Acts*, xv. 41.

Q. Are we, therefore, to regard the commandments of the Church as mere commandments of men?

A. No; but as commandments of the Lord himself, who,

through His Church, with which He always is, guides and rules the faithful; by His authority and commission the Church commands us.

Q. Why does the Church give such commandments and make such regulations?

A. To guide us in leading Christian lives.

Q. How many commandments of the Church are there that are binding on all the faithful?

A. There are five; namely,

1. Thou shalt keep the holydays or feasts instituted by the Church.

2. Thou shalt hear Mass with due devotion on Sundays and holydays of obligation.

3. Advent, Lent, Ember-days, and vigils, thou shalt fast. On Fridays, also, flesh thou shalt not eat.

4. Confess your sins at least once a year, to your pastor, or another priest duly authorized, and receive the Blessed Sacrament at Easter-time.

5. Thou shalt not solemnize marriage at certain prohibited times.

Regarding the faithful in America, where the Church of God is not sufficiently provided as yet with temporal property, the bishops deem it necessary to admonish them by a general precept, of the duty of assisting the Church and her ministers as far as possible. The first Christians did so of their own accord; but this duty rests, according to St. Paul, on the example in the Old Testament, and on the ordinance of God, that "they that serve the altar, partake with the altar;" and, "they who preach the gospel should live by the gospel." 1 *Cor.* ix. 13–14.

The First Commandment of the Church.

Q. What does this commandment ordain?

A. That we must keep the holydays, and sanctify them, particularly by the practice of Christian piety.

Q. What does this commandment forbid?

A. All servile work, and especially that by which the festival devotion is disturbed and prevented, or perhaps even derided and profaned.

Q. Why did the Church institute the feasts of our Lord?

A. In order that we might more certainly, and in a livelier manner, remember the life, sufferings and death of our Lord and Saviour, so that, meditating upon them, we may render our lives true copies of His. With this intention, the Church instituted the holy time of Advent, in order to fill our hearts with the longing desire of our fathers in the faith, and to prepare us for the coming of the Lord by the solemnity of His gracious birth. Next, the Church celebrates the commemoration of the childhood and youth of the Lord, His public ministry, His passion and death. We are put in mind of this by the holy season of Lent, which is followed by the solemnities of Easter, Ascension Day, Pentecost or Whit-Sunday, and Trinity Sunday. The feast of Corpus Christi and the remaining Sundays are to remind and exhort us, how we have to live in and through Jesus Christ, to the end, that, together with all the saints, we may celebrate the feast of the most Holy Trinity for ever in heaven.

Q. Why did the Church institute the feasts of the Blessed Virgin Mary and the other saints?

A. 1. That we might praise God for the graces which He bestowed upon them, and for the wonderful works which He wrought through them.

2. That we might the more vividly remember their example and their present glorification, and recommend ourselves the more earnestly to their intercession, that by following them upon earth, we might be united with them for ever as children of the Church triumphant in heaven.

Q. Has the Church also the power of retrenching or limiting the number of those festival days?

A. Certainly; she can do this in the same power and in the same spirit in which she instituted them; that is, if she deems it conducive to the honor of God and profitable to our salvation. For the doctrine of the Church is certainly at all times the same; but it is different with regard to the institutions and ordinances which she has made, in the course of ages, for the welfare and salvation of the faithful: in those things she is to take into account the difference of times and places.

The Church considers what is the most salutary in this respect, and makes her regulations accordingly.

Q. By what means, therefore, do we sanctify the Sundays and holydays, particularly in the spirit of the Church?

A. 1. By beginning the day with prayer and thanksgiving according to the spirit of the particular festival.

2. By assisting at the holy sacrifice of the Mass with devout attention.

3. By a good confession and a worthy communion received with due preparation, and followed by thanksgiving; remembering the mystery of the day, and ardently desiring to participate in the graces which God is ready to bestow. This is the particular way in which the first Christians sanctified the festivals of the Church; every one of them approached the holy table, having previously prepared himself with all possible care.

4. By listening attentively to the word of God when explained, the announcement of which in memory of the mysteries of grace, places it the more vividly and efficaciously before the eyes of the faithful, warms their heart and strengthens their will.

5. By assisting at divine service in the afternoon and evening, and by practicing such other exercises of devotion, as we shall deem most fit to raise our minds to God in praise, devotion, and heartfelt prayer. We should recite the acts of faith, hope, and charity, on those days, with particular energy and internal affection.

6. By pious discourses, mutually exhorting each other to good actions; by works of mercy and charity towards our neighbor, and by reading good books. Thus the day is rendered a day of rest in the Lord. Alas! that so many are anting in this respect, nay, but too often commit more sins n those days than any other.

Q. How does one sin, therefore, against the sanctification of Sundays and holydays?

A. 1. By servile work. But if such a work will not admit of delay, then we should impose upon ourselves the task of performing another good work instead thereof, and give special alms for some pious intention.

2. By publicly buying and selling, particularly during the time allotted to the public service of God.

3. By idleness, or by gaming, dancing, drinking, and keeping bad company. "I would rather, that young men should plough, and young women spin, than that they should be gaming and dancing." *St. Augustine*, lib. de 10 cord.

4. By noisy, disorderly hunting parties, particularly if they induce neglect of the service of God.

Practice.—Consider once more the exercises of virtue already recommended to you under the third commandment of God. What was there said of the sanctification of the Sunday, holds good, also, of the festival days. But study, moreover, to live, during the whole year, according to the spirit of the Church, and use every opportunity of preparing yourself worthily for these festivals, according to the circumstances of times and place, and of celebrating them with due solemnity and great recollection of mind. Follow the counsel of the venerable Thomas à Kempis: to solemnize every festival so, as if you were celebrating it for the last time in your life. Were you to keep holy, in this manner, the time of Advent and Christmas, of Lent and Easter, Pentecost, and all the other feasts of our Lord, and of His blessed Mother, for only *one* year, O, how much would that one ecclesiastical year contribute to the sanctification of your life!

THE SECOND COMMANDMENT OF THE CHURCH.

Q. What does this commandment oblige us to do?
A. It obliges us to hear, with true devotion, an entire and complete Mass on Sundays and festival days of obligation.

Q. Why are we particularly commanded to hear Mass on Sundays and holydays?
A. Because the holy sacrifice of the Mass is the most important and the most sublime part of the service of God, it being the sacrifice of the new law, in which Jesus Christ is offered anew by the hands of the priest.

Q. Who is bound by this commandment to hear Mass?
A. Every Christian who has come to the full use of reason, (generally attained about the age of seven,) unless he may have reasons that excuse him, as for instance, sickness, necessary works of charity; or a very great distance from the church, particularly if the weather be bad, necessary care of the house, etc.

Q. Does this commandment bind under pain of mortal sin?
A. Certainly, it does.

Q. In what manner are we to hear Mass?
A. We are to hear it, 1st. with due devotion and atten-

tion. St. Chrysostom says: "As often as the holy Mass is celebrated, multitudes of holy Angels surround the altars of the Lord, and adore. *Lib. de Sacerd.* Men should bend their knees also, at least during the consecration.

2. Entirely. He who does not remain present at Mass from the beginning of the offertory till after the communion of the priest, if he can do so, sins mortally.

Q. How, therefore, does one sin against this commandment?

A. If without a sufficient reason he neglects Mass either entirely or in part. Further, if during the holy sacrifice of the Mass he indulges in willful distractions, talk, sleep, laugh, gaze about, or behave irreverently in any other way, and thus disturb his own and others' devotion.

Q. Is it useful and salutary to hear Mass also on week days?

A. Very useful and salutary indeed; for, 1st. he who assists devoutly at the holy sacrifice of the Mass, participates in a multitude of divine favors, since it is the sacrifice in which Jesus Christ offers himself, supplicating His heavenly Father for us, rendering us thereby, in a particular manner, participants in the fruits of the redemption of mankind effected by His death on the cross.

2. Because by hearing Mass the temporal punishments of sin are remitted, and we obtain many graces which protect us, in the temptations of the day, against falling into sin.

3. Because, as the Council of Trent teaches us, and experience proves, "God also grants, by the holy sacrifice of the Mass, his blessing and help to us in our temporal affairs and and necessities." *Conc. Trid.*, Sess. xxii.

Q. Are we also obliged to hear the sermon and the explanation of the Christian doctrine on Sundays and festivals?

A. Certainly; if not by the letter, at least by the spirit of this commandment, and also for other reasons. For the Church desires that we should assist at the entire service of God. But since in the early times of Christianity the sermon was given immediately after the Gospel, (as it is still in some places,) the Church had no need of binding the faithful by a special command to hear the sermon.

Further, the Church desires that we be well instructed and zealous Christians, who know what they are to believe and to do, and who do it for their own sanctification and mutual edification. To this end, the hearing of the word of God, an nounced in a sermon, greatly contributes. Moreover, by neglecting to hear the word of God, we may very possibly scandalize our neighbor and induce him to commit the same neglect. "He that is of God," says Jesus Christ, "heareth the words of God. Therefore, you hear them not, because you are not of God." *St. John*, viii. 47.

Q. How are we to hear the word of God?

A. With attention and respect, without distraction or dissipation of mind, desiring ardently to understand the same, and to receive the light of the Holy Ghost into our hearts. "Blessed are they who hear the word of God, and keep it." *St. Luke*, xi. 38.

Q. Who is particularly bound to assist at the sermon, and still more to listen to the explanation of the Christian doctrine?

A. He who is not as yet perfectly instructed in the principles of faith and morals, or who is bound to do so by other rules and regulations of his ecclesiastical superiors: such as young people at school, &c.

Practice.—Impossibility or other very weighty reasons can alone excuse you from hearing Mass on Sundays and holydays. If one live in a place where there are two masses on these days, *i. e.*, an early mass and a high mass, he should, if he be married, assist at one of them, and his wife at the other: for fathers and mothers of a family do not satisfy this precept of hearing Mass, if the mother goes to Mass on one Sunday, and the father on the next: such a practice will satisfy only in a place where there is said but *one* Mass, as it frequently happens in the country. If you are a servant, servant-maid, or workman, and if the conditions of your service do not allow you to hear the parochial Mass on holydays of obligation, as may be the case in this country, you should then endeavor to be present at an early Mass, and at the evening service if possible, and practice also some particular devotions on those days, which, though they are not of obligation in this country, yet are solemnized in Catholic countries. This latter part should also be observed on those days that were formerly of obligation, but are not so at present. If the Church, adapting herself to the circumstances of the times, no longer binds us by a command to keep them, nevertheless, it is her wish that, living in accordance with her spirit, we should derive from them all the advantages in our power to obtain.

The Third Commandment of the Church.

Q. What are we obliged to do by this commandment?

A. We are obliged to observe the fast-days prescribed by the Church:

1. Lent, *i. e.*, the forty days from Ash-Wednesday till Easter, with the exception of the Sundays. The Church has ordained them since the time of the Apostles, in commemoration and imitation of the forty days' fast of Jesus Christ, in memory of his bitter passion, and as a worthy preparation for the solemnity of the great festival of Easter.

2. The Ember days, or quarterly fasts, on the Wednesdays, Fridays, and Saturdays after the third Sunday in Advent, after the first Sunday in Lent, in the week after Pentecost, and after the Feast of the Exaltation of the Holy Cross, in the month of September.

The Church ordained these fasts, in order to thank God in a particular manner, every quarter of a year, for all the graces and gifts obtained from him, and thereby to put the faithful in mind of the constant duty of penance, and to ask God for worthy priests, as it is usually on those Ember-days that the Church ordains her ministers.

3. The vigils or eves of great feasts, in order to prepare worthily for their celebration. In many places, these vigils have been transferred to some day in Advent; regarding them we are to observe the custom of the place in which we live.

Q. To what does this precept of the Church oblige us?

A. 1. To take but one full meal in a day.

2. To abstain from flesh; unless one has obtained a dispensation.

3. To observe the time for taking the meal, that is, about noon, unless we are excused by some weighty reason.

In the evening we may take a collation permitted on fast days, to the amount of about eight ounces, according to St. Liguori and other theologians of the Church.

In the morning we are not allowed any thing but some coffee or some other light drink of the kind with a small quantity of bread. This is now the common custom approved by the superiors and rulers of the Church.

With regard to the use of flesh at the full meal a great mitigation has taken place in several countries and dioceses, and the people are to observe the customs and regulations which the lawful authorities of the Church have ordained in those several places in that respect.

Q. Who is bound to observe the fasts appointed by the Church?

A. Every Catholic Christian who is not excused by age, labor, or weakness.

The following are excused from the rigorous observance of the fast:

1. Those who have not yet reached the age of twenty-one.
2. Old people who are past sixty.
3. The sick and infirm, according to the judgment of the physician.
4. Women who are in a state of pregnancy, or those who are nursing.
5. Those who are employed at hard work.
6. Those who are travelling, particularly on foot, for the greater part of the day.

If any one has a doubt on this head, let him ask his pastor or confessor; but all should endeavor to supply by other good works what they are unable to do by fasting, particularly by giving alms if it be in their power.

Moreover, all those who are dispensed from fasting are not, therefore, dispensed from the duty of abstaining from flesh, unless their state of health also requires indulgence in this respect.

Q. On what other days has the Church forbidden the use of flesh?

A. On the Friday and Saturday of every week, and this in memory of the Passion of our Lord and His rest in the grave, through a spirit of penance. However, regarding Saturday, the Church, by a general dispensation allows the use of flesh at the present time. In this respect also each one is to observe the custom of the place in which he lives.

Q. Who are bound to abstain from flesh on these days of fast and abstinence."

A. All those who are seven years of age, unless their state of health, &c., excuses them, as remarked above.

Q. Is it a grievous sin to break this commandment of fast and abstinence?

A. Yes; for we commit thereby a grievous act of disobedience towards the Church, and an open contempt of her authority.

Q. Why has the Church given this command of fasting?

A. 1. In order to exercise us in obedience and humility, the practice of which is so well adapted to strengthen us in the spirit of self-denial; a disposition of the heart without which we neither serve God nor follow Jesus Christ as we ought.

2. Because God, in the Old Testament, repeatedly inculcated the duty of fasting and Jesus Christ and the Apostles have taught the same and recommended it by their example.

3. Because by fasting we do penance, and in union with the merits of Christ atone for our sins, and satisfy for the temporal punishments due to them.

Q. Is it by the eating of the flesh that sin is committed, when we break this command?

A. No; but by the act of disobedience, of which we are guilty. "Whatsoever enters the mouth, (the flesh) does not defile man," says Christ, "but the disobedience that cometh from the heart, is it that defiles him." *Matt.* xv. 18. This also shown by the fall of our first parents.

Q. But it may be said, "Why does the Church forbid flesh particularly?"

A. He who asks thus, knows not what obedience is. For he who tries another by obedience, chooses himself the subject of obedience. Moreover, to obey in the smallest and otherwise most indifferent things, shows the greatest obedince, because then we do such things solely through obedience. Finally, nourishment is the daily want of all, and therefore the fittest and only subject to try the obedience of all men at the same time. But flesh cannot be had by all; the Church, therefore, commands the rich to place themselves, as it were, at the table of the poor, and to show themselves as their brethren, and prove themselves children of one and the same divine mother, who sets the table for all on that day. But when flesh is allowed at the principal meal, then the Church fordids the use of fish at the same meal, to show that it is our obedience, at which she principally aims, and that self-denial in which, as a wise and holy mother, she wishes to exercise us.

Q. What are we to think of those who boldly transgress this command, saying: "It is only a commandment of the Church, and what enters the mouth, does not defile the man?"

A. We are to pity them; for they know not what they say. What would parents think, if their children should say: It is but a command of father and mother, what does it concern us? How would education be possible, and what would become of the reverence due to parents? The Church is our heavenly Mother, and her power comes from God. Moreover, what would parents say, when they forbid their children to eat this thing or that, if the children would reply: "I will eat it anyhow; what enters the mouth, does not defile?" The same thing applies still more strongly to the commandments of the Church, as we have just shown.

Q. Does it suffice to abstain merely from the food or the flesh, and to fast bodily, in order to sanctify those days in the spirit of the Church?

A. No; but we should also spend them in the spirit of penance, and sanctify them by self-denial, prayer, and the exercise of good works. *Is.* lviii. 6, 7.

Practice.—Observe as far as you can, and as you are bound to do the days of abstinence and fast ordained by the Church, and if you are in any doubt, take the advice of your pastor or confessor. Be not careless or indifferent, and do not suffer yourselves to be induced by bad example to transgress the commandments of the Church; pay no attention to the ridicule of the wicked. They will respect you the more for it in their hearts, and whether or not, you should take pride in acknowledging the holy Church openly and honestly as your mother, whom you must and will obey. Think on the example of the seven children of the Machabees in the Old Testament, who preferred to suffer martyrdom, rather than transgress the command of abstinence by taking food prohibited by the law.

The Fourth Commandment of the Church.

Q. What does this commandment ordain?

A. That we should confess our sins, at least once a year, to a priest duly authorized to hear them.

Q. At what other time are we bound to confess our sins?

A. 1. As often as we wish to receive the holy eucharist, or any of the other sacraments that require in us the state of grace, if we find ourselves guilty of mortal sin.

2. In general, as soon after falling into mortal sin as we have an opportunity of confessing. If we have no opportunity, we should then endeavor to make an act of perfect contrition, and go to confession as soon as possible.

Woe to him that remains long in motal sin, for he is in danger of falling into new and more grivous sins, and of perishing therein.

The Church commands us to go to confession, at least *once* a year, that is, she thus obliges the tepid and the negligent to fulfill that duty, which, in God's designs, is to be fulfilled as often as man stands in need of receiving the sacrament of penance, to reconcile him with God. This should compel even the most wicked, but the good and zealous should not be content with this; they should try to strengthen and increase in themselves the grace of God by a frequent reception of this sacrament.

Q. Does the Church ordain any thing more by this commandment?

A. Yes; to receive communion at Easter or thereabouts. The rule is that it should be received in the parish church to which one belongs, unless he be excused from doing so by impossibility, general custom, or special permission.

The time for the paschal communion begins several weeks before Easter, and terminates several weeks after that great festival; the regulations of the place in which one lives are here also to be observed.

If any one be prevented by sickness from going to church, then it is his duty to apprise the pastor of it, that he may receive the Easter communion at home.

If any one is prevented, by a journey or other circumstances, from receiving holy communion at Easter, then he must try to receive it afterwards as soon as he is able.

Q. At what age is one obliged to commence going to confession and communion?

A. As soon as he comes to the age of discretion, and is sufficiently instructed, in order to receive the blessed sacrament worthily and with advantage, the decision of which belongs to the pastor.

Q. Why has the Church prescribed the reception of the holy eucharist at Easter?

A. 1. Because Jesus Christ instituted and first administered the most holy sacrament at that time. 2. Because Easter is the most solemn feast which the Church celebrates in the whole year, and the holy time of Lent is fittest to prepare the hearts of the faithful for a worthy communion.

Q. Does it suffice to receive holy communion once in a year?

A. No. The Church, by this command, only obliges the tepid to do at least once a year that which her zealous children frequently do, even without being commanded; so that having received the holy sacrament worthily at least once a year, they may do so more frequently for the future, of their own accord; strengthened by this banquet of love, and cheered on by the example of others and by the exhortations of God's ministers.

The Church commands as a careful mother; but she has also solemnly declared her wish in the Council of Trent, that the faithful should approach the holy table as often as possible, and even daily, after the example of the first Christians. For they lived in such a manner that the Church could, with safety, allow them this frequent and worthy reception of the most holy sacrament.

It was only afterwards, when the fervor of her children grew cold, that she was forced to give a particular command. She did it certainly with sorrow and affliction. Would to God, all Christian people, following the example of the first Christians, would become again so fervent in approaching the table of the Lord, that the Church might be enabled to withdraw this command.

Q. What sin does he commit, who, not fulfilling this command, neglects to receive holy communion at Easter?

A. He commits a grievous sin, and may be excluded from the communion of the Church; besides, he loses the right to Christian burial in consecrated ground.

Practice.—This command ought not to apply to you, for the love of Jesus, the longing desire after Him, should make you so fervent in the reception of the most holy sacrament, that you do not stand in need of a special command of the Church in this regard. But let no one imagine that he is in a safe way, and may rest contented if he does no more in this respect than what the commandment obliges him to do. Assuredly he who acts thus, is not a good or fervent child of the Church. You bear the name of Christian, but you do not live according to Christ's spirit; you do not live so that you can exclaim with St. Paul: "I live, not now I, but Christ that liveth in me." This is the effect of frequent communion.

THE FIFTH COMMANDMENT OF THE CHURCH.

Q. What is forbidden by this commandment?
A. To solemnize marriage within certain times, namely: from the beginning of Advent till the Epiphany, and from Ash-Wednesday till Low-Sunday, after the octave of Easter.

If one should be obliged to contract marriage during these times, it must be done without solemnity.

Practice.—Should God have called you to the married state, be very careful that you enter it with due preparation, so that you do not transgress this command, and that the day of your marriage may be to you a day of honor. And spend it so that you may secure the blessing of God, for it would be a frightful thing if you should spend it so as to render yourself and others guilty of an offence against God, losing by excess the graces of the sacrament, and serving the devil on that day rather than God.

As regards the support of the Church, the priests, and the schools, be liberal as far as you can, remembering the old proverb: "The laborer is worthy of his hire," and again, "Blessed is the cheerful giver." Indeed, the Lord will repay you a hundred fold whatever you do for Him, His Church, and His servants. This is what the experience of all times has taught.

PART SECOND.
ON THE MEANS OF SALVATION.

CHAPTER I.

ON GRACE.

WHOEVER is a duly instructed child of Christ's Church knows what he believes, hopes and loves, according to God's will; such a one certainly knows the way of salvation. Yet it would avail the wanderer but little to be acquainted with the way if he did not also possess the strength and the means to pursue the road pointed out to him until he reaches the end of his journey. Even so it is with man, with the Christian on the weary way to a blissful eternity. The means of attaining this happy end is grace. Christ assures us that without Him, we can do nothing. *John*, xiii. 15. We are not capable, as St. Paul says, of even pronouncing His name in a meritorious manner. 1 *Cor.* xii. 3. Grace is imparted to the faithful either interiorly, immediately, or accompanied by outward signs. Hence the necessity of grace, the sacraments and sacramentals, follows from what we have hitherto been treating of as a matter of course.

Q. What is understood by the term grace?

A. Under the term grace is understood a mark of favor, a benefit, pleasure. In the more limited sense of the term, however, we understand a gift conferred not as the liquidation of a debt or an act of justice or necessity, but solely proceeding from the spontaneous benignity and generosity of the giver. Hence St. Paul says, addressing the *Romans*, xi. 6, "and if by grace, it is not now by works, other wise grace would be no more grace." This is the sense in which the word grace is often employed in common conversation. When here treating of the means of salvation, we understand by the term grace a gift to be ascribed solely to the goodness of God. Divine grace is further divided into natural and supernatural, for a two-fold condition may be distinguished in the redeemed human race, as in our first parents, viz., the natural condition of man, in consequence of which we are rational beings endowed with manifold gifts· and the supernatural gifts imparted to our first parents by the particular favor of God, and granted also to us through the merits of Jesus Christ; whence it follows that we are children of God supernaturally gifted, and are called to the vision and supernatural possession of God in his eternal kingdom. Well adapted to illustrate our subject are the words of St. Augustine: "Our creation is not improperly termed a grace of God; for that we exist and are, not as a corpse which lives not, nor as a tree which feels not, nor as an animal which possesses no intellect, but that we are men endowed with life and feeling and understanding, and capable of thanking the Creator for these benefits; this is very justly termed a grace, as all this has not been imparted to us as the reward of former meritorious acts, but through the peculiar favor of God; yet that we are called elect, justified, and hereafter to be glorified, is a grace of a very different description." Hence we understand by the term natural grace every gift or benefit of God conferred on us as human beings in a natural way, as citizens of and wayfarers in this fleeting world. The term supernatural grace is employed to distinguish a gift of God conferred on man in consideration of Christ's infinite merits, and as citizens of a higher sphere, viz., of the heavenly kingdom.

Q. How is supernatural grace further subdivided?

A. 1. Into graces granted for the salvation of others; 2, those imparted to enable us to attain our own sanctification. Both indeed relate to man's supernatural condition, but differ from each other, in that the first is a gift of God, which by virtue of its essential qualities renders him to whom it is imparted not more perfect than before, but is rather granted for the benefit of others, as for instance, the gifts of miracles, prophecy, etc. The former, however, granted for our own sanctification is in itself adapted to promote the sanctification of him to whom it is granted, for which purpose God deigns to communicate it to man. We shall speak here of this second kind of grace. This grace rendering a man pleasing, and his acts meritorious in God's sight is again divided into exterior and interior. Exterior grace is a divine gift granted to man, through an external medium, in order to perfect his supernatural condition: for instance, the Divine Law, the announcement of the truths of the Gospel, events and misfortunes by whose instrumentality man arrives at self-knowledge and amendment. Interior grace on the contrary, is a supernatural divine efficacy which immediately, (*i. e.*,) interiorly touches, illuminates, moves, renovates, and, as it were, transforms man's spirit. Interior grace is either actual and transient, or permanent and sanctifying, which bear to each other the same proportion or relation as does a passing effect to that which belongs to the essential condition and qualities of an object. This actual grace refers to the individual good deeds performed by men, whereas sanctifying grace supposes his supernatural character of child of God. We shall now proceed to treat of both as far as the limits of our work will permit.

Of Actual Grace.

Q. What is actual grace?

A. Actual grace is a supernatural, divine efficiency, enlightening our understanding and moving our will, so that we become capable of knowing and performing good acts, or, as St. Augustine expresses himself, "It is an illumination of love, by which we fulfill in holy love what is thus revealed to us." *St. Aug. contra duas epist. Pelag.* lib. iv. c. v. It is evident that this grace extends but to individual acts. Now, these illuminations and impulses of grace belong to God, inasmuch as they are the immediate effects of this His grace in us: for as regards the good deed performed by man with its assistance, it is partially the efficacy of grace, partly the consequence of our own coöperation, as we are told by the Apostle, "Not I, but

Q. Is supernatural *actual* grace necessary?

A, Yes, it is requisite for the performance of a good and meritorious act; it is necessary for the origin of our faith, and every good and meritorious work, and for perseverance in both until the end of our mortal career. This the Saviour teaches us saying: "Abide in me and I in you. As the branch cannot bear fruit of itself unless it abide in the vine, so neither can you, unless you abide in me. I am the vine, you the branches. He that abideth in me and I in him, the same beareth much fruit, for without me you can do nothing." *John*, xv. 4, 5. Attend well to the emphasis laid on the words "you can do nothing without me." Further, let us keep in view the force of the comparison, for as the sap of the vine ascends from the interior and produces its fruitfulness, although it is far from precluding the coöperation of the vine, which is, indeed, a necessary condition, even so does grace require our coöperation for any good work in Christ.

This simile acquires peculiar force from having been employed by Jesus on that memorable evening when He instiuted the blessed Eucharist, and distributed among His Apostles the bread of life. The intention of our blessed Lord was to make them the more easily comprehend the manner in which this interior union with Christ, the author and dispenser of grace, is to be effected. This St. Paul confirms when he says, "And such confidence we have through Christ towards God. Not that we are sufficient to think any thing of ourselves as of ourselves, but our sufficiency is from God." 2. *Cor.* iii. 4, 5. And again he expressly says, "And no man can say 'the Lord Jesus,' (that is, in a meritorious manner,) but by the Holy Ghost, the spirit of all grace." 1 *Cor.* xii. 3.

Q. Does grace deprive us of or impair our liberty?

A. By no means; it, on the contrary, confirms it, and imparts to it sufficient strength duly to coöperate in good works of a supernatural order, and available for eternity.

Q. How can this be shown from Scripture and tradition?

A. The Prophets, John the Baptist, the Apostles, and Christ our Lord himself frequently exhorted their hearers to penance and perfection of life, but this they could never have reasonably done if the communication of grace deprived men of freedom. 2d. Jesus mournfully deplores the fate of the obdurate Jews: "Jerusalem, Jerusalem, how often would I have gathered together thy children as the hen doth gather her chickens under her wings, and thou wouldst not.' *Matth* xxiii. 37. This passage proves to conviction that the Jews had free will, and that Christ had granted them sufficient means of grace. The fault was entirely in themselves, as they, by the abuse of their freedom, refused to cöoperate with grace, yea, even resisted. The Holy Ghost admonishes us by the mouth of the wise man: "If thou wilt keep the commandments they shall preserve thee. He hath set water and fire before thee: stretch forth thy hand to which thou wilt. Before man is life and death, good and evil: that which he shall choose shall be given him." *Eccles.* xv. 16, 18. 3d. The holy fathers, with St. Augustine, teach the same. This distinguished doctor of grace writes in his work against the two letters of Pelagius, *Lib. II, No.* 3: "If there is no grace of God, how then does God save the world, and if we do not possess liberty how shall He judge the world?" This clearly explicit testimony of the holy father paves the way to the following elucidation of the matter, derived solely from the nature of the subject. Supposing the contrary to be the case, that is if we lost our freedom of action by grace, it becomes evident that man is neither capable of moral merit nor guilt, consequently, neither deserving of reward nor punishment. Thus he would cease to be a responsible being, as the followers of Luther, and still more those of Calvin, once absurdly affirmed. Unfortunately, this did not remain mere absurdity, for being reduced to practice, it undermined the foundation of all morality, and of all the higher sense of virtue. The Council of Trent expresses this dogma of our faith in the following solemn words: "If any man say that man's freedom, impelled and excited by God, does no cöoperate with God, who calls and moves man, and that he but passively submits, let him be anathematized." *Sess.* vi. *Can.* 4.

Q. What may be deduced from this dogma?

A We deduce from this dogma, that there is an efficacious grace, and a grace that is merely sufficient.

Q. What is efficacious, and what is merely sufficient grace?

A. Efficacious grace is that which actually confers the will and the power to accomplish good deeds. The merely sufficient grace, on the contrary, is that which indeed furnishes means and strength sufficient, but which, on account of the resistance offered by man's free will does not succeed in accomplishing the work in question. The Scriptures say that God inclines man's heart to his testimonies. *Ps.* cxviii. 36. God will give you a new heart. *Ezech.* xi. "Given repentance unto life." *Acts*, xi. 18. "I will give my law, and I will write it in their hearts." *Jeremias*, xxxi. 33. "The Lord opens the heart." *Acts*, xvi. 14. These positive and definite expressions point out clearly and unmistakeably the power of active grace, and establish its efficacy beyond all doubt. Tradition may also be brought forward in support of this doctrine. Thus St. Basil amongst other things says, writing to St Gregory of Nazianzen, "Any thing that is conferred upon us by the divine favor, we term a work of grace effective within us." All those passages of Scripture in which man is censured for his abuse of divine grace may be adduced as proofs of the real existance of merely sufficient grace. Thus, for instance, we read in *Isaias*, v. 4. "What is there that I ought to do more to my vineyard that I have not done to it. Was it that I looked that it should bring forth grapes and it had brought forth wild grapes." And Christ himself says, *Matt.* xi. 21. "Woe to thee, Corozain, woe to thee, Bethsaida, for if in Tyre and Sidon had been wrought the miracles that have been wrought in you, they had long ago done penance in sackcloth and ashes." The words addressed by St. Stephen to the Sanhedrim are likewise well adapted to illustrate our subject, "You stiff-necked and uncircumcised in heart and ears, you always resist the Holy Ghost." *Acts*, vii. 51. Compare *Matt.* xxiii. 33. Tradition concurs in bearing testimony to this doctrine, supported by which St. Augustine writes, (*Lib. de spir.*) "When compelled to explore these fathomless depths how is it that one being advised is convinced, another is left unimpressed, and unmoved? There are but two replies which I should wish to make. The first: O, sublimity of the grace of God! The second: Can there be injustice in God?" The holy doctor in these words evidently affirms the existence of efficacious and sufficient grace.

Q. On whom is sufficient grace bestowed?

A. Sufficient grace is granted to all men without exception; to the just in order to enable them to practice good works according to the commandments of God; to sinners to render them capable of doing penance; to infidels in order to bring them, either by ordinary or extraordinary means, to the knowledge of the true faith. We first stated that grace is granted to all the just in order to assist them in performing the works of the children of God. The Apostle says, "God is faithful, who will not suffer you to be tempted above that which you are able, but will make also with temptation issue that you may be able to bear." 1 *Cor.* x. 13. The theological ground for this is given by the General Council of Trent, *Sess.* vi., saying, "God commands not impossibilities but He exhorts in commanding thee to do what thou canst and to implore that which thou canst not, and He assists thee so that thou shalt be able to do it." The Council further expressly declares in the eighteenth canon, "If any man say that it is impossible for those who are sanctified in grace to keep the commandments of God, let him be anathama." We assert, secondly, that sufficient grace is offered to all sinners to enable them to return by sincere repentance to the love and friendship of their Creator, for, as the Scripture testifies, the conversion of sinners is the general will of God. So the prophet expressly says, speaking in the name of God, "Is it my will that a sinner should die, saith the Lord God and not that he should be converted from his ways and live?" *Ezech.* xviii. 23. St. Peter says, "The Lord wills not that any one should perish but that all should return to penance." 2 *Pet.* iii. Further all exhortations to penance would be fruitless were not this the case. The doctrine of the Church on this point is expressed in the General Council held at Lateran, and of course it perfectly coincides with what we have stated, that fallen man can always command sincere repentance. We further asserted that even infidels are not denied sufficient grace to obtain salvation, for the Apostle plainly says, "God will have all men to be saved and to come to the knowledge of the truth. *Tim.* ii. 4. Christ is further termed by St. John, the true light which enlighteneth every man that cometh into the world. *John*, i. 9. And this expresses such a general illumination that whoever really and sincerely desires may follow the truth. Finally, St. Paul expressly says that the heathens are not to be excused for not having arrived at the knowledge of truth; but this evidently follows from what we have previously said regarding the necessity of the general communication of sufficient grace. The Church declared her doctrine on this head, on the following occasion. Pope Alexander VII. in the year 1690, solemnly condemned the opinion that heathens, Jews, infidels, &c., are nowise influenced by Jesus Christ. Thus the grace sufficient for conversion is not wanting to infidels. If they do not turn it to account the fault is to be imputed to themselves. It is certain that as Christ has come to redeem all men, and that He wished the Gospel to be announced and promulgated amongst men by human means which was gradually done after obviating many difficulties; the sufficient grace from within must necessarily supply what is wanting in the universal announcement of the Gospel in order that all who possess the sincere will, at least the internal desire for faith, supernaturally enlightened by God may secure salvation.

"To-day if you shall hear His voice harden not your hearts." *Psalm*, xciv. 8. And again, "Behold I stand at the gate and knock. If any man shall hear my voice, and open to me the door, I will come in to him." *Apoc.* iii. 20. Oh! happy the Christian that has a heart so open to every inspiration of the Holy Ghost, that he might indeed say with Samuel, "Speak, Lord, for thy servant heareth;" and who does not permit the suggestions of grace to remain inactive, but faithfully coöperates therewith. A second principle of theology is realized in regard to so happy a soul. "He gives grace for grace," viz., for the grace faithfully corresponded with a second and greater one. Oh, how glorious and full of merit is this exchange of human and divine generosity, in which divine benignity so far exceeds human fidelity. The saints have frequently experienced this during their mortal life. Imitate their example: be not ungenerous but liberal towards your God, and you shall soon test by experience the truth of this remark. How dangerous it would be, on the contrary, shouldst thou turn a deaf or unwilling ear to divine inspiration. This act might be the means of rending a bright chain or series of graces which would otherwise have been granted thee. Let us, therefore, frequently and in all sincerity exclaim with David, *Psalm* cvii., "My heart is ready, O God, my heart is ready."

Of Sanctifying Grace.

Q. What is sanctifying grace?

A. It is the supernatural union of the soul with God in holy love, which elevates it from man's natural condition to the supernatural state of a child of God, and by which the Saviour's merits are originally applied to it.

Q. With what is the communication of sanctifying grace joined?

A. With the justification and sanctification of man.

Q. In what does justification consist?

A. In purification from every stain of grievous sin.

Q. What other term is therefore applied to sanctifying grace?

A. The grace of justification; the divine act by which it is communicated to us is styled justification.

Q. In what does sanctification consist?

A. In the communication of supernatural gifts.

Q. Which are the particular effects of sanctifying or justifying grace, tending to the sanctification and union of man with God through Jesus Christ?

A. Justifying grace imparts supernatural life to the soul, which by sin had incurred spiritual death.

"For this my son was dead, and is come to life again," says Christ in the parable of the prodigal son. *St. Luke,* xv. 32.

1. The sinner is dead by sin; by grace he again revives.

2. It imparts to the soul the radiance of supernatural purity. Hence the royal prophet says "Thou shalt wash me, and I shall become whiter than snow." *Psalm,* l.

3. It wonderfully embellishes and beautifies the soul. It is to this spiritual beauty that the words of the Holy Ghost, in the Canticle of Canticles, refer: "How beautiful art thou, my love, how beautiful! fair as the moon, bright as the sun, terrible as an army set in array."

4. It transforms man at the moment of his justification from a poor despicable sinner to one so rich and beautiful that no favored son of fortune can be compared with him, for as St. Thomas says: "The least and lowest degree of grace surpasses by far all the treasures and riches of the whole earth." *St. Thomas,* 8 *quest.* 115 *a. q.* St. Peter teaches that by grace we become in a certain sense partakers of the divine nature. 2 *Peter,* i. 4.

5. It frees and elevates man, who by sin has become as it were a child of Satan, makes him a child of grace, and, therefore, heir to his eternal kingdom and co-heir of Christ Jesus. "Behold what manner of charity the Father hath bestowed upon us, that we should be called and should be the sons of God." 1 *John,* iii. 1. "And if sons, also heirs; heirs indeed of God, and joint-heirs with Christ." *Rom.* viii. 17.

The General Council of Trent confirms all this, *Sess.* 6, *Cap.*

7, where it explicitly declares: "The preparation is followed by justification, which is not only a remission of sin, but also the sanctification and renovation of the inner man, by the voluntary reception of the grace and the gifts by which man is changed from a sinner to a just man, from an enemy to a friend, so that by hope he may become heir to life eternal. By this grace which He has conferred on us we are renewed in spirit and in heart, and are not merely considered just, but are so called, and are indeed so, by receiving within us justification, every one according to the measure imparted to him by the Holy Ghost, and according to his capacity and co-operation. And although he only can be just, to whom the merits of our Lord Jesus Christ's passion are communicated, yet this is exactly what is done in the justification of the sinner, as, by means of the merits of His holy sufferings, love is poured forth into the hearts of those justified, and dwelleth within them. Hence in justification, with the remission of sin, faith, hope and charity are infused into man's heart through Jesus Christ.

Q. Wherein consists then, according to the doctrine of the Chruch, the essence of sanctifying grace?

A. It consists in the charity poured forth into our hearts by the Holy Ghost. That this is really so, is testified by Scripture, in which all the effects of sanctifying grace are ascribed to love. Compare 1 *Pet.* iv. 8; 1 *John*, iii. 14; 1 *John*, iv. 7; *St. James*, i. 12. Tradition is not wanting in testimony on this head, for as St. Augustine writes, "The beginning of love is the beginning of justice; and the perfection of love, the perfection of justice." *Lib. de Lib. et Gratia.*

Q. What are the conditions of justification by the communication of sanctifying grace to adults?

A. Faith in God and in our Saviour Jesus Christ; consent to the suggestions of preventive grace inciting us to conversion; dread of the effects of divine justice excited by motives derived from the teachings of faith, united, at the same time with hope, in which love's dawn may already be traced, evoked by the consideration of God's mercy and Christ's merits; finally, sincere hatred and detestation of sin, and a firm resolution of amendment of life; and should the adult be already a member of the Church, the desire to receive the sacrament of penance by which in virtue of divine institution, justification is communicated. Thus the Council of Trent, *Sess.* 6. *Cap.* 6.

Q. Can man attain infallible certainty of being in the state of grace?

A. He cannot, without having been favored with a particular and divine revelation on this point, as the Council of Trent declares: "Man knoweth not whether he be worthy of love or hatred." *Eccl.* 1.

Q. Are we on this account justified in giving way to great anxiety of mind?

A. We are not; this uncertainty should serve to humble our pride and stimulate us to do all in our power in order to secure the *one great affair* of salvation.

Q. Are there particular signs which serve to console and inspire us with the blissful hope of enjoying the divine favor?

A. There are. 1. The sensible and effectual dread of sin animating us at every moment of our lives, and inspiring us with the firm resolution of enduring every imaginable torture rather than offend God by mortal sin.

2. A great and sensible love of God, accompanied by zeal in prayer, particularly mental prayer.

3. A heart which not only feels itself entirely free from all voluntary inclination to pride and envy, but which rather rejoices in its own humiliation and the exaltation of others.

4. Sincere love of our enemies, which enables us cordially to forgive every injury and insult offered to us.

5. Great compassion for neighbor's misfortunes and sufferings, and a loving readiness to alleviate his woe by alms-deeds and every other possible species of aid.

6. Great zeal for the salvation of souls, particularly when it requires sacrifices at our hands.

7. Fervor in the reception of the sacraments, with a lively faith and a tender and enduring remembrance of the presence of Jesus in the adorable sacrament. So that as He desires to dwell with us by His sacramental presence, we also may abide constantly with Him in grateful, loving adoration, and thus zealously profit by His saving and blissful presence for our greater sanctification. Well may that soul rejoice who perceives all these signs of salvation within herself. She may confidently hope that the Lord is with her, and that she lives in His grace.

Q. Why do we term the above-mentioned signs, marks of

preelection, and conclude that those possessing them are in the grace of God?

A. Because eternal life is frequently and explicitly promised to those who live in this manner.

Q. Can any one attain certainty as to whether he will persevere in grace or not?

A. No; that cannot be. "Praise not any man before his death," says the Holy Ghost by the mouth of the sage.

Final perseverance is a great and peculiar grace; yet, whoever possesses the distinctive marks of the state of sanctifying grace, possesses also the marks of final perseverance, for which grace we should humbly hope and zealously implore it of the divine clemency.

Q. Whereby is the state of sanctifying grace forfeited?
A. By the commission of mortal sin.
Q. Whereby is sanctifying grace impaired or diminished?
A. By venial transgressions.
Q. Whereby is forfeited grace recovered?
A. By sincere contrition and repentance, and recurrence to the means of reconciliation instituted by our Divine Mediator.

Q. How is sanctifying grace increased?

A. By availing ourselves of the actual graces bestowed on us, or what amounts to the same, by the assiduous practice of good works, for which actual grace strengthens and disposes us; and especially by the frequent and worthy reception of the Holy Sacraments, those channels of grace instituted by our Lord for our sanctification.

Q. Has God connected the communication of justifying grace with certain exterior signs?

A. He has; with seven symbols, termed the seven sacraments, by which sanctifying grace is either originally communicated in the ordinary way, or, when forfeited by sin, again obtained; or, if never forfeited, it is increased in us. Many other actual graces are connected with the reception of the sacraments.

Practice.—Esteem sanctifying grace as the most estimable and precious of graces; preserve it most carefully, and earnestly implore your God to grant you the ineffable grace of final perseverance.

CHAPTER II.

OF THE SACRAMENTS.

Q. What is a sacrament?

A. A sacrament is a visible, effective sign of invisible grace, *i. e.*, a sign which possesses the divinely imparted virtue of signifying and actually communicating grace for our salvation.

Q. Who instituted the sacraments?

A. Jesus Christ, our Lord and Saviour, who by his passion merited grace for us and who alone as God-man can grant it.

Q. Why did Jesus Christ institute the sacraments?

A. 1. In order that they might be visible signs of God's ineffable goodness and liberality, in our regard, and at the same time, as it were, the seal of the covenant which He deigned to make with us, and His promises in our regard.

2. Christ wished to express the communication of grace for our sanctification by exterior signs in order to present us likewise with external evidences. He wished, further, as St. Chrysostom very justly remarks, to express this grace by external signs, because we are men and not pure spirits, who, by virtue of their nature, are capable of perceiving the efficacy of invisible grace.

3. The sacraments are intended as signs and characteristic marks by which the children of the Church mutually recognize and distinguish each other from those outside her pale.

4. They are means of increasing within us sanctifying and actual grace. Thus shines forth in brilliant refulgence, from the institution of the sacraments, the admirable love and generous goodness of God towards us, His unworthy creatures.

Q. What are the essential constituents of every sacrament?

A. 1. A sign affecting the senses, called the matter of the sacraments; thus, in baptism, water is the matter or element.

2. Words, by which this sign is distinguished from common use, and set apart for this holy act, and these words are termed *the form* of the sacrament. The words are: "I baptize thee, in the name of the Father," &c. St. Augustine says the words added to the element give rise to the sacrament. *Tract* 80, *in Joan.*

3. The divine institution, for God alone is the author and dispenser of grace.

4. A certain grace expressed and conferred by the sacrament, when the matter is joined to the form, for instance, in baptism the washing away of the stains of sin from the soul of the recipient.

5. A minister and dispenser of the sacrament, and a recipient, *i. e.*, a person, who by virtue of divine institution, is capable of imparting, and another of receiving the graces of the sacrament.

Q. What, then, is to be taken into consideration when treating of a sacrament?

A. The divine institution, the matter, the form, the effects of grace, the dispenser and the recipient.

Q. How many sacraments are there?

A. Seven; all of which the Church received from her divine founder, Jesus Christ, by the instrumentality of the Apostles, and has ever since faithfully preserved and administered. They are as follows: Baptism, Confirmation, the Holy Eucharist, Penance, Extreme Unction, Holy Orders and Matrimony.

Q. What is to be observed in general regarding these seven sacraments?

A. That two of these sacraments impart grace originally to those to whom they are administered, viz: baptism and penance—hence these sacraments are called sacraments of the dead, because they bestow on those spiritually dead in in, the life of grace, sin being the death of the soul; whereas, he other five but increase sanctifying grace in those who already live in grace, hence they are styled sacraments of the living. Further, there are three of these sacraments that impress a character on the soul.

Q. What is this character?

A. This character is a supernatural invisible sign, impressed upon the soul by the reception of the sacrament, which character will eternally remain thereon, either for greater damnation or greater glory. This character further serves to secure to those who receive the sacrament and live in the state of sanctifying grace, the assistance of actual grace in the fulfilment of the duties of their station as required of them by the sacrament.

Q. Which of the sacraments impress such a character?
A. Baptism, confirmation and holy orders. These sacraments can, therefore, be received but once. The other sacraments, viz: the adorable sacrament of the eucharist, penance, extreme unction and matrimony do not impress such a character upon the soul; they may, therefore, be received repeatedly.

Q. Supposing an unworthy priest administers these sacraments, are they on that account invalid?
A. No; for it is not man but Christ, who, by the ministry of the priest, imparts grace.

Q. Does he who receives the sacraments unworthily obtain the graces they would otherwise impart?
A. No: he abuses them, although he enters the state for which the two sacraments of condition viz., holy orders and matrimony have been respectively instituted. If he enters into himself and sincerely repents he obtains the graces imparted by those sacraments which impress a character.

Q. Whence do we know that there are seven sacraments?
A. From the unanimous doctrine and practice of the Church from the earliest times. This is proved by all the sects that in the first ages departed from the communion of the Church, and which still profess their belief in seven sacraments, as do the Greeks, Russians, &c. The number and peculiar virtues which the sacraments possess, are, moreover, in beautiful and harmonious connection with the supernatural life of the soul, and with the diffusion and government of the kingdom of God upon earth. Man in the order of nature is born, increases in age and strength, is nourished, requires remedies and particularly in death's dark hour, consolation and support. God has deigned most graciously and lovingly to provide for all these wants of his children in a spiritual sense, in the order of grace and supernatural life. We are brought forth in baptism to eternal life, strengthened in the sacrament of confirmation, nourished to holy and heavenly life in the adorable eucharist, healed and cleansed in penance, and duly prepared and equiped as it were in the sacrament of extreme unction, for our lone journey to the unknown and unexplored realms of eternity. Holy orders provides for the propagation and transmission of the power to dispense these sacraments, and the sacrament of matrimony for the sanctification and propagation of the human race till the end of time.

Q. Whence are derived the ceremonies in use in the administration of the sacraments?

A. From the Church, and for the most part from the time of the Apostles, who instructed by Christ's word, taught by His example, and inspired by the Holy Ghost, instituted and ordained them either personally or by their immediate successors, in order to excite in us holy dispositions and inspire us with devotion and veneration for these holy acts.

Practice. Thank God that he has prepared for you so many consoling and most powerful means of grace in His Church; and endeavor when receiving them, to do so with due preparation, so as not to diminish their efficacy in your regard. Take heed that you do not abuse them, or what were still worse, sacriligiously profane them.

Q. Which of these seven sacraments is the greatest?

A. All the sacraments are indeed great and sublime, and each possesses peculiar excellence; but the holiest and most sublime of all is the adorable sacrament of the altar, which contains the author of all grace, Jesus Christ. The most indispensable, however, of all the sacraments are baptism and penance, these being the life-giving sacraments in the order of grace.

1. OF BAPTISM.

Q. What is baptism?

A. Baptism is the sacrament of spiritual regeneration by the ablution of water and the express invocation of the most Holy Trinity, whereby we become children of God and members of the Church.

Q. What is the matter of baptism?

Q. The remote matter of this sacrament is natural water, spring, sea, well, or rain water, as also the water obtained by melting snow, ice, or hail. The prescribed matter, however, is water blessed for baptism when it can be had. Should there exist any doubt as to whether the water employed in baptism on any emergency was pure natural water, baptism would have to be administered again with water known to be pure. Water distilled from blossoms, as for instance, rose water is inadmissible, being an uncertain matter. The immediate matter is the ablution which may be attained in three different ways, *viz*; by plunging, pour ing, and ispersion, according to the usage of the Church, from which we should not deviate. The ablution of the head only is prescribed but, in case of necessity, it is sufficient to pour the water on any portion of the body, so that it flows over the skin.

- Q. What is the form of baptism?

A. The form of baptism is this: "I baptize thee in the name of the Father, and of the Son, and of the Holy Ghost. Amen." Christ teaches us this himself, when commissioning His Apostles to go forth and preach the gospel: "Going, therefore, teach ye all nations, baptizing them in the name of the Father, and of the Son, and of the Holy Ghost." These words of command prove clearly the divine institution of baptism. There are three points to be taken into consideration in the administration of this sacrament, and these points ought to be well and generally known, because (as will be shown hereafter) any one not only may, but should baptize, in case of necessity, hence it is indispensable for every one to be duly instructed on this head.

1. True natural water must be employed in baptism, and poured on the recipient.

2. While the water is being poured on the person baptized, the prescribed words, "I baptize thee, in the name of the Father, and of the Son, and of the Holy Ghost," are to be pronounced.

3. It is indispensable to the validity of the sacrament that its dispenser intends really to baptize, i. e. to administer the sacrament instituted by Christ, and which the Church, when baptizing, administers.

Q. Who is the minister of this sacrament?

A. Any one at all may validly administer this sacrament, be his condition, religious profession, or persuasion, what it may, supposing—and this must be carefully borne in mind, —that he intends doing what the Church does. The ordinary minister, however, is he who administers it in virtue of his office, that is to say, either the parish priest, or some other priest or deacon intrusted with this duty.

Q. May there not be, at the same time, several ministers of the sacrament?

A. Supposing that one pour the water and the other pronounce the words, the administration is not valid, because the one who pronounces the form does not do what he says. "I baptize thee (wash thee)," and he who actually performs the ceremony does not pronounce the words accompanying his act. This is confirmed by what the council of Florence decree in the time of Pope Eugenius, concerning the requisites for the validity of the sacrament, in which we find the following: "The sacrament is made up of three constituents, of things which form the matter, of words which constitute the form, and of the person of the minister who confers it, not the *persons* of the *ministers*, but in the singular form, the *person* of the *minister*.

Q. Should every one know this?

A. Most assuredly; since in cases where there is danger of death to one unbaptized, any one may and should baptize.

Q. Can the baptism of water be in certain cases, otherwise supplied, so that man obtains without it the grace of justification?

A. Yes; either by the baptism of desire, or of blood.

Q. What is the baptism of desire?

A. It is the justification by desire, the unbaptized adult earnestly and fervently longing to receive this sacrament, joined to perfect contrition and supreme love of God, whereby he arrives at justification. Should such a person be unable to realize his sincere desire regarding baptism, he will yet be saved as a child of the Church.

Q. Wherein consists baptism in blood?

A. It is the martyr's death for the sake of Christ and the true faith, which of course is usually accompanied by the shedding of blood, and it possesses the same virtue as baptism with water, when that cannot be procured. This is the teaching of the holy fathers and doctors of theology, as also of the Church, who venerates as martyrs and champions of the faith the unbaptized catechumens who have given up their lives for Christ.

Q. What are the effects produced by baptism?

A. The effects of baptism are—

1. The remission of original sin and of actual sin committed before the reception of the sacrament, as also the punishment attached to them, so that if a person were to die immediately after having been purified by the regenerating waters of baptism, he would be forthwith admitted to the beatific vision; hence we profess in the creed, "I believe in baptism for the remission of sins." *Council of Trent*, 5 sess. 5 cap.

2. Sanctification communicated by supernatural grace, is imparted to us; the soul is, in particular, rendered capable of exciting the three theological virtues, faith hope and charity, in a meritorious and supernatural manner. *Council of Trent,* 6 sess. 7 cap.

3. We are in this manner spiritually regenerated to life eternal. *John,* iii. 5.

4. We are adopted as children of God. *Gal.* iii. 26.

5. We become members of the Church, and by the communion of saints, partakers in all her goods and graces. *Acts,* ii. 41.

6. We are elevated to the dignity of heirs of heaven. *Mark,* xvi. 16.

Of the Ceremonies used in the Administration of Baptism.

Q. Why does the Catholic Church make use of various ceremonies in baptizing?

A. Partly as emblems of the effects of baptism, and partly to remind us thereby of the obligations we take upon ourselves by its reception.

Q. Is the use of these ceremonies of ancient date?

A. Yes; it is derived from the primitive Church, as we shall presently show.

Q. May baptism be administered without employing the usual ceremonies?

A. The omission of the prescribed ceremonies is prohibited under the pain of sin, when a case of necessity does not nullify the prohibition, and should this have occurred in such an emergency, the ceremonies must, if possible, be afterwards performed.

Q. Why is the catechumen brought first to the Church door?

A. Because he is still defiled by the guilt of sin, and hence unworthy of entering the house of God. "Holiness becometh Thy house, O Lord!" says the royal prophet. Further, because baptism admits him to the Church. The exorcisms are performed at the portal and the doctrines of the Church briefly explained, so that the catechumen may know what he in future has to believe and practice. He is also prayed over and the holy gospel is read; he is then breathed upon, hereby, as St. Augustine says, "The inimical might of Satan, who has hitherto had the unbeliever in his power, is broken." *St. August. Lib.* 1 *de Symb.* cap. 1.

Q. Is the practice of exorcising catechumen ancient in the Church?

A. Most certainly; for St. Augustine refuting the sophistries of Pelagius, proves from this custom, that children are born under the dominion of Satan, and in another place he says that this custom has been universally adopted in the Church. *Lib.* 2. *de nupt. et concup.* cap. 18.

Q. Why is breathing on the catechumen joined to the exorcism?

A. When Christ imparted to his disciples the Holy Ghost he breathed upon them. *John*, viii. 20. The priest's breathing on those to be baptized express the expulsion of the evil one, and the approach of the Holy Spirit. St. Augustine also speaks of this ceremony. *Lib.* 6. *contra Julian*, cap. 2.

Q. What is then done with the one to be baptized?

A. The sign of the holy cross is impressed on the brow, breast, eyes, ears, and the remaining senses of the catechumen, to show, that in the sacrament of baptism a character of Jesus Christ, *i. e.* an indelible character is impressed.

2. That his senses are sanctified by faith in Christ to the true worship of God and our Lord Jesus Christ.

3. That he must endeavor with all his natural and spiritual endowments to profess openly his faith in Christ and His Church even at the sacrifice of his life.

4. That as a Christian he must be at the cross of Jesus Christ.

5. Finally, that the life of a Christian is not to be a voluptuous and sensual one; according to the dictates of the flesh, but a life of self-denial, and hence that he is not to be surprised, if, as an adherent of the crucified God, he meets on his journey through life, with many trials and adversities, as this is the probation to which all are subjected, and which, when patiently and resolutely borne will obtain for us an exceedingly great reward in the mansions of eternal joy and glory.

Q. Why is blessed salt placed on the catechumen's tongue?

A. 1. To signify that he is to be delivered from the corruptions of sin, that he is never more to admit it to the shrine of his heart, but that he is to remain pure and inviolate in order to fit himself for the reception of greater graces.

2. That he is to acquire a relish for things spiritual.

3. That by true faith that divine wisdom is conferred on him, which he is to prove in all his actions, so that he may never have to reproach himself with precipitation, imprudence or crime. Salt is an emblem of prudence.

4. That by the graces communicated in baptism, the body may once more be freed from all corruption.

Q. What is signified by the imposition of the minister's hands?

A. The imposition of the dispenser's hands signifies the reconciliation in virtue of which he who was formerly secluded from the pale of the Church, is now admitted to her maternal bosom. It is further used, as St, Augustine says, in order that henceforward the evil one may not presume to re-enter the dwelling from which he has been expelled. *St. Augustine, Liber* 2. *de pec. mer.* cap. 26.

Q. Why are the ears and nostrils of the catechumen moistened with spittle?

A. The priest who administers the sacrament moistens the catechumen's ears and his nostrils with spittle while pronouncing the words used by Christ when touching the ears and the tongue of the man possessed by a dumb devil, "Epheta."

1. To show that man has become a true and living member of Christ united with the divine head.

2. That the spiritual ear of the heart has been opened, and that man is no longer deaf to the divine promises, threats, and warnings, but that he readily recognises the voice of His Lord and shepherd and distinguishes it from strange voices as Christ says, "My sheep know my voice. *John,* ix.

3: The nostrils are moistened with the spittle to signify, as St. Ambrose says, that one baptized, spiritually receives the fragrance of piety. *St. Ambrose, Lib. de Sacra.* cap. 1.

Q. What ceremony now succeeds?

A. The abjuration; the person baptized is asked, "Do you renounce the devil and all his works?" to which he, or the sponsors in his name, reply, "I do renounce him." That the usage has been derived from the apostolic times is attested by the Holy Fathers in various passages; we also find it mentioned in the *Apostolic Constitutions, Lib.* 1.

Q. Why is this abjuration pronounced before the reception of baptism?

A. In order that all the faithful may know that the principal duty imposed by their Christian profession is that, " They are not of the world, as I (Christ) also am not of the world:" *John*, xvii. 16; *i. e.* that they abandon the pernicious maxims of the world and all it contains, and ever live spiritually united with the God who so graciously deigns to adopt them as his children, " *In the expectation of the blessed hope, and the coming glory of the great God.*" That they may further understand that this renunciation of all that is opposed to the divine will and ordinance is so essentially and immediately united to the Christian name that he who lives not up to its dictates incurs great guilt and likewise *perjures himself.*

Q. Why does the priest demand of the catechumen at the font, " Dost thou believe in God the Father?" upon which he, or his sponsors reply, " I do believe?

A. To remind us that baptism without true faith, will be of no avail to us. "*He that believeth and is baptized shall be saved; and he that believeth not shall be condemned.*" *Mark*, xvi. 16. The sponsors are also reminded that when the infant shall have arrived at the use of reason, they are bound to have it duly instructed in the principles of the Holy Catholic faith.

Q. What is meant by annointing the catechumen's breast, and shoulders with holy oil?

A. To denote that he has now entered the lists as a champion of Christ against the devil, the world, and the flesh; that he is to preserve a pure heart and resolutely crush in the germ every thought unworthy of his high calling, and bear with fortitude the pressure of whatever afflictions or burdens it may please his Lord and Master to inflict upon him.

Q. Why is the head of the person baptized anointed with chrism?

A. To show that he has now received in baptism, the grace of the Holy Ghost; further that as he is internally annointed with the joy and grace of the Holy Ghost and externally with chrism, he may be more forcibly reminded of the reasons why he is called a Christian.

Q. What is signified by the white garment with which the priest clothes the neophyte?

A. It signifies that he has put off the old man and put on the new. *Ephes.* iv. 24. Further, the spotless innocence obtained after the washing away of the stains cleaving from birth to our souls. This purity we should carefully guard against every breath of sin and corruption, so that we secure our salvation, for nothing impure is admitted into the kingdom of God. *Apoc.* xxi. 27.

Q. What is signified by the candle given to the neophyte?

A. The holy rite is concluded by giving to the neophyte a burning candle, with the words, "Receive this burning candle and preserve unsullied thy baptismal robe, observe the commandments of God, that when the Lord comes to the wedding feast, thou, with all the saints of the heavenly host, mayst come to meet Him and enter into the possession of life everlasting. The burning candle is further emblematical of the three theological virtues, infused into the heart in baptism. Faith is symbolized by the light, hope and charity by the flame. The candle is put in the neophyte's hand, because it suffices not to preserve faith, hope and charity in the heart, when not manifest in the works, remembering what the Apostle says: "Being mindful of the work of your faith, and labor, and charity, and of the enduring of the hope of our Lord Jesus Christ, before God and our Father." 1 *Thess.* i. 3. The neophyte is then dismissed in peace. It is intended as an admonition that he shall press forward from virtue to virtue, and soar ever upward to the regions in which is enthroned the source of celestial life and purity unstained, God, the Saviour.

Q. Must there be at least one sponsor, or more, at baptism?

A. There must, according to the ordinance and practice of the Church from the earliest ages.

Q. How many sponsors are required?

A. A godfather and godmother, or a godfather or godmother, according to the ordinance of the *Council of Trent*, sess. xxiv., can. 2. The Church is averse to more than two sponsors, on account of the spiritual affinity, arising between the parties, being an obstacle to the validity of matrimonial alliance. When others, besides one godfather and godmother, are called upon to act as sponsors, the others are merely witnesses or honorary sponsors.

Q. Who contracts this spiritual alliance, and with whom?

A. He who administers the sacrament, enters into a spiritual relationship with the neophyte and its parents; the sponsors, the one for whom they act in this relationship, and the neophyte's parents; so says the Council of Trent. This affinity is an impediment to marriage.

Q. What are the duties imposed on sponsors?

A. They are manifold and of great importance, for,

1. They are bound to answer for the child the questions, if it renounces the devil, the world and the flesh, 'if it believes all the Church proposes, just as if the child pronounced the words itself with the full determination of realizing them in work.

2. They bind themselves to instruct the child; hence they pledge themselves, and become security and witnesses to the Church that they will do their utmost to have the child instructed in the faith, on arriving at the age of reason, and to cause it to persevere therein. This duty becomes still more binding when parents either neglect or become in any way disqualified for or incapable of fulfilling their paternal duties.

3. They are to give the neophyte a name.

Q. What kind of names should sponsors select for their god-child?

A. They should see that heathen names are not chosen, but rather the names of the saints, solemnly venerated in the Church, or the names of angels mentioned in the Holy Scripture, so that by their intercession the children may be guarded and protected, stimulated to imitate their example, to endeavor to arrive at perfection, and at length to join them in the realms of unfading bliss.

Q. May persons not in communion with the Church be admitted to act as sponsors?

A. No; because they cannot possibly fulfil the duties imposed by the sponsorship. How can they instruct a child in a faith which they neither know nor profess?

Q. What is the baptismal covenant?

A. The baptismal covenant is a covenant which God deigns to make with man in baptism. God promises and grants by baptism the greatest gifts, goods and graces, on condition that the recipient preserves his faith, and strives after justice He who receives the sacrament, accedes to these conditions, and promises to live in holiness, and to persevere to the end therein. When adults are admitted to the sacrament of regeneration, sponsors are required to attend as witnesses, whereas at the baptism of infants they are securities. Speaking on this subject, St. Augustine says: "Infants profess their faith by the words of those in whose arms they are borne, and the Church, as mother, grants them speech by her faithful." *St. Augustine, Lib. de peccato. merit. c.* 19. This is the covenant made between God and the neophyte. We adopt this term, because we consider it peculiarly adapted not only to express our object, but also the obligations which man takes upon himself: furthermore, because it is authorized by scriptural usage; for we frequently find in the inspired pages the term "covenant," particularly in passages relating to the Church of Christ. As this covenant lasts as long as our mortal pilgrimage, we should frequently renew it, particularly on the festival of our patron Saint, on our birthday, and similar occasions. We cannot recall too frequently the duties imposed on us by baptism. St. Ambrose says, speaking on this subject: "Thou hast entered the sanctuary of regeneration, repeat the questions put to thee on this occasion, and ponder well on the answers thou hast given. Thou hast renounced the devil and his works, the world with its pomps and pleasures. Reflect well on thy words then spoken, and never lose sight of the obligations thou hast taken on thyself." Herein principally consists the practical utility as regards our spiritual lives, of what we have said of this first, and most essential of sacraments. Live up to thy baptismal pledge, deviate not a hair's breadth from the path marked out to thee by the law of Him, whose co-heir thou hast become, and then thou needst not fear for thy salvation. Deplore sin bitterly, bewail thy misfortune, shouldst thou have already sullied thy baptismal robe, and forfeited thy ineffable dignity, as heir of the Most High, by the commission of grievous sin, and endeavor by redoubled zeal, fidelity and penance, to atone for thy past transgressions.

Of Confirmation.

Q. What is the Sacrament of Confirmation?

A. It is the sacrament in which those baptized receive by the unction with chrism, united with the word of God, the strength of the Holy Ghost, in order that they may profess their faith with fortitude, and live according to its dictates.

Q. How is the divine institution of this sacrament proved?

A. From Holy Scripture. The Holy Evangelist Luke expressly says, that the faithful received extraordinary graces by the imposition of the hands of the Apostles. *Acts,* viii. 17; x. 17. The bishops being the successors of the Apostles, and their representatives, the same effects are essentially wrought by the imposition of their hands, as St. Cyprian says: "The truth is in this symbol and the spirit in this sacrament." *Sehm. de unct. chrism.* The earliest Fathers, such as Tertullian, St. Cyprian, St. Cyrel, speak of the general use of Confirmation, to which also the oldest Councils, as those of Laodicea and Teliberis, oblige the faithful. *Cyprian. Epist. ad Ub., Cyril, Cat. 3 Tert. de Bap. c. 7.*

Q. What is the matter, and what the form of the sacrament of confirmation?

A. The matter of the sacrament is a mixture of oil and balsam, blessed by the bishop, and known from the most ancient times under the name of chrism. With this the brow of the recipient is anointed; that the imposition of the hands of the minister of the sacrament is united to the unction anointing, is proved by the manner in which this holy act is performed, and in this sense must the passages of Scripture and the Holy Fathers, referring to this subject, be understood. As to the definite form of the words pronounced, the bishop, whilst imposing his hands and anointing, says these words: "I sign thee with the sign of the cross. I confirm thee with the chrism of salvation, in the name of the Father, and of the Son, and of the Holy Ghost. Amen."

Q. Who is the ordinary minister of the sacrament of confirmation?

A. The bishop, as we are taught by the example of the Apostles, and by the tradition of the Church. A priest, however, may validly become the minister of the sacrament in an extraordinary case, and with the special permission of the Holy See. The words of St. Jerome to Ereginus, tend to prove this: "What does the bishop do, that the priest may not do, excepting only the conferring of holy orders?" Thus it is only the sacrament of orders that can never be conferred by a simple priest. It is even quite customary in the Greek Church, with the privilege and consent of the Holy See, that the priests who administer baptism, immediately after, confer the sacrament of confirmation. The same privilege has been granted by the Pontiffs in the Latin Church, not unfrequently to missionaries.

Q. Who may and should receive this sacrament, and when does it become incumbent on the faithful?

A. Every baptized Christian is capable of receiving this sacrament for we read of the Apostles that they imposed their hands on all those baptized, and it was customary in the primitive days of the Church to confirm immediately after baptism, without regard to the age, sex or condition of the neophyte. And is it not most just that all should receive the sacrament, which is the strength and confirmation of the Spirit? It is true, indeed, that infants are not obliged to take the field against the enemies of their salvation, yet they are called upon to prepare for the approaching combat, and arm themselves for the all-deciding ordeal of temptation and suffering, which, unless immediately taken to the bosom of their Heavenly Father, they shall certainly have to go through, so that they may receive the perfection of this grace, to the end that when the critical moment arrives, they may more surely be victorious. Still, it is advisable to postpone the reception of this sacrament, unless in case of necessity, till the age of seven or, according to the different circumstances of time and place, until after the reception of the adorable Eucharist, and this for the following reasons:

1. On account of the greater veneration paid to the sacrament, when received after due preparation.

2. Because it is more efficacious when imparted to those duly prepared.

3. In order that the profession made by sponsors in baptism, may be personally renewed and confirmed by the person to whom the sacrament is administered.

4. In order to obviate the danger of receiving the sacrament twice, the repetition being of course invalid; when the sacrament is administered to those arrived at the age of reason, this cannot easily occur.

Q. What is the preparation required for receiving this sacrament?

A. The candidate for confirmation must be in the state of sanctifying grace; hence, should he have forfeited his baptismal innocence by a formal transgression of God's commandments, he must approach the tribunal of penance. Those, therefore, who are about to receive this sacrament should be exhorted to strive to obtain the utmost purity of conscience, in order to prepare a fit dwelling for the Holy Spirit.

Q. Why does the bishop give to those confirmed a slight blow on the cheek?

A. To signify that they have now enrolled themselves under the banner beneath which victory is obtained, not by repelling violence by violence, but by bearing patiently insult, indignity and injustice, for Christ's sake, as it is written of the Apostles: "And they indeed went from the presence of the council rejoicing that they were accounted worthy to suffer reproach for the name of Jesus." *Acts,* v. 41.

Thus was it that the martyrs struggled against their persecutors and Christ's enemies, joyously and tranquilly turning one cheek to the heartless scoffer and persecutor who struck them on the other, cheerfully and patiently enduring every torture for Christ's sake.

Q. Why are sponsors chosen in confirmation?

A. Sponsors are admitted at confirmation in order that by their virtuous example they may encourage the neophyte in the spiritual combat. The sponsors of course must have already received this sacrament. This act cannot be wantonly deferred and neglected, without incurring the guilt of sin.

Q. Is the sponsorship attended in this sacrament also by the contraction of spiritual affinity?

A. It is; this affinity is contracted with the minister of confirmation, the person confirmed, and his parents.

Q. What are the advantages afforded by the reception of his sacrament for spiritual life?

A. 1. It endues us with strength and high courage, and powerfully moves us to thank God for the inestimable grace of having been admitted to the knowledge of TRUTH.

2. It inspires us with zeal in co-operating with the suggestions of grace, so that we may never be unfortunate enough to sadden the spirit of God within us. It also admonishes us frequently to renovate in ourselves the graces received in this sacrament, and to conduct ourselves resolutely, under the banner of the cross, as faithful soldiers of Christ.

3. We are reminded that our bodies are temples of the Holy Ghost, and that we should ever treat them accordingly.

Of the most Holy Sacrament of the Altar.

Q. What is the holy sacrament of the altar?

A. It is the sacrament of the body and blood of our Lord Jesus Christ, and, under the form of bread and wine, instituted by Him as the spiritual food of our souls.

Q. What then is the term applied by excellence to this sacrament?

A. It is called the Eucharist. This is a Greek word, equivalent to a grateful remembrance or thanksgiving, because in this sacrament is solemnly and gratefully celebrated the glorious passion of Christ our Lord, and the endless benefits conferred by Him on the human race; also, because our true and loving Saviour is given us as our spiritual nourishment, consolation, strength, and all, for which ineffable benefit we certainly owe God our most fervent thanks. Indeed, so inconceivably great is this grace and gift, that man, in the boldest aspirations of hope, might have never presumed to imagine that Jesus Christ, seated at the right hand of God in the kingdom of His glory, should so perfectly give himself to us, that we ourselves are His, and by this divine sacrament are in a manner so unspeakably intimate, holy and blissful, united and incorporated with Him. Hence the reception of this adorable sacrament is termed *communion, i. e.,* union, because it unites us to each other as members of one and the same body. It is also known by the name of *viaticum*, because it is the celestial food by which we are nourished and supported on the way through life, and particularly when about to leave earth's thorny path and pass on to the unknown realms of eternity, there to meet our judge and hear our doom.

Q. Who instituted this sacrament, and at what time?

A. Our Lord and Saviour Jesus Christ instituted this sacrament at the Last Supper, as we learn from the Evangelists. *Math.* xxvi. 26; *Mark*, xiv. 22; *Luke*, xxii. 19; *Cor.* xi. 23–26. At that solemn moment, He delivered to the chosen few His own adorable body under the form of bread, and His precious blood under the form of wine, commanding them and their successors to do the same in commemoration of Him.

Q. What are the principal points demanding our attention, when treating of this august sacrament?

A. The five following: 1. Of Christ's true and real presence in the sacrament of the altar; 2. Of the transubstantiation of the bread and wine; 3. Of the sacrifice made thereof; 4. Of the Holy Communion; 5. Of the adoration and veneration to be paid to this greatest of sacraments.

Of Christ's real presence in the most Holy Sacrament of the Altar.

Q. Who is truly and really present in the sacrament of the altar?

A. Christ the Lord, as God and man, body and soul, whole and entire, truly and actually, and under the form of bread and wine. This is incontestibly proved by the words of institution, for Christ, taking at the Last Supper the bread, and then the chalice into His hands, and wishing to assure us of the truths of this sacrament, spoke as the great lawgiver of the New Testament, as one making a last will and testament, the solemn and definite words: "Take ye and eat, for this is my body." "This is my blood that shall be shed for you." *Matth.* xxvi. Of this institution He has previously asserted and solemnly confirmed His assertion: "My flesh is meat indeed, and my blood is drink indeed; I am the living bread that came down from heaven, whoever eats of this bread shall live for ever, and the bread that I will give is my flesh for the life of the world." *John,* vi. Whoever then holds sacred the words of Christ, will, with the Apostles and the tradition of the Church, believe and steadfastly profess with us these words of the Divine Legislator, by which He left in this testament His true, real, and essential presence in the adorable sacrament. St. Cyril professes with the Holy Fathers in the following words, his faith in this mystery: "Since Christ himself declares of the bread: 'This is my body,' who shall dare to doubt it; since He declares, 'This is my blood,' who presumes to doubt its being really His blood?" At the nuptial feast of Cana in Galilee, He once transformed water into wine, which much resembles blood, and shall we presume to hesitate in believing that He changes wine into His blood? Look not, therefore, on the bread as mere bread, or the wine as mere wine, for it is the body and blood of Christ, as is evident from our Blessed Lord's own words. Even should thy senses furnish thee with a different testimony in this regard, thy faith should so strengthen thee, that thou wilt judge, not by the taste, but firmly believing, without yielding to even the slightest doubt, that Christ's body and blood have been given to thee." *Catech.* 9.

Q. How is Christ present in the adorable sacrament?

A. Christ is wholly present in the fullness of His glory under each form individually; wholly and entirely under the form and appearance of bread, wholly and entirely under the form and appearance of wine, because He is present in both as He is and exists in heaven. He is, moreover, wholly and entirely present under each and every particle of the sacramental species, be they ever so minute; were not this the case, He should be separated and broken in the Holy Communion, which is an absurdity to suppose. " For Christ," as says the Apostle, " dies no more after having risen again." *Rom.* vi. 9.

The incomprehensibility of this holy presence should not perplex us, as every reasonable person will readily assent to what the great St. Augustine says, viz.: "That God, in His omnipotence, is able to do more than our understanding is capable of comprehending." The essence of even the common objects surrounding us is, and remains to us an impenetrable mystery; for who can explain the manner in which bread, and nourishment in general, is changed into the substance of our own body and blood. How then shall we presume to fathom the mystery of transubstantion? The manifestation of God's omnipotence and infinite wisdom naturally far surpasses the limited powers of our understanding. Let it suffice for us to know, that God does or has done any thing, in order to believe and profess it as undeniably true.

Of Transubstantiation.

Q. In what consists the change, or transubstantiation, occurring in the Holy Sacrament of the Altar?

A. It is the change of the whole substance of the bread and wine into the substance of the body and blood of Christ. This transubstantiation is effected by Divine omnipotence, through the medium of the duly pronounced words of consecration by a lawfully ordained priest.

Q. How is this transubstantiation proved?

A. It is proved on the same grounds as Christ's real and true presence in the august sacrament.

1. From the words of institution, for Christ expressly says, "This bread(which I hold in my hand and which you see me hold) is my body." Whoever heard these words pronounced by Christ's own divine lips, could not possibly have attached to them any other signification than that which Christ gives them. He says, as it were, "This which I hold in my hand, and which has the appearance of bread, is not bread, but my body." Just as if Christ, at the nuptial feast in Cana of Galilee, had pointed to the stone jugs, saying, "This is not water, but wine;" every one who was aware of the pitchers having been filled with water, must necessarily have come to the very just conclusion that it had been changed into wine. The same remarks apply to the chalice.

2. Had the substance of the bread and wine remained, Christ must necessarily have employed a very different form of speech. He would have been obliged to say, "*in,* or *amongst* the particles composing the bread," or "*with* the bread," or "*here* is my body." For the institution of a new law, covenant, or testament, such as Christ was then making, urgently required fixed, clear, and accurately defined language; and this so much the more, as a misinterpretation of the departing Saviour's words would infallibly lead to idolatry, or, as it is generally styled, the adoration of bread, or "bread worship." Christ speaking of His flesh, which He proposes leaving us as food, and of His blood, as our spiritual drink, says, "My flesh is meat indeed, and my blood is drink indeed." *John,* vi.

From this it is sufficiently evident that it is not of bread and wine He speaks, but of the reality of His sacred body. An example will serve to illustrate this. We read in holy writ that Lot's wife was changed into a pillar of salt. Now, as in this transformation the inner substance of the body was changed, and the exterior form remained so also in this august sacrament, for the substance of the bread is changed to the body of Christ, while the exterior form and appearance remains unaltered. The same holds good of the chalice. The form, the taste, the scent, all the accidents of the wine remain, without its substance, as a veil for the blood of Christ, yea, Christ whole and entire. This is the constant and unanimous doctrine of the Church and all the Holy Fathers. St. Cyprian says, treating of this subject: "The bread which the Lord gave to His disciples, is not figuratively but essentially changed by the omnipotence of 'the word made flesh.'" *Serm. de cœna Domini.*

St. Ambrose says: "Thou wilt, perhaps, say, 'I see something else, and yet thou declarest that I receive the body of Christ.'" To this he replies: "The sacrament which thou receivest is called forth by God's own words. If the words of the Prophet Elias were sufficiently powerful to call down fire from heaven, shall not the words of Christ be powerful enough to change the species of the elements? Thou hast read of the works of creation: 'He spoke, and it was done. He commanded, and the whole world immediately existed.' Now, the words of Christ, which made of nothing that which was not, are they unable to transform that which already *is*, into that which *it was not?* It is no less a work of omnipotence to call new beings into existence than to change the substance of those already existing." *Lib. de Initiandis* c. 3. St. John Chrysostom says: "He who sanctifies and changes these gifts is Christ himself." *Homil. 83 in Matt.* St. John Damascene teaches: "Bread and wine are changed into the Body and Blood of the Lord. If thou inquirest how this is accomplished, attend to the reply given thee by the Holy Spirit." *Lib. 4 de Fide Orth. c.* 14.

The Church pronounces this dogma in the *Council of Trent* in the following terms: "If any one say, that in the most holy Sacrament of the Altar, the substance of bread and wine remains present with the substance of the Lord Jesus Christ's Body and Blood, and denies the wonderful and peculiar change of the whole substance of the bread into the Body, and the whole substance of wine into the Blood, so that the appearances of bread and wine only remain, which change the Catholic Church terms, with peculiar propriety, *transubstantion*, let him be anathema." *Sess.* 2.

Of the Holy Sacrament of the Eucharist as a Sacrifice.

Q. When does the holy sacrament of the altar possess the qualities of a sacrifice?

A. At the consecration, by the transubstantiating words of the priest; for at that moment Jesus is, as it were, immolated in an unbloody manner, as a holocaust of praise, adoration and thanksgiving, and likewise as a propitiatory victim for the salvation of the living and the dead.

Q. What is the name applied to this sacrifice?
A. The Holy Mass.

Q. What is the sacrifice of Mass considered in itself?
A. It is the transubstantiation, immolation, and participation of the body and blood of Jesus Christ instituted in commemoration of the bloody sacrifice consummated by our Lord on the bloody tree of the cross in pain ineffable, and ignominy unexampled. It is the same sacrifice as that offered by Christ on the cross, and its representation. For it is the same sweet and loving Saviour who on Calvary's Mount and on our altars immolates himself a victim of praise and propitiation for us, his sinful brethren. It is also the representation of this great sacrifice, because Christ's bitter death is emblematically expressed by the consecration of the two species, and the body of Jesus Christ being offered up, as it were, separated from his precious blood.

Q. Who instituted this sacrifice?

Christ himself, at the last supper, saying: "Do this in commemoration of me." *Luke,* xii. This is the doctrine of the Church and all the Fathers, and is confirmed by the *Council of Trent,* 22 Sess., in the following words: "If any one assert that Christ by these words, 'Do this in commemoration of me,' did not constitute the Apostles priests, and command them and other priests to offer up His body and blood, let him be anathema." And again, "If any one say that there is not a true and real sacrifice presented to God in the Holy Mass, let him be anathema." *Canon,* 1, 2.

1. The sacrifice of the Mass is the oblation which replaces the numerous victims of the Old Law. It is now offered up by all nations of the earth, in order, as we read in the prophet *Mal.* k 11, "*Worthily to praise God, and the name of our Saviour.*"

It is the great sacrifice of which all former oblations were but types, and from which they received their efficacy. Let us consider what the Holy Fathers say on this subject. St. Cyprian writes thus: "We behold the same sacrament and sacrifice of the Lord symbolized in the priest Melchisedeck, for who can be more justly termed the priest of the Most High God than our Lord Jesus Christ who presented to the Father the great victim, his own body and blood, under the form of that which Melchisedeck once offered bread and wine." *Ep.* 63 *ad Cæcilium.*

St. Gregory of Nyssa teaches: "He offers himself up as an expiatory victim for us, and as a victim immolates himself; thus he is at the same time a priest and the Lamb of God which taketh away the sins of the world." And when did He do this? When on giving to the assembled Apostles His body as food and his blood as drink, he declared that the sacrifice of the Lamb was already consummated." *Orat.* 1. *in Christ resurr.* St. Austin says: "Before this sublime and only true sacrifice all false sacrifices depart." *Lib.* 10, *de civit Dei.*

Q. To whom is the sacrifice of the Mass offered?
A. To the triune God alone.
Q. Why is this oblation made?
A. The reasons for the oblation of this holy and spotless victim are thus enumerated by the *Council of Trent.* "If any one assert that the sacrifice of the Mass is merely an oblation of praise and thanks or a mere commemoration of the sacrifice consummated on the cross, and not also an expiatory victim, or that it benefits only those who partake of it, or that it should not be offered for the living and the dead, for sins, punishments, atonements and other necessities, let him be anathema." 22. Sess. 3. Canon. In this canon of the Church the following dogmas are included and pronounced.

1. That the sacrifice of Mass is a victim of adoration and praise.

2. That it is offered to God in thanksgiving, or in other words, that it is a victim of thanksgiving.

3. That it is a deprecatory sacrifice, and may be offered to the Father of Mercies for all the necessities of the Church militant and suffering.

4. That it is an expiatory sacrifice, and not a mere commemoration of Christ's bloody death on the cross, and that hence,

5. It benefits not only those who partake of the sacrament, but those also who assist at the celebration of this sacrifice of the New Covenant.

6. Finally, that it is offered up for the necessities of the living and the dead.

St. Cyril's beautiful words serve us as sufficient proof, since they but re-echo the sentiments of all the Fathers and Doctors of the Church. The perfect spiritual sacrifice of the unbloody worship having been consummated, we implore God, for the sake of the great Victim thus immolated, to grant unity and peace to His Church, true peace to the world, grace for potentates, soldiers, allies; for those who are stretched on the bed of sickness; for all who stand in need of assistance do we all pray and present this sacrifice, during which we also call to mind those who have departed this life, firmly believing that the souls for whom we pray will derive great benefit, when this holy Word and Victim, fruitful in grace and in blessings, reposeth on our altars. Christ, who immolated himself for our sins, we offer up, in order to propitiate our good God in our behalf and theirs." *Cath.* 24.

The most perfect proof that the adorable sacrifice should be offered to the Divinity, for each and all of these ends, is derived from the fact that Christ, who is priest and victim, certainly contains within himself more than sufficient grounds for the offering up of this sacrifice for all these intentions.

Q. What does the Mass, with its ceremonies, signify and represent?

A. It is not only the commemoration of our Saviour's most bitter Passion and death; it also calls to our minds the whole economy of our salvation. The *Introit* is emblematic of the yearning of the patriarchs, prophets and all the just of olden times for the advent of the Messiah. The "*Kyrie Eleison*" is an emblem of their prayers and sighs for His appearance, and their longing to offer Him up to God as an expiatory sacrifice. The "*Gloria*" recalls the joyful event of our Saviour's birth; the *Collects*, which immediately follow, His presentation and oblation in the temple. The *Epistle* which is read on the left side of the altar signifies the mission of the Baptist, who instructed and admonished man. The *Gradual*, the preparation made by his exertions for the arrival and knowledge of Christ Jesus. The *Gospel*, which is read on the right side of the altar, signifies Christ's apostolic office of teacher, by which he has led us over from the left to the right hand, *i. e.*, from things temporal to things eternal, from the dominion of sin, beneath the sweet sceptre of grace. Lighted tapers and incense are used during the chanting of the Gospel, in order to signify that the Gospel enlightens the world and fills it with the fragrance of God's glory. The *Credo* is emblematic of the election and mission of Jesus Christ, his apostles and disciples. The *Offertory* and *Secret*, immediately following the *Credo*, refer to the voluntary oblation and preparation made by Christ for his approaching sufferings. The *Preface*, which is entoned in a loud voice and concludes with an exulting strain of "Hosannas," signifies the triumphant entry of Christ into Jerusalem on Palm Sunday. The *Canon*, recited in a low voice immediately after the *Preface*, calls to mind the desolation attending Christ's bitter sufferings. The elevation of the sacred Host reminds us that the meek Lamb of God bore His unexampled torments in silent resignation, and offered Himself up to His Father, on the cruel cross, bathed in blood and tears, for us, ungrateful sinners. The *Pater Noster* represents Christ's dying prayer; the breaking of the holy Host, Christ's expiatory death on the cross; the *Agnus Dei*, the mourning of those who believed in the Redeemer when his mangled body was taken from the cross; the priest's communion, our sweet Saviour's sad interment; the Canticle following the communion, and styled the *Post-Communion*, the joy called forth by the Lord's glorious resurrection; the "*Ite Missa est*," Christ's farewell to earth, and His ascent to the dwelling of His glory; the priest's *benediction*, the descent of the Paraclete; the Gospel, which is read at the conclusion of the adorable sacrifice, the preaching of the Apostles, when replenished with the power and the fullness of the Spirit of Truth, they hastened to announce to all nations, tribes and peoples the glad tidings of salvation, and, by the conversions thus made, propagated Christ's Kingdom (Church) on earth. Whoever directs his attention immediately or mediately to all this during the celebration of the Holy Sacrifice, will undoubtedly assist with devotion and much spiritual benefit.

Of Holy Communion, or the Participation of the Mystery of our Altars.

Q. Are the faithful obliged to receive this sacrament?
A. Most assuredly, as is evident from Christ's words: "Do this in commemoration of me." *Luke*, xii.; 1 *Cor.* i. 24. For by these words Jesus not only constituted the Apostles priests of the New Covenant, and commanded them and their successors in the priestly office to present the sacrifice of His Body

and Blood, by the change of bread and wine, but He also thereby enjoins its personal reception on all the faithful. He instituted this sacrament as the spiritual food for the children of His Church. The doctors of the Church justly conclude from this passage that the participation in this sacred banquet is to be looked upon as a Divine precept, even had not our Holy Mother, the Church, given any law on the subject.

Q. Must this sacrament be received under both forms?

A. That the officiating priest must communicate under both forms, is beyond the slightest doubt, as the sacrifice is offered under both forms. However, it is to be observed of the priests, when not celebrating the Divine Sacrifice, but merely assisting, and of the laity, that it suffices to receive this blessed sacrament under one form, and that there is no command binding us to receive under both. We are to observe whatever the Holy Church, our wise and good mother and teacher, may think proper to decree, according to the time and circumstances. The Holy Scripture vouches for the correctness of this remark, for in many passages in which this adorable mystery is mentioned we find the Body and Blood both explicitly named, and in others merely the reception of the bread, because, under this form, both body and blood are present; for, in the passage in which we find the words, "Unless you eat the flesh of the son of man and drink his blood you shall not have life in you" (*John*, vi. 54), we immediately after see, "He that eateth this *bread* shall live for ever." *John*, vi. 59. And when Jesus said, "He that eateth my *flesh* and drinketh my *blood* hath everlasting life" (*John*, vi. 55), he adds: "And the *bread* that I will give you is my flesh for the life of the world." *John*, vi. 52. He who said, "He that eateth my *flesh* and drinketh my *blood* abideth in me and I in him," (*John*, vi. 57), also said: "If any man eat of this *bread*, he shall live for ever." Christ's own example proves the truth of this conviction, for, although at the last supper He dispensed this adorable mystery under both forms, He gave this sacrament to the two disciples of Emmaus only under one form, as the Holy Fathers unanimously interpret this passage. *Luke*, xxiv. 30, 31. Hence we find from the earliest ages of Christianity the custom of administering the sacrament also under one form. We learn from history that it was received now under one and again under both forms. Those, for instance, who could not bear the taste of wine, received under the form of bread alone;

this occurred frequently during the times of persecution, when it was customary to give the consecrated bread to the faithful, to be carried to their dwellings where they might partake of this celestial banquet according to their devotion and convenience. A drop from the consecrated chalice was given to infants. It is deserving of remark, that in the Acts, when the holy communion is spoken of, we find mention only made of *breaking the bread. Acts*, ii. 46.

Somewhat later the Church, actuated by very weighty reasons, ordained that this sacrament was to be administered to the laity in the Western Church under the form of bread only. This prevented much irreverence that was wont to occur from the accidental spilling of the consecrated wine. Moreover, the sacrament is much more easily administered under the form of bread alone, laying aside the fact, that in many places wine cannot be procured in sufficient quantity for general distribution. These reasons may be regarded as of greater weight, when the circumstance is taken into consideration that the laity lose not in the slightest degree the fruit of the sacrament, for Christ is wholly present under both forms, and is only consecrated, immolated and partaken of by the priest in as far as it is a sacrifice. Further, because there appeared heretics who maintained that this sacrament must necessarily be partaken of under both forms, the adorable blood of Jesus not being present in the Host, which is evident absurdity and falsehood. Supposing it for a moment correct, it must lead to the conclusion that we receive not Christ's living body, but his corpse, which of course is preposterous, for Christ, once risen from the dead, "dieth no more."

Q. What preparation is required for the reception of this adorable sacrament?

A. The apostle admonishes us: "Let a man prove himself, and so let him eat of that bread." 1 *Cor.* xi. 28. This self-probation consists in an earnest examination of the state of one's conscience, followed by a contrite confession to a duly authorized priest, by which the guilt-stained soul is restored to purity. Many persons, however, who go frequently to confession, have recourse to the tribunal of penance, out of devotion and reverence, before approaching this august mystery, when the state of their conscience would not in itself render confession imperative, but in order to prepare the better for so great a guest.

2. A lively act of faith should be excited in the breast so soon to become the throne of the Lord of glory, that, in the Holy Host, truly He is present who was born of the stainless Virgin for our sakes, bled and died on the ignominious tree of the cross, and now sitteth in power and majesty at the right hand of God the Father, whence He shall come in the fullness of His might to judge the quick and the dead.

3. A firm purpose of amendment is to be renewed.

4. We should be particularly careful to renew our sincere and hearty forgiveness of every injury or offence offered us.

5. We are to be fasting from midnight, *i. e.*, we are carefully to abstain from partaking of anything in the form of food, drink or medicine. The slightest particle or drop thus taken renders us unfit to approach the Holy Table for the time in question. Should we when rinsing the mouth accidentally swallow a drop of water mixed with spittle, it does not prevent the reception of the adorable sacrament.

6. Acts of humility, desire and love for Jesus, in the mystery of ineffable love, are to be excited immediately before receiving, with the utmost devotion and fervor. Suitable prayer-books will be found to give efficient aid in this respect.

Q. Is it a grievous sin to approach this Holy Table in the state of mortal sin?

A. Certainly; it is a crime of so heinous a nature that the Holy Ghost says, by the mouth of the Apostle, of those who incur this guilt: "He that eateth and drinketh unworthily, eateth and drinketh judgment to himself, and shall be guilty of the body and blood of the Lord." 1 *Cor.* xi.

That is, as St. Chrysostom interprets this passage, "He becomes guilty of the body and blood of the Lord, just as if he had slain Christ, and His blood stains his guilty soul as if he had shed it as His murderer and executioner. O God, how horrible a crime! As often as we peruse the doleful history of our sweet Saviour's bitter Passion, our hearts are filled with indignation against Judas, Caiphas, Pilate, and all who with such fiendish rage and cruelty outraged the Lord's adorable person; and yet more grievous are the indignities and sufferings inflicted on this meek Lamb of God by an unworthy reception of His adorable body and blood than all that was inflicted upon Him by the perverse and wicked Jews. The wanton malice of such a wretch is rendered more daring and horrible by the clear knowledge he possesses of what he does. Do such unhappy beings consider the enormity and horror of the crime they wickedly commit, of the Divine wrath which they defy, of the punishments impending over them? With what great respect did not the Lord wish the Ark of the Covenant to be treated, in which the Tables of the Law were preserved? No one, not even the priest, was permitted to touch it unless covered. *Ex.* xxv. No one might presume to touch or carry it, even when covered, except the Levites, who were obliged, while thus engaged, to act with the utmost care and reverence. The Philistines, who had taken it in battle and carried it about from place to place, were smote by the Lord with disease and tribulation. Fifty thousand Bethlamites were suddenly snatched out of life, for having presumed to gaze irreverently upon it. 1 *Kings*, vi. Oza rashly stretched forth his hand to prevent its falling, and he was struck dead on the spot. If, then, God so strenuously insisted on the Ark being duly honored, and so severely punished those who were guilty of but slight irreverence, what punishment have those to expect who treat the adorable mystery with indignity or who presume to partake unworthily of the Body and Blood of God's only begotten Son? How shall they one day stand before Him, their Judge, whom they now so cruelly insult and dishonor as Saviour? God has not unfrequently punished such wanton and presumptuous wickedness, even here on earth.

Q. What should we do when receiving the adorable Sacrament?

A. We should approach the Holy Table with devoutly folded hands and downcast eyes, and, after having made a genuflection with the utmost reverence, the cloth is taken from the rails and rested on the hand, the head moderately raised, the cloth put under the chin, so that if the Holy Host might be dropped by the priest it may rest on the cloth; the mouth is to be reverently and sufficiently opened, the tongue laid on the lower lip, where it is to be quietly kept till the consecrated particle reposes on it. The adorable Sacrament having been received with the greatest possible devotion, the recipient rises and with folded hands again makes devout genuflection, and returns to his place with downcast eyes and clasped hands as he came.

Q. What is to be done after Holy Communion?

A. We should carefully avoid hurrying immediately from the church. Let us rather recall to mind the example of the beloved disciple at the Last Supper, and endeavor to profit by our sweet Saviour's adorable presence, by keeping all the powers of our minds in a calm and collected state, and adore Christ, truly and really present, with the utmost humility, striving wholly to unite ourselves with Him in faith and love.

2. Acts of the most fervent thanksgiving and oblation are to be excited, in union with the infinite merits of our beloved guest, Jesus, our Lord and Saviour.

3. We should renew our purposes of amendment and sanctification of life, by earnestly avoiding the occasions of sin, and struggling against temptations, and by the most zealous practice of the duties of our state.

4. We should recommend to the divine clemency the living and the dead, for whom we are bound by duty and gratitude to pray. Let all this be done with the tenderest and most confiding love, saying, with the patriarch Jacob: "I will not let thee go unless thou bless me." *Gen.* xxxii.

This confidence will undoubtedly increase the graces conferred on you in this adorable sacrament.

Q. How should we further seek to sanctify the day of our communion?

A. The day on which the soul has united itself with Jesus in this august mystery, should be wholly employed in thanksgiving and praise, and more time than usual set apart for prayer and other practices of piety, particularly when this day is a Sunday or holyday, as is frequently the case.

Q. What is further to be observed after the reception of this saving sacrament?

A. After confession and holy communion, every one is strictly bound to guard most carefully against a relapse into his former sins, in order that he may not prove himself unworthy of so inestimable a favor, and thus increase his own damnation; remembering the words addressed by Christ to the man sick of the palsy, whom He restored to health: "Behold thou art made whole: sin no more lest some worse thing happen to thee." *John*, v. 14. This, however, should not suffice for us; we should zealously seek to improve the immense graces conferred by this sacrament, for securing the great affair of our salvation, so that we may be able to say in truth with the great Apostle: "I live, now not I; but Christ liveth in me." *Gal.* ii. 20.

Q. What is understood by spiritual communion?

A. We understand by spiritual communion, a fervent desire to receive Jesus Christ in the sacrament of His love, expressed by reciting with ardor the three theological virtues, as if about in reality to partake of this celestial food.

Q. What are the benefits derived from spiritual communion?

A. It procures us. 1. Participation in the graces conferred by this divine sacrament, according to the teaching of St. Augustine and St. Thomas. 3 *p. q.* 80, 1 *ad.* 3.

2. It is a very suitable means of preparation for the reception of the adorable mystery, as it exercises the soul in those acts of piety the best calculated to fit us for sitting at this banquet of celestial sweetness.

3. It further serves to insure our daily assisting at the celebration of the august mysteries, with more fruit and greater devotion.

Q. How is the spiritual communion to be made?

A. The most proper manner of preparing to receive our divine Lord spiritually is from the "*Agnus Dei ;*" first, to excite sentiments of sincere contrition for the many sins committed against Him, who loves us so fondly and so constantly, then we should humbly join the priest in the thrice-repeated words: "O Lord, I am not worthy that Thou shouldst enter under my roof; say but the word, and my soul shall be healed." Thereupon let us excite acts of faith, hope, and charity in this mystery. This being done, we should, while the priest is communicating, invite Jesus to enter into our hearts, with these and similar burning sighs of fervent love: "Oh my Jesus, my Saviour, Thou life of my soul, come and give thyself to me! Ah, would that I might now receive Thee! O my Jesus! my sweet love, come." We should now say with the most ardent love and humility, as if Jesus had really entered our hearts:

"Soul of Jesus, sanctify me. Blood of Jesus, wash me. Passion of Jesus, strengthen me. Wounds of Jesus, heal me. Heart of Jesus receive me. Spirit of Jesus, enliven me. Love of Jesus, inflame me. Mercy of Jesus, spare me. Cross of Jesus, save me. Cross of Jesus, support me. Thorns of Jesus, crown me. Sighs of Jesus, plead for me. Agony of Jesus, atone for me. Lips of Jesus, bless me in life and death, in time and eternity. Amen."

Q. What are the fruits produced in the soul by the worthy reception of the adorable Eucharist?

A. The fruits of a worthy communion are numerous, inexpressibly great and important; for this is the bread that came down from heaven, imparting life to the world; the bread which vivifies, strengthens and refreshes our souls in the life of grace. This sacrament further symbolizes and effects the union of all the faithful as members of one body, united together by the merits of the saints and all pious souls. Further, what is still more important, it intimately unites those members with Christ, their divine head, so that He abideth in them, and they in Him, the fullness of supernatural life. It is the food and refreshment furnished us by infinite love, in our weary pilgrimage over the thorny paths of life, surrounded by dangers, toils, and enemies, with whom we have to contest every step in our advance towards our glorious goal, the heavenly Jerusalem; a manna containing in itself all that is delicious, much superior to that given to our fathers in the desert; a food, rich in heavenly delights, containing for us the germs of undying bliss and glory. St. Bernard beautifully expresses himself on this subject: "The worthy reception of this sacrament diminishes the inclination to even the slightest sins, and removes entirely the tendency to more grievous transgressions. If, then, a person no longer experiences such violent temptations, emotions of anger, envy, and the like, he may thank the body and blood of the adorable physician of his soul, to whom he is indebted for this favor, for the virtue of the sacrament has begun to operate within him. He may rejoice, for his cure is not far distant." *De cœna Domini.* And again he says: "The body of Christ is a remedy for the sick, a path for the traveller, it strengthens the weak, refreshes those who are of a good and earnest will, and cures tepidity. Man becomes milder in admonishing, more patient in labor, more fervent in charity, more cautious in protecting, readier in obedience, and more devout in thanksgiving." The great St. Ignatius, the martyr, very justly exclaims, addressing Christians in general: "An immortal remedy is this bread, an antidote to death, so that we may live in God, through Jesus Christ." *Epis. ad Eph.* This is the sacred banquet of which the Church speaks in her solemn hymns: "O holy banquet in which Christ is received, the memory of His passion renewed, the soul filled with grace, and a pledge of future glory is given us."

Of the Adoration of the Most Holy Sacrament of the Altar.

Q. Should we adore the most holy sacrament of the altar?

A. Yes; for is it not Jesus Christ himself concealed beneath the sacramental forms? Now, Holy Writ itself calls on us to adore Jesus Christ, for it is written of Him: " Let the angels of God adore Him." *Heb.* i. 6. And in the Psalms we find the following passage : " And all the kings of the earth shall adore Him, all nations shall serve Him." *Ps.* lxxi. 11. The royal seer having been favored with a vision of this most sublime mystery, does not consider it sufficient to say : " The poor shall eat and shall be filled, they shall praise the Lord," but adds : " And all the kindred of the Gentiles shall adore in His sight." *Ps.* xxi. 27, 28. The Magi from the East, and many others paid to the Lord divine honors, while He was still on earth, fell down before Him, and adored Him. *Math.* viii. 2, ix. 2, xiv. 15 ; *Mark,* v. 6, xv. 19 ; *Luke,* xxiv. 52 ; *John,* ix. 8. Now in the august mystery of our altars, we believe the same Christ present, not in mortal flesh, but in immortal though veiled glory, worthy of benediction and honor in the fullness of His power and glory. This our faith we seek to testify by reverently prostrating ourselves before this adorable sacrament in humble and devout transports of love. St. Chrysostom says: " The Magi bowed down in adoration before Christ in the crib, and worshipped Him with great fear and trembling ; thou beholdest Him not in the crib, but on the altar ; we are, therefore, bound to offer much greater proofs of respect and adoration than did these heathens." *Hom.* 24 in Ep. 1 ad Cor. The Apostle St. Paul, speaking of the glory of Christ and the worship due to him, says : " For which cause God also hath exalted Him, and hath given Him a name, which is above all names ; that in the name of Jesus every knee should bend, of those that are in heaven, on earth, and under the earth." *Phil.* xxix. 10. If this veneration is to be paid to the mere name, shall we refuse it to Him, the mighty and divine One present on our altars ? The Council of Trent thus expresses this dogma : " If any man say that Christ, the only Begotten, is not to be also exteriorly adored and honored with peculiar and festive solemnity, further, that He is not to be, according to the universal and laudable usage of the Church, borne from place to place in processions, or exposed to the public adoration of the people, or that His adorers are idolaters, let him be anathema." *Sess.* xiii. *Can.* vi.

Practice.—Magnify and praise the Lord with all the heavenly hosts; thank Him in union with the aspirations of Mary's sinless heart, and of all the saints in heaven and on earth, for the institution of the most adorable sacrament of the altar; for this greatest proof of the ineffable love He bears thee; for this sublimest of His gifts, and devote yourself entirely to the adoration, veneration, and love of Jesus on our altars. Hasten to cast thyself down before His lowly dwelling in our tabernacles, tarry there as long as is permitted thee, and receive thy sweet Jesus as often and as worthily as thou canst with sentiments of strong faith and fervent love; treat Him not with neglect who establishes His throne in thy heart; give thyself entirely up to Him, let all the faculties of thy soul be absorbed in His sweet love, and thou shalt certainly begin to lead a life hidden with that of Christ in God, and enjoy in communing with Jesus, a foretaste of the joy of heaven, and the graces pre-ordained for thee from all eternity, shall certainly be poured down upon thee through Jesus Christ, with whom thou art so intimately united by this sacrament.

Of Penance.

Q. What is penance?

A. It is the sacrament in which the remission of sins, committed after baptism, is granted to the sincere penitent by the absolution of the priest.

Q. Who instituted this sacrament?

A. Jesus Christ, who after His resurrection, breathed upon the Apostles, saying: "As the Father hath sent me, I also send you. Receive ye the Holy Ghost: whose sins you shall retain, they are retained, whose sins you shall forgive, they are forgiven." *John,* xx. 21–23. The *Council of Trent* thus express itself on this head: "If any one assert that in the Catholic Church the institution of penance is not for the faithful a true and real sacrament instituted by Christ, to reconcile them with God, as often as after Baptism they fall into sin, let him be anathema." Sess. xiv. Can. 1.

Q. Was this power to survive the Apostles?

A. Undoubtedly, for the Church founded by Christ was to continue to the end of time, and with it, the spiritual powers granted to the Apostles, not for their personal advantage, but for all who believe in Christ's name; now, there will unfortunately be sinners found on earth to the end of time, languishing for the forgiveness of their transgressions;. this Christ clearly foresaw, hence He instituted this remedy of grace for all men and all ages, as the second and last saving plank after the shipwreck of sin, as the holy Fathers term the sacrament of penance.

Q. To whom, then, was this transmitted?

A. To the bishops as legitimate successors of the Apostles, and the priests they may please to appoint.

Q. Do priests really forgive sins?

A. Certainly; not, however, by human power, but empowered and authorized by God, who confers on them this privilege for the benefit of the faithful.

Q. When does the priest remit, when does he retain sins?

A. He remits sins when he gives absolution in the tribunal of penance; he retains them when he refuses or delays it.

Q. May every sin, without exception, be remitted in the Church of God by the sacrament of penance?

A. Yes; provided the sacrament be received with due dispositions.

Q. What are the principal constituents required for the worthy reception of this sacrament?

A. Contrition, confession, and satisfaction, as we are taught by Scripture; these requisites may easily be deduced from the nature of a sincere conversion, for if a man have injured or offended his neighbor, and sincerely wishes to be reconciled with him, he acknowledges and repents of the evil done him, he goes in quest of the injured person, acknowledges the wrong done him, and expresses his sorrow for what has occurred, and declares his willingness to atone for it. Our confession and reconciliation with God, require the same of us. The Church pronounces this dogma in the *Council of Trent* as follows: "The matter, as it were, of this sacrament, is the three acts of the penitent, viz., contrition, confession, and satisfaction. These are, therefore, called the parts of the sacrament of penance, in as far as penance requires them for the perfection of the sacrament and the full and perfect remission of sins, according to the divine ordinance." Sess. xiv. Cap. 3. We shall here add separately the most necessary remarks on each.

Contrition.

Q. What is contrition?

A. It is an interior grief and horror of sins committed, with the firm resolve never more to relapse into our evil habits, as is said by the *Council of Trent*, in Sess. xiv. Cap. 4. True contrition thus includes in itself two acts; sorrow of the heart, and the purpose of the will.

Q. What qualities must contrition possess in order to obtain forgiveness of sin?

A. It must, first, be interior, *i. e.*, genuine sorrow and detestation, not pronounced merely by the lips; but, on the contrary, proceeding from the heart.

2. Supernatural, *i. e.*, this sorrow and detestation must be excited by supernatural motives and considerations taught us by faith. We are to detest and reject sin above all things, as an insult and offence directed against the divine majesty, and not purely from considerations prompted by temporal motives; for instance, the many temporal chastisements incident to sin. Thus a drunkard may heartily regret that he has been intoxicated, when the fit, being over, leaves in its train nauseousness, depression, and sickness, &c.; a gamester, after having lost his money; a libertine, when his excesses have entailed disease upon him, or robbed him of the good name he enjoyed in the world. Such sorrow, generated as it is by mere natural causes, suffices not for the remission of sin, being unaccompanied by any real detestation of the sinful act. This was the regret experienced by Saul when he said to the prophet: "I have sinned; yet honor me now before the ancients of my people." 1 *Kings*, xv. Antiochus repented on his sick couch in a similar manner, of the wicked deeds committed in Jerusalem. It was but a natural sorrow and detestation of his crimes, called forth by the approach of death, which he recognized as a consequence and punishment of his sins. His heart, however, remained unchanged, hence we find written of him: "He laid himself down upon his bed, and fell sick for grief, because it had not fallen out to him as he imagined." 1 *Mach.* vi. 8. God beheld his unconverted heart. The sorrow expressed by the royal prophet was different, when, penetrated with remorse, he exclaimed: "I have sinned." He experienced the deepest regret for having

offended God, and therefore merited to hear those consoling words from the lips of the prophet: "The Lord hath taken away thy sin."• 2 *Kings*, xii.

Now contrition, when true and so qualified as to enable us to obtain remission of our sins, must be excited by motives furnished by faith, in virtue of which we repent of and detest all that we have done against the Divine commandments. Faith is also, in this respect, the ground of all justification. Contrition must, further, be universal, *i. e.*, extending to all the sins we have committed; at least, to all the mortal sins, without exception, to which we may have unfortunately consented. Should one not be truly contrite, for any one mortal transgression, his confessions would be invalid, and instead of obtaining the forgiveness of his sins, they would, as before, weigh down his soul with their enormity, with the addition of the horrible guilt of sacrilege.

4. Contrition must, further, be accompanied by the earnest purpose of amendment.

Q. What is to be observed of this purpose of amendment?

A. It must be interior and true, *i. e.*, it suffices not merely to pronounce it with the lips, we must make it with a strong and energetic will, and firmly resolve to adhere to it. It must be universal, *i. e.*, extending to all sins. This is requisite for a true and sincere amendment of life, viz.:

1. To avoid sin and all occasions of sin.
2. To avoid the temptations to sin; and should they, notwithstanding, continue to importune us, to resist them resolutely and generously from their first appearance.
3. Further, to repair injuries done to the honor and property of our fellow men to the best of our ability.
4. Seek to make due amends for every known and wilful scandal given.
5. Forgive each and every offence done us, and become heartily reconciled with all men.
6. Fulfil with the greatest punctuality the duties and obligations imposed by your state of life, and resolutely press forward on the path of Christian virtue and piety.
7. Faithfully perform the penance enjoined us in the tribunal of penance.

Q. What is understood by immediate occasions of sin?

A. That which is generally a cause of temptation to us, whether it be a person, diversion, occupation, &c.

Q. Are we strictly bound to avoid the immediate occasions of sin?

A. Certainly; for "he who loves danger shall perish therein" (*Eccles.* v.), as Scripture and daily experience testify. He loves danger, who voluntarily puts himself under its influence, or flies not when he might do so, even should he not have sought or exposed himself to it.

Q. What is to be done when our circumstances will not immediately permit us to fly such occasions?

A. We should strive to render the immediate occasion remote, that is, less imminent; arming ourselves with the weapons of prayer, vigilance, mortification and prompt resistance. If this cannot be done, it becomes imperative on us to avoid it, even should it entail on us some temporal loss; yea, at the expense of all our earthly goods, even of life itself, according to the words of our Lord: "If thy right eye scandalize thee, pluck it out and cast it from thee; if thy hand or foot scandalize thee, cut them off and cast them from thee." *Matt.* v. 30. That is, if a thing were as necessary to us as hand or foot, still we are imperatively bound to avoid it, at whatever loss and peril, rather than remain in danger of falling into sin.

Q. What should persons take into consideration who procrastinate in resolving to avoid occasions of sin?

A. That the absolution obtained in the sacrament is altogether invalid, and serves but to increase their guilt.

Q. How is supernatural contrition further distinguished?

A. By perfect and imperfect contrition or attrition.

Q. When is contrition perfect?

A. When proceeding solely from love and sorrow, for having offended a God infinitely good, perfect and amiable in himself.

Q. When is it merely attrition?

A. When our sorrow does not immediately proceed from grief, excited by love, for having offended a God infinitely amiable and perfect in himself, but from love of God called forth by his being for us the supreme good, from whom we have received and do still expect so many benefits, and by other motives subordinate to love, such as fear of the judgments of God, as affecting our temporal and eternal well being.

Q. Is perfect contrition indispensable, in order to obtain forgiveness of sin?

A. It is, when we cannot receive the sacrament of penance;

joined with the reception of this sacrament, attrition suffices. We should, however, earnestly endeavor to obtain perfect contrition, which prepares and, as it were, enlarges our hearts for greater and more precious graces, and increases within us the fruit and efficacy of this pledge of God's ineffable mercy.

Q. When, in particular, are we bound to excite contrition?

A. 1. Before confession, or, at least, before absolution.

2. As often as we have been unfortunate enough to fall into some grievous sin.

3. In danger of death. It is, moreover, very laudable and salutary to excite perfect contrition daily; at least, before retiring, after having examined our conscience. Thus shall we be enabled to live and die in greater security, increase within us the treasures of sanctifying grace, and increase the merits gone before us to our blessed home beyond the dreary portals of the tomb.

Q. What will be found peculiarly adapted to excite in our hearts sincere and supernatural contrition?

A. 1. Earnest reflection on the infinite majesty of God, whose glory fills heaven and earth, and our own nothingness in His sight, being called into existence by His fiat, and unable to perform the slightest action unassisted by His power and His love.

2. The infinite goodness God has deigned to manifest in our regard: for do we not owe all we possess to His bounty; every gift, every breath we draw, every cheering sunbeam, our whole being and all our faculties? The infinite mercy of God, recalled to our minds by the Holy Cross and Him who bled thereon, our dearest Jesus—all that God has done for us after our having forfeited, by the sin of our first parents (to which we have added so many actual transgressions), all claims to heaven, and incurred damnation; and yet Jesus awaits us with such patient, untiring love, opens wide His arms, in order to fold us to His breast in forgiving love, if, like Magdalen, the loving penitent of old, we cast ourselves contrite at His blessed feet.

3. The lively remembrance of the bitter Passion of our dear Jesus and His expiatory death on the cross; on the bitter tears mingled with blood, shed for us on that couch of pain; on the heavy sighs, wrung from his tortured breast by our ingratitude, in the dark, dreary hours of his agony on Calvary. His doleful exclamation, the streams of blood, the gaping wounds, His heart pierced after death by the cruel lance.

4. The earnest consideration of eternity and approaching judgment; on the fearful consequences entailed by sin, dwelling for ever in the flames of hell; and also on the ineffable joys of heaven, the raptures and delights there awaiting the eternal possession of God, in the company of the just made perfect.

Of Confession.

Q. What is confession?
A. An express, contrite, but secret self-accusation, before a duly authorized priest, of, at least, all the grievous sins committed after baptism, as far as we can recall them to memory, in order to obtain their remission by the priest's absolution. The words of St. John are to be understood as referring to this sacrament when he writes: "If we confess our sins, He is faithful and just to forgive us our sins, and to cleanse us from all iniquity." 1 *John*, i. 9.

We say that confession is an express self-accusation, in order to show that the penitent is bound to confess his sins, as he believes them to be, in the Divine sight, without palliation, exaggeration, diminution, disguise or concealment. We have further stated confession to be a secret accusation, in order to distinguish it from the public penitential accusation, at times practised in the primitive Church, but which, on account of scandal, was in course of time abolished. The accusation for sacramental confession is to be made in secret. We have said that every known and remembered grievous sin, at least, is to be confessed; for whoever willingly and knowingly conceals but *one* grievous sin has made his accusation in vain, and instead of obtaining the benefits to be derived from this saving sacrament, incurred the enormous guilt of sacrilege. As regards venial sins, they may be confessed, and this accusation is accompanied with great spiritual advantages; yet we are not bound by any precept to confess them, and they may be washed away without confession by acts of contrition and penance, and by the merits of Christ's Passion. Should a person, however, not be sufficiently instructed to enable him accurately to distinguish a mortal from a venial transgression, he is bound to lay his doubts before his confessor, in order that he may not incur the guilt of grievous sin by culpable ignorance. Venial sins are, moreover, confessed in the tribunal of penance, as an act of humility, and in order to draw down greater and richer graces on the recipient, particularly when one is so happy as to lead a life undefiled by mortal sin. In this case, however, we must be very careful to excite true contrition and a firm purpose of amendment; for without sincere contrition there can be no remission of sins, either in or out of the tribunal of penance. Thus whoever confesses venial sins alone, and repents not heartily of at least one of them, draws upon himself, by his confession, the guilt of sacrilege.

Q. May sins once confessed be repeated, and the grace of the sacrament obtained?

A. Certainly; supposing that one should have been so happy as to fall, since the last confession, into no sin: for contrite self-accusation of sins once committed, alone is necessary for the validity of the sacrament. This self-accusation may be as frequently repeated as we wish. The grace of the sacrament consists in its effacing the stains of sin when our consciences are thereby defiled, or in imparting, when this is not the case, new treasures of sanctifying grace, as water cleanses us from the stains contracted or, when we are free from such, serves to promote the cleanliness of the body; and again, as one light dispels the darkness of a room, but if a second be added the light will be much increased.

Q. When is it particularly advisable to renew our self-accusation of sins once committed?

A. When we have not to accuse ourselves of sins, or at least of mortal sins consented to since the last confession, it is well in this case, in order to obviate all fears respecting true contrition, to add at the end of our accusation: "I include and accuse myself of this or that grievous sin, into which I unfortunately fell."* The sin is then specified. We are, however, to be on our guard against repeating, in detail, the sins committed against the sixth commandment, provided they have once been confessed, with due dispositions, as this might, perhaps, lead to a new carnal temptation. Should any one wish to renew their self-accusation on this point, it is to be done in general terms.

Q. When does it become incumbent on us to repeat the sins once confessed?

A. When we wish to receive the sacrament of penance, and have not since its last reception incurred the guilt of either a mortal or a deliberate venial sin; as also when making a general confession, or when we have reason to fear that our former confessions were not accompanied with the due dispositions.

Q. What is general confession, and what class of persons have recourse to it?

A. General confession is a detailed and full accusation of all the sins committed since we arrived at the age of reason. A confession of this kind should be made by those who approach for the first time the table of the Lord, those who are entering on a new state of life, and those who find themselves admonished either by serious illness or advanced age to prepare for their passage from this land of exile to their eternal home.

Q. On whom is general confession incumbent?

A. On all those who have not sincerely and contritely confessed their evil deeds, and particularly such as are the slaves of evil habits.

It will, moreover, be found a salutary custom, after having made a good general confession, to make a confession annually of all the faults committed since the general confession: this will be found highly conducive to a knowledge of ourselves, and will also serve as a security for the validity of our ordinary confessions. General confessions, however, proceeding from scruples or mistaken devotion are neither to be commended nor practised.

It is much better to confess frequently, with careful preparation, and earnestly to strive to progress in virtue, to think of the good which we can and should yet perform, instead of morbidly brooding over the evil once committed, and now unfortunately beyond the power of recall.

Q. Who instituted the sacrament of penance?

A. Jesus Christ, who expressly declares: "Whose sins ye shall forgive, they are forgiven; whose sins ye shall retain, they are retained." *John,* xx. 3.

By these solemn words, Jesus Christ appointed the Apostles and their successors in the holy ministry, the priests and bishops, as judges in matters of conscience, possessing the power of retaining or remitting sins according to right and justice. The appointment of this judicial tribunal likewise imposes on the faithful to the end of time the obligation of entirely and sincerely revealing the wounds of conscience. For how could the Apostles and their successors duly exercise the powers granted them, if they were not made acquainted with the spiritual infirmities and miseries of those who apply for the exercise of this saving power? Christ, however, never gave to the Apostles, or never does to their successors, any revelation as to the spiritual condition of those who have recourse to them for the remission of sins; this being denied the judges, it follows that the applicant must disclose the state of his conscience to him from whom he solicits aid. The necessity of this obligation becomes apparent from the solemnity with which Christ imparted this power to his Apostles. He breathed upon them and said: "As the Father hath sent me, so also do I send you. Receive ye the Hóly Ghost; whose sins ye shall forgive," &c. The import of these words is evidently this: "As I have received from the Father the power to forgive sins, so also ye, by the power of the Holy Ghost, whom I impart to you." Had not these words made it a duty for the faithful to disclose to the Apostles the state of their conscience, the stupendous power thus conferred would have been a vain, though pompous declaration, for why confer authority which can neither be exercised at all, or, at least, in any rational manner? Had Christ merely conferred on his Apostles the power to forgive sins, the case would be different, but this was not the only authority with which He invested them; He likewise expressly empowered them to retain guilt. The exercise of a power of this nature necessarily supposes a thorough knowledge of the disposition of the heart and the state of the conscience, and not merely of the exterior, which is so often deceptive. The penitent may, indeed, be a hypocrite, or he may conceal or gloss over his guilt; in this case, however, he must describe to himself all the dread consequences involved by the receipt of an invalid absolution, obtained from the priest on false pretences.

Q. Has confession been practised ever since the times of the Apostles?

A. It has; we find this practice alluded to in Holy Writ. St. James exhorts us: "Confess ye your sins one to another" that is, those who have fallen into sin, to those who have the power to free them from their guilt. *James*, v. In the Acts we find that many of the faithful came and confessed, and acknowledged what they had done. *Acts*, xix. 18. The tribunal of penance was, indeed, less frequently resorted to in the primitive ages of the Church, when the first Christians were characterized by such distinguished purity of life, than after the lapse of ages and increasing degeneracy of the people had cooled the first fervor of charity. The small number of priests and bishops, whose whole time and attention was devoted to the announcement of the Gospel, likewise precluded the possibility of confessions being practised as at present. That confession was in use in the times of the Apostles, is clear from what we have cited; particularly, when the testimony of Scripture is taken into account, in conjunction with what tradition and history have to offer on the subject.

Q. How do the Fathers of the first centuries express themselves on this head?

A. They speak of confession as a duty generally known and complied with, the origin of which may be traced to the times of the Apostles. Tertullian, who flourished in the second century, writes of confession of sin made to a priest, and adds: "Some there are who shun this, as an exposure of self, and defer it from day to day, being more afraid of the shame than desirous of a cure, like to those who affected by some malady conceal it from the physician, and thus perish, falling victims to false shame." *De Pœnit.* 9 and 10. Nothing can be more explicit than the words of Tertullian.

St. Cyprian, bishop of Carthage, observes: "I entreat ye, beloved brethren, every one of ye confess his sins, whilst yet life is spared to the sinner, and his accusation may be received; whilst satisfaction may be made and absolution obtained." *Cyp. Tract. de Lapsis.* Origen writes on the same subject: "Behold, Scripture teaches that we should not conceal sin in our bosoms. Those who suffer from indigestion, or the presence of diseased matter in the stomach, feel relieved when they have vomited it up; so those who have sinned and conceal their guilt within themselves are internally oppressed, as it were suffocated, by the poisonous effluvia of sin. When the sinner, however, becomes his own accuser, when he denounces himself and confesses, he vomits forth the crime and removes the cause of his malady." *Orig. Hom.* ii. *in Ps.* 37. St. Basil teaches: "We must reveal our guilt to those who are intrusted with the administration of the mysteries of God." *St. Bas. in Resp. ad Quest.* 228. St. Ambrose warns us: "Some are anxious to be admitted to penance, so as to have communion speedily dispensed to them. Such persons rather seek to bind the conscience of the ministers of reconciliation, the priests, than to free themselves; for their own consciences are not eased, and those of the priests burthened; for the command, 'Set not holy things before swine,' is not observed." *Lib. 2 de Pœnit.* St. Augustine admonishes the faithful of his time to approach the tribunal of penance, saying: "Do penance as the Church prescribes, in order that the Church may pray for you." Let no one say to himself, "I do it secretly before God. He from whom I expect pardon knows it, as I do myself." To what purpose, then, the following words: "'Whatsoever ye shall loose upon earth shall be loosed in heaven?' Have the keys been delivered to the Church in vain? Has the Gospel been set at nought, and Christ's words proved futile, of no avail?" *Hom.* 49, 50. St. Chrysostom assures us "that whoever is ashamed to confess his sins to a priest, but is not ashamed to commit them, in the sight of God, if he do not confess and repent, shall be covered at the last dread day with shame and confusion, not before one or two individuals, but before the whole world." *Orat. de Muliere Sam.* St. Leo the Great says: "The manifold mercy of God so aids human frailty, that not only by the grace of baptism, but also by the remedy of penance, the hope of life eternal may again be secured, so that those who have profaned the grace of regeneration, being judged by their own judgment, may obtain remission of their sins; and herein has it pleased the Divine goodness to decree that mercy and pardon are only to be obtained by the mediation of the priests. The Mediator between God and man, "the man Christ Jesus," imparts to the ministers of the Church the power to impose the satisfaction of penance on those who confess, and again admit them, purified by this atonement, to pass to the reception of the other sacraments through the gate of reconciliation. The *Council of Trent* pronounces this dogma in the following solemn decision:

"If any one deny that sacramental confessions is divinely instituted and necessary for salvation, let him be anathema." Sess. xiv. can. 6; and, again: "If any one shall say, that in order to receive the remission of sin, according to divine institution, it is not necessary to confess each and every mortal transgession which after due and assiduous examination can be remembered, let him be anathema." Can. 7. This divine institution and constant practice of confession since the time of the Apostles, is also most clearly and amply proved from the fact, that according to the doctrine and practice of the Church, it is not only the laity who are bound to have recourse to penance, but also priests and bishops, and even the Pope himself. The priesthood, however, would never have submitted to an act in itself so painful and humiliating, had not confession been ordained by Christ himself, and continually practised in the Church from the primitive ages. If confession had been introduced by mere human agency, history would surely be able to point out the date of its introduction, as well as the name of him who possessed such magic influence or boundless power over men as to induce them willingly to submit to that which costs human pride so severe a struggle. History is, however, silent on this subject: no trace of the introduction of confession is to be discovered; it follows, therefore, that the practice of confession is coeval with the existence of the Church. According to the very correct principle of Tertullian, "that which is universally practised in the Church, and whose origin and introduction cannot be pointed out, must be regarded as an apostolic institution or ordinance." *Lib. de Præscript.* We know exactly, for instance, when and by whom public penances were done away with; and when Catholic apostates, under the name of Protestants, declared against confession; but we do not know by what Pope or council confession was introduced, or has any one as yet been able to discover it. The introduction of such a practice would certainly have excited general attention, supposing it to be introduced by human caprice or policy in the course of ages. And would not the great ones, the proud ones of the earth, on whom this duty is as binding as on the lowliest mendicant, rebel against it? Can it be supposed they would tamely and silently have submitted to an innovation so humiliating and so painful. The eastern sectaries who severed themselves in the primitive ages from the communion of the Church, fully agree with her in practising confession as necessary and salutary for the obtaining of life eternal. The Greek schismatic Russians of to-day, as well as those earlier sects, may be adduced to prove the truth of our position, that confession is not a known invention or ordinance introduced in progress of time into the Church, but a divine institution.

Q. Has Christ made self-accusation in the tribunal of penance a condition for the remission of sin, as well as a means of atonement?

A. Yes; the sinner having presumed insolently to rise in rebellion against his Lord and Master, by the commission of sin, it is just and proper that he should be obliged to humble himself before Christ's representatives (1) in order to pluck out more effectually the root of all evil within us, which is pride, and to excite and confirm in our hearts those dispositions which form the fundamental condition of our reconciliation with the divine majesty, viz., humility, and sincere and humble contrition.

2. To inspire us with dread of falling or relapsing into sin, which even here below has produced consequences so humiliating and painful.

3. To assist, by confession, in arriving at self-knowledge, and to encourage and incite us to make more rapid and successful progress in the way of virtue by the admonitions, intructions, and paternal exhortations of the confessor.

4. In order not to expose us to the danger of deluding or deceiving ourselves in so momentuous a matter which might easily occur were we constituted sole judges of our own interior.

Our dear Lord wills, furthermore, for our consolation and encouragement, that our reconciliation with Him be confirmed and attested by the judicial sentence of His anointed minister. Even the heathens have some idea of this, as we learn from Seneca, who advises us to unbosom ourselves to a judicious and virtuous friend; to lay open before him our infirmities and evil propensities, and also our falls, in order that we may live in unblemished morality. Sincere and thinking Protestants cannot deny, and do frankly acknowledge the beneficial effects resulting from a secret self-accusation made to the minister of God. Leibnitz, one of their clearest and most profound thinkers, unhesitatingly declares that nothing is more admirable and divine in the Catholic Church than the practice of confession. *Syst. Theolog.*

Q. May not the practice of confession be accompanied by abuses?

A. It certainly may; but this is not to be imputed to the sacrament, but to the unworthy and ill-disposed recipient.

Q. What are the qualities of a valid confession?

A. It must be, 1. Entire; 2. Sincere; 3. Explicit; 4. Contrite; 5. Humble and respectful.

Q. When may confession be termed *entire?*

A. When we accuse ourselves of all the grievous transgressions—at least, which we can call to mind; with their number, kind, and such circumstances as alter the nature of the crime.

Q. Are we bound to mention the number of times we may have fallen into any particular sin or sins?

A. We are, as far as we can remember and are capable of exactly determining. We have also to mention the number of persons with whom we have sinned, or whom we may have injured, for God wills that we confess every sin committed. This includes the number of sins; for each renewed transgression, even should it be of the same commandment, is a new sin. If we are not able to determine the number of times we have committed any sin, we are to specify it as nearly as possible; to state how often we have daily, weekly or monthly committed it, and whether or not it be a sin of habit.

Q. What circumstances are we obliged to mention, in order that our confessions may be entire?

A. 1. Those which change the nature of sin; for instance, unlawful intercourse, whether with a single person or one married: in the latter case, it is not only impurity, but likewise adultery.

2. Those which render a transgression mortal which is in itself venial; for instance, if we were aware that an individual could be so incensed by a slight affront as to break forth into blasphemous language and imprecations, or that by the utterance of a slight falsehood we should materially and grievously injure our fellow-man in his good name or property, and yet did not shrink from the act.

3. It is, in general, advisable to state what is calculated to enable the confessor to obtain a clearer insight into the state of the penitent's conscience, so that he may be the better able to guide and advise him. Long narrations, accompanied by the mention of names, and all irrelevant matters are, however, to be guarded against.

The confessional is intended for contrite self-accusation, and not for long stories and useless digressions. No mention is to be made of others—at least, by name. We are, moreover, to guard against confessing other people's faults, instead of our own.

Q. When is confession *sincere?*

A. When we accuse ourselves precisely as we think the sin is in the Divine sight, and with the same candor as if we were confessing to the all-knowing Judge, without concealment, palliation, exculpation or embellishment, false excuses, exaggeration or diminution.

Q. What consequences attend an intentional concealment of even one mortal sin, the number of mortal transgressions, or the circumstances which change their nature?

A. The whole act is invalid, and, far from obtaining the remission of the sins of which we have accused ourselves, we but add to our crimes the fearful guilt of sacrilege.

Q. What considerations should the penitent make use of, in order to put false shame to flight, and enable himself candidly to lay open the state of his conscience?

A. 1. That there exists no cause for us to be ashamed. St. Chrysostom observes, it is shameful to sin, but honorable before God and his representative contritely to acknowledge the evil done. The confessor is certainly well aware of the great self-denial required, in order to confess our sins and frailties, and must, therefore, when he sees that the penitent humbly and sincerely acknowledges his faults, be filled with gratitude toward God, who assists him in the performance of this act, and admiration and sympathy for his penitent, whose heart he beholds stirred with love, contrition and humility towards God, and confidence in him. He rejoices when the penitent freely unbosoms himself to him, and thus places greater trust in him than in any earthly friend, and he feels himself honored that God has chosen him as an instrument of His mercy to remit to the contrite penitent his guilt, rescue him from impending perdition, snatch him from the jaws of hell, and unlock again for him, the prodigal, the golden gates of his Father's glorious mansion, the heavenly Jerusalem.

2. Should this sincerity be wanting, the whole confession is null, and tends only to add the guilt of sacrilege to the other transgressions, the absolution pronounced being null and void.

3. That it is better to confess secretly to a priest, delegated by Divine authority, the sins committed, than to carry constantly about with one the undying worm of conscience; to live in constant danger of eternally perishing, which would inevitably be our lot should a sudden and unprovided death overtake us.

4. That it is better that one individual should be made acquainted with the fault into which we have fallen, than that it should be made manifest on the last day to the whole world as a sin unconfessed and unrepented of.

5. That since we must, sooner or later, prevail on ourselves to acknowledge our transgressions sincerely, unless we are

prepared to renounce all hopes of salvation, it is more prudent to do it at once, rather than after having long been lashed by remorse of conscience and exposed to the peril of eternal damnation.

6. That the priest is strictly bound, under pain of mortal sin, to keep inviolably secret whatever has been disclosed to him under the sacramental seal; that he is not even permitted to mention the sins confessed to the penitent himself out of the confessional, and is to prefer death, like St. John Nepomucenes, to a violation of the sacramental seal. Moreover, that God so wonderfully provides for this secrecy that priests, even in delirium, or when laboring under mental diseases, still observe perfect silence concerning the disclosures made in the confessional. Even apostate priests respect the secrecy of the confessional. Luther and the other reformers, although they sneered at, condemned and rejected the use of confession, are not known to have violated the secrecy it imposed.

Q. What is to be done, should one experience peculiar difficulty in confessing some particular sins?

A. We may request the priest's permission to commit the matter in question to writing; it is, however, better to call to mind the four last things, to take courage, and simply and humbly to confess our sins; even though the priest should reproach us severely and sternly, we should continue, candidly, to enumerate our sins; he certainly intends whatever he may say, or impose upon us, for our greater good; and is much edified and consoled by our sincerity and humility.

Q. What is to be done when we are at a loss how to express ourselves in regard to some matter of confession?

A. We are to notify it to the priest, who will not fail to lend his assistance.

Q. What are we to do when we have omitted some grievous fault?

A. 1. Should this omission have been unintentional, either from forgetfulness, or from not being aware of the fault in question, we have to repeat it in the next confession, should we have no opportunity of confessing before approaching the holy table.

2. Should this omission have been culpable, induced by false shame, or want of proper self-examination, we are bound to state the number of confessions made during the concealment, and likewise to repeat each of them.

Q. When may confession be termed *clear* and *explicit?*

A. When the faults committed are confessed in a manner so intelligible and precise, that the priest can hear and fully understand the disclosures made; it does not, therefore, suffice to couch our self-accusation in general terms, or to make it unintelligible, by speaking in an ambiguous manner, leaving the nature of the sin undetermined; for instance, where we do not specify whether the sin was one of thought, or desire, or what particular exterior act against the Divine law we have committed. Care, however, is to be taken not to raise the voice too high, so that those without the confessional may not hear, and be scandalized at our sins. Confession must, finally, be contrite and humble, as those dispositions of the heart are requisite as we have said when treating of contrition; attention must, further, be paid to express ourselves as modestly as the nature of the sin, in question, will permit.

Q. In order that confession may possess these qualities, by what should it be preceded; and how should we prepare for it?

A. We should humbly and fervently implore of the Divine clemency, the grace to discover the extent of guilt, humbly to acknowledge and resolutely to amend. 2. We should withdraw as much as may appear necessary to us, from the cares of business, from worldly pursuits and pleasures, in order to prepare with recollection and fervor, our reconciliation with God by penance. Those who confess frequently, are wont to live in the presence of God, and they who often and lovingly visit Christ in the adorable sacrament, will find but little difficulty in preserving recollection of spirit in the hurry of their daily avocations. 3. Let us call to mind that the confession in question may be the last we shall make, and let us endeavor to perform this holy act with the fervor, humility and contrition, we should wish to have, if required immediately after to appear before the tribunal of the Omniscient Judge, the dread avenger of sin, the loving Father and forgiver of sinners and humble penitents. 4. We are then seriously and carefully to examine our conscience.

Q. In what does examination of conscience consist?

A. In the earnest and sincere examination of what we may have thought, wished, uttered, done, or omitted since arriving at the use of reason, or since the last confession.

Q. How should we proceed in this examination, in order that it may be properly made?

A. We are to recall to mind when we last confessed, consider whether our confession was accompanied by any defect, either in the accusation, contrition, or restitution. If the penance was performed, and how; if and into what new faults and sins we have fallen, in thoughts, words, works and participation in the sins of others. We are to examine ourselves regarding the commandments of God; the precepts of the Church; the seven capital sins, and the duties imposed by our calling.

Q. With what degree of strictness should this examination be made?

A. With the same degree of exactitude, that a reasonable and prudent individual would devote to any affair of the very first importance.

Q. What length of time should we allot to this examination?

A. That depends on the capacity of the persons in question and the manner of life led. There are persons who have a retentive memory, there are others who experience difficulty in recalling the past; there are persons who lead a very uniform life, others are immersed in cares and perplexities, and overwhelmed by business and exposed to distractions without end; some have to encounter few temptations, others have much to suffer from interior and exterior seductions; some frequently examine their conscience and approach the tribunal of penance, others without a care or thought for spiritual things adding sin to sin, and, perhaps, not within the lapse of years resorting to the confessional. The first class need a comparatively short time for the examinaiton of conscience; the second requires more time. No one, however, should go to excess in this respect. We are only required to give the same care and attention to this, that we should to any other serious business; should some fault occur to our recollection after confession, notwithstanding our having duly examined ourselves, we have only to mention it in the next confession. God never requires impossibilities of us; further, confession is not intended as a rack for the contrite sinner, but to give him consolation and peace of heart, as says the *Council of Trent*, Sess. xiv. c. 3. The penitent should place confidence in his ghostly father, who will not fail to assist, by proposing questions, to which he should candidly reply.

Q. What faults, in particular, are we to guard against in the examination of conscience?

A. We are to guard against a light and superficial examination. 2. We should never seek to excuse and palliate all our faults, but judge them in our own case as severely as we should had they been committed by others. 3. That we estimate our sins according to the law of God and the teaching of morality, and not according to the prejudices and false maxims of infidels and worldlings, who consider nothing reprehensible, excepting murder and theft. 4. It is not sufficient to examine ourselves, solely, concerning the sinful words or works committed, we should carefully scrutinize our thoughts and desires, and also to endeavor to discover in how far we have been a stumbling-block to our fellow-men, how we have been accessory to other's sins. 5. We are to seek, to ascertain the number of our grievous transgressions, and earnestly reflect on the most efficacious means of amendment, as also on the sources and occasions of our faults, so as in future to stop the one and avoid the other; finally, what measures are to be taken in order to repair the damage ourselves or others have sustained from our sins, in order to avoid further evil consequences.

Q. What tends to facilitate this re-examination of conscience?

A. Daily and careful scrutiny of our acts, words, thoughts and omissions, together with frequent confession.

Q. What is to be done after having completed the examination of conscience?

A. To excite contrition for all known and unknown transgressions, accompanied by the sincere and firm purpose of amendment. Should the penitent be obliged to wait a considerable time before the confessional, let him meditate on the sufferings and death of Christ; think of death, the poor souls in purgatory, how gladly they would wait some hours, and how fervently they would employ them, could they enjoy the happiness and privilege of confessing; recite the Penitential Psalms, keep a strict guard over the senses, particularly the eyes, and commend himself to the protection of our blessed Mother Mary and the guardian angels. Should any thing be heard of others' confession, he who has accidentally heard it is as strictly bound to secrecy as the priest to whom the disclosure was made. It would be a grievous sin to speak of what one has thus accidentally learned. Care should, therefore, be taken not to place one's self too near the confessional. It were also better to apprise the confessor of the fact, should the penitent's accusations be overheard by other persons. On entering the confessional, we should cast ourselves, in spirit, with Mary Magdalene, at the bloodstreaming feet of the Redeemer, as if present on Calvary; recall to mind the last judgment in which all that has not been effaced by the sacraments shall be made manifest. We should then sign ourselves with the sign of the cross and say:

"Father, pray give me your blessing in order that I may entirely and truly confess my sins: I, poor sinful creature, accuse myself before the Almighty God, and you, Father, as God's representative, of the following sins:" to be then mentioned. Should we be happy enough to have preserved ourselves free from every deliberate fault, we are to notify it to the priest, and accuse ourselves of some sin of our former life. Should we have but venial faults and imperfections to confess, we add: "I accuse myself of this sin —— committed in my former life." The confession is then concluded in the following terms: "For these and all the sins of my whole life, I am most heartily sorry, I hate and detest them, because I have thereby offended God, the Supreme and most amiable Good; I am fervently resolved never more to sin, and carefully to avoid all occasion of relapse; I humbly beg pardon of God, and salutary penance and absolution of you, my Father." The instructions given by the confessor are then to be attentively heard, and the questions he may think proper to ask candidly and respectfully answered. Care must be taken to hear distinctly and to understand the penance imposed, and in conclusion, the confession, contrition and purpose of amendment are again to be united with the infinite merits of our Redeemer, praying and bleeding for us on the cross, to which our crimes have nailed Him. While the sacred words of absolution are being pronounced, we should represent to ourselves our Saviour's heart opening, as it were, to receive us, and wash us with the blood flowing from it; we should invoke the name of Jesus, our deliverer, with sentiments of faith, humility and confidence. After confession, we should devote some time to returning thanks, and implore grace to avoid sin for the time to come. We are to perform the penance imposed upon us with as little delay as possible, reciting it with downcast eyes and clasped hands. These acts should be performed with a heart stirred by the most grateful emotions, full of fervor and devotion. We should further endeavor, on leaving the Church, to preserve recollection of spirit, as a necessary condition for a worthy communion.

Q. What is to be done when the priest refuses, or defers absolution?

A. We should humbly submit to the decision of our spiritual father, and faithfully perform whatever he may impose upon us, in order to prepare and dispose ourselves for receiving absolution.

Satisfaction.

Q. What is sacramental satisfaction?

A. It is, so to speak, the indemnification or reparation the penitent has to offer to the outraged majesty of God, by his penitential works, conformably to the decision of the confessor and in union with the infinite merits of Christ.

Q. Why does God require this satisfaction of the converted sinner, pardoned and cleansed by the merits of Christ?

A. The wisdom and justice of God demands this, in order, to prevent those, who, after baptism, fall into sin from becoming careless or presumptuous, which might easily occur were the sinner required neither to do nor suffer any thing, in order again to be reconciled to Him, whom he has wantonly and ruthlessly offended, for Christ, himself, assures us that if we do not penance, we shall all perish. *Luke,* xv. 13. Further, we are to bear in mind that these penitential works, to be imposed by the confessor, derive all their efficacy from the infinite merits of Christ, with which they are to be united.

Q. How is the satisfaction imposed in the confessional, distinguished?

A. It may either be coercive or healing. The first consists in works of a penitential character, and require self-denial; these are calculated to chastise the sinner and serve as a reparation for the offence his sin has offered to the Divine

Majesty; for instance, prayers, fasting, almsgiving and other good works. Healing penance, on the contrary, consists in practices calculated to insure the avoidance of all occasions of sin, and to guard him against relapse. As to the reparation we owe our neighbor, should we have injured his reputation, or the restitution to be made in case we have defrauded or otherwise injured him in his property, as also the removal of scandals and enmities, these belong rather to the indispensable conditions for true conversion than to satisfaction.

Q. What is to be observed about the penance imposed in the confessional?

A. It is to be humbly and willingly accepted and conscientiously performed.

Q. When the penance is not performed is confession thereby rendered invalid?

A. When we fully and sincerely intend performing the penance imposed, but afterwards neglected so doing, the confession already made does not become null, but still we commit a sin of which we shall have to accuse ourselves in the next confession, particularly when the penance in question was imposed for grievous sins confessed. Satisfaction is termed the complement of confession. It were a bad sign, and the cause of serious doubt as to whether our confession were made with the due dispositions, were we slothfully and lightly to postpone performing the penance enjoined, or altogether neglect it. It is best to commence it, if possible, immediately after confession, and do what may be done at once, the remainder as soon as we possibly can. It must be eventually done, and the sooner, therefore, the better.

Q. What is to be done, when the penance imposed appears too difficult?

A. We should earnestly consider how light the satisfaction imposed in the tribunal of penance is, when compared with the enormity of sin, as an offence against the Divine Majesty, the severity and length of the penitential exercises, imposed on penitents, in the first ages of the Church; the austerities practiced by the saints and by holy persons, even in our own times, in atonement of sin. Should there, however, exist a moral impossibility to perform some satisfactory work enjoined, we are respectfully to acquaint our father confessor with the fact, and request him to give another in its stead.

Q. Why are the penitential exercises imposed in our times so easy of performance?

A. It is the indulgence of a wise mother towards the frailty of her children. The Church justly apprehends, that if she adhered to the rigor of her early penitential code, it would deter sinners from repentance, or should they approach the tribunal of penance they might neglect performing the penance enjoined. Our holy mother the Church, therefore, in consideration of our weakness, prefers imposing by her ministers light, satisfactory works, and advising the penitent to take voluntarily upon himself more arduous and painful ones, by which, alone, the sinner can escape temporal chastisements, to be borne either here on earth, or hereafter in the flames of purgatory.

Q. Do there then remain temporal punishments to be borne after the guilt and eternal punishment of sin has been remitted in the tribunal of penance?

A. Yes, certainly.

Q. Whence do we derive this knowledge?

A. From the testimony of Holy Scripture and the teachings of the Church.

Thus when Nathan said to the penitent David: "The Lord also hath taken away thy sin." He adds: "Nevertheless, the child that is born to thee shall surely die!" 2 *Kings*, xii. 13, 14. Moses was also pardoned the doubts he entertained of the fulfillment of the Divine prophecy; yet, in punishment thereof he was debarred from entering into the land of promise. *Deut.* i. 38. Does not the whole earth remain, even after our redemption is accomplished, a valley of tears, of bitterness, affliction and toil, in consequence of the sin committed by our first parents, in Paradise? This is, moreover, the express teaching of the holy Church; the *Council of Trent* solemnly declares it in the following terms: "If any one assert, that to every sinner after the grace of justification the guilt is so remitted, that no load, whatever, of temporal punishment remains to be canceled here on earth, or hereafter, in purgatory, before entering the kingdom of heaven. let him be anathema. *Trid. Sess.* i. *can.* 30, c. And so it behoveth the Divine justice, wisdom and goodness, as the Council further defines. "Verily, did it behove the Divine justice, that those who sinned ignorantly before baptism, should be restored to grace in a different manner from those who, once delivered from the servitude of sin and Satan, after having received the gift of the Holy Ghost, knowingly defile the temple of God, and hesitate not to sadden the Holy Ghost. But it also behoves the Divine goodness that sins be not remitted entirely without satisfaction, lest on the next occasion, considering sin but a slight evil, we may again relapse into, perhaps, greater transgressions without fear and as it were, presumptuously, against the Holy Ghost, and thus heap up treasures of anger for the day of judgment. For these menacing chastisements of satisfaction, doubtless, inspire fear of sin, hold us back as with a bridle, and render us more cautious and vigilant for the future. They also heal the remains of sin and destroy the evil inclinations incurred by sin, by the practice of the opposite virtues. *Con. Trid.* 1. *c.*

Q. By what means may these temporal punishments be canceled here on earth?

A. Partly by the satisfaction imposed in the tribunal of penance, by the patient bearing of sickness, poverty and other afflictions of life; further, by voluntary prayers, penitential practices, particularly by the exercise of the spiritual and temporal works of mercy: finally, by obtaining indulgences. In this sense the Apostle says: "I fill up those things that are wanting of the suffering of Christ in my flesh," *Coloss.* i. 26, that the full efficacy of His redemption be applied to us.

Q. Where shall we have to undergo these temporal punishments if they are not cancelled on earth?

A. In purgatory.

Q. Which is to be preferred: to do penance here for our sins, or suffer for them hereafter, in the flames of purgatory?

A. We should prefer to suffer for them here on earth, for the penitent thus secures himself against relapses into sin, when he has learned to overcome himself, resolutely and firmly; further, because the penitential works undertaken here, are not to be compared to the pains of purgatory; to which we shall have to submit hereafter. Were Christians to reflect on the example of the first Christians, on the austerities practiced by the saints, and particularly on the fearful torments awaiting them in purgatory, they would certainly be more assiduous in the practice of penance, at least, they would cease to complain of the penance imposed in the sacrament. To such slothful and effeminate individuals the words once addressed by Naaman, the Syrian, to his lord, may be properly applied: "If the prophet had bid thee do some great thing, surely thou shouldst have done it: how much rather what he hath now said to thee, wash and thou shalt be cleansed?" 4 *Kings*, v. 13. How trifling is the toil of the short journey, compared to the burthen of leprosy. How gladly should the sinner here satisfy the Divine justice, principally by the excellent virtue and power of sacramental penance, when he considers how great are the pains of purgatory! Whoever reflects, maturely, upon the subject, will not fail to exclaim, as did the penitent Augustine: " Here burn, O Lord, here cut, but spare me in eternity !"

Q. Which are the principal effects of the valid and worthy reception of the sacrament of penance?

A. 1. It effects a perfect remission of the guilt of sin, and delivers us from the eternal punishment thereby entailed. 2. It imparts to those who have grievously sinned instantaneous restoration to the state of sanctifying grace, or increases it in those who have not forfeited it by mortal transgressions. 3. It elevates those reconciled to God to the ineffable dignity of His children, if, unhappily, they have become children of Satan, by mortal sin; or it renders them, if already children of God, more similar to their Divine Father and more amiable and lovely in his Divine sight. 4. It affords joy and exultation to all the saints and angels of God in heaven, and particularly to the most tender and loving hearts of Jesus and Mary. 5. It produces tranquillity, consolation, and many powerful graces in the penitent's heart for a new and better life, and inspires the confessor with joy and hope, as also all who truly love God and us, and who perceive in our conduct the effects of this sacrament, so rich in grace. 6. It procures, for those reconciled with God, the merit of their former good works, lost by sin. 7. It imparts to them that ineffable peace of conscience, of which Jesus Christ says: " the world can neither give nor take it away," and of which Saint Paul testifies " That it far surpasseth all the joys and delights of the world." *Phil.* iv. and *St. John* xiv. 29. This, however, only holds good on condition of our not again relapsing into sin.

Q. What will be found the best preservative against relapses into sin?

A. 1. The faithful observance of the rules laid down by our confessor for the regulation of our conduct, with his admonitions and warnings. 2. The careful avoidance of sin and its occasions. 3. Living and acting in the presence of God. 4. The vigilant guard of our senses, particularly our eyes and tongues. 5. Frequent prayer, particularly mental prayer, fervent thoughts, short ejaculations and aspirations to God during the day. 6. The remembrance of the four last things, particularly certain and approaching death. 7. Frequent worthy confession and communion. 8. All the practices calculated to preserve us from temptation, or to aid us in withstanding it. These have been enumerated in treating of the sixth petition of the Lord's prayer.

Practice.—Hast thou properly understood and duly reflected on all that has been said of the sacrament of penance? "Do this and thou shalt live." Confess frequently, but with the due dispositions, for this sacrament certainly produces the most beneficial spiritual effects that can be conceived. It is, as it were, the beacon on the gloomy shore of thy path to eternal happiness, diffusing cheerful and radiant light over the whole weary way. Choose as confessor and counselor in matters of conscience an experienced and zealous priest. Fix, as he may direct, the time for thy confession, and adhere faithfully thereto. Confess at least monthly, and, if possible, more frequently. We read of saints who were wont to confess daily with great spiritual benefit, and this holy practice wonderfully added to their glory in heaven by the increase in sanctifying grace thereby obtained. Endeavor, then, to go to confession as often as you possibly or conveniently can, and on the other hand to avoid the faults and defects which prevent those beneficial results and seriously injure the soul.

The utility of frequent and well made confession consists principally in the knowledge we obtain of ourselves, and in the increase of sincere humility and contrition of heart; in the greater purity of conscience, in the perfect purity of intention and the more careful avoidance of occasions of sin; in the increase of sanctifying and active grace, so that assisted by both, we may rapidly increase in zeal by virtue and all the practices of Christian perfection. The faults which impede these beneficial results, and which are to be shunned with peculiar care, are a superficial examination of conscience, when one confesses rather as a matter of custom, without a fixed, definite and firm purpose of amendment; a morbid anxiety in examination of conscience, and want of confidence in Christ's infinite merits, joined with which we are in faith to prepare for the reception of this important sacrament. Therefore, let me impress once more upon thy heart, confess frequently, very frequently, with the due dispositions, as thou hast been directed in this instruction, and as thy confessor may think proper to advise, and be assured the great affair of thy salvation will be secure now and in the hour of thy death.

Of Indulgences.

The doctrine of Indulgences is most intimately connected with the sacrament of penance, which is that of the remission of sins. We shall, therefore, treat here, as the most proper place, of this means of grace.

Q. What is an indulgence?

A. An indulgence is a remission, conferred by the power of the Church, of temporal punishment, remaining after the guilt of sin has been canceled in the sacrament of penance, and which, otherwise, we should have to endure either here or hereafter.

Q. How many kinds of indulgences are there?

A. There are two kinds, a plenary and partial indulgence: a plenary indulgence is the remission of all temporal punishments incurred by the commission of sin, even after our reconciliation with God by penance. A partial indulgence is the remission of a portion of the merited chastisement.

Q. What does faith teach respecting indulgences?

A. 1. That the Church possesses power to grant them. 2. That the proper use of indulgences is salutary for the faithful. This is the doctrine of the Church in the *Council of Trent, Sess.* 25, *Decret. de Indulg.*

Q. Whence does the Church derive the power to grant indulgences?

A. From Christ the Lord, who expressly declares:

"Amen, I say to you, whatsoever you shall bind upon earth, shall be bound also in heaven, and whatsoever you shall loose upon earth shall be loosed also in heaven." *Matt.* xviii. 18. The Church has further, as we have just shown, the power to cancel sin and its eternal punishment, why then should she not be authorized by Christ to remit temporal punishment to those possessing the due dispositions; this is, certainly, an inferior exercise of authority.

Q. Whence have indulgences their virtue and efficacy ?

A. From the treasure of Christ's infinite merits, and from the superabundant satisfaction and merits of His saints, in whose communion we live. Respecting the merits of Christ, they, of course, can never be exhausted, as they are infinite: as to the Saints, it is known that many of them performed greater penances and made more satisfaction than their own sins required. This satisfaction and these works of supererogation are not to remain inactive in the Church of God as is evident from the dogma of the communion of saints, yet so that their virtue and efficacy is conditioned by Christ's merits, by whose assistance and grace, they have obtained sanctity and practiced so many acts of virtue and penance. And oh, how great is the treasure of Mary's virtues and sacrifices—that virgin Mother of our Redeemer and refuge of sinners! There is, indeed, in the Church of God, a treasure of satisfaction whose administration God has intrusted to the supreme power of the Church.

Q. Who has power to grant indulgences ?

A. The successor of him to whom the Lord expressly said : " To thee I deliver the keys of heaven, whatsoever you shall loose on earth shall be loosed in heaven. *Matt.* xviii. 18. He, who is Christ's representative and vicar, the Roman Pontiff, the head of the Church. The bishops may also grant indulgences, with the approbation and consent of the Holy See, on certain occasions, as far as appears salutary for the faithful.

Q. Was the custom of granting indulgences always practiced in the Church ?

A. It certainly was ; we find this custom alluded to in St. Paul's Epistles and confirmed by the example of the Doctor of the Gentiles, as St. Ambrose, Theodoret and Anselm very justly remark in support of the doctrine and practice of the Church. We refer to the indulgence granted by St. Paul to the incestuous but penitent Corinthian. Writing to the Corinthians, he says: " For what I forgave, if I have forgiven anything, for your sakes I have done it in the person of Christ."
Cor. ii. 10. The Apostle alludes, in these words, to the treasures of merits possessed by the Church, viz.: the merits

of Christ and his faithful members, in virtue of which he could deal indulgently with the contrite delinquent. Had this been, merely, a remission of canonical penance, it would not, in itself, have been a benefit, in imparting which, the Apostle acted in the person of Christ; and had the temporal punishment yet remained to be borne, here or hereafter, the Apostle could not reasonably have spoken as acting in the person of Christ, in whose name he exercised this beneficent power. The same holds good of two instances we find in the writings of St. Cyprian and other eminent ecclesiastical authors; that apostates and other notorious sinners truly contrite for their crimes, were pardoned and declared free from punishment, at the instance of the martyrs. Had such penitents, however, merely exchanged the temporal punishment imposed by the Church for the punishment awaiting them in purgatory, they would have but little cause for self-gratulation. This was, then, real indulgence granted by the power of the Church through the merits of Christ and the holy martyrs, possessing efficacy for time and eternity. (*S. Cyp. ep.* 10, 12, 30.)

Q. What are the conditions necessary in order to gain an indulgence?

A. 1. He who desires to do so must be in the state of grace. 2. He must fulfil the prescribed conditions; from this it is evident that it is a calumny fabricated by sectarians, that an indulgence is a permission and approval of sin; before sin has been removed, there can be no thought of obtaining an indulgence, which is but the remission of the temporal punishment incurred by sin after its guilt has been forgiven. We see from this, that in order to obtain a plenary indulgence we must be perfectly free from every voluntary sin, be it ever so trifling; because as long as any sin, even venial, remains, man is not in a condition to profit by indulgences. The remission of mortal sin is obtained in the sacrament of penance, of venial transgressions, by fervent acts of contrition and other exercises of penance. Whoever wishes to profit duly by a plenary indulgence, must have the grace of God, and in order to insure his being in this happy condition; first approach the tribunal of penance, or go to confession every week. Should there remain in the heart any wilful inclination to venial sin, then the plenary indulgence is not obtained entirely and perfectly, but only in proportion to the degree of preparation; should we have been in the state of sin, or have sacrilegiously approached the sacrament of penance, of course there can be no idea of deriving any benefit whatever from the indulgence. As for the indulgences attending jubilees and missions, we have to comply carefully with the conditions laid down for obtaining them. The giving of alms has certainly been, and may again be proposed, as one of the conditions for obtaining an indulgence, but to say, therefore, that indulgences are to be sold at a certain rate, is a foul slander. If ever any thing of the kind has transpired, it is attributable to the wickedness and cupidity of individuals, and not to the doctrine, ordinance or approbation of the Church.* *See Additions*, p. 405.

Q. May indulgences of every kind be applied to the souls in purgatory?

A. Certainly, since intercession may be made in their behalf, as is proved in the article on the Communion of Saints.

Q. Is the proper use of indulgences salutary?

A. Without doubt; for, 1. Indulgences cancel the temporal punishments incurred by sin. 2. They encourage us to seek reconciliation with God, by supplying the severe canonical penances of former days by works of piety, less arduous and painful. 3. They, on the other hand, inspire us with zeal for doing penance and amending our life, as they cannot be obtained without these dispositions. 4. They promote the frequent reception of the holy sacraments and the practice of other godly works, and finally they dissipate the anxious fears entertained by zealous penitents with regard to the divine judgments. The use of indulgences, therefore, far from destroying the spirit of penance and austerity, and rendering the faithful careless and remiss, is, on the contrary, the very means of bringing those to true penance to whom other-

---

* It is a gross calumny that the Church sold indulgences in Luther's time, in order to obtain means to prosecute the erection of St. Peter's Church. Whoever makes such an assertion, either proves his ignorance of historical facts, or the malignancy of his character in adhering to and propagating falsehood. We plainly see from the communication directed by Leo X., who then governed the Church, to Archbishop Albrecht of Ments, that the Church held and taught of indulgences exactly what she now does, and so with the conditions necessary in order to obtain them. She then, as now, required a contrite and humbled heart, reconciled to God in the sacrament of penance. But if his Holiness wished to have the alms given by the faithful appropriated to the erection of a temple, common to all Christendom, it was assuredly a grand and sublime idea, viz., that all Christendom should unite in building a magnificent temple, to the God of one and all; an idea which every one must admire and commend, save those who are partakers in the sordid and hypocritical sentiments of Judas.

wise the idea would have never occurred, and to strengthen and encourage them to persevere in piety and virtue.

Practice.—Esteem highly the indulgences offered by the Church, and endeavor to obtain them. Keep in mind the advice given by the virtuous and learned Bellarmine, who very truthfully, wisely and correctly admonishes all : " Let every one be as zealous in obtaining indulgence as if penitential exercises possessed for him no virtue—let every one be as zealous in these practices of penance as if he possessed no hope of obtaining indulgences. Whoever acts thus, has truly chosen the shortest and surest road to heaven."

Of Extreme Unction.

Q. What is extreme unction ?
A. It is the sacrament by which those dangerously ill receive peculiar grace for the welfare of body and soul by the holy unction.

Q. Who instituted this sacrament ?
A. Jesus Christ.

Q. Is there any mention made of it in the Holy Scriptures ?
A. There is; St. James says, " If any man be sick among you, let them bring in the priests of the Church, and let them pray over him, anointing him with oil in the name of the Lord, and the prayer of faith shall save the sick man and the Lord shall raise him up, and if he be in sins he shall be forgiven them." *James,* v. 14, 15.

Q. Has the sacrament of extreme unction been administered from the earliest times, and without interruption in the Church of God ?

A. It has; *St. Cyril* mentions it Lib. 2, 40. And *St. Chrysostom* lib. 3, *de Sacerdotio.* Innocent I., thus writes to Decentius : " There exists no doubt that what is written by St. James is to be taken and understood of the faithful who are sick." The same Pontiff also declares it to be a sacrament of the living, thus pre-supposing the recipients being in the state of sanctifying grace, as he prohibits it being administered to sinners previous to their having approached the sacrament of penance, for he says : " Why should we administer extreme unction to one to whom the other sacraments are denied ?"

Q. Why is this sacrament termed extreme unction ?

A. Because the sick person is anointed with blessed oil, and this unction is the last administered by the Church to her children as preparation for a happy death.

Q. What are the advantages imparted by extreme unction for the spiritual welfare of the sick?

A. It increases, 1. sanctifying grace. 2. Remits venial and mortal transgressions, should we have forgotten to confess them or otherwise been unable to do so, and which are hence termed the remains of sin. 3. It imparts strength to the sick to bear patiently and meritoriously the pains and other disagreeable circumstances attendant on sickness, and enables him nobly and victoriously to sustain the last hard combat, and to give up life in fervent and loving conformity to the divine ordinance. When extreme unction is administered to those who have lost consciousness, it is under the supposition that the heart is truly contrite, and that the recipient would possess the requisite dispositions for absolution, otherwise extreme unction could not be administered. This sacrament, however, having in itself the virtue of cancelling sins, which have never, from ignorance or incapacity of any kind, been submitted to the binding and loosing power of the Church, is to be considered as the perfection of the sacrament of penance, and is, therefore, mentioned immediately after it.

Q. What corporal benefits are conferred by this sacrament?

A. It frequently alleviates the pains of sickness, and at times perfectly restores health.

Q. Why is this sacrament explained in the Christian doctrine before holy orders and matrimony?

A. Because, on account of its possessing the power to remit the remains of sin, it is more appropriately placed after penance; and, further, because all the sacraments just mentioned concern only individuals of particular states.

Q. Who is the minister of this sacrament?

A. The Priest.

Q. What are its matter and form?

A. The matter is the oil blessed for this particular purpose by the Bishop, (*Trent, Sess.* 14, *Ext. Unct.*), the words used in applying the unction are the form:

"By this holy unction and his gracious mercy may the Lord forgive thee whatever thou hast sinned (———);" the sense is named, &c., its organs anointed.

Q. Who may and should receive extreme unction?

A. Every Catholic Christian, who, after having attained the years of discretion, falls dangerously ill; this sacrament, however, cannot be received except in cases of dangerous sickness. Death resulting from any other cause than disease, even when foreseen, precludes its reception.

Q. When should extreme unction be received?

A. As soon as we have reason to consider the illness of a dangerous character, in order that we may receive it with so much the greater profit and preparation.

Q. What preparation should precede it?

A. We must be in the state of grace, therefore the sacrament of penance is to be first resorted to; we are further to excite, in particular, sentiments of sincere contrition for all the sins committed by the senses, accompanied by the most ardent desire to purify ourselves from every, even the most hidden stain of sin, by this sacrament. Those present, when this sacrament is administered, should aid the sick person by fervent prayer, in order that he may obtain all the graces the sacrament confers.

Q. How often may this sacrament be received?

A. As often as we are dangerously ill, or should the disease be of long duration, as often as a new danger of death occurs.

Q. Is it not imprudent to postpone the reception of extreme unction from fear of death?

A. Certainly; this is as absurd as it is dangerous, for first, extreme unction has been, at least, partly instituted by God in order that the sick may more rapidly and certainly recover their health if it be conducive to their eternal welfare. Should the illness be really mortal, what is more desirable than the grace to die happily and secure salvation, to which end the sacrament of extreme unction is administered. This should be duly considered by the children, parents, friends and relatives of the sick, that they may not be tempted, by postponing the reception of extreme unction, to injure, so materially, the souls of those dangerously ill, from motives of false and sensual tenderness.

Practice.—Take care to inform your friends and relations, when occasion offers, whilst you are still in health, that they need be under no apprehension with regard to having this sacrament administered to you in case of dangerous illness. When you find yourself seriously ill, do not wait to be admonished to prepare for extreme unction. You should, rather, ask to have it administered in good time. Live so, that when once the priest anoints you, you may console yourself with the conviction that your senses have ever been employed in the service of God. It is a very salutary practice to call to mind, several times in the year, and better still, as often as you approach the holy table, to think of extreme unction, and consider how you would wish to have lived when that solemn moment comes for you to receive it. Regulate your life by that thought, and when the final moment comes, your wish will not be in vain or too late.

OF HOLY ORDERS.

Q. What is the sacrament of holy orders?

A. It is a sacrament by which a particular grace and power is conferred on priests and other ministers of the Church, for the spiritual office they have to perform in the Church of God.

Q. Who instituted the sacrament of orders?

A. Christ the Lord, at the Last Supper, when he instituted the adorable sacrament of the altar, and imparted to the Apostles the power to change the bread and wine into the substance of his sacred body and blood, and constituted them dispensers of the mysteries of the new law. *Matt.* xxvi. 1; *Cor.* xi. 26. The *Council of Trent* expressly declares, if any one say that holy orders is not a real and true sacrament instituted by Christ, let him be anathema. *Sess.* 23, *Can.* 3.

Q. Why is this sacrament termed orders?

A. Because it comprises several definite and subordinate grades, as so many steps to higher degrees, which are to be successively ascended, in order to rise from the minor, to the higher or greater degrees.

Q. What is the matter and form of this sacrament?

A. The essential matter is the imposition of the bishop's hands, joined in the Latin Church to certain exterior signs, emblematic of the spiritual power imparted; for instance, in ordaining a priest, the chalice, patten, wine and bread, are given him; the essential form is the prayer recited by the bishop, while imposing his hands on the recipient.

Q. Who is the minister of this sacrament?

A. The bishop, as St. Jerome writes: "What does the bishop confer that the priest may not, holy orders, alone, excepted?"

From this we naturally deduce that all those sects which have not validly consecrated bishops have no priests, and consequently no sacraments, of which God has constituted the priests the ministers, according to the words of St. Paul: "Let every one consider us as servants of Christ, and dispensers of the mysteries of His grace." 2 *Cor.* iii. 6.

Q. How does Scripture confirm the institution of the sacrament of orders?

A. By many passages in which the institution, ordination and mission of the servants of the holy Church, by the imposition of hands and the prayers accompanying this act, are expressly mentioned. Thus St. Paul writes to Timothy, a bishop consecrated by him, and reminds him of the graces of the sacrament, admonishing him: "Neglect not the grace that is in thee; what was given thee by prophecy with imposition of the hands of the priesthood," *Tim.* iv. 19, "and again I admonish thee, that thou stir up the grace of God which is in thee by the imposition of my hands." 2 *Tim.* i. 6. But as so much depends on the holy office being filled by worthy ministers of God, the same Apostle warns every bishop: "Impose not hands lightly upon any man, neither be partaker of other men's sins." 1 *Tim.* v. 22.

Q. How does tradition confirm this truth?

A. St. Basil says, when speaking of the validly ordained servants of the Church: "They received by the imposition of hands spiritual grace," *in epi. ad. Tim.* St. Ambrose, in his work on the dignity of the priesthood, says: "Man imposes his hands and God imparts his grace." Theodoret exhorts: "Let first the lives of those who are admitted to orders be examined, and then the grace of the Holy Ghost invoked." 1 *Tim.* v. Leo the Great, says: "Fasting and praying they imposed their hands on them in order that we may understand with what devotion minister and recipient conferred and received this sacrament, that a sacrament of such great blessing may not appear to be negligently dealt with." *Ep.* 81, *ad. Dioscorum.* The *Council of Trent,* therefore, justly declares and decides: "It being evident from the testimony of the Holy Scripture, apostolic tradition, and the unanimous agreement of the holy Fathers, that by holy orders, which is consummated by words and exterior signs, grace is imparted, no one is allowed to call into question that holy orders is one of the seven sacraments." *Sess.* 23, *e.* 3.

Q. How many grades does the sacrament of Orders embrace?

A. There are, in general, seven grades, distinguished by the terms Minor and Major orders; the minor orders comprise four degrees, the order of cross-bearer, or porter, the lector, the exorcist and the acolyte. These grades have been instituted by the Church as preparatory steps for the higher degrees, and are not in themselves sacraments, although they partake in the effects of the grace it brings forth. The higher degrees include the grades of sub-deacon, deacon and priest. As to the grade of sub-deacon it is but a preparatory grade established by the Church, and as it were, an extension of the deaconship. The Church so disposed of these various offices for the convenience of the deacons, who, particularly in the first ages of the Church, stood in need of so much assistance, their whole time and attention being taken up in converting, heathens and propagating the knowledge of God's true Church. These grades were also introduced in order to insure more worthy preparation for the reception of the higher sacramental orders. As to the deaconship, it was instituted by the Apostles, and the ordination conferred on deacons, as servants and assistants of the priests; it is divine, of apostolic intstitution, and a sacrament.

The priesthood comprises in itself two orders, viz.: priests of the first and second class. Priests of the first rank are called bishops and are the immediate successors of the Apostles, and receive their appointment directly from the successor of St. Peter, the supreme head of the Church, to govern and direct the faithful, to ordain and place over the different congregations priests of the second class. *Acts*, xx. 28. The priests of the second order are, as it were, the successors of the seventy-two disciples, who, under the supreme direction of the bishops, perform the duties of the holy office, yet without possessing the power of imparting the sacrament of ordination to others.

Q. Can all these grades of the different ecclesiastical and sacramental orders be traced to the first ages of the Church?

A. They can, for Pope Cornelius enumerates them precisely as at present, 1600 years ago when writing to Fabius of

Antioch, against the heretic Novatian, he says: "He knew not that there must be a bishop in every church, though he knew that there are in the same (Church) forty-four priests, seven deacons, as many subdeacons, forty-two acolytes, exorcists and lectors, with the porters, fifty-two." *Ep.* 9, *Apud Constantium ep. Hom. Pont.* The letters and writings of the most ancient Fathers of the Church also bear evidence to the existence of these different grades; Dionysius, Anaclet, Ignatius, Cyprian and others. The *Council of Trent* justly decides: "If any one assert that there is in the Catholic Church no divinely appointed hierarchy, consisting of bishops, priests and ministers, let him be anethema." *Sess.* 23, *Can.* 6.

Q. Are there then several sacraments of orders since there is more than one degree?

A. Assuredly not; the sacrament of orders is but one, the species of power conferred being one, imparted in different degrees, but referring to one and the same object, viz.: the true body of our Lord in the adorable sacrament of the altar, and to the one holy ministry of Divine worship in the true Church of Jesus Christ. All these grades of orders, instituted by Christ, that is to say, diaconal, sacerdotal and episcopal, are so many different sacraments, for each of them confers by the imposition of hands and the accompanying prayer, a particular and distinct grace and spiritual power; yet, as they all tend to the same object, they are but one and the same sacrament, called holy orders. St. Thomas thus expresses himself on this subject: "The difference of orders is the difference of a collective power, whose essence consisting in the fullness of power is contained in one, and in the others a participation therein. The fullness of the Sacrament is in the priesthood, the others possess a participation in this power, hence, they form but one sacrament of orders." *St. Thomas*, 4 *Dist.* 24. The episcopal order was the first instituted by Christ, so it also is the source and centre of all the other orders. Christ, the Lord, did not gradually introduce his Apostles into the ministry by different orders as is now the custom, but as God called our first parents into existence, not as helpless infants, but in the fullness of their growth, as the progenitors of the whole human race, so also did Christ when about to receive the human race as children of God immediately impart to the Apostles the plenitude of the priestly power. In these days, man must be born first and pass through different stages before he attains to mature manhood, so also must the successors of the Apostles increase gradually or by different grades till they obtain the fullness of the priesthood. A priest, however, may be validly ordained without having been a deacon, as the priesthood includes the deaconship. But no one could be a validly consecrated bishop who had not previously received priestly orders, for he who has not himself been a priest can never obtain the power to ordain priests and thus become their spiritual father.

Q. Of how many kinds is the spiritual power conferred by Christ on the priests?

A. It is twofold: the one extends to His own adorable body, by the power to change bread and wine into the substance of His body and blood, and distribute it to the faithful; the second, over His spiritual body, the Church, particularly by the power to forgive sins. Both justly excite our highest admiration, seeing that God should grant to man a power so far surpassing all the power of the angels and the great ones of the earth. Each of these powers is, in itself, a miracle far surpassing the wonders of creation; the transubstantiation of bread and wine into Christ's adorable body and blood, and the justification of sinners. St. Ignatius, the martyr, therefore, justly terms the priesthood "the climax of all honors." *Epis ad Smyrn.* St. Dionysius, "a dignity, surpassing all conception." *De Cœlesti Hier.* c. 3. St. Ephraim, "a divine office;" "God has preferred you to the angels." - Thus exclaims St. Bernard, addressing priests, "to God alone art thou inferior, O priest!" says the ancient spiritual teacher Cassian, *Catal. Glor.* We must naturally conclude that the life of one so highly favored should correspond with the sublime dignity to which he is exalted.

Q. Which are the fruits of this sacrament?

A. 1. Those who are ordained Priests receive great graces on account of their intimate union with Christ in the exercise of the ministry, and of their close relation to the kingdom of God. None can conceive how much sanctifying grace is increased in the soul of him who receives holy orders; he holds God's place on earth, and is the dispenser of His graces. 2. This sacrament imprints an indelible character on the soul of the person ordained. "As Baptism cannot be reiterated, so holy orders cannot be conferred twice," on account of this character. Thus St. Gregory the Great to John of Ravenna.

This character secures likewise to those ordained the particular assistance of actual grace in the exercise of the sacred ministry. 3. Those ordained participate, moreover, in numerous gifts of grace when administering the holy sacraments and fulfilling the other functions of their holy calling. 4. The individuals are also determined by ordination, who are appointed by Christ under the auspices and direction of the supreme head of the Church, to guide and govern the faithful. The kingdom of God on earth would not be the perfect organization which it really is, were not the grades and orders of ordination closely adhered to, or if hirelings were permitted, uncalled and unauthorized, to intrude themselves into the holy ministry, and the government of the Church of God. Christ by thus fixing and determining holy orders, has opposed a formidable and insurmountable barrier to such intrusions. Thus the sacrament of orders is a glorious and distinctive characteristic of the truth and visibility of the Church, presupposing that those ordained can prove that they have lawfully entered the sanctuary of the Church by legitimate bishops.

Practice.—Manifest towards the priests and ministers of the altar on every occasion, in words and in actions, due honor, and reverence, particularly in the exercise of their functions. Seek thus to atone for the manifold insults and indignities to which the ministers of God are exposed, particularly in our own times and in this country. Shouldst thou be called to this holy state, and have lived up to your thrice-blessed vocation, rejoice at this election of grace, examine your heart carefully and prepare with the utmost assiduity by prayer, sanctity of life, and earnest study to enter upon a state so fraught with dread responsibility. Woe to him who has overrated his strength, and who presumes, in obedience to the prompting of human motives, persuasion, or passing inclination, to take upon himself the fearful burden imposed by the priesthood, a burden which God's angels would shrink from lightly accepting; woe also to him who, being called, still buries his talent, or, after having laid his hand upon the plough, looks back.

CHAPTER III.

OF MATRIMONY.

Q. What is matrimony?

A. It is the divinely-appointed connection and most intimate union between man and wife for the propagation of the human race.

Q. When and where did God institute matrimony?

A. Immediately after the creation of the first human pair in paradise, as the book of Genesis informs us. *Gen.* ii., 18.

Q. Did matrimony continue to maintain its primitive integrity and sanctity?

A. No, after the fall of our first parents into sin, the bonds of wedlock were loosened and the indissolubility of marriage, between one man and one woman, no longer observed.

Q. Who brought matrimony back to its primitive unity, purity, and indissolubility?

A. Jesus Christ, who further elevated this union to the dignity of a sacrament. "Because Moses, by reason of the hardness of your heart, permitted you to put away your wives, but from the beginning it was not so. Behold I say to you, that whosoever shall put away his wife, and shall marry another, committeth adultery, and he that shall marry her that is put away committeth adultery." *Matt.* xix., 8; *Luke* xvi., 18; *Mark* x., 11.

Q. What, then, is matrimony in the new law?

A. A sacrament, by which man and wife are joined in conjugal union to obtain an increase of sanctifying grace and the peculiar assistance of God, to enable them to fulfil the duties of their station, and to bear its toils and difficulties in a meritorious manner.

Q. Whence do we know that Christ elevated matrimony to the dignity of a sacrament?

A. From revelation. Christ's presence at the nuptial feast of Cana, of which we are informed by John the Evangelist, on which occasion Christ wrought the first miracle of His divine mission, serves to prove the sanctification of marriage as the holy Fathers and interpreters of the Scriptures justly observe.

This doctrine of faith is positively confirmed by St. Paul in his Epistle to the Ephesians, in which he terms marriage a great sacrament in Christ and His Church. *Eph.* v., 32. The union of wedlock is an emblem of Christ's spiritual union with His Church. Tradition confirms this. St. Chrysostom writes in his 56th Homily on the book of Genesis: "Matrimony is a sacrament and a figure of the love which Christ entertains for His Church." St. Augustine teaches, "The benefit of marriage amongst all nations consists in the propagation of the human race, but in regard to the people of God it consists in the sanctity of the sacrament. *Lib. de bono conj.* c. 24. This has ever been the faith and doctrine of the Church from the times of the Apostles, hence the Council of Trent very justly decreed: "If any one assert that marriage is not one of the seven sacraments, instituted by Christ, let him be anathema." Sess. 24, Can. i.

Q. Whereby is marriage contracted?

A. By the free consent of the parties concerned, which consent must be legitimately expressed, either by words or gestures. Hence to enter into the married state, the requisites are:—1. Parties capable of receiving the sacrament. 2. The freely expressed, mutual and legitimate consent of the parties. This contract forms the matter of the sacrament. 3. The reciprocal expression of this consent by words or signs, constituting the form of the sacrament. 4. The presence of the lawful pastor and two witnesses, that is, in places in which the decrees of the Council of Trent have been promulgated, for that council, for very weighty reasons, declared marriages otherwise contracted as invalid.

Q. Is the blessing of the priest indispensably requisite for the validity of the sacrament?

A. No, only the presence of the pastor, as the Council of Trent desires nothing more for the validity of the sacrament. The parties concerned contract marriage by their lawful and free consent, and this is the sacrament. The priest's benediction merely contributes to the greater sanctification of the act. But, even where the decrees of the Council of Trent have not yet been published, as in many parts of the United States, the parties, if they have any claim to Christian feeling and virtue, will of course seek to obtain the priest's blessing, and enter this holy state in his presence, unless great distance render it impossible. This is, moreover, the express ordinance of the bishops in such dioceses.

Q. What is understood by parties capable of entering into the matrimonial state?

A. Such as are not prevented by natural or legal impediments from validly receiving the sacrament.

Q. What is an impediment to marriage?

A. Such circumstances as by the law of nature or the decrees of the Church prevent one from legally entering upon this state.

Q. How are impediments to marriage distinguished?

A. 1. Into such as render marriage unlawful, for instance, a simple vow of chastity; a promise of marriage given to another; marriage with heretics, without a due provision for the Catholic education of the children who may be born of the marriage. 2. Into such as render marriage null and void, as affinity or consanguinity within the fourth degree; a solemn vow of chastity, the solemn religious profession of one of the parties, or being unbaptized.

Q. What precautions have been taken by the Church in order to discover impediments of marriage more easily and surely?

A. The publication of the banns; this imposes on each and every one, who is aware of any impediment to marriage existing between the parties named, the duty of informing the pastor. As the state, moreover, frequently imposes conditions under which it allows or prohibits the contraction of marriage, the candidates for matrimony are to be on their guard against transgressing any of them, especially in protestant countries, so that they may avoid entailing upon themselves unpleasant consequences.

Q. Can impediments to marriage, in no instance, be obviated?

A. Such as have their source in the laws of nature never can, yet others may, on weighty grounds, be removed and be dispensed with by the Church; this is to be further treated of with the respective pastors.

Q. Whence does the Church derive her judicial power in matrimonial matters concerning impediments?

A. From Christ the Lord, who exalted matrimony to the dignity of a sacrament, and thus placed it under the jurisdiction of the Church.

Q. What qualities and what preparations are requisite for a Christian couple entering the marriage state?

A. They should, first, seriously consider and duly and im

partially examine themselves in order to discover whether or not God has called them to this state. 2. They should not thoughtlessly plight their faith, but duly consider and examine whether the person with whom they wish to enter into the conjugal union be so qualified as to render the matrimonial state a means of salvation. 3. They should be properly instructed and certain of entering this state unencumbered by impediments to matrimony. 4. They are to live in innocence and piety as betrothed, and avoid private interviews and conversations with the other party; they are not to believe that greater freedoms are permitted them, particularly, after a promise of marriage has been given and received; they should, on the contrary, be upon their guard more than others, so that they may not draw down the divine malediction upon their future union. Persons betrothed are expressly forbidden to dwell in the same house. They should be sure to enter upon this state from pure intentions and motives pleasing in the divine sight. "We are the children of saints, and we must not be joined together like heathens that know not God." *Tob.* viii., 5.

Would to God that every bride might, in truth, declare with the chaste Sarah: ". Thou knowest, O Lord, that I never coveted a husband, and have kept my soul clear from all lust. Never have I joined myself with them that play, neither have I made myself partaker with them that work in lightness. But a husband I consented to take, with Thy fear, not with my lust." *Tob.* iii., 16-18. Before the reception of the sacrament of matrimony they should approach the holy sacrament of penance and the blessed Eucharist with great devotion. It is, therefore, a very laudable custom, and one to be recommended to all who enter upon this state, first to make a general confession in order to purify their consciences as far as possible, and to approach the table of the Lord on their wedding-day, in order to dispose themselves for the reception of the rich graces imparted by the sacrament of matrimony.

Q. How is marriage contracted?

A. The parties solemnly declare in the presence of their pastor and two witnesses that they take each other in marriage, upon which the priest blesses their intention and the contract they make. This should, if possible, be done during the celebration of the holy sacrifice of the Mass, which is offered up for the bride and bridegroom.

Q. Do those grievously offend who, without having confessed, or after having made a sacrilegious confession, receive the sacrament of matrimony in the state of mortal sin?

A. They commit a most grievous crime and become guilty of a great sacrilege, by which they profane, instead of receiving, the graces attached to this sacrament.

Q. What is understood by plighting one's faith, betrothment, or engagements?

A. The earnest serious promise of future marriage.

Q. Is this promise binding, and are those who have given it obliged to fulfil it?

A. Certainly, and this under pain of a heinous sin, unless both parties are willing to retract the promise given, or should motives or circumstances justify the refusal of either party to fulfil their promise—a matter to be left to the decision of spiritual superiors. Amongst these circumstances we may mention, in particular, the call to a religious life.

Q. What is understood by light and inconsiderate promises of marriage?

A. 1. Promises given by those who neglect consulting with God in prayer, or who pay no regard to the counsels of their parents, guardians and pastors. 2. Those who in their choice make less account of religion and virtue than of temporal advantages and the like. 3. Who do not first duly consider whether they possess the necessary qualifications to take upon themselves the numerous and arduous duties imposed by this state and the charge of a family.

Q. What are the duties imposed by the conjugal state?

A. 1. Sincere and holy affection, as the Apostle so strongly admonishes: "Husbands love your wives, as Christ also loved the Church, and delivered himself up for it." *Ephes.* v., 25. "No man ever hated his own flesh but nourisheth and cherisheth it, as also doth Christ the Church." *Ephes.* v., 25. He admonishes wives in terms equally explicit: "Let women be subject in love to their husbands, as is the Church to Christ." *Ephes.* v., 22. "They shall be two in one," says the Lord, when instituting as well as when elevating matrimony to the dignity of a sacrament. Mutual support and aid in domestic life, particularly concord and peace. 3. Mutual edification in Christian piety, as the Apostle so earnestly exhorts all. 4. Great solicitude for the Christian education of their family and the due government of the household for the glory of God and their own salvation. *Ephes.* vi., 4. 5. By the careful avoidance of every abuse of marriage, as the Apostle admonishes, where he says: "Marriage is honorable in all." *Heb.* xii., 4.

Q. What crime is directly opposed to the marriage contract?

A. Adultery: we have touched slightly on the heinousness of this crime in treating of the sixth commandment. Oh! if the guilty person would but think how holy a bond he severs, how he undermines the happiness of his family if his guilt be detected; how bitter the serpent fang of repentance he conceals in his bosom, even if his crime be laid open to no eye but that of the All-seeing Avenger. What dreadful maledictions are pronounced on adulterers in Holy Writ, what heavy chastisements he entails upon himself, what dread consequences he heaps upon his head, he would certainly not sin, but rather manfully overcome the temptation which lures him recklessly to plunge into such a labyrinth of crime and misery! "He that is an adulterer for the folly of his heart shall destroy his own soul; he gathereth to himself shame and dishonor, and his reproach shall not be blotted out." *Prov.* vi., 32.

Q. Is marriage indissoluble?

A. It is, when actually consummated; thus did God institute marriage in paradise, as is evident from the words of Holy Writ. "A man shall leave father and mother and shall cleave to his wife, and they shall be two in one flesh." *Gen.* ii., 24. Christ the Lord confirms this, when He makes Adam's declaration His own. "What, therefore, God hath joined together let no man put asunder." *Matt.* xix., 6. And again, every one that putteth away his wife, and marrieth another, committeth adultery, and he that marrieth her that is put away from her husband, committeth adultery." *Luke* xvi., 19.

St. Paul solemnly declares in his Epistle to the Corinthians the indissolubility of marriage amongst Christians in the following terms: "But to them that are married, not I, but the Lord commandeth, that the wife depart not from her husband, and if she depart, that she remains unmarried, or be reconciled to her husband. And let not the husband put away his wife." 1 *Cor.* viii., 10, 11. He adds: "The wife is bound by the law as long as the husband lives." The same remark holds good of the husband. Neither is polygamy permitted amongst Christians; no man may have two or more wives; no woman two or more husbands. "They shall be two in one flesh." This is the primitive institution of marriage, and Christ ordained unity of marriage in the new law, as a type of His union with the one Church, who went forth from the wound of His blessed heart, on the wood of the cross, as the Eve of the new Covenant with Him, the heavenly Adam, under the symbol of water and blood. So says St. Augustine, treating of this subject. *Tract* 120 *in Joan*, and *St. John Chrysostom, Hom.* 84. Should one of the parties after the celebration of the nuptial ceremony, and before the marriage is consummated, resolve to enter the religious state, the matrimonial contract is thereby dissolved, according to the decision of the *Council of Trent*. Sess. 24, Can. 6. The high state of perfection embraced and the spiritual nuptials celebrated with Christ, are the grounds on which this privilege is based. The Pope can further, in the plentitude of apostolic power, dissolve marriage on motives of consequences, provided it has not been actually consummated. When, however, the marriage debt has been once paid, no one, not even the Pope, can dissolve it; it is binding till the death of one of the parties.

Q. What, then, is to be done when married persons cannot, from various weighty reasons, live together?

A. They may in this case be separated in bed and board by their spiritual superiors, but they must remain unmarried till the death of one of the parties severs the link which human power can not presume to touch.

Q. What are the conditions of a happy marriage?

A. 1. A proper choice. 2. A good intention. 3. Due preparation, particularly the worthy reception of the holy sacraments. 4. Zeal and Christian piety, particularly in bearing and forbearing, self-abnegation, and good example. 5. Invincible patience, in bearing with the frailties and defects of the other party. 6. Anxious and unremitting solicitude for the proper training and instruction of their offspring from earliest youth. 7. Domestic habits and social family life, also the avoidance of pride with the vain pomp and pleasure of the world.

Q. What are the sources of unhappy and unfortunate marriages?

A. A rash and inconsiderate choice of those to whom one

unites himself; this occurs, principally, when one takes into account nothing save a pleasing exterior, a large fortune and good connections; the bright delusions vanish but too speedily, and leave nought behind but bitterness, disappointment, and hopeless regret. 2. The want of a good intention, as many only marry for the sake of being married. 3. The levity with which many receive the sacrament of matrimony without having previously endeavored to put themselves in the state of sanctifying grace, and secure the blessing of heaven by having recourse to the sacrament of penance and the holy Eucharist. Those who thus enter upon marriage draw down upon themselves the curse of God by the sacrilege of which they become guilty, instead of obtaining grace and strength from on high to fulfil the grave and responsible duties awaiting them. 4. The want of virtue in general, and a vicious course of life indulged in up to the reception of the sacrament. "Piety is profitable to all things," says the Apostle, "having promise of the life that now is, and of that which is to come." 1 *Tim.* iv., 8. This declaration is fully and in a particular manner confirmed in the conjugal state. There can be no happier union here below than when the husband exclaims in truth and security, "O, that I were as worthy and virtuous as my wife," and the wife in return, "Had I but my husband's virtues!" 5. The difference of religion in mixed marriages, frequently produces mutual discontent and unhappiness, and causes the religious and moral training of the children to be but indifferently, if at all, attended to.

Q. In what light is marriage between parties of different creeds to be considered?

A. First, should they have been formed without express contract and provision, that the issue, if any, is to be brought up in the Catholic faith, they are altogether inadmissible; but even when this has been duly provided for, such marriages are never to be commended.

Q. Why does the Church disapprove of such unions?

A. 1. Because the Catholic party is always exposed to the danger of losing the faith, or at best becoming lukewarm and indifferent. 2. Because the Catholic education of the children is generally defective, and not unfrequently impracticable. 3. Because the dissenting party can procure from the state a divorce, and then contract a new alliance, which is contrary to faith, and may expose the Catholic party to great hardship and misery. 4. Because such a marriage can never present a true emblem of Christ's union with His holy Church. 5. Where there is no communion of faith there never can be as intimate a union and concord as the conjugal state justly claims, particularly in the mutual sanctification of life.

Q. What conditions are laid down by the Church, in case her children should contract such marriages notwithstanding her disapproval?

A. 1. That the Catholic party must be left at perfect liberty to practice his or her religion. 2. That he or she should zealously endeavor as long as they live together, to bring the dissenting party to acknowledge and embrace the truth. 3. That the children, without distinction of sex, be brought up in the Catholic faith. How, indeed, could the Catholic party consent to have their offspring trained to any other religious profession than the only true and hence only saving Catholic faith? Such an agreement, on their part, would betray a lamentable want of principle, as also a want of heartfelt conviction of the truth of the faith they profess, as also a want of affection for the children with whom they hope to be blessed. Should one of the parties have neglected before marriage to have this contract made, he or she still remains bound in conscience to observe it strictly in every particular, if they wish to obtain salvation and qualify themselves for approaching the sacrament.

The Catholic father of a family is bound to employ all his paternal authority to ensure the Catholic education of his children, and the mother should leave nothing undone to effect the same desirable object. The baseness and folly of the contract that some of the children should be brought up in the exercise of the father's religion, and others, in that of the mother's, is too evident to require further illustration. A couple who act thus, consider religion as a garment with which they clothe their daughters in a different manner from their sons, and prove but too clearly by such perverse conduct, their perfect indifference in matters of religion, and their woeful ignorance and want of judgment.

Q. Is marriage, being a sacrament, allowable and advisable for all?

A. No; for the Church requires continence of those consecrated to the service of the sanctuary by the sacrament of holy orders. She also considers the state of virginity as higher and more perfect than that of matrimony, according to the express words of the doctor of the Gentiles: "He that giveth his virgin in marriage doth well, and he that giveth her not doth better." 1 *Cor.* vii., 38. A double error is here to be combated.

The first is that which, with Jovinian, so exalts marriage as to place it on a level with and even elevates it above virginity. Tradition, Christ's own blessed example and that of His spotless mother, are all opposed to this. The Council of Trent, therefore, very justly decides as follows: "If any one shall affirm that matrimony is to be preferred to virginity, or that it be not better and more blessed to live in virginity than in the married state, let him be anathema." Sess. xxiv. can. 10. The second error is broached by those who declare and maintain it to be impossible to live in a state of celibacy. Those who speak so are strangers to the omnipotence of grace and the virtue of prayer. Nothing is too difficult for those who persevere in prayer before the Lord, and confidently ask Him for the grace of chastity. "God is faithful," as the doctor of nations assures us. "Who will not suffer you to be tempted above that which you are able, but will make also with temptation issue, that you may be able to bear it." 1 *Cor.* x., 13. St. Augustine, therefore, justly remarks, when treating of these words: "Pay your vows to the Lord." "Of yourselves," says he, "ye are too weak, but if you put your trust in Him to whom you have made your vows, you will assuredly receive strength to do it." *Ep.* lxxv. And in another passage he exclaims, when considering this state of life: "Happy necessity which binds to that which is better." *Ep.* 45.

Q. What is this unmarried state termed which the Church imposes on those she advances to the higher orders?

A. It is called celibacy.

Q. Is the perpetual chastity required by the Church of her consecrated ministers just and reasonable?

A. Without doubt. The sanctity of the holy office and the obligations it imposes, demand of those who have taken it upon themselves, undivided affections and general solicitude for the welfare of their fellow men, and the state of celibacy alone can qualify man to enter upon it. Candid and upright protestants both acknowledge and declare this. They have so expressed themselves even in public documents. The Helvetic confession, as also the Anglican Church, express in their ordinances the wish to behold men in the sacred ministry untrammelled by the bonds of wedlock. *Conf. Helv.* 2, c. 29. *Edw.* c. 21. Even in the Old Testament the priests were obliged to observe continence during the time appointed for them to sacrifice and ministry in the temple. Even the heathens, by an intuitive and correct feeling, received and acknowledged the excellence of virginity in the divine ministry. The Egyptian priests were either unmarried, or had but one wife, contrary to the general custom of the people of those times. And in Rome and Athens the sacred fire kept constantly burning in Minerva's honor was attended by virgins only. What stainless purity does not Christian sentiment demand of those who present to the divine majesty the spotless victim of the New Testament, the immaculate Lamb of God, Jesus, the purest and holiest, conceived in the womb of Israel's lily, by the cooperation of the Holy Ghost. In truth, it is only chastity that can in any degree qualify the priest to offer this most holy sacrifice, the august victim of the new law; he thereby becomes a visible and worthy representative of Christ, a worthy minister of the Lord on earth, whose life and deportment draw the hearts of the faithful heavenward, and inspires them with full confidence in the priest as their common spiritual father. How different would it not be were the ministers of the sanctuary incumbered by the bonds of wedlock. The contemptible and despised condition of the priests of the Greek Church, afford a striking example of the truth of this remark, as every one knows who has had opportunities of learning anything on this subject. *De Maistre on the Pope*, iii. book, iii. chap. How greatly is the perplexity of such a situation increased when the wife or children of these parties scandalize the flock. The spirit of God certainly guided and directed the Church in ordaining and strictly enforcing the celibacy of her priests, and the two inferior grades of deacon and sub-deacon.

Practice.—Let no other motive induce thee to decide on a state of life, than the divine will and the salvation of thy immortal soul, and then thou mayst hope to know and fulfil the will of thy Lord and God in this respect. Should it please the divine majesty to call thee to the married state, thou wilt endeavor to make a prudent choice, prepare thyself properly for the reception of this sacrament of matrimony, and in that state thou wilt strive to live in such a manner as to procure thy own salvation and promote that of those intrusted to thy care.

CHAPTER IV.

OF THE SACRAMENTALS.

BESIDES the means of grace instituted by Christ himself, for the sanctification of the faithful, that is the seven sacraments, the Church in virtue of the powers imparted to her by her divine founder, has ordained other consecrations, benedictions and ceremonies, in order to assist her children in the attainment of that priceless good, for which alone they have been created, that is to say, salvation in the possession of God.

These are all included under the term of sacramentals, because, like the sacraments, they impart grace, although not in the same degree, nor with the same efficacy. These consecrations, benedictions, and ceremonies, do not always and infallibly take effect by virtue of their institution, as do the sacraments, but are frequently emblems fraught with deep and holy meaning, as rights and acts calculated to heighten the solemnity of divine worship. Their efficacy moreover depends on man's free co-operation. The Church can change, increase, or diminish these blessings, consecrations and rites, but over the sacraments instituted by Christ himself, she has not the same jurisdiction. They may in this respect be compared to the washing of the feet, recommended to the faithful by Christ's own word and example, although he did not elevate this touching and beautiful act to the dignity of a sacrament, or declare it necessary for all. *See* p. 406.

OF THE BENEDICTIONS OF THE CHURCH.

Q. What do we understand by this term?
A. The application of those prayers and ceremonies of the Church, by which persons and things are peculiarly appropriated or set apart for the divine service.
Q. Which are the principal benedictions?
A. 1. The consecration, dedication and benediction of

churches and all that is necessary and proper for the celebration of divine worship;

2. That of the objects used in divine service;

3. That imparted to clerical and religious persons.

We shall briefly add the essential characteristics of these benedictions.

The Dedication of a Church.

Q. What is understood by the dedication of a church?

A. The solemn act by which a temple is consecrated for divine worship. This consecration may take place by a simple benediction, which may be imparted by a priest with the prelate's permission, or it is performed with the unctions and all the other ceremonies prescribed by the ritual. This is called consecration, and in this case a bishop must officiate.

Q. Is it an ancient custom to dedicate or consecrate churches?

A. It is; we can trace it to the earliest ages of Christianity, and we find its type in the dedication of Solomon's temple, performed in the Old Law, and recorded in the 3d book of Kings.

Q. How is this rite performed?

A. The vigil of the consecration is to be observed as a fast; the vesper service is chanted before the relics of saints to be placed on the altar, and in the interim preserved in a proper repository becomingly ornamented. Early on the morning of the following day the bishop goes thrice round the church, sprinkling it with holy water; he then enters the church and writes the Greek and Latin alphabets upon the floor, which is covered with blessed ashes in the form of St. Andrew's cross; those two languages being the principal ones of ancient times, and those in which the Old and New Testaments are written and read, being the tongues, moreover, in which our faith was chiefly announced in primitive times; the altars are then anointed and consecrated with the blessed oils, whilst psalms selected for the occasion are chanted, and prayers full of unction and fervor recited, accompanied by the performance of ceremonies fraught with deep and holy meaning. The same ceremony is performed on the walls of the church, which, in memory of the twelve gates of the heavenly Jerusalem are marked with twelve crosses. The altar being the favored spot on which the Immaculate Victim of the New Covenant is daily to be immolated, is consecrated with the utmost solemnity. The whole edifice loses its consecration if the altar be removed from its original position.

Of the Blessing of Church Bells and Vestments.

Q. Why are the church bells blessed, and why is this act called baptism of the bells?

A. The bells attached to our temples are blessed, being as it were the heavenly voices inviting the faithful to divine worship. Their benediction is termed *baptism;* on this occasion the name of a saint is given them in order that the saint may join to the pealing of the bells fervent prayers for the willing and zealous acceptance of the invitation to assemble and worship the Lord of heaven and earth. The sound of our church bells is intimately connected with the most important moments of our earthly pilgrimage, so the ablution with water and the unction with chrism and the holy oil of the sick, seem to allude to the bells being destined to take part in the most solemn affairs of our life and death. The church bell is, according to the expression used by the Synod of Cologne, "the trumpet of the church militant." It appears to praise the Most High with us; to raise with us the voice of supplication to Him who sits enthroned above the fleeting clouds of earth. The bells seem to peal gladly out when joy animates our hearts; to toll sadly and heavily when grief weighs them down. To the faithful who live in the state of grace their sound is of heaven; to the infidel and libertine it is gloomy and insupportable. It welcomes us on our first appearance in the temples of our God, and on our last unconscious journey to our narrow homes it sends after us a thrilling and mournful farewell. At times it is entirely silent, viz., when the Church is employed in bewailing the agony and death of her Divine Spouse, or smarting under the wounds inflicted by some great crime committed by her unfaithful children. This is the case during an interdict, at which time public worship is suspended. The silence of death then seems to reign on earth, and ominous terror burthens every heart. When, on the contrary, the smallest bell sends forth its silvery strain from the church steeple, every thing in the ecclesiastical sphere seems to rejoice in renovated existence. We need not, therefore, be surprised that a German poet should have felt so warmly and written so beautifully on this subject. An ancient verse declares the destination of our church bells to be as follows:

> "Laudo Deum verum, plebem voco, congrego clerum,
> Defunctos ploro, nimbum fugo, festaque honoro."

Q. Why are the furniture, the holy vessels, vestments and linen used in the celebration of the divine mysteries all blessed?

A. Because they are set apart for divine service and are often brought into immediate contact with the adorable sacrament. That certain vestments of finer and more beautiful texture are set apart to be worn by the priests and ministers of the sanctuary, during the celebration of divine worship is both proper, reverent and edifying. The peculiar form and material of the holy vessels tends to promote devotion, and keep the spirit in pious meditation during the celebration of divine service. God himself prescribed most minutely the vestments, furniture, vessels for the tabernacle, and these were all to be of such costly materials and elegant workmanship as to excite our astonishment. Let those in particular take this remark into consideration, who, having inherited a portion of the sentiments of Judas, consider nothing too rich or costly for secular representations and celebrations, but are much afraid of extravagance in decorating the temples of the Lord, and think any thing good enough for that purpose.

Of the Benediction of Burial-Grounds.

Q. Why are grave-yards or church-yards blessed?

A. 1. In order that the bodies of the faithful, which in life were temples of the Holy Ghost, and shall one day arise in glorious immortality, may be deposited in a fitting and holy resting place.

2. In order to remind us that the souls of the faithful reposing in the unbroken tranquility of the tomb, in our burial-places, are united with us, in the holiest bonds of hope and affection, and to encourage us by the sight of the holy place in which their remains lie, to make supplication for them at the throne of mercy.

3. That the consecrated ground allotted for their burial-place may remind us of the one faith which so intimately unites the departed with us. It is a just and holy ordinance of the Church, in virtue of which only such as have in life been united in the same one holy faith, rest after death in the same consecrated ground, from which they are excluded by great and heinous crimes, or if they severed themselves from the communion of the Church by heretical or schismatical opinions, or open infidelity. When frivolous and thoughtless worldlings loudly complain that men who have never cared for religion, but on the contrary were to their fellowmen a stumbling-block and cause of scandal are denied burial in consecrated ground, they show their own want of judgment and sense of right. Wherefore should the Church acknowledge and impart her maternal benediction after their death to men who have lived and died in sentiments and opinions totally opposed to her teaching and practice?

The Benediction of Objects used in Divine Service.

Holy Water.

Q. Is the use of blessed water ancient?

A. We can trace it to apostolic tradition; it is mentioned in the so-called *Apostolic Constitutions*, l. vii. ch. 15. Symbols of this blessing are found in the Old Testament: *Levit.* Those who attentively peruse the fervent prayers, so full of force and unction used by the Church in blessing water, will easily understand why the faithful so carefully preserve holy water in their dwellings, and so confidently and devoutly make use of it before retiring or arising, leaving their dwellings, and such like, unless, indeed, they imagine it possible for the Church to pray and bless in vain. The ecclesiastical writers of the fourth century mention a vessel of holy water placed at the entrance of Christian temples. *Euseb. Hist.* c. 10.

Blessed Candles.

Q. Why does the Church bless candles?

A. They are blessed to serve as symbols of the spiritual joy of the Church and the interior illumination of the Holy

Ghost. Lighted tapers are emblematic of *faith*, which enlightens, *hope*, which imparts genial warmth, and *love*, which inflames. The burning tapers, placed upon our altars during Divine service, remind us of the bloody persecutions with which the infant Church had to contend in days when the voice of praise and supplication arose from vaults and caverns where her Divine rites were celebrated. We find our blessed tapers symbolized in the old law. God himself commanded a golden candlestick with seven branches bearing lights to be placed in the tabernacle, and Solomon had the temple furnished with several candlesticks of the finest gold. 2 *Paralip.* iv. Is it not more proper, then, for us to seek to honor the presence of our sovereign Lord and Master in the sacrament of His love, during the celebration of the Divine mysteries and in acts of worship generally, by the use of blessed tapers?

Q. On what occasion, in particular, does the Church bless tapers?

A. On the Feast of the Purification of the Blessed Virgin Mary, commonly called Candlemas. This, as an emblem of our deep conviction of her inviolate purity, the radiance of which, far from being dimmed by the birth of her Divine Son, became the brighter and more effulgent.

Q. Why are processions held on this festival?

A. In order to represent to us in a more lively manner the journey of the Blessed Mother, St. Joseph, Anna and Simeon to the temple, and as a tribute of love and homage to our sweet heavenly Queen.

Q. When are blessed candles employed?

A. During the administration of holy baptism and extreme unction, on account of their symbolical signification, and in order to put the powers of darkness to flight by the virtue of the blessed candles.

The Blessed Ashes.

Q. Why does the Church bless ashes on Ash-Wednesday, the first day of Lent?

A. 1. In order to excite to do penance, by the remembrance of an approaching and certain death. This is the reason why the priest, when sprinkling the heads of the faithful therewith, employs the words of the Divine sentence, pronounced on man after his first transgression, and extended to all his posterity :

"Remember, man, thou art but dust, and unto dust thou shalt again return."

2. In order to call forth in us the spirit of humility, without which no penance, however severe, is acceptable in the Divine sight. Ashes have been, from the earliest times, a symbol of penance and humiliation. Job did penance in dust and ashes. Micheas and other prophets called on the people to do penance in sackcloth and ashes. The Ninevites wept and lamented their crimes in sackcloth and ashes, and found favor in the Divine sight. *Jonas*, iii.

Of the Blessed Palms.

Q. Why does the Church bless palm branches?

A. 1. In memory of Christ's solemn and triumphant entry into Jerusalem, on which occasion the exulting populace strewed the way with palms.

2. On account of their symbolic signification, the palm being an emblem of the victory which Christ gained over sin, hell and death, and for which we, in imitation of Him, have also to struggle. *Apoc.* vii. 9. They are, therefore, borne in procession as memorials of Christ's triumphant entry, after which they are preserved in our dwellings until the commencement of Lent, when they serve for the preparation of the ashes with which the faithful are marked on Ash-Wednesday.

The Paschal Candle.

Q. What does the paschal candle recall to our minds, and when is it blessed?

A. The paschal candle is a symbol of Christ, the conquering King, the mighty vanquisher of death, the valiant lion of Juda, who freed us from the slavery to which sin and Satan had reduced us, and its radiant effulgence, the fiery pillar which in days of yore preceded the children of Israel from the land of bondage to the promised inheritance. It is blessed with great solemnity on Holy Saturday, and used during the paschal time at the celebration of the Divine service. After the Gospel on the Festival of Christ's Ascension, it is extinguished, in memory of that event.

Of the Holy Oils.

Q. What is understood by this term?

A. The holy oils blessed on Maundy Thursday by the bishop, particularly the holy chrism, the oils used in baptism and in administering extreme unction. The two first are employed in the baptismal rite, and chrism in the consecration of churches and church bells. The oils for the sick are used in administering extreme unction. St. Basil mentions the consecration of these holy oils on Maundy Thursday. 1 *De Sp. S.* cap. 17.

Of Incense.

Q. Why does the Church employ and bless incense?

A. Incense is an emblem of adoration and prayer, in the fragrance of devotion wafted heavenward by the ministry of kindly angels. We find mention made of incense in the Old Testament. *Levit.* iv. 7. Besides these objects blessed for Divine service, in general, the Church is wont to bless various objects for the private devotion of her children and attach Indulgences to the godly use made of them. To this class belongs the blessing of the so-called *Agnus Dei.*

Q. What is the blessed *Agnus Dei?*

A. It is a particle of wax stamped with the figure of the Lamb of God. This is the interpretation of the word *Agnus Dei*. These small waxen images of the Lamb of God are so highly prized on account of their being blessed only by the Pope himself, and that but once in seven years. The sight of the image should remind him who wears or uses it of the innocence, gentleness, and patience which should characterize all our actions, as imitators of the meek Lamb of God, Christ the Lord. If this be our earnest endeavor, the solemn benediction imparted to the Agnus Dei will certainly not be wanting in efficacy in our regard. Besides this, God imparts to the faithful, by the devout use of the Agnus Dei, more special protection and richer blessings. The learned Baronius traces the use of the Agnus Dei to the year 58 A. D. See his annals of the year 58.

2. The blessing of crosses, rosaries, pictures and medals, so that, by the zealous and devout use thereof, we may more frequently and meritoriously renew within us the memory of Christ, His blessed mother and glorified servants.

3. The blessing of plants on the festival of our blessed Lady's Assumption, as symbols of the aromatic fragrance of her virtues, according to the words of the Canticle of Canticles: "Who is she that goeth up by the desert, as a pillar of smoke, of aromatical spices, of myrrh, and frankincense, and of all the powders of the perfumer." *Cant.* iii. 6.

Of the Benedictions of Persons.

Q. What individuals are installed in their respective offices by peculiar dedication or consecration?

A. 1. Those who by the sacrament of Orders and the ordinance of the Church are separated from the mass of the people and devoted to the service of God and the sanctuary; of these we have already treated in speaking of Holy Orders. The Church has instituted, besides the rites of ordination, various other peculiar dedications of persons to the Divine service, accompanied by prayers full of unction, and ceremonies replete with deep meaning. We may here mention the elevation and coronation of our supreme head, the holy Pontiff. The newly-elected successor of Peter is solemnly borne to the place distinguished by the appellation of *Confessio Petri*, where thousands of Christians formerly expired in tortures for Jesus' sake, and where the remains of the two glorious princes and pillars of the Church, Peter and Paul, still rest. Many prayers are here pronounced by several bishops over the newly-elected Pontiff, in order to draw down upon him from the Father of mercies the fullness of celestial benediction, Divine strength and courage from on high to discharge the duties of his awful trust. The pallium worn on the shoulders is given him with the words: "Receive the pallium, the plenitude of the pontifical authority, for the honor of Almighty God, the glorious Virgin Mary, the mother of His Son, the blessed Apostles Peter and Paul, and the holy Roman Church." During the celebration of the Divine mysteries by the Holy Father, personally, the Epistle and Gospel are chanted in the Greek and Latin tongues, to signify that he is the supreme head of both the Eastern and the Western Church, and of all Christendom. When the ceremony of the coronation is performed, the tiara is placed on the Pontiff's head with the words: "Receive the tiara adorned with a triple crown, and know that thou art the father of princes and kings, the ruler of the earth and Vicar of Jesus Christ our Saviour." Thus crowned, he doubtless receives a particular communication of grace and strength to enable him duly to perform the duties attached to this most important office in the Church of God. The solemn elevation of the Cardinals to the dignity of assistants of the Holy See and counsellors of his Holiness the Pope, is certainly accompanied by heavenly grace and favor.

2. As regards the inauguration of abbots, abbesses and religious of both sexes, as also that of kings and emperors of Christian states, inasmuch as the office and calling of such persons is peculiarly allied to the Divine worship, they are enrolled in the holy state by peculiar benedictions. The rulers of nations likewise have an office which when properly discharged, may be the source of rich blessings to the Church of God. The Church reminds princes and people of this duty by the holy unction she administers. The Old Testament furnishes instances of the unction given to kings by Divine ordinance.

OF THE BLESSINGS OF THE CHURCH.

Q. What is meant by the blessings of the Church?
A. The different prayers of blessing and protection privately pronounced by the Church over individuals and objects.

Q. Over what manner of persons does the Church usually pronounce such prayers?
A. Over those who are exorcised. By such prayers the faithful are protected against the malignity of the devil, or delivered from his power, should he have unhappily acquired any over them. These prayers are generally pronounced over persons baptized, as has been shown when treating of the ceremonies accompanying the administration of baptism. Further, when just apprehensions are entertained of a person being possessed by Satan, or exposed to exterior influences proceeding from this inveterate enemy of man; public exorcisms, however, can only be resorted to with the approbation of ecclesiastical superiors.

2. The Church pronounces prayers of benediction and protection over the betrothed, particularly during the celebration of the bridal mass.

3. She does the same when churching women. Women after childbirth are not indeed bound by a commandment to be churched; yet they should, in imitation of Mary, take the child, with which heaven has blessed them, to the house of God, there dedicate it to His Divine service, make an offering according to their ability, and ask the blessing of the Church. It were erroneous, however, to imagine that churching must be submitted to under pain of sin, and it were further an error of faith to suppose, or assert, that the birth of a child impresses a stain of guilt on the soul of a Christian mother.

4. The apostolic benediction imparted by priests and bishops in general, and particularly the blessing given by the supreme Pontiff as Vicar of Christ on earth. We find that priests have been accustomed to give their blessing from the earliest ages of the Church. Thus, the Emperor Justinian knelt before St. Sabbas, and craved his blessing. And did not Melchisedeck bless Abraham, the father of the faithful? *Gen.* xv.

Q. Why does the Church also bless a variety of objects?

A. She blesses them in order to impart to them spiritual virtue and dedication. That this is attained by the benediction of the Church is evident from the words of St. Paul to Timothy: "Every creature of God is sanctified by the word of God and prayer." 1 *Tim.* iv. 4.

Q. Are not all things good according to the Divine declaration made on the Sabbath of creation?

A. This certainly was the case when first the creation proceeded from the hand of God; man, however, on whose account alone the visible creation was called forth, having violated God's command, drew down upon earth the Divine malediction. Hence it is quite proper to bless our fields and dwellings, and also our food, and our holy mother the Church pronounces over each particular prayers and benedictions.

Q. Is this custom ancient?

A. It may be traced to the patriarchal times. Christ himself blessed the loaves and fishes, which He ordered to be distributed amongst the people. *Luke,* iii. 16. St. Chrysostom and Theophilus both remark, when treating of St. Paul's words, quoted above, that the custom of blessing certain objects is very ancient. St. Basil expressly assures us, that this practice is grounded on apostolic tradition. *Epist.* i. ch. 27. The holy fathers, Clement, Dionysius, Cyril, Ephrem and Augustine concur in the same testimony. Several kinds of nourishment, bread, fish, eggs, etc., are blessed at Easter. Wine is blessed and partaken of as an emblem of mutual love and friendship on the festival of St. John.

Of the Ceremonies and Rites of the Church.

Q. What is understood by Church ceremonies and rites?
A. Significant emblems and acts belonging to the celebration of Divine worship.

Q. What induces the Church to employ ceremonies?
A. 1. By these man very properly and justly testifies in an outward manner the interior affections and emotions of his heart, his devotion to and adoration of his supreme Lord and Master.

2. These rites and ceremonies are peculiarly adapted to render Divine worship more solemn, to fix our attention, enliven our devotion, and render the impression more permanent. These ceremonies are, therefore, not mere exterior and vain observances, but full of meaning and, when rightly understood, powerfully influence the heart to raise its affections heavenward, and adore God in spirit and in truth. If an ignorant and thoughtless person is satisfied with merely gazing on the acts performed, without taking pains to fathom their meaning, the Church is not to blame, but rather the individual who neglects to procure instruction concerning the signification of these ceremonies so replete with meaning and beauty. The *Council of Trent*, therefore, very justly remarks: "Man's nature being so constituted that he does not easily, without external aid, soar to the contemplation of things Divine, our holy mother the Church has instituted and ordained peculiar usages and ceremonies, which have been handed down to her by tradition. The Church admonishes pastors to instruct the faithful carefully in the nature and signification of the rites which she deems it proper to employ. We are all aware that God himself commanded numerous ceremonies to be observed in the Old Law. We also see our Divine model, Christ the Lord, employing ceremonies in the New Testament; for instance,

when healing the deaf and dumb man, (*Mark*, vii.) restoring sight to the man born blind, (*John*, ix.) imparting the Holy Ghost to His Apostles, (*John*, xx.) and also when instituting the adorable sacrament of the altar. He further prescribed the manner in which the sacraments were to be administered during the forty days He remained on earth after His resurrection. When treating of the ceremonies of the Church, it is proper to mention all those prescribed for the celebration of the august sacrifice of the Mass, so full of deep signification and so admirably adapted to render that holy act more solemn and impressive.

3. All the ceremonies prescribed in administering the sacraments; these are all most intimately connected with the nature of these channels of grace, and well calculated to prepare the hearts of the faithful to derive grace and benediction from their devout reception.

4. The ceremonies used on various festive occasions, and the consecrations, dedications, and benedictions before referred to, such as the washing of the feet on Maundy Thursday, which reminds us of our blessed Saviour's infinite self-humiliation; in stooping to wash the feet of His disciples before giving them His own precious body and blood, as we learn from the Evangelist who relates this most winning example. He added the express admonition to do as He had done. When this act is performed in the spirit of Jesus Christ, and according to the ordinance of the Church, it is certainly fraught with peculiar graces. *See the Additions: The ecclesiastical year.*

SOLEMN ECCLESIASTICAL PRACTICES.

Regarding the solemn practices of the Church, we mention in general all those acts of devotion performed throughout the world for the consolation and encouragement of the faithful, in effecting their sanctification. Amongst these the exposition and adoration of the sacrament of the altar deservedly occupies the first rank; then follow the vesper services and devotions held in honor of the saints, particularly the Blessed Virgin Mary, which are so calculated to excite, nourish, strengthen, and elevate the spirit of piety and devotion in a Christian heart. As the Church is aware of these devotions, and approves of them, what we have said of them appears to us very properly introduced. Processions, pilgrimages, missions, and sodalities belong also to these practices.

Processions.

Q. Have processions been long in use?

A. They have. We learn that Josue passed around the walls of Jericho several times in procession, after which, on the sounding of the trumpets, the walls fell to pieces. David brought the ark of the covenant from the house of Obededom in solemn procession. 1 *Paral.* xiii. The prescribed visit to the temple, so strictly enjoined on all males, on the great festivals, from the twelfth year upward, naturally formed processions through all Judea, the people being accustomed to journey to the holy city in groups, praying and chanting psalms as they went. Christ's triumphant entry into Jerusalem on Palm Sunday was also a most solemn procession. We find that processions were in use in the first ages of Christianity. The solemn procession, ordained and led on by Gregory the Great in Rome during the prevalence of the plague, in order to propitiate the Divine clemency, is well known, as also the success which attended it, for scarcely had the procession ended when the angel of death departed from Rome, and the pestilence ceased its ravages. The great procession ordained by Procleus in Constantinople, in the thirty-sixth year of the reign of Theodosius, in order to implore of heaven deliverance from the earthquake which threatened destruction to the whole city: finally, the processions of rogation, introduced by Mamertus, Bishop of Vienna in France, and which were shortly afterwards extended to the whole Church and made annually on the three days preceding the festival of our blessed Lord's ascension. O how glorious will be the procession called forth by Christ's words to the just: "Come, ye blessed of my Father, possess the kingdom prepared for you from the foundation of the world!" *Matt.* xxv. 34. It is not to be wondered at, therefore, that our hearts are filled with sweet and solemn joy when we take our place in the festive train. This is particularly the case in reference to the solemn procession on Corpus Christi.

Q. Why are crosses, or crucifixes, and banners borne in processions?

A. In order to make open profession of our faith in Christ and the triumph of the Holy Cross.

Q. Why were the relics and images of the saints borne in procession?

A. In order to signify that we are firmly resolved to tread the path they have trodden, and to imitate their virtues.

Q. Why are processions formed in lines consisting of two individuals?

A. To remind us of the great command, which enjoins on us to love and acknowledge all men as fellow-servants of our dearest Master, Christ Jesus, and dear brethren in the Lord.

Q. Why do processions pass through public squares and streets?

A. So that we may boldly declare before heaven and earth that we are not ashamed of our holy religion, and to impress on our minds that we are pilgrims on earth and should constantly walk before the Lord.

On Pilgrimages.

Q. What is understood by this term?

A. Journeys undertaken in order to visit various shrines and holy places.

Q. Are pilgrimages laudable, commendable and useful?

A. They certainly are, when undertaken and performed with the proper dispositions. It is true that God is everywhere present, and that from every corner of the earth the loving and contrite sighs of a Christian soul reach His ear and touch His paternal heart. Still, it may please Him to bestow greater favors in certain places and at certain periods, according to the decrees of his wisdom and unbounded freedom of will and action, to those who petition Him in humility and confidence.

The united prayer of many, and the virtuous example of our brethren, on such favored spots are highly conducive towards animating and strengthening our confidence and devotion. Should any one find by experience, however, that making pilgrimages but distracts him, he will certainly do better to abstain from so doing in future, seeing that he is of so peculiar a temperament that what tends to advance others in spiritual life only retards his advancement, perhaps adding sin to tepidity and want of recollection. The perversity of our fallen nature is so great, that perhaps no practice has escaped misapplication and abuse. This, however, does not justify our censuring such practices, but rather those who misapply them. Pilgrimages are in themselves good and salutary, but they have certainly been abused, and may again. The fault, however, is not to be ascribed to them, but to those who undertake and perform them without the proper dispositions.

Q. Which are the principal and general places of pilgrimage?

A. 1. The Holy Land; 2. Rome; 3. To Loretto, and other places in which the Blessed Virgin has shown herself particularly gracious.

The tomb of St. James, at Compostella, was in former times a famous resort for pilgrims. There are in every Christian country particular places in which heaven seems to lend a more willing ear to our supplications. These are well known, at least, in the vicinity, and may be visited with great spiritual benefit.—See the additions: missions.

Sodalities.

Q. What are sodalities?

A. Pious confraternities generally approved of, and enriched with great treasures of grace and many privileges by the supreme head of the Church. Their end is mutual encouragement in works of virtue and charity. As the rules of these sodalities do not bind under pain of sin, and when duly observed tend to animate us with zeal in the performance of our Christian duties, every one should endeavor, according to his circumstances and state of life, to enroll himself in one or more.

Practice.—Take care to venerate whatever the Church blesses and sets apart for the celebration of Divine worship. Manifest this veneration of the heart by outward tokens of respect towards such objects and rites. This is, as it were, the test of the liveliness of our faith, the measure of the extent to which the life of the Church has penetrated us. A truly Catholic heart feels intuitively, as it were, the virtue of these blessings, dedications and ceremonies without further consideration, and finds itself powerfully attracted by all that the Church has ordained in this respect. This should be the case with thee.

PART THIRD.

THE CARE OF SALVATION.

IN THE PRECEDING PARTS OF THIS WORK, WE HAVE EXPLAINED THE WAY OF SALVATION, AND THE MEANS WHICH RENDER SALVATION POSSIBLE; BUT WE SHALL NOT BE SAVED WITHOUT THE CARE OF SALVATION, OR WITHOUT THE PRACTICE OF CHRISTIAN JUSTICE.

CHAPTER I.

ON THE AVOIDANCE OF EVIL.

Q. IN what does Christian justice consist?
A. In the avoidance of evil and the practice of good. The Psalmist admonishes us: "Decline from evil and do good." *Ps.* xxxvi. 27. This is what Isaias requires of us when he exclaims: "Abandon wickedness and practice goodness." And this is what St. Paul terms, "putting off the old man who is corrupted according to the desires of error, and putting on the new man who according to God is created in justice and holiness of truth." *Col.* iii. 8–10; *Eph.* iv. 22.

The evil which we are to avoid is sin, the only moral evil. The good which it is incumbent on us to do consists in the practice of Christian virtue, in striving after perfection, and earnestly seeking to model our lives on that of our dear Lord and Saviour, Jesus Christ. Now, as sin, according to the words of St. John, renders us like unto the author of sin, "He that committeth sin is of the devil." *John,* iii. 8. So also does the practice of justice render us like to God and secure to us His possession in the joy of the just made perfect. "He that doeth justice is just, as He, God, also is just," says St. John. Christ the Lord confirms this assertion when addressing sinners, "You are of your father the devil." *John,*

viii. 44. He assures us, on the contrary, when speaking of the just, who make His Divine teaching the rule of their lives: "My Father will love him and we will come to him and will make our abode with him." *John,* iv. 23. So that the just man may joyfully exclaim with St. Paul: "I live, yet not I, but Christ in me." *Galat.* ii. 20.

On Sin.

Q. What is sin?
A. It is a voluntary transgression of the Divine law.

Q. Is sin of various kinds?
A. It admits of two principal divisions, original and actual sin. In the first part of our work we have treated of original sin committed by Adam in paradise, and which we take upon ourselves in connection with our human nature. We shall here speak of actual or personal sin.

Q. How is it committed, how distinguished?
A. It is committed by thoughts, desires, words, works and omissions, and is either a mortal or a venial transgression.

Q. What is mortal sin.
A. It is a voluntary transgression of the Divine law in a matter of moment, or the violation of a commandment which we are bound under pain of eternal death to observe.

Q. Why is a sin of this nature termed mortal sin?
A. Because it deprives the soul of the spiritual life of grace: "Sin when accomplished generates death." *Jam.* xi. 15. "Thou hast the name of being alive, and thou art dead." *Apoc.* iii. 1.

Q. What is venial sin?
A. A transgression of the Divine law, in a lighter matter, (if we may imagine the expression) when the command neither enjoins, nor prohibits, under pain of damnation, or, should the matter amount to a mortal transgression, when there is not full knowledge, or not complete deliberation and full consent. These are the sins meant by St. James, when he says: "In many things we all offend. *James,* iii. 2. To these lesser faults the Sage refers when he asserts, that, "The just man falls seven times," *i. e.* frequently. *Eccles.* vii. 21.

Q. Why are such transgressions termed venial sins?

A. Because man may obtain their remission by the merits of Christ without approaching the tribunal of penance, providing he sincerely detests them.

Q. What are the consequences of mortal sin ?

A. Sanctifying grace departs, man becomes a child and slave of the devil, and thus forfeits his dignity of child and heir of heaven. He is deprived of all merits acquired for eternal life, and remains as long as he perseveres in mortal sin incapable of doing aught that is meritorious in the Divine sight. "If the just man turn himself away from his justice and do iniquity, all his justices which he has done shall not be remembered." *Ezech.* xviii. 24. "If I should distribute all my goods to feed the poor, and if I should deliver my body to be burned, and have not charity, it profiteth me nothing." 1 *Cor.* xiii. 2. Moreover, man becomes by sin the executioner of Christ, and tortures him as much as in him lies in his own foul bosom, for he profanes Christ's infinite merits, crucifies the Lord anew in his heart, and tramples his blood under foot, as St. Paul declares, writing to the Hebrews, chap. xvi. He therefore becomes an object of aversion and abomination in the Divine sight, and renders himself miserable in this world by the pangs of a seared conscience, and the numerous other evil consequences attendant on sin and passion, even in this life. He, moreover, exposes himself to the imminent danger of eternal death and ruin, should he in this unhappy state be summoned before the tribunal of God, to account for his ill-spent life. This most awful of dangers accounts for the warnings of scripture : "And all the days of thy life have God in thy mind, and take heed thou never consent to sin." *Job,* iv. 6. "Flee from sins, as from the face of a serpent." *Eccles.* xxi. 2. "Sin maketh nations miserable." *Prov.* xiv. 34. The Psalmist says, "Many scourges overtake the sinner." "To God, the wicked and his wickedness are baleful alike." *Wisd.* xiv. 9. How numerous are the instances of the intensity of God's hatred of sin, and the fearful judgments it has called forth, as recorded in scripture. What has been said will enable us to form an idea of the enormity of a mortal transgression ; but, in reality, we shall never be able to fathom the wickedness and enormity of a mortal sin, until we have gazed on God face to face, in the realms of bliss. We shall then be able to estimate the horrid wickedness of sin, as a direct opposition to, and negation of God, the supreme good.

Q. What presents in the liveliest colors and most striking manner to our minds the wickedness of mortal sin ?

A. 1. Due reflection on the perversity of the sinner, who dares to ask, with Pharaoh: " Who is the Lord, that I should obey him ?" or with the rebellious Israelites mentioned by Jeremias, exclaim virtually, if not actually : " I will not serve." *Jer.* ii. 20. Thus preferring creatures to the Creator—a shameful pleasure, to the supreme good. Let us consider how detestable a person would appear in our eyes who, in all his words, works, thoughts and affections, manifested nothing but pride, covetousness, hatred, envy and the like. This consideration causes even heathens to look upon a violation of the laws of nature with so much horror, that they considered it alone a sufficient barrier against evil. So it was with the Stoics, but their sentiments and their acts did not correspond.

2. Meditation on the judgments of God ; the eternal damnation of the fallen angels, incurred by consenting to one mortal transgression ; the expulsion of our first parents from paradise, on account of one sin of disobedience, and the whole misery and fearful maledictions resting on the world, the awful consequences of this transgression.

3. The consideration of the incarnation and death of Christ, with the sufferings endured by Him during His whole mortal life and His bitter Passion, in order to reconcile us again with the Divine justice, had we been separated from God only by a single mortal sin.

4. Earnest consideration of the pains of the damned, to which the commission of one mortal sin exposes us.

Q. To what conclusion should these reflections lead us?

A. That we should gladly embrace every loss, suffering and pain, even death itself, rather than offend God by the commission of a grievous sin.

Q. Is there a distinction to be made regarding grievous sins, and may some exceed others in enormity ?

A. Certainly ; in proportion as the command of charity towards God and our neighbor is more or less grievously transgressed.

Q. What is it that makes sin so enormous in the Divine sight ?

A. 1. The full knowledge of the evil committed.

2. The relapse.

3. The greater number of graces received from God, which,

of course, render the sinner's ingratitude of a deeper dye. St. Peter's words of complaint allude to this subject, "It had been better for them not to have known the way of justice, than after they have known it to turn back from that holy commandment which was delivered to them." 2 *Pet.* ii. 21. There remains, as it were, for wanton sinners no atoning victim; they have nought to expect but the full severity of Divine justice, as St. Paul teaches, when writing to the Hebrews, ch. x. Christ's expiring prayer on the cross was made in vain for them: "Father, forgive them, they know not what they do." Such sinners are well aware what they are doing, with full clear knowledge, against the Holy Ghost. It is written that those who knowingly sin against the Divine Spirit, shall not be forgiven. These declarations of Christ and His Apostles should suffice to open the sinner's eyes to the imminent dangers to which he exposes himself by his crimes. Although there is no sin, no matter how dark its dye, which, if sincerely repented of and confessed with the due dispositions, may not be remitted in the tribunal of penance.

Q. What are the consequences entailed by venial sin?

A. Venial sin diminishes charity in our hearts, and renders us displeasing in the Divine sight; it is, next to mortal sin, the greatest of evils.

Q. What contributes to give us a clearer insight into the malice of venial sin?

A. 1. The fact that since it is an offence against the Divine majesty, it is, for instance, not allowed to utter even a slight falsehood, were it even to deliver ourselves or others from the utmost misery, or from death itself.

2. That not all the tortures which human ingenuity, aided by satanic cruelty has ever devised, all the sufferings ever endured by man, are capable of effacing the guilt of one venial sin; nay, not even the merits of all the Angels and Saints—nothing save Christ's own precious blood can wash this dark stain away—nothing but His infinite merits repair the injury it has done the soul.

3. That venial sin forms the transition from the narrow path which leads to life eternal, to the broad way whose end is destruction. Thus it is *written:* "He that contemneth small things shall fall by little and little." This induced St. John Chrysostom to assent without hesitation, that we should fear venial, even more than mortal sins, for the latter are in

themselves appalling, the former are less so, and yet they lead but too frequently to perdition, by preparing the way and disposing us for the commission of mortal transgressions. St. Hilary very justly remarks: "It will be very difficult for him to preserve himself from mortal sin who despises venial faults." *Epist. de Tnit quadrag.* The grace of God decreases with the commission of every new venial sin and the passions increase in strength and violence.

4. Venial sin at the very least must be atoned for in the flames of Purgatory, and the tortures we shall have to undergo in this prison, according to St. Augustine, so far exceed all earthly torments that they will bear no comparison with them. *Serm. 42 de Sanctis.* Venial sin debars us from the vision and enjoyment of God, until its last trace has been removed by these intense flames.

5. Venial sins deprive us for all eternity of the merit and reward of the good works we may have performed with the assistance of those graces of which venial sin deprived us.

Q. What consequences are to be deduced from what we have said?

A. That no earthly consideration should be powerful enough to induce us to commit a voluntary venial sin.

Q. Is it possible for us to remain free from venial transgressions?

A. It is not, without a peculiar grace conferred only on St. John the Baptist, St. Joseph and perhaps some other special favorites of God. It is written in the Old Testament: "The just man falleth seven times;" that is, he falls frequently. *Eccl.* viii. 21. St. James expressly says: "In many things we all offend." *James,* iii. 2. St. John says: "If we say we have no sin we deceive ourselves, and the truth is not in us." *John,* i. 8. These passages, however, are not to be understood of voluntary transgressions, but of frailties and defects, accompanied by a certain degree of deliberation, though not with full consent and immediately repented. When we seek to repair the spiritual loss sustained by increased zeal; every true Christian assisted by God's grace, can thus live. God permits us to experience our weakness in order to preserve and confirm us in humility.

Q. How does sin usually penetrate to the soul?

A. By presentation, pleasure in the object thus contemplated and consent. The soul at first represents to itself a thought or imagination, or the world, the flesh, or the devil make some impression on it by means of the senses. If man do not promptly and resolutely oppose the seductive thought or imagination, pleasure succeeds, and consent to that which flatters and gratifies is, of course, not long withheld. Representation thus begets pleasure, pleasure consent, consent the deed, and the deed when repeated soon becomes a habit, habit generates obduracy, obduracy, despair, as the last step to the dread regions of torture into which the devil will draw us ever deeper and deeper down on the broad road of sin.

Q. Which are the general means of defence, the preservatives against sin?

A. 1. The fear of God; "The fear of the Lord driveth out sin." *Eccles.* i. 27. Who would presume after due reflection to offend God, so just, so holy, so great and good a Being? "*Who is like unto God?*" this was the motto (battle-cry) of Michael and the good Angels when opposing the tempter, and by it they gained the victory over the infernal dragon. "There is no fear of God before their eyes," says the royal Prophet mournfully. Hence so many and such grievous transgressions. The same complaint might be made of men in our own days. Sin is committed wantonly and without any fear of the Divine judgments, without a thought of the piercing, unslumbering eye which from the realms of inaccessible light takes note of it. "Hear, O ye Heavens, and give ear, O earth, for the Lord hath spoken, I have brought up children and exalted them but they have despised me." *Isaias,* vi. 2.

2. The remembrance of God's presence, "God sees me." Whoever endeavors to live in the presence of God will not dare to offend Him. "We cannot," says Clement of Alexandria, "otherwise remain free from sin, than by considering God ever present." I. 3. *Pedag.* c. 5. St. Jerome declares, "the remembrance of God puts every vice to flight."

3. The recalling to mind the bitter passion and death of our blessed Lord Jesus which is renewed by sin.

4. The lively remembrance of the four last things as the Holy Ghost admonishes us: "Remember, man, thy last things and thou shalt never sin." Who could sin when penetrated with the fear of death and hell, particularly when we consider that very many die suddenly, and many in the state of sin. "If thou wert now about to die, what wouldst thou do?" asks St. Bernard. *Spec. mon.* This thought defends and rescues.

5. The love of prayer, particularly the practice of meditation.

6. The frequent and worthy reception of the holy sacraments.

7. Shunning the occasions of sin. Those who live thus avoid sin and free themselves from numberless temptations. We have already spoken of how temptations are to be withstood and overcome, when explaining the sixth petition of the Lord's Prayer.

Q. How many kinds of mortal sin are there?

A. 1. The seven capital sins; 2. Sins to which we become accessory; 3. Sins against the Holy Ghost; and 4. Sins which cry to heaven for vengeance.

Of the Seven Capital Sins.

Q. Name the seven capital sins?

A. 1. Pride; 2. Avarice; 3. Lust; 4. Envy; 5. Gluttony; 6. Anger; 7. Sloth.

Q. Why are these termed capital sins?

A. Because they are the prolific roots from which many branches shoot forth—the parent streams which receive and contain, as it were, many others.

Q. Are these sins always deadly?

A. They are not, excepting lust; in that sin there can be no indulgence that is not mortal. The other sins become deadly, when they cause us, in serious matters, to act contrary to the love we owe our Maker and our fellow-creatures.

On Pride.

Q. What is pride?

A. Pride is an inordinate desire for distinction before men, on account of real or supposed advantages, which induce a person to prefer and exalt himself above his fellow-men, and take to himself the honor due to God alone.

Q. When does pride amount to a mortal sin?

A. When, with full, clear knowledge and deliberation, we assail God's honor, as did Lucifer, and exalt ourselves as if we were not dependent on God; or when man is prepared to sacrifice duty and virtue, in matters of moment, at the shrine of pride, and to commit some other mortal sin at its suggestion.

Q. What is said in Holy Writ of the sin of pride?
A. "Pride is the beginning of all sin." *Eccl.* x. 15. "God resists the proud." 1 *Peter*, v. 5.

Q. What sins, in particular, have their source in pride?
A. Disobedience, contumacy, vanity, boasting, a domineering spirit, harshness towards inferiors, envy and strife, cruelty, extravagance, injustice, hypocrisy, heresy, infidelity, hatred of God, and the like.

Q. What is to be deduced from this?
A. 1. The malice of this vice, which prompts man to act in direct opposition to the end of all created things; man, a creature of God's omnipotence, presumes to arrogate to himself the honor belonging to the Supreme Being only.

2. The folly of this vice; for man is proud either of real advantages of mind or body: in this case, he boasts of what has been given him, and of which he shall have to render a strict account, or he prides himself on imaginary excellencies, and this is evident folly and presumption.

3. The danger into which this vice plunges us. It is, as the Holy Ghost testifies in the Scriptures, the root of all evil, and it is evident from the idea of this sin, which is rebellion against God. This crime plunged one-third of the heavenly hierarchy into the flames of hell, and the deceitful promise, "Ye shall become like to God," was the occasion of Adam's fall. Pride seals for us the fountain of grace, and thereby casts us down into the pit of reprobation. This vice is further accompanied by numberless dreadful consequences, even here below, for ourselves and others, and has reduced innumerable families, yea, even whole kingdoms to ruin.

Q. What are the preservatives and antidotes against pride?
A. 1. The earnest consideration of what we just said of the malice, folly and danger of this vice. "What hast thou that thou hast received, and if thou hast received, why dost thou glory as if thou hadst not received?" inquires the Apostle. *Cor.* iv. 7. Thou art a being who from eternity was "nothing," until God's fiat called thee forth to life and light. Thou hast nothing of thyself, save sin, of what then wilt thou boast?

2. The remembrance of the sins we have committed, and the uncertainty in which we must remain as to their remission: "Man knoweth not whether he be worthy of love or hatred." *Eccl.* ix. 1. Still less when he is perfectly conscious of having once grievously sinned.

3. The thought of the silent tomb, in which the king and the beggar alike sleep the long last slumber, and the terrible trial to be undergone at the bar of the Omnipotent and Omniscient Judge.

4. The attentive consideration of the consequences which this sin involves. It deprives us of all the merits we might acquire by works in themselves good, and is, as St. Gregory the Great declares, a sign of eternal reprobation, as humility on the contrary, is one of the works of pre-election.

5. A lively remembrance, on the one hand, of the fall of the Angels, and on the other of the infinite humility and humiliation of the Incarnate Son of God.

6. The zealous practice of humility and humiliation kept alive and guarded by assiduous self-examination.

Practice.—Eradicate every fibre of this vice from your hearts, and be particularly on your guard against self-commendation; be ready to extol your neighbor's good deeds and qualities, but concerning yourself be silent. Rejoice when unmerited humiliations are allotted you, and regard them as peculiar graces.

On Avarice.

Q. What is avarice?

A. It is the inordinate desire to obtain and possess temporal goods.

Q. When is avarice a mortal sin?

A. When man really prefers his money and property to God and heaven, and this is the case when he would rather grievously sin, than forfeit his possessions, or when he does not hesitate to commit grave offences against the Divine law in order to increase his fortune.

Q. What does the Holy Scripture say of avarice?

A. "There is no one worse than he that envieth himself." *Eccl.* xiv. 6. "Avarice is idolatry." *Gal.* v. 20.

Q. What vices have their source in covetousness?

A. Deceit, falsehood, hardheartedness, violence, usury, perjury, injustice, theft, simony, superstition, witchcraft, treasure-seeking, manslaughter and murder. There have been men who have made over to Satan their eternal inheritance by written documents, in order to procure wealth.

Q. What conclusion may be drawn from this?

A. 1. The malice of this vice; by covetuosness man devotes to riches all the love and regard which he should entertain for God; wealth is the object of his desires and his affections, and with blind devotion he clings to it from the depth of his heart, with his whole soul and all its powers. Avarice is, therefore, in the strictest sense of the word, idolatry.

2. The folly of avarice. The covetuous man gives up his affections to gold, which is so infinitely beneath him, and which, far from procuring him happiness, loads him with grief and anxiety. He, as the wise man says: "Eateth his bread in darkness and in many cares." *Eccl.* v. 16. "Thou fool, this night do they require thy soul of thee, and whose shall those things be which thou hast provided?" *Luke*, xii. 20. These are Christ's own words.

3. The great danger to which this vice exposes our salvation. Christ the Lord, teaches, that we "cannot serve God and mammon," and again, "How hardly shall they that have riches enter into the kingdom of God: for it is easier for a camel to pass through the eye of a needle than for a rich man to enter into the kingdom of God." *Luke*, xviii. 24, 25. For, as the Apostle says, and daily experience confirms, "those who wish to obtain wealth fall into many temptations, and snares of the devil." They expose themselves to all the evil consequences and the train of sins already enumerated, attending avarice. This passion increases with years, and is so violent and so fraught with danger that it plunged an Apostle into the abyss of hell, to say nothing of the oppressions, insults, injuries, it causes us to commit against our fellow-men. The avaricious man, no matter how great his wealth may be, lives in a kind of poverty, and cannot be induced to part with his gold, even to procure the necessaries, much less the comforts of life; thus his own existence and that of all connected with him is made miserable.

Q. What are the remedies to be employed against avarice?

A. 1. Frequent visits to the church-yard and the daily remembrance of approaching and certain death, the ruthless spoiler of all the treasures which man loves and joys.

2. The consideration of the goods of heaven, immense in value and permanent as God himself, and which those forfeit who here below give themselves up to inordinate love of earthly possessions.

3. The remembrance of the extreme poverty of Jesus, "who

being rich became poor for our sakes, so poor that He had nought whereon to lay His head." *Luke*, ix. 58. The practice of Christian liberality and generosity, the virtue directly opposed to avarice; this generosity should be extended to the suffering poor and to the zealous promotion of pious purposes; giving to the poor, as Christ assures us, lays up treasures for us in His eternal treasury, with high interest for their temporary use. *Luke*, xvi. 9.

On Lust.

Q. What is lust?
A. Inordinate concupiscence to satisfy the sinful flesh.
Q. Is lust in itself a mortal sin?
A. It is; in this matter there is no venial sin, neither of thought, wish, desire or outward act dictated by concupiscence. Venial sin is in this respect only possible, when we do not indeed consent but yet withhold the consent in a cold and tepid manner.
Q. What does Holy Writ say of impurity?
A. "If you live according to the flesh you shall die. They who do such things shall not obtain the kingdom of God."
Q. Name some of the effects of impurity?
A. Blindness of the understanding, ruin of the health of the body, undermining domestic happiness, extravagance, enmity, duels, suicides, unnatural lewdness, frenzy, and despair.
Q. What becomes evident from this?
A. 1. The abominable nature of this vice which induces man to lower himself beneath the animals, and to prefer the filthy pleasures of the flesh, to God, and all his advantages of mind and spirit.
2. The folly of this crime which leads man to seek delight in a transgression which plants in his guilt-seared soul the thorn of remorse, and in his body the seeds of destruction and disease.
3. The danger of eternal and temporal ruin, to which it exposes its votaries, for of all vices, there is none which so degrades and enslaves man, none which binds him in stronger chains of guilt, misery and chastisement, neither is there any sin to which man is more violently and more constantly tempt-

ed than this. When man once falls into a sin of this nature, numberless relapses follow, and he is in the greatest danger of damnation, if not rescued by a peculiar grace. "Know you not that neither fornicators nor adulterers shall possess the kingdom of God?" 1 *Cor.* vi.

Q. What are the preservatives against sins of impurity?

A. 1. The avoidance of dangerous occasions, particularly private interviews with persons of the other sex.

2. A vigilant guard over our senses, particularly the sense of sight. "I made a covenant with my eyes, that I would not so much as think upon a virgin," says the chaste and patient Job; xxxi. 1.

3. A temperate mode of life, with mortification and self-denial. "I chastise my body and bring it under subjection." 1 *Cor.* And again: "But those who belong to Christ have crucified their flesh with its lusts."

4. The avoidance of idleness. "Idleness hath brought much evil," saith the wise man.

5. Prayer, and the frequent reception of the sacrament of penance, immediate recourse to God by prayer on the approach of temptation, the invocation of the holy name of Jesus, and the use of the sign of the cross. Thus it was that St. Justina triumphed, as St. Gregory Nazianzen assures us, over the united powers of hell.

6. The remembrance of the fearful judgments of God called down even here below by the crimes of the lewd and debauched. In order to purify the earth from the filth of lust, God opened the floodgates of heaven, nor were they closed until the whole human family, eight persons alone excepted, slept beneath the surging billows. Fire fell from heaven and consumed the lewd inhabitants of Sodom and Gomorrha, and hell swallowed up alive the people of the five cities mentioned in Scripture, on account of their unnatural lusts.

7. The earnest consideration of the pangs of conscience, which usually succeed the commission of crimes of this nature.

8. The woful state, to which indulgence in these beastly excesses reduces even the body, that too many, who have given themselves up to it, become living masses of corruption, odious in the sight of God and man, burthens to themselves, nuisances, or rather pests in society.

9. The thought of the body's approaching dissolution and

the punishments of hell. "As much as she hath glorified herself, and lived in delicacies, so much torment and sorrow give ye to her." *Apoc.* xviii. 7. So says St. John, speaking of Babylon, the queen of nations, and so will the angry Judge say to the licentious soul which has lived and acted for the flesh, not for Him.

Practice.—Endeavor to obtain angelic purity, and confess on this point, even that which appears most trifling, with the greatest humility and candor. Avoid all dangerous occasions—whether company, or immoral writings, and be careful to reject temptations of this kind promptly and decidedly.

Envy.

Q. What is envy?

A. Envy is pain or displeasure felt at sight of our neighbor's excellence, advantages, or good fortune, joined with inward satisfaction on perceiving his defects, and malicious joy on learning that he has experienced some accident or misfortune. The envious man, therefore, beholds with discontent and displeasure the good fortune of others, because he is not similarly favored; he looks with an evil eye upon those who are his equals in fortune, and regards those who possess nothing, with the fervent and heartfelt wish that they may never be any better off than they are at present.

Q. Is it envy when we wish to possess that which others have?

A. No; but it is envy when we are not satisfied at others having as much or more than us.

Q. Name the sins into which envy plunges those addicted to it.

A. Injustice, cruelty, backbiting, detraction, lying, calumny, hatred, desire of revenge, perjury, enmity and murder. St. Cyprian says that "envy is the nursery of all vice."

Q. Is envy a mortal transgression?

A. Envy is, in itself, a grievous offence against the charity we owe to God and our neighbor; and therefore in itself mortal, unless it be diminished by precipitation, want of free, deliberate consent, or the smallness of the fault into which it hurried us.

Q. What does Holy Writ say of envy?

A. " Envy is the rottenness of the bones." *Prov.* xiv. 30. And again : " But by the envy of the devil, death came into world." *Wisd.* ii. 24.

Q. What may we learn from this ?

A. The malice of this crime ; for, says a holy Father : " How can we expect any bounds to malice, where our neighbor's good fortune is considered our own misfortune ?" " The envious man virtually," as Salvianus remarks, " persecutes and decries the gifts of God in his brother who possesses them." What deplorable perversity ? It is a vice most directly opposed to charity, and where it exists no thought of heaven can rationally be entertained ; that blessed abode would be, itself, to the envious a place of sorrow, a rack of torture.

2. This vice bears not only the stamp of malice, but also of folly, for it is a crime which procures for those who indulge it neither advantage nor pleasure, not even here below, but only pains and blinds them. " Envy torments the sinner, clouds his understanding, infects his heart, and sours his temper," says St. Isidore. 42 *Solil.* Wherefore this torment ? If he were free from envy, if he rejoiced in his neighbor's good fortune, he would acquire the merit of love, and enjoy without bitterness the goods and blessings awarded to him. The heathens were accustomed to represent envy under the form of an old hag, blind and decrepit, feeding on vipers, and supporting herself on a pointed staff, which inflicts upon her at every step a new wound.

3. The danger of eternal damnation, to which envy exposes man. " Envy is," as St. Augustine, commenting on the fifth psalm, remarks, " the twin brother and the inseparable companion of pride." Accordingly, what is said of the danger of pride may also be said with regard to envy. The Holy Scripture assures us, that " by the envy of the devil, death came into the world." *Wisd.* ii. 24. Those who belong to his party zealously imitate his works, as we read in *St. John's Gospel,* viii. 44. It was envy which made the first-born of the human race a fratricide ; envy, that nailed the Lord of heaven to the cross, after glutting itself by inflicting the most excruciating tortures upon Him. Envy is peculiarly, and still more strikingly even than pride, a mark of damnation, for it is directly opposed to charity ; for we read in Holy Scripture : " He that loveth not, abideth in death." 1 *John,* iii. 14. St. Chrysostom exhorteth us : " Let us flee the contagion of envy, for we can-

not possibly escape hell without being free from this vice."
Ad pop ant. hom. 53. To say nothing of the great temporal misery it brings on ourselves and others, it is wholly destructive to peace and fraternal kindness.

Q. When is envy, in particular, a mortal sin ?

A. When we envy our neighbors on account of their spiritual goods and virtues, and hence seek to annoy and injure them, or maliciously rejoice when we see them fall into sin or wanting in virtue.

Q. Name the preservative and antidote against envy ?

A. 1. The fear of being stigmatized as the child of Satan.

2. The thought of the futility of this vice, and our folly in not acquiring merit by participation with holy joy in the privileges and advantages of grace or nature possessed by our neighbors, and which might be of greater service to us in obtaining salvation than even our own.

3. The frequent particular and careful consideration of the distinctive characteristics of charity, which the Apostle thus enumerates: "Charity is patient, is kind: charity envieth not, dealeth not perversely, is not puffed up, is not ambitious, seeketh not her own, is not provoked to anger, thinketh not evil, rejoiceth not in iniquity, but rejoiceth with the truth." 1 *Cor.* xiii. 4–7. Whoever, aided by careful, particular examination of conscience, implants in his heart the ramifications of holy charity, will not fail to eradicate every fibre of envy.

On Intemperance, or Gluttony.

Q. What is intemperance, or gluttony ?

A. It is the excess committed in eating or drinking, when persons exceed the bounds of moderation, either in quantity or by haste, and also when they partake of food and drink merely on account of the pleasure derived from eating and drinking.

Q. Is intemperance, in itself, a mortal sin ?

A. It is not; but it may become one, when one so gives himself to food and drink that he makes the gratification of his sensual appetites the end of his being, and deserves to be reckoned amongst those of whom St. Paul says: " Whose God is their belly, whose end is destruction, that they are enemies of the cross of Christ." *Phil.* iii. Or when, in order to gratify our appetites, we do not hesitate to transgress God's commandments in a matter of moment.

Q. What does Holy Writ say of intemperance?

A. "Be not greedy in any feasting, and pour not out thyself upon any meat. By surfeiting many have perished." *Eccl.* xxvii. 32. "Lustful appetites transformed the children of Israel into ungrateful rebels, who were made to feel the full weight of the Divine chastisements." *Rom.* xi. "The kingdom of the Lord is not meat and drink." *Rom.* xiv. 17.

Q. What sins are generated by intemperance?

A. Sloth and negligence in the Divine service, neglect of the duties of our calling, forwardness, wantonness, impurity, strife and murder, the ruin of fortune and health.

Q. What conclusion is to be drawn from this?

A. That intemperance is an abominable, degrading, and ruinous vice, which dishonors human nature, debases it to the level of the brute, and injures soul and body.

Q. In what light should drunkenness be considered?

A. Drunkenness is even more abominable and more dangerous than gluttony: Holy Scripture warns us repeatedly against this vice: "Woe to the drunkards and those that sit in judgment and strength staggering with wine." *Isaias*, xxviii. Christ himself admonishes us: "Take heed to yourselves, lest perhaps your hearts be overcharged with surfeiting and drunkenness." *Luke*, xxi. 34. "Do not err," says the Apostle to all: "Neither drunkards nor railers shall possess the kingdom of God." 1 *Cor.* vi.

The magnitude and enormity of this vice become particularly apparent,

1. By its depriving man of the use of his noblest attribute and endowment, *viz.,* his reason.

2. Because drunkenness is wont to cause transgression of all the Divine commandments at once. The inebriate sins against the first and second commandments, because he makes an idol of intoxicating liquors, prefers and serves them rather than God; on such occasions, too, he is wont to curse and swear and profane the holy name of God. He sins against the third commandment, because he frequently absents himself from Divine worship, in order to indulge his beastly appetite. He sins against the fourth commandment, because, by his unworthy conduct, he grievously offends and mortifies his parents, if they are still alive. Against the fifth, because the

drunkard generally injures his health and implicates himself in disgraceful broils, and thus scandalizes all who hear of his having so degraded himself, or who see him in this shameful situation. Against the sixth, because every drunkard is more or less tempted to indulge in carnal pleasures. Against the seventh, because such persons are generally inclined to employ, in procuring liquor, money belonging to others, and to contract debts without the prospect of being able to pay them. Against the eighth, by calumny, detraction, and other sins of the tongue. Against the ninth and the tenth, because he places no restraint on his concupiscence and renders himself incapable of governing himself.

3. He renders himself and others miserable both here and hereafter, for drunkenness impairs health and hastens death, deprives him of honor, fortune and domestic happiness, lessens his susceptibility to the inspirations of grace, and renders his conversion very questionable, it being a rare occurrence for a confirmed drunkard to renounce the immediate occasions of intemperance.

Q. When is drunkenness a mortal sin?

A. When man by excess in drinking, deprives himself of the use of reason, and also when in order to indulge his passion for liquor, he neglects duties binding him under pain of grievous sin, as, for instance, the duties devolving on him as a husband and father, which are certainly sadly neglected, when, instead of attending to his daily avocations, governing his household and duly training his children, he spends his time in taverns and such places.

Q. Name the preservatives against drunkenness?

A. 1. The shunning of occasions; 2. Frequent confession; 3. The earnest consideration of the woful consequences, entailed even here below by this vice; 4. The thought of the quenchless and excruciating thirst, by which, drunkards, in particular, shall certainly be racked in hell for all eternity; 5. A promise made in presence of a priest.

Practice.—Observe the maxim: "Too little seldom proves hurtful, but too much, very frequently;" thus you will preserve your health, lengthen your life, and retain unimpaired the strength so necessary for the discharge of the duties of your calling. When partaking of liquors not prohibited, such as wine, beer, cider and the like, be careful never to go to excess; abstain constantly from distilled liquors, except in cases of necessity, or on account of their medicinal virtues.

Anger.

Q. What is anger?

A. An inordinate motion or excitement, called forth by some resistance offered us, or by some real or imaginary insult offered, or injury done us. When this inordinate state of our mind is joined to the desire of taking revenge, and making our neighbors feel in turn the injury or mortification we have received at their hands, it is termed revenge.

Q. Is anger of every description sinful?

A. No; our definition is an *inordinate motion*, for there is a just indignation directed against sinful acts or sentiments, in opposition to the just and holy decrees of God. Hence the admonition of the prophet: "Be angry and sin not." *Ps.* xlv. Our indignation in this case must be directed against the sin, and the sin only, not against the sinner, whom we are bound to love as ourselves, though he be our mortal enemy, and whom we dare not injure either in thought, desire, word or deed, but rather should commiserate, and whom we may punish and chastise only to lead to amendment, when the office we occupy and the authority we possess, render this a duty. It would be sinful to regard the commission of crime with indifference; and in this sense Holy Writ speaks of God's anger, which is but another name for the infinite abhorrence He entertains for sin, and the expression of His just indignation.

Q. When is anger a mortal sin?

A. When this passion induces us to commit a serious transgression in a matter of importance, against the charity we owe to God and our fellow-men. This would be the case if a man were so far to forget himself as to rise up against God, who permits certains evils to befall him, and break forth into imprecations and revilings against the Divine majesty, or when in anger we hate our fellow-men and either wish a great misfortune to overtake them, or injure them in a matter of importance.

Q. What does Holy Writ say of this vice?

A. "Let all bitterness and anger and indignation be put

away from you." *Eph.* iv. 31. "Whosoever is angry with his brother, shall be guilty of the judgment." *Matth.* v. 22. "Put away anger from you, and give not place to the devil." *Eph.* iv.

Q. What sins originate in this vice?

A. Anger incites the person who indulges it, to many sins of thought, desire, word and deed, *viz.*, hatred, enmity, implacability, cursing, reviling, imprecations and insults. It induces strife, feuds, frays, quarrels, violence, ruin of health and domestic peace, scandal, injury to our fellow-men in their property and persons, and even murder.

Q. What signification is to be drawn from this?

A. 1. The wickedness of this vice. Anger is as directly opposed to holy charity as pride or envy; anger violently seeks its destruction and leads to enmity, it is also the death of fraternal affection.

2. The folly of this vice, for how very insignificant in themselves, are, generally speaking, the occasions which call forth these ebullitions of passion; anger far from amending things, or setting matters to rights, only tends to blind our understandings, and to wound and exasperate our fellow-men.

3. The pernicious nature of anger and the imminent risk to which it exposes our salvation. The angry man, of course, while laboring under the influence of passion, imagines that he is doing no evil. But, let him consider how very correct and important is the remark of the great Bellarmines on this subject: "A grain of patience is worth more than a cart-load of right and justice." Anger, cursing and enmity generally go hand in hand; cursing is, as we know, in the truest sense of the word, the language of devils, and enmity is an insurmountable obstacle to salvation. We have proved in the first part, when treating of the Lord's Prayer, the calamities this passion has heaped on families, communities and even whole nations, to say nothing of how it embitters the existence of those who indulge in it. Let us but recall to mind the horrors of so many wars which may be generally traced to anger and desire of revenge, as their fountain-heads.

Q. What means should be taken against the passion of anger?

A. 1. Earnest reflections on eternity, and that things earthly and transitory do not deserve that we should so violently disturb and excite ourselves.

2. The remembrance of our sweetest and mildest Saviour, Jesus Christ.

3. The thought of the sins we have committed, and the torments of hell thereby justly incurred, in comparison with which whatever injuries or insults may be offered us, are as nothing.

4. Immediately pronouncing the sweet name of Jesus, at least mentally, when we perceive ourselves agitated by passion; calling to mind, that we shall, perhaps even before long, be stretched cold and lifeless in the grave, alike indifferent to praise and censure, to injuries and favors.

Practice.—Endeavor to preserve equanimity, a gentle and even temper, and sweetness of manners and disposition. Think frequently of the beautiful example of mildness left us by St. Francis de Sales, and implore his intercession at the throne of God, in order that you may be strengthened to imitate him in his amiable and gentle manners. Overcome yourself so that no one can ever remark, whether you are in good or bad humor, but rather let all see that you are ever the same, full of self-possession and holy mildness. Let this be the subject of your particular examination, and do not give it up until you have mastered your anger. This you owe to the charity you should bear your neighbor, and you know where charity is wanting, every other virtue is hollow and worthless.

Of Sloth.

Q. What is sloth?

A. The laxity of the will, which prevents us from fulfilling the duties imposed upon us, and inspires us with disgust for and unwillingness to overcome the obstacles to be encountered on the road to heaven.

Q. When is sloth a mortal sin?

A. When tepidity has grown so far on a person, as to cause him to wish that he had not been created, rather than secure eternal bliss by self-abnegation, or when this unhappy state causes him to neglect important duties, or occasions his fall into sins of a grievous nature.

Q. What says Holy Writ with regard to sloth?

A. "Cursed be he that doeth the work of the Lord deceitfully." *Jer.* xlviii. 10. "Every tree that yieldeth not good fruit, shall be cut down, and shall be cast into the fire."

Matth. vii. And again: "The unprofitable servant, cast ye out into exterior darkness." *Matth.* xxv. 30. "I know thy works; that thou art neither cold nor hot; but because thou art lukewarm, and neither cold nor hot, I will vomit thee out of my mouth." *Apoc.* iii. 15, 16.

Q. Name the sins which have their source in sloth?

A. Negligence in the Divine service, despondency, idleness, coldness and indifference in religious matters, want of confidence in God, omission of the works of Christian charity, weariness of life, impenitence, &c.

Q. What does this prove?

A. 1. The malice of this sin; for this condition is directly opposed to the fundamental duty devolving on us as creatures of God, which is to accomplish His will, and that in all things without exception, because He wills, how He wills and when He wills. Sloth, however, will bear nothing of this.

2. The folly of sloth. A slothful person is over-careful to avoid trouble, and thereby increases his trouble. A common proverb says: "Where there is a will, there is a way." And again: "Blithe begun, and half is done."

3. The misery and ruin into which sloth plunges its votaries, even here on earth; the fulfilment of his duties becomes more arduous and painful, and he exposes himself to severe reproaches from persons better disposed than himself. He stops the fountains of grace, and easily loses Divine grace by the omission of duties of importance. In this case, on account of the perverse dispositions of his mind, there can be but little hope entertained of earnest repentance and amendment.

Q. What preservatives should we make use of against sloth?

A. 1. The remembrance of our last end, the value of time, and the certainty of death's approach.

2. The perusal of the lives of the saints.

3. Earnest reflection on the pains of purgatory awaiting a slothful person, should he be happy enough to die in the state of sanctifying grace, which is very questionable.

4. The consideration of how much better and easier and more meritorious it is to perform good actions in a proper manner, rather than by halves, coldly and tepidly, which perhaps robs us of whatever merit we might have acquired, and draws down chastisement upon us.

Practice.—Attend daily to Christ's exhortation: "Be ye

perfect, as your heavenly Father is perfect." Think, immediately on awaking in the morning : " A new day is granted me—a day which I am determined to employ better than those hitherto granted me." It passes quickly, and never again returns; and if you employ it properly, O how happy you will be in eternity ! with what pleasure will you look back upon it! To live once for an eternity—O how encouraging is that thought ! Keep steadily in view the lives of the saints, and say to yourself, with the great St. Austin : " If others have been able so to do, why not I ?" Reflect on that which is presented to your consideration on the festival of All Saints ; attend punctually and steadfastly to the times set apart for prayer and the reception of the sacraments. Guard, particularly, against indulging in sloth on awaking ; arise quickly, with the dawn, and thus crush the serpent's head. This will keep your zeal alive the whole day.

OF THE WAYS OF BEING ACCESSORY TO ANOTHER'S SIN.

Q. How may one become accessory to the sins of others ?

A. By exciting others to commit them. The Psalmist says : " From my secret sins cleanse me, O Lord, and from those of others spare thy servant." *Ps.* xviii. 14. " Be not partakers of other men's sins." Thus St. Paul admonishes his beloved disciple Timothy. 1 *Tim.* v. 22.

Q. How do we most frequently fail in this respect ?

A. 1. By advice ; when we suggest evil to others, and seek to have them carry it out. Thus Herodias advised her daughter to ask the Baptist's head of Herod as the meed of the pleasure she had caused him by her graceful dancing. *Mark*, vi. ; *Matt.* xiv. Thus the Scribes and Pharisees persuaded the people to demand that the Lord should be given up to death.

2. By command ; when we go so far as to dare enjoin the commission of evil on others. Thus David commanded his generals to expose Urias in such a manner to the darts of the enemy in battle that he should surely fall, and thus incurred the guilt of wilful murder. 2 *Kings*, x. Those who frame bad laws belong likewise to this class.

3. By assent ; when we express our approbation of the evil our neighbors are about doing. Saul thus sinned, by taking under his charge the garments of those who stoned Stephen.

Acts, vii. 57. The magnitude of this sin is increased by others being encouraged in the crime. St. Paul says, when speaking of this subject: "Not only they that do them, but they also that consent to them (that do them) are worthy of death. *Rom.* i. 32.

4. By provocation or incitement. This occurs, particularly, in sins of anger and impurity.

5. By commendation and flattery, viz., when we praise or extol our neighbors on account of this or that evil done by them. This excites in the breasts of those to whom we address such pernicious flattery a certain pleasure, in view of what they have done, and encourages them to repeat similar shameful and sinful actions, perhaps even worse: "For the sinner is praised in the desires of his soul, and the unjust man is blessed." *Ps.* ix. And we read in the prophecies of Isaias: "O my people, they that call thee blessed, the same deceive thee, and destroy the way of thy steps." *Isaias*, iii. 12. How often are we not obliged to witness such perversity?

6. By silence; when a person commits an unlawful act, which he would not have done had we, in accordance with justice and duty, expressed our disapprobation. "When I say to the wicked: Thou shalt surely die; if thou declare it not to him, nor speak to him, the same wicked man shall die in his iniquity, but I will require his blood at thy hands." *Ezech.* iii. 18. These words we find in a passage of Ezechiel. The omission of paternal correction, which the Lord expressly admonishes us to practice when occasion offers, *Matt.* viii., is also to be noticed here.

7. By permission; when we do not employ the authority we possess or the esteem in which we are held in repressing or preventing the commission of evil. This occurs, particularly, when we connive at the faults committed by those of whom we have charge. Heli sinned in this way, by over-indulgent treatment of his wicked sons. The great Apostle warns us against this, as follows: "Know you not that a little leaven corrupteth the whole lump." 1 *Cor.* v. 6. "Woe to them that sew cushions under every elbow, and make pillows for the heads of persons of every age, to catch souls." *Ezech.* xiii. 18.

8. By participation; when we actually aid and take part in the commission of sin, which occurs particularly in sins against justice, such as cheating and theft, also in anger and sins against

purity, or when we afford refuge and shelter to thieves and debauched persons, and thus connive at their wicked and disgraceful conduct.

9. By defence; when we strive to justify and exculpate the evil committed by our neighbors. "Woe to you that put darkness for light and light for darkness, that put bitter for sweet and sweet for bitter." *Isaias,* v. 20. We thus become, in most cases, accessory to their sins, and generally add to the guilt thus incurred that of scandal. Scandal is the most general and common way in which we cause the sins of others and participate in them. We have already shown the enormity of this crime, when treating of the ten commandments. No palliation of such faults will be admitted at the bar of Divine justice; neither the number of delinquents, public opinion, common practice, or any thing else. The first question is, if the matter is founded on equity and truth, or on injustice and falsehood. "Thou shalt not follow the multitude to do evil; neither shalt thou yield in judgment to the opinion of the most part, to stray from the truth." *Exod.* xxiii. 3. Did not the whole Jewish populace clamor against the Lord himself, and unite in one fearful cry: "Crucify Him! crucify Him!" "Every one," as the doctor of the gentiles reminds us, "shall one day appear at the tribunal of the eternal, inexorable Judge, to account for what he has done or caused others to do against the law of God." *Rom.* x.

Practice.—Avoid, with the utmost care, incurring the guilt of the sins of others; fear nothing more than injuring the souls of thy fellow-men: endeavor, on the contrary, as much as in thee lies, to encourage others in the practice of virtue, by advice, encouragement, commendation, exhortation, permission, assistance and example; succor and defend persecuted virtue, and thus seek to participate in the good works done by thy fellow-men, in their sanctification and deliverance from sin and its consequences.

SINS AGAINST THE HOLY GHOST.

Q. Which sins are, in general, termed sins against the Holy Ghost?

A. Known, continued and deliberate resistance to the illuminations of grace offered us by the Divine benignity. As the effects of grace are mainly attributed to the Holy Ghost, this sin is termed an offence against the Holy Spirit. "With a stiff neck, and uncircumcised heart and ears, you always resist the Holy Ghost," were the words addressed by the holy deacon, Stephen, to the Jews, who, in order to prevent themselves from being touched by his words, stopped their ears. *Acts,* vii.

Q. What says the Lord of this sin?

A. He explicitly declares, that "it shall neither be forgiven here nor hereafter." *Mark,* iii.; *Luke,* xii. The reason of this is, that the sinner, by this sin, voluntarily closes the gates of repentance and pardon on himself. Woe to those who plunge themselves in this dreadful state, who have so perverted and corrupted their hearts, and who, as the Scripture says, will not know the truth, fearing lest they should be forced to amend. *Ps.* xxxv.

Q. In how many ways may we offend the Holy Ghost by this kind of sin?

A. 1. By presumption; by wantonly sinning against the teaching of reason and revelation, in the foolish hope that the Divine clemency will not permit our ruin, although aware that God, being infinite sanctity and justice, must necessarily be the avenger of evil. The admonition of the Holy Ghost, by the mouth of the wise man, should be followed by sinners of this description: "Be not without fear about sin forgiven; and add not sin upon sin. And say not: the mercy of the Lord is great: He will have mercy on the multitude of my sins. For mercy and wrath quickly come from Him: and His wrath looketh upon sinners." *Eccl.* v. 5–7.

The consideration of God's benignity and goodness should rather serve to move us to speedy and sincere repentance. Should it not melt and touch our hearts with remorse, that we have sinned against so loving and tender a father? St. Paul says, in his Epistle to the Romans, ii. 4. "Mercy and judgment I will sing to thee, O Lord," says the Psalmist. *Ps.* c.

2. By despair; when we go to the opposite extreme and forget God's mercy, although faith and reason furnish us with so many proofs thereof, and say to ourselves with the reprobate Cain, "My sin is greater than I may deserve pardon." *Gen.* iv. 13. Christ prayed for his executioners, and explicitly says to the Apostles and their successors: "Whose sins ye shall forgive, they are forgiven: whose sins ye shall retain, they are retained." *John,* xx. 23.

3. By obstinately calling into question and opposing the

known truth in matters of faith and morality. The Holy Ghost being the spirit of truth, this sin is very appropriately termed an offence against Him. These were the dispositions of Elymas, whom St. Paul thus addresses: "O thou full of all guile and of all deceit, son of the devil, enemy of all justice, thou dost not cease to pervert the right ways of the Lord." *Acts*, xiii. 10. He calls such persons, in his Epistle to Timothy, "defenders of error, judged by their own judgment." 2 *Tim.* iii.

4. By envying the spiritual graces conferred by the Holy Ghost: this is evidently the disposition of Satan, by whose envy sin entered into the world; and those who participate in this malice bear his livery and character in the fullest sense of the word. They have defaced the image of God, and engraved that of Satan in its stead.

5. By obduracy; which is the state of those who perceive the necessity of amendment of life, and yet persevere in the commission of sin, and strive to prevent the efficacy of grace. These were Pharao's dispositions, and were also the sentiments entertained by the perverse and obdurate sinner whom Job quotes: "Depart from us, we desire not the knowledge of thy ways." *Job*, xxi. 14. "The wicked man, when he is come into the depth of sins, contemneth." *Prov.* xxviii. 3. These words of Scripture are particularly applicable to such persons.

6. Impenitence; which is manifested by man's knowingly and deliberately stifling and rejecting every thought of repentance and atonement, although he feels the enormity of his crimes. "But according to thy hardness and impenitent heart thou treasurest up to thyself wrath, against the day of wrath and revelation of the just judgment of God." *Rom.* ii. 5.

These are the most common ways in which sins against the Holy Ghost are committed; their peculiar character and enormity consist in the circumstance of man's resisting and repelling, with full knowledge and deliberation, the motions and lights of grace, the promptings of the spirit of truth and love. Such belong to the number of those who, in the times of Isaias, wantonly and sacrilegiously declared: "We have entered into a league with death; and we have made a covenant with hell." *Isaias*, xxviii. 15. Only a miracle of Divine grace can snatch sinners of this description from the jaws of hell.

Practice.—Take well to heart the Apostle's serious warning: "Grieve not the Holy Spirit of God, whereby you are sealed unto the day of redemption." *Ephes.* iv. 30. O rather open thy heart readily and fully to the inspirations of the Holy Spirit; keep alive within thee the love of truth, so that thou mayest be able, at every moment of thy life, to declare before the Lord thy readiness to obey His will, saying: "Speak, Lord, thy servant heareth. Lord, what wilt thou that I do?" and that thou mayest belong to the number of those of whom the Apostle writes: "Children of God are impelled by the Holy Spirit." Burning with desire not to offend the infinite mercy of God; replenished with confidence in the Lord, who is mighty to raise up children to Abraham from the stones; full of zeal in defence of the truths of religion; full of gratitude and joy in beholding the good by which God is known, praised and magnified by others; all eagerness in attending to every inspiration of the Holy Ghost; animated by the spirit of Christian penance and self-denial: this will consecrate thee a temple of the Holy Ghost.

OF THE SINS WHICH CRY TO HEAVEN FOR VENGEANCE.

Q. Which sins are thus termed?

A. Those of which the Scriptures declare, that on account of their enormity and malice, they cry to heaven for vengeance on their perpetrators.

Q. Name the sins which belong to this class?

A. 1. Wilful murder. "What hast thou done? The voice of thy brother's blood crieth to me from the earth. Now, therefore, cursed shalt thou be upon the earth." *Gen.* iv. 10, 11. Thus saith the Lord to the fratricide Cain. It were too superfluous to expatiate upon the heinousness of this crime; every humane mind is filled with horror at considering it, and the wretch who has imbrued his hands in human blood is so racked by remorse of conscience as not unfrequently to deliver himself up to justice, in order to escape internal torment.

2. Sodomy; the name applied to those excesses into which human depravity is drawn by the long indulgence of unbridled licentiousness, which finally sinks, as it did with the Sodomites, to the practice of unnatural lusts. The book Leviticus severely condemns crimes of this nature. *Lev.* xviii. 22, 23. "The cry of Sodom and Gomorrha is multiplied, and their sin is become exceedingly grievous." *Gen.* xviii. 20. "Therefore," said the angels to Lot, "we will destroy this place, because their cry is grown loud before the Lord, who has sent us to destroy them.

And the Lord rained upon Sodom and Gomorrha brimstone and fire from the Lord out of heaven, and he destroyed the cities and all the country about." *Gen.* xix. 24. God in the same manner destroyed Onas, who presumed in the sight of heaven so far to degrade his dignity, as image of God, as to sin in an unnatural manner. The words of the Psalmist are to be applied particularly to such polluted sinners. "Man when he was in honor did not understand: he is compared to senseless beasts, and is become like to them." *Ps.* xlviii. 13.

3. By oppression of the poor, particularly widows and orphans. "You shall not hurt a widow or an orphan. If you hurt them, they will cry out to me, and I will hear their cry: and my rage shall be enkindled." *Exod.* xxii. 22, 23. God in many other passages of Holy Writ threatens those with temporal and eternal chastisement who oppress the poor, and refuse justice and relief to helpless orphans and widows. "Wo to them that make wicked laws: and when they write, write injustice: to oppress the poor in judgment, and do violence to the cause of the humble of my people: that widows might be their prey, and that they might rob the fatherless." *Isaias*, x. 1, 2.

4. By defrauding laborers of their justly, and generally hard-earned wages. "Thou shalt not refuse the hire of the needy and the poor; but thou shalt pay him the price of his labor the same day, before the going down of the sun, because he is poor, and with it maintaineth his life: lest he cry against thee to the Lord, and it be reputed to thee for a sin." *Deut.* xxiv. 14, 15.

Practice.—Live in such a manner that thou needest be under no apprehension of thy sins crying to heaven for vengeance; but rather that the perfume of thy virtues, united with the infinite merits of Christ, may rise to heaven, and render thee pleasing in the sight of God. Endeavor, in general, to penetrate further into the meaning of whatever thou hast read of sin, its different ramifications, and the preservatives against it, so that thou mayest be able to clear up both thy own doubts and those of others; that thou mayest be in a condition to understand and explain to others the danger of sin, the great evils it entails, and the best means of avoiding its consequences and preventing its entrance into the heart. "A wise man feareth and declineth from evil: the fool leapeth over and is confident." *Prov.* xiv. 16. And again: "The path of the just, as a shining light, goeth forwards, and increaseth even to perfect day. The way of the wicked is darksome: they know not where they fall." *Prov.* iv. 18, 19. Hence when they have fallen the carelessness and negligence in rising from the pit into which they are plunged, and their indifference as to whether they become reconciled with the Divine Majesty or not.

OF THE MEANS OF ATONING FOR SIN.

Q. Whereby are we cleansed from sin?

A. Speaking in general, there is but one principal fount in which we are purified from sin, viz., the merits of Christ our Lord, as we have endeavored to show, in the first part, when treating of the creed. We appropriate to ourselves, so to speak, these infinite merits of faith, which, joined with the sacrament of baptism, raises us to the dignity of children of the only true Church of God. The sacrament of penance, in the Church of God, is the means of reconciliation and of recovering the grace of God, lost after baptism by grievous sin. There are, nevertheless, other practices of piety which serve to efface the stains incurred by our daily falls and frailties, and which are peculiarly adapted to fit us for the worthy reception of the sacrament of penance, viz.: prayer, offered to God from a contrite heart. "He hath had regard to the prayer of the humble, and He hath not despised their petition." *Ps.* ci. 18.

2. Fasting and other penitential works, or acts of self-abnegation and humiliation. "God saw their works, that they were turned from their evil ways: and God had mercy with regard to the evil which He said He would do them." *Jonas*, iii. 10. This we find written of the Ninevites, who did penance in fasting, sackcloth and ashes.

3. By alms deeds: "For alms deliver from all sin." *Tob.* iv. 11. So we read in the book of Tobias, and the prophet says: "Redeem thou thy sins with alms, and thy iniquities with works of mercy to the poor." *Dan.* iv. 24. Presupposing, of course, that in these and the works yet to be mentioned, the heart really turns in abhorrence from its sinful ways, and offers its trifling expiatory works to God, united with the infinite merits of the great High Priest and Victim.

4. The sincere forgiveness of injuries and offences: "For

if you forgive men their offences, your heavenly Father will also forgive you your offences." *Matt.* vi. 14.

5. Works of true spiritual zeal. "He who causeth a sinner to be converted from the error of his way, shall save his soul from death, and shall cover a multitude of sins." *James*, v. 20.

6. Acts of extraordinary love of God, joined with fervent contrition. "Many sins are forgiven her, because she hath loved much." "Charity covereth a multitude of sins." *Luke*, vii. 47; 1 *Pet.* iv. 8.

Practice.—Zealously avail thyself of all these means in order to purify thy heart more and more from sin. Be particular in receiving the sacrament of penance frequently, and always with the due dispositions. Recall to mind the instructions given above when treating of this sacrament of reconciliation. In the possession of these promises the Apostle exhorts: "Having, therefore, these promises, dearly beloved, let us cleanse ourselves from all defilement of the flesh and of the spirit, perfecting sanctification in the fear of God." 2 *Cor.* vii. 1.

CHAPTER II.

ON THE PRACTICE OF VIRTUE.

WHAT we have hitherto taught concerning the avoidance of sin and the shunning the occasions of it is indispensable for the practice of Christian justice. In order to secure salvation, we are to avoid even the shadow of a voluntary offence of the Divine Majesty. This, however, is far from being the sum of Christian perfection, on the contrary, the practice of good works and virtuous acts is an indispensable and essential requisite, in order to imitate truly our Lord Jesus Christ, who not only avoided evil, but practised justice in its highest perfection. The Apostles admonish and encourage both the faithful of the first ages, and us their degenerate descendants, to emulate each other in the imitation of Christ, in order that, as St. Peter desires: "We being dead to sins, should live to justice, and thus secure our calling by good works." 1 *Pet.* ii. 24. And as St. Paul writes: "Denying ungodliness and worldly desires, we should live soberly, and justly, and godly in this world, undefiled and holy, gleaming as lights in this world obscured by the night of wickedness, for God's honor, Christ's glory, our own salvation, and the sanctification of our fallen race." *Tit.* ii. 12; *Colos.* i. 10. Otherwise, of what utility were faith to us, as St. James says: "By works a man is justified, and not by faith only: for even as the body without the spirit is dead, so also faith without works is dead." *Jam.* ii. And as the Apostle says: "Not the hearers of the law are just before God, but the doers of the law shall be justified." *Rom.* ii. 13. We will treat here of these two principal points in replying to the two main questions:

What are the conditions of a good work meritorious for eternal life. What qualifications we should possess in order that we may perfectly and easily perform these, and all other good and meritorious acts, or what the practice of Christian virtue requires of us.

Q. What is termed a good work?

A. An act performed by man according to the Divine law; it follows from this, that there are likewise natural good works, when man, guided by the light of reason does that which he recognizes as good, and in accordance with the Divine law.

Q. What term is applied to a work both good in itself and meritorious for salvation?

A. An act performed in conformity with the Divine law by persons living in the state of sanctifying grace.

Q. Which are the principal conditions required in a work of this description?

A. 1. The state of sanctifying grace.
2. Purity of intention.
3. Perfect agreement with the form of command.

Q. What is understood by the state of sanctifying grace?

A. The state of man superior to the natural order, brought about by his supernatural union with God, through the merits of Jesus Christ. This becomes evident from what we have said in the first chapter when treating of sanctifying grace.

Q. What is understood by the term pure intention?

A. The will to perform or omit some specified act because such is the will of God; or in other words, that we refer the work either silently and mediately, or explicitly and immediately to God's honor. "Whether you eat, or drink, or whatever you do, be it all to the greater honor of God," says St. Paul. 1 *Cor.* x. Christ the Lord warns us, saying: "Take heed that you do not your justice before men, to be seen by them: otherwise you shall not have a reward of your Father who is in heaven." *Matth.* vi. 1. The motto of St. Ignatius, "*All for the greater glory of God,*" relates to this subject. By thus referring all our works to the honor of God, every act otherwise of an indifferent or natural character, as also the discharge of our daily avocations, becomes meritorious and well pleasing in the Divine sight; for instance, sleep, recreation, labor, etc. This is a fact which we are wont to consider too little and in too superficial a manner. Did we but take it to heart, how easily might we become rich in good works. When on the contrary purity of intention is wanting, when, in the last instance, we refer all to ourselves, or in order to elicit the esteem and applause of our neighbor, or solely to benefit him, we shall have no merit at all in the Divine sight, how good soever in themselves, how glorious and heroic our works may have been. "Amen, I say to you, they have received their reward." This will be the sentence pronounced on such persons by the eternal Judge. *Matth.* vi. 2. The virtuous acts performed with an impure intention are therefore very aptly compared to the fruits growing near the Dead Sea, which are indeed beautiful to the eye, but contain in themselves only dust and ashes, and are unfit to serve as nourishment or refreshment. Such works, no matter how glorious in the eyes of men, are nothing else but rapid strides, made *from* not *on* the path to life eternal. They are, according to the expression of Scripture, a "bag with many holes," out of which that falls that has been placed in it.

Q. What is understood by perfect conformity with the Divine law?

A. That the work be not solely with respect to itself, and the actuatory motives, just, pure, and according to the Divine will, but also that with regard to the circumstances of time, place and persons it be performed duly and in full conformity with the Divine will. Hence the principle of theologians and moral philosophers: "Good is measured by the whole, bad by every defect."

Practice.—Search diligently and frequently into the state of thy conscience, according to the marks we have stated characterizing the true children of God, and endeavor with still greater diligence than heretofore to excite purity of intention, so that thy good works may not be rendered fruitless by vanity, tepidity, self-love, or the like.

Q. Is it sufficient to practice good works in any manner at all?

A. It is not: they should be performed as often as possible, and with all care and assiduity, in the best possible manner, with ease and joy, which is the essence of virtue.

Of the Virtues.

Q. What is virtue?

A. Aptness and facility in good works acquired by practice, and realizing what we know to be good and pleasing in the Divine sight.

Q. What are the chief divisions of virtue?

A. Virtue is divided into two grand classes; theological and moral.

Of the Theological Virtues.

Q. What virtues bear this name?

A. Such as have their immediate scope and exercise in God. We must here observe that the theological virtues presuppose a Divine endowment which renders us capable of practising them; they are, therefore, said to be divinely infused, because by the sacrament of baptism, man receives immediately from the hand of God, the capability of practising these virtues, viz: Faith, Hope, and Charity. We do not mean, however, to be understood as implying that man by constant practice may not acquire greater facility in the practice of these virtues.

Q. In this sense, then, in what does the virtue of faith consist?

A. It consists not only in firmly believing all that the Church proposes, but also in keeping before our eyes the truths of faith in all our actions and omissions.

Q. In what does the virtue of hope consist?

A. It consists not only in the expectation of divine assist ance, but also in constantly thinking of our destiny, and in caring more for it than for any other thing upon earth.

Q. In what does the virtue of charity consist?

A. It consists not only in preferring God to all other things, but also in thinking of Him at all times, yielding up to Him every affection of our heart, and aspiring after union with Him in prayer.

Q. How may we increase the efficacy of these virtues?

A. 1. By repeating frequently the acts of these virtues. 2. By considering frequently the motives which were mentioned above, concerning our holy faith, hope, and love. 3. By conversing with God in prayer, particularly during meditation.

Q. How do you make acts of faith, hope, and charity?

A. As follows:

An Act of Faith. I believe in Thee, one God in three persons, and in Jesus Christ, the Son of God made man, and the Saviour of the world. I believe all that the one, only true, Catholic Church, instituted by Jesus Christ, proposes. I believe because thou, Oh my God, art the eternal truth; and I am ready to shed my blood for this holy faith. Oh God, strengthen my faith.

An Act of Hope. Oh my God, I hope to obtain heaven and all the means necessary to reach it through Jesus Christ our Lord, who has redeemed me and gained heaven for me. Oh God, strengthen my hope!

An Act of Love. Oh my God! I love Thee with all my heart, with all my soul, with all my mind, and with all my strength, because Thou, oh my God, art the supreme good, infinite beauty, and love, who didst create me for thyself, from whom I hold all I possess. Oh my God and my love, I will sin no more. Increase, oh God, my love for Thee.

Q. Should these acts be frequently made?

A. Certainly; they should be excited in the heart at least once daily at morning prayer; the same should be done on Sundays and holydays more at length with renewed attention and devotion. We should be so penetrated by the spirit of these three virtues that they may accompany all our actions and omissions, and according to the spirit we should live and breathe in faith, hope and charity.

Of the Moral Virtues.

Q. Which of the virtues bear this appellation?
A. Those which more immediately refer to our conduct and manners, and serve to regulate them according to the prescription of the Divine law; as faith, hope and charity, and even reason present them to our view, and recommend them to our practice.

Q. How are moral virtues distinguished?
A. They comprise the four cardinal or fundamental virtues, the seven capital virtues, and those which lead us up the ascent of Christian virtue to the summit of perfection expressed in the eight beatitudes.

Of the four Fundamental or Cardinal Virtues.

Q. What is understood by the four fundamental virtues?
A. Those virtues which support the edifice of virtue as ground pillars, and which must be present in every other good act, in order to impress upon it the genuine stamp of virtue.

Q. How many virtues are there of this kind?
A. Four: prudence, justice, temperance, or moderation, and fortitude.

Q. Why are these virtues termed cardinal?
A. The word is of Latin origin, and signifies *hinge;* and as the hinge supports the door and makes it useful, so do these support the other moral virtues and enable us to reduce them to practice. These virtues are the sources of various duties, and all the general maxims of life, according to the variety of callings, or are derived from them. So says St. Ambrose: *Lib. off. c.* 23. St. Augustine says: "The knowledge of all human things is that which recognizes the light of *prudence,* the ornament of *temperance,* the strength of *fortitude,* and the sanctity of *justice.*" *Lib. cont. academ. c.* 7.

Q. What is understood by the virtue of prudence?
A. Prudence is that virtue by which we easily discern what

is to be done or avoided in every particular case in the service of God, and which easily recognizes and properly applies the suitable means in order to arrive at the desired end.

Q. What follows from this?

A. That no truly virtuous act can dispense with the assistance offered by prudence; that real virtue is not found coupled with indiscretion. This virtue further requires full conformity with the Divine law.

Q. In what terms does Scripture recommend this virtue?

A. "My son, do thou nothing without counsel, and thou shalt not repent when thou hast done." *Eccl.* xxxii. 24. And again: "A wise heart, and which hath understanding, will abstain from sin, and in the works of justice shall have success." *Eccl.* iii. 32. "Be prudent as serpents." This admonition Christ himself gives us, and He speaks of the virgins admitted to the nuptial banquet as "prudent," thus characterizing their virtuous, and in the Divine sight well pleasing lives, by the one word, prudent. *Matt.* x. and xxv. "See therefore, brethren, now you walk circumspectly: not as unwise, but as wise: wherefore become not unwise, but understanding what is the will of God." *Ephes.* v. 15–17.

Q. What is understood by justice, as one of the cardinal virtues?

A. Justice is that virtue which induces its possessor to give every one his due.

Q. What conclusion is to be drawn from this?

A. That all true virtues require the aid of justice; for when a virtuous act withholds from our fellow-men what they may justly claim, it forfeits its character of virtue.

Q. How does Scripture recommend the virtue of justice?

A. The Psalmist represents his ideal just, and consequently blessed man, in the following terms: "Blessed is he that walketh without blemish, and worketh justice: he that speaketh truth in his heart, who hath not used deceit in his tongue: nor hath done evil to his neighbor: nor taken up a reproach against his neighbors." *Ps.* xiv. 1–3. "Render, therefore, to all their dues: tribute to whom tribute is due: custom to whom custom: fear to whom fear: honor to whom honor." *Rom.* xiii. The words of the Holy Ghost refer to this justice: "Justice exalteth a nation," *i. e.*, the people of God striving after the perfection of virtue. *Prov.* xiv. 34.

Q. What is implied by the virtue of moderation?

A. Moderation is that virtue by which man keeps in proper bounds, and represses all inordinate lusts and desires.

Q. What do you conclude from this?

A. That all true virtue must necessarily be accompanied by moderation: for virtue without measure or order ceases to be virtue.

Q. What says Scripture of this virtue?

A. We read in the Old Testament the following admonition, which should be duly taken to heart: "Be not over-just." *Eccl.* vii. 17. The prince of the Apostles admonishes all the faithful to be temperate and sober, so as to leave no opening for the fiend. This alludes not only to sobriety in meat and drink, but of temperance in general. This command was already addressed to the first-born of the human race. "The lust of evil shall be under thee, and thou shalt have dominion over it." *Gen.* iv. 7. "Decline not to the right hand nor to the left." *Prov.* iv. 27. There are temptations under the specious garb of virtue, as the Apostle assures us, when he says that Satan appears under the form of an "angel of light." 2 *Cor.* xi. This is particularly the case in going to extremes in practices of virtue.

Q. What is implied by the term *fortitude?*

A. Fortitude is that virtue which enables us resolutely and magnanimously to overcome all the obstacles we meet with in the way to heaven.

Q. What does Scripture say of fortitude?

A. "The just man," says the Scripture, "is like a lion, full of confidence." *Prov.* xiv. The exhortations and declarations of the Psalmist serve to inspire us with the same sentiments: "The Lord is the protector of my life; of whom shall I be afraid? If armies in camp should stand together against me, my heart shall not fear." "For though I should walk in the midst of the shadow of death, I fear no evils, for Thou art with me." *Ps.* xxvi. 2. And again: "Do ye manfully, and let your heart be strengthened, all ye that hope in the Lord." *Ps.* xxx. "Beloved brethren, be ye steadfast and immovable, always abounding in the work of the Lord, knowing that your labor is not in vain in the Lord." 1 *Cor.* xv. 58.

Of the remaining Moral Virtues.

Q. Name the virtues which rank next to the cardinal virtues?

A. Those directly opposed to the seven capital sins: 1. Humility; 2. Generosity, or liberality; 3. Chastity; 4. Benevolence; 5. Temperance; 6. Mildness; 7. Zeal in the practice of good works. These virtues might with propriety be termed capital virtues, because a number of other virtues have their source in them as their fountain-head.

Q. In what does the virtue of humility consist?

A. In that we sincerely and in every instance ascribe whatever good qualities or traits we may perceive in ourselves solely to God, and that, penetrated with the lively consciousness of our sins and defects, we entertain a low opinion of ourselves, and observe with pleasure that others consider us entitled to no distinction.

Q. In what does the virtue of generosity, in the sense of liberality, consist?

A. In the constant readiness to assist others beyond their expectations with the goods conferred on us by fortune, and to reward liberally the services they may have rendered us.

Q. In what does the virtue of chastity consist?

A. In the resolute repression of all inordinate emotions of the flesh, and carefully guarding our imagination and all our senses.

Q. In what does the virtue of benevolence consist?

A. It consists in our rejoicing at the goods possessed by our fellow-men, and that we sincerely sympathize in whatever they may have to suffer, and rejoice at their happiness just as if the case were our own.

Q. In what does the virtue of temperance consist?

A. In perfectly controlling our inordinate appetites and refraining from all excessive indulgence in the pleasures of the table.

Q. In what does the virtue of mildness consist?

A. In the acquired facility of repressing courageously every inordinate emotion of anger and impatience, and to preserve one's equanimity without giving way to sullenness or caprice.

Q. In what does the virtue of zeal consist?

A. In the acquired facility attained by continued co-operation with the Divine grace, in attending to the inspiration of grace, and seeking to realize without delay, by the practice of good works.

Q. In what terms does Scripture recommend the practice of these virtues?

A. " Unless ye become as little children, ye shall not enter into the kingdom of heaven." *Matt,* xviii. " Give and it shall be given to you." *Luke,* vi. 38. " Blessed are the clean of heart for they shall see God." *Matt.* v. " Love one another with the charity of brotherhood. Rejoice with them that rejoice, weep with them that weep." *Rom.* xii. " Let us walk boldly as in the day, not in rioting and drunkenness." *Rom.* xiii. " Learn of me, because I am weak and humble of heart." *Matt.* xi. 29. " In spirit fervent serving the Lord." *Rom.* xii. 11.

Q. What means are to be employed in the acquisition of these virtues?

A. Those which we have mentioned above in treating of the seven capital sins, for those practices which eradicate vice implant the opposite virtues in the heart.

Q. What virtues should we practice with peculiar zeal in order to preserve our consciences undefiled by sin, and to become fruitful in good works, and thus gradually to arrive at Christian perfection?

A. Those to which Christ has in particular annexed the promise of eternal life, and which are on that account commonly termed the eight beatitudes, viz.:

1. Blessed are the poor in spirit, for theirs is the kingdom of heaven.
2. Blessed are the meek, for they shall possess the land.
3. Blessed are they that mourn, for they shall be comforted.
4. Blessed are they that hunger and thirst after justice, for they shall be filled.
5. Blessed are the merciful, for they shall obtain mercy.
6. Blessed are the clean of heart, for they shall see God.
7. Blessed are the peacemakers, for they shall be called the children of God.
8. Blessed are they that suffer persecution for justice' sake, for theirs is the kingdom of heaven.

Q. What is meant by poor in spirit?

A. Those deserve the name of poor in spirit who possess hearts free from all inordinate longings after the goods and possessions of this world. Whoever is thus qualified journeys on to heavenly bliss unencumbered and unimpeded by oppressive and harassing cares, following the admonition of the Apostle: "Seek the things that are above, and not the things that are upon earth." *Colos.* iii. 1, 2.

Q. Who deserve the name of mild?

A. All who have obtained the mastery over angry and impatient emotions. The soil of their hearts is thus freed from the destructive influence of this passion, and their souls are constantly prepared, like a cloudless sky, or a crystal stream, to reflect in their lives the genial beams of Divine inspiration, so powerful in leading them to the practice of perfection.

Q. What kind of mourners does Christ term blessed?

A. Those only who are afflicted with sorrow for having themselves so often offended God, and at beholding Him offended by others. Such persons by their tears purify their hearts from every sin, and their virtues from every blemish.

Q. Who may be said to hunger and thirst after justice.

A. Those who not only wish, but feel that they ardently wish one thing only, viz.: the attainment of the highest degree of Christian virtue, to progress daily and hourly therein; a disposition of heart which impels them to move rapidly forward on the way to perfection.

Q. Christ says, "Blessed are the merciful." To whom may this beatitude be applied?

A. To such as zealously fulfil the works of Christian charity.

Q. Into how many classes may works of this order be divided?

A. Into two principal classes, works of corporal and works of spiritual mercy. The first refer to the corporal necessities and miseries of our neighbor, the latter to his spiritual wants, or the welfare and salvation of his soul.

Q. Which are the principal works of corporal mercy?

A. They are seven in number. 1. Feeding the hungry. 2. Giving drink to the thirsty. 3. Clothing the naked. 4. Ransoming captives. 5. Visiting the sick. 6. Harboring strangers. 7. Burying the dead.

Q. In what terms does Scripture recommend the works of corporal mercy?

A. "Deal thy bread to the hungry, and bring the needy and the harborless into thy house. When thou shalt see one naked cover him." *Is.* lviii. 7. "Turn not away thy face from any poor person." *Job* iv. 7. "My son, shed tears over the dead, and neglect not his burial." *Eccles.* xxxviii. 16. "Be ye, therefore, merciful, as your father also is merciful." *Luke*, vi. 36. "Be ye kind one to another, merciful, forgiving one another." *Eph.* iv. 32.

Q. What are the menaces contained in Scripture against those who neglect practising these good works?

A. Eternal reprobation, frequently preceded by temporal want and misery. "He that stoppeth his ear against the cry of the poor, shall also cry himself and shall not be heard." *Prov.* xxi. 13. And St. James writes: "Judgment without mercy to him that hath not done mercy." *James*, ii. 13. Christ the Judge, already pronounces sentence of reprobation against them, in these words: "Depart from me, ye cursed, into everlasting fire; for I was hungry, and you gave me not to eat. I was thirsty, and you gave me not to drink. Then shall they also answer him saying: Lord, when did we see thee hungry, or thirsty, or a stranger, or naked, or sick, or in prison, and did not minister to thee? Then the Lord shall answer them, saying: Amen I say to you, so long as you did it not to one of these least ones, neither did you do it to me." *Matt.* xxv.

Q. What promises does Scripture make to those who are zealous in the practice of these good works?

A. 1st. Temporal blessings: "He that giveth to the poor shall not want." *Prov.* xxviii. "Give and it shall be given unto you a full measure, a well heaped measure." *Luke*, xvi.

2nd. Spiritual blessings, the pardon of sin, by the grace of repentance and amendment granted to us. "Alms deliver from all sin and death, and will not suffer the soul to go into darkness." *Tob.* iv. 11. Further, most efficacious graces to enable us to attain Christian perfection: "And thy justice shall go before thy face; and the glory of the Lord shall gather thee up." This is the assurance given by the Holy Ghost by the mouth of *Isaias*, lviii. And St. Paul writes: "He that administereth seed to the sower, will both give you bread to eat and will multiply your seed and increase the growth of the fruits of your justice." 2 *Cor.* ix. Experience confirms this assertion, in regard to those who practice mercy not only from motives of natural compassion but prompted by charity to God and man, as the lives of the saints prove. Such persons may justly confess with holy Job, "From my youth compassion grew up with me; I was an eye to the blind, and a foot to the lame, I was the father to the poor." *Job*, xxix. Finally, the particular grace of perseverance in virtue and a judgment of mercy and reward. " Blessed are the merciful : for they shall obtain mercy." *Math.* v. 7. "Give alms, and thus lay up for yourselves imperishable treasures in heaven." *Luke*, xii. "Come, ye blessed of my Father, possess the kingdom prepared for you from the foundation of the world. For I was hungry, and you gave me to eat," &c. *Matt.* xxv. 34.

Q. Which are the principal spiritual works of mercy?

A. 1. Admonishing sinners. 2. Advising those in doubt. 3. Consoling the afflicted. 4. Bearing patiently with injustice. 5. Forgiving those who offend us. 6. Instructing the ignorant. 7. Praying for the living and the dead. Do whatever lies in your power in order to prevent your neighbor from committing sin, and to promote within him the growth of virtue and piety.

Q. How may this be done?

A. By instruction, example, direction, reproof, correction, and the exercise of the just authority possessed by parents and superiors, as also by prayer. Whoever is thus zealously attentive to promote his neighbor's salvation, strives himself after Christian perfection; for the truths of faith, which impel him to labor for the spiritual welfare of his fellow-men, incite him with still greater zeal to strive to secure the great object of his own salvation. If God so richly rewards the works of corporal mercy by graces here and glory hereafter, how much richer and more glorious must be the recompense awarded in eternity to spiritual works of mercy. This is clearly manifested in the lives of the saints.

Q. What does Holy Scripture say of these works of spiritual mercy?

A. "God gave to every one of them a commandment concerning his neighbor." *Eccle.* xii. "He must know that he who causeth a sinner to be converted from the error of his way shall save his soul from death, and shall cover a multitude of sins." *Jam.* v. 20. "In this we have known the charity of God, because He hath laid down His life for us: and we ought to lay down our lives for the brethren."— *John*, iii. 16. "I have become all to all, in order to gain all for Christ." 1 *Cor.* ix. 22.

Q. What motives are best calculated to inflame our zeal in the practice of works of spiritual mercy?

A. 1. Reflection on the great dignity of human nature, man being the image of God.

2. The consideration of man's priceless value in the sight of the Divinity, as he has been bought, redeemed, and sanctified by the blood of the Messiah.

3. The relation in which our neighbor stands to us as a brother or sister in Adam and in Christ.

4. The reflection of the inestimable value of spiritual works of mercy according to the words of St. Chrysostom: "A spiritual work of mercy surpasses in value all the corporal works of mercy which a person might exercise in one act towards all mankind."

5. The infinite pleasure with which God regards such works; they may even be said to elevate us to the dignity of co-operators with God when zealously and lovingly performed. Oh, with what unbounded delight do not Jesus and Mary look upon the endeavors of such as strive to prevent Christ's merits and sufferings from proving fruitless to the souls of the redeemed!

6. The guarantee for salvation thus obtained.

7. The ineffable reward in heaven, and the eternal participation in the joys of those who have been delivered from a sinful condition or sanctified by our efforts. Whoever will meditate on these and similar considerations will, without doubt, feel his heart inflamed with a burning desire to procure the salvation of souls. He will frequently exclaim, with St. Francis Xavier, from the depths of his fervent heart: "O Lord, give me souls."

Q. Who may be said to possess purity of heart?

A. All who endeavor to keep far from every voluntary sin and imperfection, and in order to attain this end zealously employ the means ordained by God in order to remove the danger of contracting these stains; but more particularly those, who by resolutely overcoming every temptation to impurity, obtain a heart perfectly united to God in love, and free from all concupiscence of the flesh; the grace of interior intercourse with God sanctifies the lives of those thus qualified.

Q. To what class of persons may the term "meek" be applied?

A. Those who not only themselves harbor no trace of enmity in their hearts, but who, moreover, live amongst their fellow-men as angels of peace, and thus diffuse this blessed peace around them. Great graces accompany such virtuous endeavors to enable us to live in uninterrupted peace with God, and render us in the highest degree susceptible of the blessings of charity, which is the bond and the pledge of Christian perfection.

Q. Who may be said to suffer for justice' sake?

A. Those who are reviled, insulted, and ill-treated by others on account of the performance of their duties, and because they realize their character of children of God in word and work. Those who have the happiness and the courage thus to suffer, obtain the grace of unbloody martyrdom, and are in the most eminent degree followers of Christ and His saints.

Q. What may be observed of each of these grades of virtues?

A. 1. That each in a particular manner leads man to the perfection of virtue, and that they are mutually connected, so that whoever increases in the one, receives thereby grace and assistance for the more perfect practice of the others.

2. That there is a peculiar promise of reward and beatitude for time and eternity annexed to each.

3. The consideration of all these virtues renders more striking the great contrast existing between the spirit of Christ and the spirit of the world. The spirit which governs the world and its votaries, clings to the very opposite of these virtues, and thereby leads its deluded followers down to the gloomy labyrinths of vice and misery. Those are blessed in the eyes of the world who strive after wealth, honor, sensual pleasure, and the applause of men. In a word, a life made up of the paltry enjoyments afforded by a fleeting world, and bearing but one characteristic, viz., entire forgetfulness of their nobler destiny, the possession of God.

Practice.—Meditate frequently on the eight beatitudes pronounced by our Lord's own blessed lips when treating of these virtues, and you will find yourself powerfully encouraged in endeavoring to obtain them; you will joyously resolve to give your whole heart with all its affections to Him who is alone worthy of it, and not be satisfied with mediocrity in virtue, but endeavor to become daily more exemplary by a true and resolute effort to root out some old evil, and implant in its stead some new virtue.

CHAPTER III.

THE STATE OF CHRISTIAN PERFECTION.

Q. What is understood by the term Christian perfection?
A. That condition of life and disposition of heart in which man keeps himself aloof from every deliberate venial transgression, and cherishes the earnest desire of becoming daily more like to his Divine Model by the perfect practice of the above-mentioned virtues according to his calling and condition.

Q. Is this a general vocation?
A. Without doubt, for all are called to follow Christ, who says: "I am the way, the truth, and the life." *John*, xiv. 6. To this perfection Jesus invites all without exception. "Be you, therefore, perfect, as also your heavenly Father is perfect." *Matt.* v. This loving Saviour further promises to all a rich reward in His heavenly kingdom. The Apostles in their Epistles exhort all Christians without distinction to lead holy and unblemished lives, as we have before observed. This vocation and obligation becomes evident from the character and marks of the Church, as she both is, and is termed *holy*. Whoever, then, does not endeavor to obtain sanctity, is not a living branch on the tree of the Church, and is, therefore, exposed to the imminent danger of drying up, and being cast into the flames. The ninth article of the Creed, by which we profess our belief in the communion of saints, refers to this vocation and obligation. To this communion in eternal life, we never shall be admitted until our souls are perfectly purified from even the slightest stain of sin, either here in the ordeal of penance, or hereafter in the flames of purgatory, and we have acquired the perfection of virtue.

The same motives impel all Christians to strive after sanctity of life, viz., the holy will of God, and the great increase of grace and glory to be thus obtained: "That is the will of God, your sanctification." 1 *Thess.* ii. 12. "He who soweth in blessings shall also reap of blessings." 2 *Cor.* ix. 6. Christ has prepared and left in His Church the most efficacious means of acquiring these virtues in each and all.

Q. What is the principal condition for the practice of Christian perfection?

A. The grace of God and our co-operation. "Not I, but the grace of God with me." 1 *Cor.* xv. 10.

Q. Which graces are in this respect the most efficacious?

A. Those which in us, and with our co-operation, establish a permanent condition which is joined with numerous illuminations and impulses of actual grace.

Q. What is the term applied to these graces?

A. The seven gifts of the Divine Spirit.

Of the Seven Gifts of the Holy Ghost.

Q. Name these seven gifts?

A. 1. Fear of the Lord. 2. Piety. 3. Knowledge. 4. Fortitude. 5. Counsel. 6. Understanding. 7. Wisdom. The Prophet Isaias thus characterizes Jesus, He who is the author and finisher of our salvation, our teacher and model on the way to Christian perfection: "And the spirit of the Lord shall rest upon him, the spirit of wisdom and of understanding, the spirit of counsel and of fortitude, the spirit of knowledge and of godliness, and he shall be filled with the spirit of the fear of the Lord." *Isaias*, xi. 2. As to us who are but mere wayfarers in this valley of tears, on the way to the reward of virtue, these gifts bear an inverted relation; supported by these gifts of the Holy Ghost and our own cooperation, we may be able to ascend the ladder leading from a dreary desert of woe to the glorious city of God. The first step is that of salutary fear, that what has already caught the halo of heaven's glory, wisdom. Thus is formed the heavenly ladder upon which Jacob beheld the angels of God ascending and descending; with that zeal, fidelity in the practice of Christian perfection, and longing to fulfil the holy will of God which animates these angelic spirits, are we to endeavor to fill our hearts.

Q. In what does the gift of the fear of the Lord consist?

A. It is the grace which places man in the permanent state in which he dreads but one thing, viz.: offending God by sin.

Q. In what does the gift of piety consist?

A. Piety is that grace and gift by which man approaches God, and arrives at the state of seeking his only joy and consolation in communing with Him in prayer; he permanently finds what he thus seeks.

Q. In what does the gift of knowledge consist?

A. It is a gift enabling those who seek and love God alone, to arrive at a supernaturally enlightened state of acquaintance with the will of God and fulfilling the same. They, therefore, in all their acts and omissions, keep the great affair of salvation constantly in view.

Q. In what does the gift of fortitude consist?

A. It is the grace by which man is nerved resolutely to adhere to, and undauntedly to execute, whatever he recognizes as the Divine will and the voice of duty, without permitting himself to be disturbed or intimidated by the storms raised by the voice of concupiscence, the attacks of Satan, and the allurements of the world.

Q. What is the gift of counsel?

A. It is a gift and grace which renders man permanently capable of advising himself and others in intricate questions, and deciding correctly what the affair of our salvation requires of us in this or that particular circumstance, and what is in accordance with the Divine will.

Q. What is the gift of understanding?

A. It is the gift by which man arrives at such a knowledge of the truths and mysteries of religion, that his life is perfectly grounded on faith, and all his actions and omissions spring from motives presented by this fundamental virtue.

Q. What is the gift of wisdom?

A. This is the gift and state of well-ordered charity, which so regulates and frames all our desires and actions as to make them perfectly coincide with all that the Divine love requires of us. The derivation of this word is profoundly and clearly explained by St. Bernard in treating of the Latin word *sapientia*, from *sapia scientia*. The state of perfection is thus established and within us, on a permanent basis, and to those who arrive thereat, may the words of the teacher of nations be applied: "Whoever is led by the spirit of God, they are the sons of God." *Rom.* viii. 14. When this is the case, the richest and fairest fruits on the tree of virtue cannot be wanting. To this perfection our life grows up, according to the simile used by the royal psalmist in comparing man with a tree which in due time blossoms as the palm-tree, and immediately brings forth rich fruits. *Ps.* i. 3.

Q. Name the fruits of this class particularly eulogized in Scripture?

A. The twelve fruits of the Holy Ghost, viz.:

1. Charity, which must impart life to every fruit of virtue, for that which is not performed in obedience to the promptings of holy love is of no real value, as we have already shown.

2. Joy, which causes us to perform cheerfully the good we find ourselves bound in conscience to undertake. *Phil.* iv. 4.

3. Peace, which causes us to practice virtue calmly and with tranquillity of heart. *Luke,* il. 14; *Phil.* iv. 7; *Ps.* cxviii.

4. Patience, to be exercised in bearing the difficulties and pains encountered in the discharge of duty. *Luke,* xx. 19; *James,* i. 2.

5. Longanimity, which enables us steadily to pursue the path of virtue without being discouraged by the obstacles placed in our way by the enemies of salvation. *Heb.* ii. 4; 2 *Cor.* vi. 4; *Matt.* x.

6. Benignity, which prevents us from injuring or wounding the feelings of our fellow-men, and induces us to aid them as much as in us lies. *Eph.* v. 8.

7. Amiability or goodness, which diffuses over our deportment so much gentleness and suavity, that we win upon the affections of those with whom we associate, and thus induce them to attend with greater zeal to the one great affair of salvation. *Colos.* iii. 12.

8. Meekness, which enables us to preserve equanimity and gentleness of deportment, even when we have been injured or insulted.

9. Candor, which is opposed to all deception and double-dealing, with regard to our neighbors, and causes us to act frankly and openly. *Tim.* iii. 11; *Prov.* xii. 22.

10. Modesty, which will check our zeal from degenerating into presumption. *Phil.* iv. 5

11. Continency, which will enable us to perform all this in unvarying self-denial. *Thess.* v. 22.

12. Chastity, which will keep us far removed from the contamination of whatever might sully the virginal lustre of this virtue, and leave not even the slightest room for suspicion of our having, by even the most transient thought or slightest act, incurred the degrading guilt of the opposite vice. *Wisd.* i. 1; *Cor.* vii. 34.

These are the fruits of the Holy Ghost, as enumerated by the Apostle when addressing the Galatians, and they mature all the other fruits of virtue on our tree of life. They are directly opposed to the fruits of the flesh, which render the lives of the wicked like trees fruitful in vice and perdition, growing in the fruits of the evil spirit, in enmity, inordinate grief, restlessness, impatience, impetuosity, violence, envy, severity, hostility, infidelity, presumption, lust and unchastity.

Practice.—Examine your conduct well, and see if, and in what degree, these gifts of the Holy Ghost, as proofs of your spiritual condition, influence your conduct; and frequently beseech the Spirit of life and love to increase His gifts within you. Sit also in judgment on your exterior deportment, your actions and omissions, if, and how abundantly, the fruits of the Spirit are visible in your life. Oh, nourish and cherish them with the utmost solicitude! Destroy, on the other hand, in the very germ, the pernicious fruits of the flesh, taking to heart the admonition of the great Apostle: "They who are Christ's have crucified their flesh, with its vices and concupiscences." *Gal.* v. 24. And again: "For what things a man shall sow, those also shall he reap. For he that soweth in his flesh, of the flesh also shall reap corruption: but he that soweth in the Spirit, shall reap life everlasting." *Gal.* vi. 8.

The Evangelical Counsels.

Q. Are there any other exercises of piety by which we are eminently strengthened and encouraged in the imitation of Christ, so that we may here below so model our lives on His as to be most intimately united with Him, hereafter, in the mansions of His glory?

A. There are; viz., *the observance of the evangelical counsels.*

Q. Name these?

A. 1. Voluntary poverty; 2. Angelic chastity; 3. Obedience to a spiritual superior.

Q. Why are these termed evangelical counsels?

A. Because their observance has not been enjoined on us by command, but merely recommended by Christ and His Apostles to the faithful, as powerful means of attaining greater perfection here, and the enjoyment of more exquisite bliss and greater glory hereafter. Before any one resolves, however, to bind himself to observe these counsels, he must have obtained the serious and passionless conviction, grounded on pure motives, that he is called thereto by God. St. Augustine says: "A command is one thing, an advice another." *Serm.* 16 *de temp.* And again: "Whoever hearkens to and follows the advice, will receive greater glory: whoever, on the contrary, does not fulfil the command, shall not escape punishment unless he repent." St. Ambrose says: "The counsel invites the willing, the command imposes obligations even on the refractory." *Lib. de Vid.* St. Jerome teaches as follows: "When counsel is given, every thing is left to the good pleasures of the person advised; a command, however, implies necessity on the part of those to whom it is lawfully directed: yet greater merit is to be obtained by voluntary sacrifice." *Lib. adv. Toc.* This becomes more evident when we consider well what each of these evangelical counsels requires of us in imitation of Christ.

Q. In what does evangelical poverty consist?

A. Voluntary poverty is the renunciation of all temporal goods, so that no property is possessed and no self-empowered disposal of things temporal is allowed.

Q. How did Christ recommend the practice of evangelical poverty by precept and example?

A. In that being rich, he, out of love to us, became poor, as the Apostle says: 2 *Cor.* viii. 9. And Christ himself declares: "The foxes have holes, and the birds of the air nests; but the Son of man hath not where to lay his head." *Luke*, ix. 58. He wished at His entrance into the world to behold its light in a miserable stable. And when He left this world, after the hardships of a poor life, He hung, the poorest of the poor, on the holy cross; His nakedness covered only by the purple garment of His precious blood. To this state of perfection Jesus exhorts and encourages us particularly in the answer given to the young man who asked him: "Master, what shall I do, in order that I may obtain life eternal?" Christ replied: "If thou wilt enter into life, keep the commandments." To this He added: "If thou wilt be perfect, go, sell what thou hast, and give to the poor; and thou shalt have treasure in heaven: and come, follow me." *Matt.* xix. 21. With this admonition the Apostles implicitly complied, for they could all with Peter declare: "Behold, we have left all things, and have followed thee: what, therefore, shall we have?" *Matt.* xix. 27. Jesus answers, promising a hundred-fold here below, and particular glory hereafter. Hence we behold the faithful of the infant Church laying their fortunes at the feet of the Apostles, so that none of their number called any thing his own, as St. Luke testifies, *Acts*, iv. 32.

Q. In what consists this reward of an hundred-fold here below, as promised by Christ to those who embrace evangelical poverty?

A. In the multitude of graces granted us by the Lord in consideration of this sacrifice, and in the great advantages for salvation obtained by this voluntary renunciation of the gifts of fortune. Man thus frees himself from the innumerable cares and anxieties entailed by the possession of, or longing after, wealth and honors, as also from the great temptations to which he is exposed by the treasures, pleasures and goods of this world. Genadius, therefore, wisely remarks: "It is good to give to the poor a portion of our property; better, to dispose of it entirely in their favor, and at once to live in and with Christ in poverty." *Lib. de En. dogm.*

Q. In what does angelic chastity consist?

A. In voluntary abstaining from marriage, in order to live in human flesh pure and unsullied as the angels.

Q. How did Christ by word and example commend the practice of perfect virginal chastity?

A. He, the king of virgins chose as mother the spotless Mary, the queen of virgins; this His sweet, pure mother, He gave in charge to His virgin disciple when expiring on the cross, in order that imitating Him the favored one, might worthily act as His substitute. On one occasion, Peter said that such being the case it would be better not to marry. Christ asserted, saying: "He that can receive, let him receive." *Matt.* xix. 12. Thus signifying, that abstinence from the marriage state is merely a counsel, which, nevertheless, when followed, will be found of great advantage. All the Apostles obeyed the loving invitation of Jesus: "Follow me, live in continence," and advised the faithful to do the same. "I have no commandment of the Lord," says St. Paul, "concerning virgins, but I give counsel, I think, therefore, that it is good for a man so to be. He that giveth his virgin doth well, he that giveth her not, doth better." And again: "It is good for a man not to touch a woman." And of the widow he says: "Let her marry," but he adds, "more blessed shall she be, if she so remain, according to my counsel; and I think that I also have the spirit of God." 1 *Cor.* vii. That is, the advice I here give is rather in accordance with the promptings of the Holy Ghost, than my own judgment. This is further the unanimous teaching of the Holy Fathers. St. Ambrose writes on this subject: "A good wife is justly commended, yet a pious virgin is preferred to her, according to the words of the Apostle: "He that giveth his virgin doth well, he that keepeth her doth better. The virgin thinks of the service of God; but she that is married thinketh on the things of the world." The former is bound in the bonds of wedlock, the latter is unfettered; the one is under the law, the other under the influence of grace. Matrimony by which the propagation of the human race is secured, is good, but better is virginity which enters on the possession of a celestial inheritance, and draws upon itself the succession of heavenly merits. By a wife comes care, by a virgin salvation." *St. Amb. ep.* 81, *ad Syrie et ep.* 82, *ad Vercell.* The Church declares and solemnly decides in the *Council of Trent:* "If any one maintain that matrimony is to be preferred to virginity, and that it is not better to and more blissful to remain in virginity, than to contract a matrimonial alliance, let him be anathema." *Con. Trid.* Sess. xxiv. c. 18.

Q. In what does the advantage afforded by the observance of chastity consist?

A. In freeing us from the cares and anxieties incident to the matrimonial state, and devoting one's self, mind, body and soul to the service of God and the faithful fulfilment of His holy will. "He that is without a wife is solicitous for the things that belong to the Lord, how he may please God; but he that is with a wife, is solicitous for the things of the world, how he may please his wife, and he is divided. And the unmarried and the virgin thinketh on the things of the

Lord, that she may be holy both in body and in spirit. But she that is married, thinketh on the things of the world, how she may please her husband." 1 *Cor.* vii. 32–35. "Blessed are the poor in spirit, for they shall see God." This promise of Christ refers particularly to souls who live in the strict observance of chastity, and in prayer are peculiarly illuminated by the inspirations of the Divine spirit. There awaits these favored ones, moreover, in the mansions prepared for them by their heavenly Lord, a peculiar reward and a closer union with Jesus their blessed Spouse. We find in the revelations of St. John: "I saw: and, behold a Lamb stood on Mount Sion, and with Him a hundred and forty-four thousand, having His name and the name of His Father written on their foreheads. And they sung as it were a new canticle, before the throne and before the four living creatures, and the ancients, and no man could say the canticle, but those hundred and forty-four thousand, who were purchased from the earth. These are they who are not defiled with women: for they are virgins. These followeth the Lamb whithersoever He goeth." *Apoc.* xiv.

Q. In what consists the practice of voluntary obedience?

A. When out of love to God we renounce our right to the exercise of free will in admissible matters, in order to do that which is commanded us by a superior given or chosen.

Q. How does Christ recommend to us by word and example the practice of obedience?

A. Jesus, although in person true God, and in His sacred humanity far superior to every other created being, would not enter into the world in full manhood, but appeared in the ordinary way as a helpless infant, dependent on, and subject to His blessed mother and holy foster father, St. Joseph. Jesus further recommended this virtue to the practice of His followers by His whole hidden life in Nazareth, of which we find in the gospel no other record than this: "He was subject to them." *Luke*, i. 50. Jesus freely submitted to the ordinance of the Old Law, and even to the decrees of earthly potentates. He, the King of kings and Lord of lords, while yet in His mother's womb, obeys the decree of the Emperor Augustus, and induces her to journey to Bethlehem; submissively, too, He accedes to the unjust and tyrannical will of the earthly judge Pilate, in the last stage of His mortal existence. Legions of angels were in readiness to defend Him against the violence and malignity of His enemies, yet Jesus preferred submitting to whatever Pilate might ordain in his regard, as he had received power from the Father over His person; thus, as the Apostle says: "Humbling (annihilating) himself and becoming obedient even unto the death of the cross." *Matt.* xxvi. 53; *John,* xix. 11; *Philip.* ii. 8. In a word, Christ particularly recommends the practice of this virtue in His exhortation to the faithful, and to His disciples, to submit to the divinely-acquired authority of the Old Testament, as long as a shadow of it should exist: "The Scribes and Pharisees have sitten on the chair of Moses, all, therefore, whatsoever they shall say to you, observe and do." *Matt.* xxiii. 2. Christ refers us in this passage to the source of this obedience, viz., that it is not man as man whom we obey, but only in as far as he is delegated to act in our regard as God's representative, according to the Lord's declaration: "He that heareth you, heareth me." This declaration holds good particularly when the superior in question possesses, by his ecclesiastical office or mission, authority and power over us. "Obey your prelates, and be subject to them. For they watch, as being to render an account of your souls." *Heb.* xiii. 17.

Q. In what does the value of perfect obedience, and the advantages it affords for a life of perfection consist?

A. 1. In that man freely and lovingly immolates himself to the Lord, thus becoming, with all the powers and faculties of soul and body, a living holocaust of Divine love. By the vow of poverty, man offers up and renounces, for God's sake, the possession of things temporal, the whole outward world; by the vow of chastity, the possession of his body; by obedience, the possession of his intellectual and spiritual powers, by entirely devoting to the service of God his will and understanding in the boundless desire of doing naught save what God wills, and to strive after the accomplishment of what is good.

2. That man, by this obedience, frees himself from all anxiety in choosing between good and better, as he is guided by obedience in all cases not prohibited by the law of God, and has only to attend to the will and wishes of his superior, in whose person he obeys not man, but Christ the Lord, out of love to whom, he has taken upon himself the obligation of perfect obedience, and whose representative and organ the

superior is in his regard. Thus, says St. Ignatius, in his epistle on obedience in accordance with the unanimous teaching of the fathers and doctors of the Church.

3. This obedience increases the merit of every virtuous act, because in performing them, we have solely in view the wish of God, which is the law and the plenitude of all sanctity. The words of the Holy Ghost in the Old Testament have reference to this: "Obedience is better than sacrifice." And again: "An obedient man shall speak of victory." The promise of Christ is justly considered as also referring to this virtue. "Whoever shall humble himself, shall be exalted." Matt. xxiii. 12. Here in the order of grace, hereafter in the order of glory. For there is no greater voluntary humiliation than the voluntary submission of the understanding to the will of another, because he is our superior, although we may otherwise far surpass him in judgment and virtue.

Q. Are we allowed to obey a superior in sinful matters?

A. No; obedience refers only to things which are left to our free choice, and not to such as are defined, commanded, or prohibited by the express decree of God.

Q. Who is bound under pain of sin to observe the evangelical counsels?

A. Whoever binds themselves thereto by vow, voluntarily and with free consent.

Q. Can these vows be observed in the secular state?

A. Partially they can, when we have promised to do so, and in as far as such a vow is admissible and practicable.

Q. Where are these evangelical counsels practised and observed?

A. In the different orders of the Church.

Q. What is an order?

A. A congregation of persons, which by a rule approved by the Holy See, bind themselves by a solemn vow to observe these counsels. When such community has received but a temporary approval from a bishop, or when its members are admitted only to simple vows, it is not termed an order, but an assembly or congregation.

Q. What is the difference between solemn and simple vows?

A. Solemn vows are accepted by the Church; simple vows, on the contrary, bind the individual in conscience, without having been accepted by the Church as such. The consequence is, that when any member of an order violates the vows or quits the order, he becomes liable to the censures and penalties denounced against such apostates. This is not the case with those who take simple vows, unless particular ordinances in that regard have been made by the Holy See.* Solemn vows render the contraction of marriage null and void, simply illegal.

Q. Are orders of great antiquity in the Church?

A. Their existence is coeval with that of the Church of God, they may even be traced to the Old Law. We read of the schools of the prophets, who lived in community as religious do at present. Particularly worthy of remark is what is recounted by the historian Philo, of the life led by the Assinner, as also what the traditionary chronicles of the Carmelites relate; this order derived its name from Mount Carmel, on which godly men are said to have lived in community since the time of Elias. Immediately after the gospel had been announced, religious societies were formed, particularly in the deserts of Egypt. After the Church had obtained liberty under Constantine, religious communities began to flourish in the East, under the auspices of St. Anthony and other virtuous men. Soon after, it sprung into life and pristine vigor in the West beneath the fostering hand of the great St. Benedict and his spiritual children, rich in the most glorious fruits of piety for the benefit of the whole Church, the salvation of souls, and the well-being of civil society, for whose cultivation and instruction these zealous servants of God incessantly labored. Many new orders arose in the course of time, which according to their different callings strove in the most efficacious manner to manifest by the life of Christian perfection their solicitude for their own salvation and that of their fellow-men. According to the motto of St. Ignatius, the founder of the Society of Jesus: "All for the greater honor of God." And does not the essence and aim of Christian perfection live in this?

Q. What are orders on this account called?

A. The state of Christian perfection.

Q. Is it to be accounted a great favor and happiness, when one finds himself called to a religious life?

---

* Thus the members of the Society of Jesus, although they bind themselves only by simple vows, are called religious, members of an order, hence all the consequences attending an infringement of solemn vows are incurred by a violation of the obligations taken by Jesuits, according to a decree of the Holy See.

A. Assuredly, but the duties imposed by this vocation are to be fulfilled, after we have once attained certainty concerning the reality of our higher calling. Whoever actuated by temporal motives, human respect, or inclination, would refuse compliance with the suggestions of grace would place his salvation in imminent danger by this opposition to the Divine decree. Those were remarkable words addressed by Christ to the youth who inquired what was to be done in order to secure salvation: "If thou wilt be perfect, go, sell what thou hast, and give it to the poor: and come, follow me." And when the young man had heard this word, he went away sorrowful: for he had great possessions. And Jesus said to His disciples: "Amen, I say to you that a rich man shall hardly enter into the kingdom of heaven." *Matth.* xix. 19–24. These words, however, are in their strictest sense to be applied to this young man, whom Christ called in a particular manner to the observance of poverty. Unfaithful souls, who but half comply in following the movings of Divine grace, when called from a worldly life to a religious state, should seriously reflect on the Lord's threatening words: "No man putting his hand to the plough, and looking back, is fit for the kingdom of God." *Luke,* ix. 62.

Q. What practical lesson is to be deduced from this?

A. That every one is bound earnestly and carefully to examine what state of life he may be called to, and that having once recognized the Divine will, he is to let no earthly consideration deter him from fulfilling it. Resolutely and steadily he is to obey the voice of God when by prayer, interior illumination, exterior circumstances, and particularly in accordance with the advice of a holy and experienced spiritual guide, he has attained moral certainty of his being called to the religious state. He is then, in spite of every obstacle, and no matter how tender and how strong the ties that bind him to earth, to sever them and obey the voice of God. Those who are not called to this holy and Divine state, should be very careful not to deter or dissuade those who are favored with a religious vocation from following it. This perverse conduct would certainly render them highly culpable in the Divine sight. Parents and relatives are to take this particularly to heart, since they, as also brothers and sisters, are but too apt, out of natural affection and motives founded on human respect and consideration, to seek to prevent entrance into the religious or clerical state. The justness of Christ's warning is here proved in its full force: "And a man's enemies shall be they of his own household." *Matt.* x. 36. Let those favored by a Divine call consider the Apostle's words: "We ought to obey God rather than man." *Acts,* v. 29. According to the unanimous teaching of the Fathers and Doctors of the Church, with St. Alphonsus Liguori, parental authority must give way. The Church even grants time for reflection to those joined in matrimony by her priests, and permits them, should they find themselves called, still to enter the clerical or religious state, provided matrimony has not been actually consummated. Should either party feel called to enter orders or the religious state, the marriage contracted is dissolved: so great is the esteem in which religious life is held, in the sight of God and His holy Church.

Q. Which are the principal means of animating ourselves with ever-renewed zeal in striving after the perfection of Christian virtue?

A. 1. Prayer, and communing with God in pious meditation. "In my meditation," says the Psalmist, "a fire shall flame out." *Ps.* xxxviii. 4. This is the fire of Divine love; if it glow in our hearts, that zeal for the practice of virtue, without which we cannot please God, will certainly be enkindled. Whoever is not devoted to prayer, whoever finds not this holy exercise in regard to his spirit's life what breathing is to that of the body, shall never experience the promptings of holy zeal.

2. Constant remembrance of the presence of God, a condition of meditation, and continued prayer in spirit and in truth. "Walk before Me, and be perfect," said God himself to Abraham. *Gen.* xvii. 1.

3. The lively remembrance of our sweet Saviour; earnest reflection on His life, passion and death; particularly, on His uninterrupted presence with us in the adorable sacrament of His love. This, united with meditation on and veneration of the virtues of His most sacred heart; oft-repeated visits to the blessed sacrament; frequent reception of the holy communion, and careful and fervent thanksgiving for this priceless boon, will lead us into the sanctuary of mental prayer, and procure a knowledge and love of Jesus Christ to which neither written nor spoken human words can ever enable us to arrive.

4. Great and tender devotion to the spotless Virgin, as the dispenser of Divine grace, of whom it is written: "I am the Mother of fair love, and of fear, and of knowledge, and of holy hope. In me is all grace of the way and of the truth; in me is all hope of life and virtue: come over to me, all ye that desire me, and be filled with my fruits." *Eccl.* xxiv. 24–27.

5. The resolute practice of *sincere* and heart-felt humility; for whatever we are, or may become in the service of God, we are by grace. 1 *Cor.* xv. "But God communicates His grace to the humble." 1 *Pet.* v. 5. Humility ensures for us the practice of virtue, by the purity of intention.

6. The constant practice of self-denial, corporal austerities and penance, with victories over self and passion. "If any man will come after me, let him deny himself." This is the admonition of Christ. *Luke,* ix. 23. And the Apostle assures us: "They who are Christ's have crucified their flesh, with its vices and concupiscence." *Gal.* v. 24. "But I chastise my body." 1 *Cor.* ix. 27. "Overcome thyself," was the frequent exhortation of St. Ignatius to St. Francis Xavier, and through him to all. To the question, Why so? the Saint used to answer, Because this alone suffices. This is interior abnegation, to be required by repeated acts of heroic virtue, for the practice of which daily life affords us numberless opportunities, and thus unseals to us a fountain of the richest graces and merits. This is particularly true of victories obtained over our curiosity in seeing and hearing, as also in conversing on useless and distracting subjects.

7. The observance of silence, and a strict guard in general over the tongue.

8. Due appreciation of adversities and crosses, and unalterable patience in bearing them.

9. Zeal in whatever tends to promote the salvation of our fellow-men.

10. Diligent examination of conscience.

11. Frequent confession.

12. The example of the saints who so zealously practised all this as we read in their lives. Whoever takes this into consideration and duly ponders upon it, will find himself touched by the same emotions that stirred St. Augustine's heart when he exclaimed: "If others have been able to do this, why not thou, oh, Austin?"

13. Constant consideration of the four last things, particularly the certainty and proximity of death. The thought of the judgments of God, that avenging Judge, who will probe our every act, word, and even the most secret thought. The remembrance of the eternity of woe to which the wicked are hastening, and the awful uncertainty as to the attainment of salvation. "There exists a possibility of my being eternally damned." These words all the saints were obliged, during life, to address to themselves. What degree of zeal in the practice of virtue, could be considered too great in order to escape eternal torment! And, on the other hand, can any exertion, made to obtain possession of eternal joy, be considered too much?

14. The annual spiritual renewal, or retreat, prescribed by St. Ignatius. This is a certain time spent in solitude, during which the eternal truths, the life, sufferings, and death of Jesus Christ are taken into consideration, in such an order, as is found most adapted to enlighten our understanding, inflame our heart, and strengthen our will.

These spiritual exercises, are furthermore, means and channels of grace, chosen by Divine Providence, as their confirmation by the Holy See attests, and the experience of thousands confirms. Happy the person who can find time and opportunity to make this retreat for the appointed length of time, viz., a month; the meditations being divided into four grand divisions, one for each week. The path on which one is guided by these meditations, so admirably and systematically digested, is distinguished by the terms—the Purgative, Illuminative, and Unitive Way; man being thus strengthened and encouraged to remove from his soul whatever stain of sin and imperfection may be cleaving to it, and at the same time irradiated and enlightened by the refulgence of Christ's adorable virtues, and by a particular and plenteous infusion of grace united with God. Eight or ten days are then annually spent in solitude, in order to repeat these holy exercises. They will be found most efficacious means of reviving our zeal in the practice of virtue, and enkindling within our breasts the earnest desire and the firm purpose of striving resolutely and perseveringly after perfection.

The time spent in this spiritual retreat may well be termed days of the Lord. 1 *Cor.* vi. This, then, dear Christian, is the substance of the Catholic Religion, the way of salvation; walk steadfastly in that path, as you are admonished by this work. Pursue it in and through Him, whose example guides and fortifies us in striving after perfection—Jesus Christ, the Founder and Perfecter of our Faith, who is the " Alpha and Omega." *Amen.*

ADDITIONS.

THE JUBILEE.

Q. What do you mean by a Jubilee?
A. By a Jubilee we mean that year of grace in which our Holy Father, the Pope, grants an extraordinary plenary indulgence to those who make a pilgrimage to Rome. By the grant of Boniface VIII., the jubilee was to take place every hundred years; by that of Paul II., every twenty-five years. What the jubilee was for the Jews, in a temporal point of view, viz: a year of deliverance from servitude, a year of rest; it was intended to be for Christians in a spiritual point of view, viz: a year of deliverance from the servitude of sin, and peace of conscience. The jubilee takes place first at Rome; the year after, the indulgence of the jubilee can be gained throughout the whole Church. This year is called the "Holy Year." In modern times the Popes are accustomed to grant a plenary indulgence in the form of a jubilee on other particular occasions.

As in our days, wickedness spreads more rapidly than ever, the Popes oftener afford these important opportunities of penance and sanctification.

Q. What do you understand by an indulgence of so many days, or so many years?
A. The remission of a certain amount of temporal punishment to be endured either on earth or in purgatory.

OF THE SACRAMENTALS.

If we attentively consider the blessings made use of by the Church, we shall observe that they were of a two-fold character, some belonging to things and persons, relating to the public divine service, others, which the church imparts rather for the private advantage of the faithful. We may very properly distinguish them by calling those of the former kind *Benedictions*, and those of the latter kind simply *Bless-*

ings. We do it for the sake of clearness, without pretending that this distinction should be observed in common usage. It is also to be observed that most of the benedictions, where an anointment takes place, are usually called *Consecrations.*

(See page 326.)

The Ecclesiastical Year and its Festivals.

Q. What is understood by the Ecclesiastical Year?
A. That division of the year which the Church adopts in commemorating the most important mysteries of our Redemption.

Q. Why do we mention the ecclesiastical year and its festivals under the head of Sacramentals?
A. Because the festivals of the Church are not only commemorative of past events, but also a kind of participation in the graces connected with the great events which we commemorate. These festivals, therefore, are for those who celebrate them in the spirit of the Church, like a tree bearing its yearly fruit, and yielding its spiritual food of sanctification. The prayers used by the Church confirm this doctrine, for she prays as if the events commemorated occurred on the day of their celebration.

Q. When does the ecclesiastical year begin?
A. It begins on the first Sunday of Advent.

Q. Which are its principal parts?
A. Advent, Lent, Easter-time, and the time from Trinity-Sunday to Advent.

Q. When does Advent begin?
A. On the Sunday preceding the feast of St. Andrew, the Apostle.

Q. Of what do the four weeks of Advent remind us?
A. Of the four thousand years preceding the coming of Christ, and of the expectation and longing desire of men, particularly the patriarchs and prophets, for the coming of the Redeemer.

Q. Why was Advent instituted by the Church?
A. In order to prepare the faithful for the festival of the birth of our Lord.

Q. What does the Church do for this purpose?

A. She is accustomed to sing a solemn High Mass, at an early hour, in honor of the Blessed Virgin, during which the faithful unite their sighs for the coming Redeemer to those of Mary the Queen of Prophets and the Mother of Jesus Christ.

Q. Which are the principal feasts which the Church celebrates at the close of Advent?

A. Christmas, Circumcision, and the Epiphany.

Q. What do we commemorate on the Sundays that follow?

A. We commemorate the youth and hidden life of Jesus Christ.

Q. Of what does the holy time of Lent remind us?

A. Of the forty days' fast, and of all the labors of our Lord in His apostolic life; and particularly, at the close of Holy Week, of His bitter passion and death.

Q. What do we commemorate on Palm Sunday?

A. We commemorate the solemn entrance of Jesus into Jerusalem.

Q. Why does the Church begin the "Tenebræ" in Holy Week on Wednesday?

A. Because, on this day, Christ was betrayed by Judas to the Pharisees and Scribes.

Q. Of what does Maunday-Thursday remind us?

A. Of the Last Supper, and of the institution of the blessed Sacrament.

Q. And Holy Friday?

A. Of the crucifixion and burial of our Lord.

Q. And Holy Saturday?

A. Of the resurrection of our Lord.

Q. Why does not the Church commemorate the resurrection during the night from Saturday to Sunday?

A. On account of the many ceremonies that accompany the celebration.

Q. What does the Church bless on Holy Saturday particularly?

A. The fire, the paschal candle, and water for baptism.

Q. What does this blessed fire signify?

A. The renovation of fervor, which should be a fruit of the holy time of Lent, for the worthy celebration of Easter.

Q. What is the signification of the paschal candle?

A. It signifies Christ the light of the world, and the life of those who rise with Him from the dead.

Q. Why is water blessed for baptism on this day?

A. Because it was on this day that Catechumens was ordinarily baptized.

Q. Of what does the time intervening between Easter and Ascension remind us?

A. It reminds us of the forty days which Christ, after His resurrection, spent on earth in instructing His disciples how to direct His Church.

Q. Why has the Church established the three Rogation-days preceding the feast of the Ascension?

A. To beg the blessing of God upon the fruits of the earth, and his grace for the sanctification of the hearts of men which have been prepared for His grace during the holy time of Lent and Easter; and to put us solemnly in mind that it is principally by prayer that we obtain and increase the grace of God for following Christ and winning heaven.

Q. Of what do the ten days intervening between Ascension and Whitsuntide remind us?

A. Of the Apostles assembled together with the other disciples of our Lord, with Mary and the holy women, in the Cenacle at Jerusalem, and of their preparation for the descent of the Holy Ghost.

Q. Does Whitsuntide remind us of anything?

A. Yes, of the descent of the Holy Ghost upon the Apostles and upon all the disciples of the Lord assembled on that occasion, and of the founding of the Church.

Q. Why does the Church, on the following Sunday, celebrate the feast of the Holy Trinity?

A. In order to remind us and impress us deeply with the truth, that one day we are to celebrate in heaven this feast of feasts, viz: by the vision of the Holy Trinity, provided we shall have made good use of the graces which God bestowed on us whilst we were on earth.

Q. Why does the Church solemnize the festival of Corpus Christi on the Thursday after the feast of the Holy Trinity?

A. In order to return special thanks for the institution of the most august Sacrament of the Altar, the greatest of all gifts bestowed on earth through the redemption, as this could not be done becomingly in Holy week; and in order to admonish us that it is through Christ our Lord alone that we believe, hope, and love, and whose presence in this adorable Sacrament renders our worship truly worthy of God.

Q. What does the Church commemorate on the remaining Sundays after the feast of the Holy Trinity?

A. The periods of time gone by since the foundation of the Church, during which the Providence of God has shown itself so wonderfully in the preservation and propagation of the Church.

Q. Of what are we reminded by the feast of All Saints?

A. Of the glorious triumph which the blessed in heaven enjoy now and forever.

Q. Of what does the feast of All Souls remind us?

A. Of the souls suffering in Purgatory, in order that we may be stimulated to help them by means of our prayers, etc., and be spurred on by the memory of them to conclude the ecclesical year in a worthy manner, and to begin the next with greater fervor.

(See page 326.)

Missions.

Q. What do you understand by Missions?

A. By missions I understand a renovation of spirit to be effected by a whole congregation at a particular time, during which the people assist at meditations, sermons, and other spiritual exercises especially adapted to the occasion.

Q. Which are the meditations, instructions, and spiritual exercises principally belonging to a mission?

A. Meditations on eternal truths, considerations and instructions concerning the state of life; general confessions and communions; thorough reconciliations; a visit to the churchyard accompanied by the pious recollection of the departed; the institution of the confraternity of the Sacred Heart of Jesus; the choosing of Mary for our Mother; the renovation of the promises made at Baptism; making a public atonement before the Blessed Sacrament; finally, the blessing and erecting of the Holy Mission-cross.

Q. Since what time have missions been in use?

A. In their essence they are as ancient as the preaching of the Gospel itself. We find a type of them in the preaching of penance by St. John the Baptist. His insisting on the eternal truths, on the conditions of a true reconciliation with

God, on the example and the imitation of Christ, are so many indications of the nature and order of missions.

After him, Christ Himself and His Apostles, gave the great mission for the conversion of the world, by which they traced out the way to be followed by Missionaries, in order to propagate the kingdom of Christ and increase the fervor of Christians.

Q. Since when have missions been given in the manner in in which they are given now?

A. Chiefly since the time when St. Ignatius wrote his book of Spiritual Exercises. For missions are the application of them to the people. Missions were given by the Fathers of the Society of Jesus, and other religious orders since the time of St. Ignatius, consequently, since the sixteenth century.

Q. Are missions useful?

A. According to the testimony of experience, they are the most efficacious means for the conversion and sanctification of entire congregations.

www.ingramcontent.com/pod-product-compliance
Lightning Source LLC
Chambersburg PA
CBHW022117290426
44112CB00008B/703